ISLANDS OF THE LAGOON
Murano, Burano and Torcello

Venice

0   400 m
0   400 yds

KU-013-288

S. Michele

Isola di
S. Michele

Cimitero

S. Mic

THE MINOR ISLANDS

Canale delle Fondamente Nuove

rina
Gesuiti

oli

Campo
S. M. Nuovi

S. S. Giovanni
e Paolo

Campo
S. Maria
S. Maria
Formosa

S. Francesco
d. Vigne

vador

Fondaz
Querini
Stampalia

CASTELLO

CASTELLO

Canale di Porta Nuova

Vecchie

Basilica di
San Marco

S. Giorgio
del Greci

Darsena
Grande

Piazza
S. Marco

S. Zaccaria

La Pietà

Riva degli Schiavoni

S. Giovanni
in Bragora

Isola di
S. Pietro

atie Nuove Palazz
Ducale

Arsenale

S. Pietro
di Castello

THE MINOR ISLANDS

nta della
gana

a Dogana
rary Art Centre

Museo
Navale

Via G. Garib

Canale di San Marco

Rio del Sette Martiri

EASTERN CASTELLO

Monumento a
Garibaldi

S. Giorgio
Maggiore

Biennale

Darsena
di
Sant'Elena

Teatro
Verde

Isola di
San Giorgio
Maggiore

QUARTIERE
S. ELENA

S. Elena

CAMPO
DI MARTE

PARCO

DELLE

RIMEMBRANZE

Isola di
Sant'Elena

ISLANDS OF THE LAGOON
The Lido

Santa Maria
delle Grazie

San Servolo

INSIGHT  GUIDES

VENICE
CITY GUIDE

⊙ Walking Eye App

YOUR FREE DESTINATION CONTENT AND EBOOK AVAILABLE THROUGH THE WALKING EYE APP

Your guide now includes a free eBook and destination content for your chosen destination, all for the same great price as before. Simply download the Walking Eye App from the App Store or Google Play to access your free eBook and destination content.

HOW THE WALKING EYE APP WORKS

Through the Walking Eye App, you can purchase a range of eBooks and destination content. However, when you buy this book, you can download the corresponding eBook and destination content for free. Just see below in the grey panels where to find your free content and then scan the QR code at the bottom of this page.

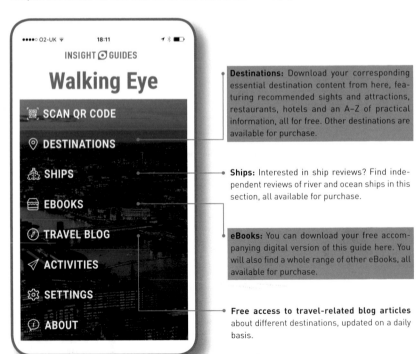

Destinations: Download your corresponding essential destination content from here, featuring recommended sights and attractions, restaurants, hotels and an A–Z of practical information, all for free. Other destinations are available for purchase.

Ships: Interested in ship reviews? Find independent reviews of river and ocean ships in this section, all available for purchase.

eBooks: You can download your free accompanying digital version of this guide here. You will also find a whole range of other eBooks, all available for purchase.

Free access to travel-related blog articles about different destinations, updated on a daily basis.

HOW THE DESTINATION CONTENT WORKS

Each destination includes a short introduction, an A–Z of practical information and recommended points of interest, split into 4 different categories:

• Highlights
• Accommodation
• Eating out
• What to do

You can view the location of every point of interest and save it by adding it to your Favourites. In the 'Around Me' section you can view all the points of interest within 5km.

HOW THE EBOOKS WORK

The eBooks are provided in EPUB file format. Please note that you will need an eBook reader installed on your device to open the file. Many devices come with this as standard, but you may still need to install one manually from Google Play.

The eBook content is identical to the content in the printed guide.

HOW TO DOWNLOAD THE WALKING EYE APP

1. Download the Walking Eye App from the App Store or Google Play.
2. Open the app and select the scanning function from the main menu.
3. Scan the QR code on this page – you will then be asked a security question to verify ownership of the book.
4. Once this has been verified, you will see your eBook and destination content in the purchased ebook and destination sections, where you will be able to download them.

Other destination apps and eBooks are available for purchase separately or are free with the purchase of the Insight Guide book.

Contents

Introduction

The Best of Venice 6
Venice's Allure 19
The Venetians 21

History

Decisive Dates 26
City in the Lagoon 31

Features

Saving the City 49
Architectural Style 54
Artists of Colour and Light 63
The Operatic Tradition............ 70
Carnival 75
Eating Out 83

Insights

MINI FEATURES

Marco Polo 36
The Doge 40
Dams and Deadly Floods 53
The Venetian Palace 61
The Return of La Fenice......... 73
Commedia dell'Arte 79
Café Society 87
Gondolas and
    Gondoliers....................... 132

Antonio Vivaldi 154
The Arsenale 166
The Biennale......................... 171
The Scuole 182
The Jewish Ghetto 196
Venice Film Festival 232
Cruising the Brenta Canal ... 240

PHOTO FEATURES

Artists' Trails........................... 68
Regattas and
    Water Festivals.................. 80
The World's Grandest
    Private Chapel.................. 122
The Accademia 212

Places

Introduction 95
Around San Marco 99
The Grand Canal 125
Castello 146
Eastern Castello............... 163
San Polo and
    Santa Croce.................... 173
Cannaregio....................... 189
Dorsoduro 200
Islands of the Lagoon 217
The Minor Islands 236

Travel Tips

TRANSPORT

Getting There **246**
  By Air.............................. **246**
  By Rail............................. **246**
  By Sea............................. **246**
  By Coach **246**
  By Road **246**
Getting Around................... **247**
  The Airports................... **247**
  Car Parks....................... **247**
  City Ferries.................... **247**
  Gondolas **248**
  Water Taxis **248**
  Boat Holidays **248**

A – Z

Accommodation **249**
Admission Charges............. **249**
Addresses **249**
Budgeting for Your Trip........ **250**
Children............................. **250**
Climate.............................. **250**
Crime and Safety **251**
Customs Regulations **251**
Disabled Travellers **251**
Embassies/Consulates **251**
Etiquette **251**

Festivals and Events........... **251**
Gay and Lesbian
  Travellers **253**
Health and Medical
  Care **253**
Internet **253**
Maps **253**
Media **253**
Money **253**
Opening Hours.................... **254**
Postal Services **254**
Religious Services **254**
Smoking............................. **254**
Student Travellers.............. **254**
Tax **254**
Telephones **255**
Time Zone........................... **255**
Toilets................................. **255**
Tourist Information **255**
Tourist Offices in Venice **255**
Travel Agents...................... **255**
Visas and Passports **255**
Weights and
  Measures **255**

LANGUAGE 256

FURTHER READING 260

Maps

Venice **96**
San Marco............................ **100**
The Grand Canal **126**
Castello **148**
Eastern Castello **165**
San Polo and
  Santa Croce.................... **174**
Cannaregio **190**
Dorsoduro **202**
Giudecca and
  San Giorgio Maggiore **220**
Torcello, Burano and
  Murano............................ **224**
Lido **234**
The Minor Islands............... **236**
Inside front cover Venice
Inside back cover Venice
  vaporetti network

THE BEST OF VENICE: TOP ATTRACTIONS

Here, at a glance, are the sights you really must not miss, from the Palazzo Ducale and 18th-century palaces to some of the finest art galleries in the world.

△ **Basilica di San Marco.** With its five domes, glittering mosaics and treasures of inestimable value, Venice's grand basilica is a mix of styles from Romanesque and Byzantine through to Gothic and Renaissance. See pages 101 and 122.

▽ **Punta della Dogana.** Once the customs house of the Venetian republic, the low-slung buildings on the Punta della Dogana have been transformed into Venice's leading contemporary art showcase. See page 202.

▽ **I Frari.** This soaring brick Gothic church, beautiful in its graceful simplicity, is the setting for a couple of masterpieces by Titian. See page 181.

▽ **Accademia.** For a crash course in the Venetian Old Masters, with works by the Bellinis, Tintoretto, Titian, the Tiepolos, Veronese, Canaletto and more, the Accademia is second to none. See page 212.

◁ **Guggenheim collection.** Peggy Guggenheim amassed a remarkable eclectic private collection of modern art, ranging from Picasso to Max Ernst, in what was long her home on the Grand Canal. See page 130.

▽ **Ca' Rezzonico.** This magnificent 18th-century palace affords a glimpse into noble lifestyles and has some fine frescoes by the Tiepolos. See page 133.

▽ **Palazzo Ducale (Doge's Palace).** In white stone and pink marble, this masterpiece of High Gothic style was the command centre of empire and remains the home of paintings by Titian and Veronese. See page 106.

▽ **La Fenice.** The world-famous opera house has been restored to its former glory. See pages 73 and 114.

▽ **Ca' Pesaro.** This baroque Grand Canal mansion, formerly home to one of Venice's grand families, today houses an extensive modern art collection and, upstairs, one of Europe's museums of Japanese Edo-period art and objects. See page 141.

▽ **Carnival.** The best-known event in Venice is the carnival, an extravaganza of colourful masks, costumes and music held in the 10 days before Shrove Tuesday. See page 75.

THE BEST OF VENICE: EDITOR'S CHOICE

Unique attractions, festivals and events, top palaces and islands, best bars and boat trips, family outings... here are our recommendations.

BEST PALACES AND ART MUSEUMS

Palazzo Ducale (Doge's Palace). A masterpiece of graceful High Gothic style. See page 106.

Accademia. The world's finest collection of Venetian art. See page 212.

Guggenheim collection. *The* museum of modern art. See page 130.

Ca' d'Oro. Gothic palace with beguiling museum of art. See page 139.

Ca' Pesaro. Kandinsky, Chagall and co in a splendid baroque palace. See page 141.

Ca' Rezzonico. Sumptuous 18th-century palace with art to match. See page 133.

Palazzo Mocenigo. Showcase of 18th-century living and interior decoration. See page 179.

Palazzo Vendramin-Calergi. Both a patrician palace and casino. See page 142.

San Rocco. Virtuoso Mannerist display by Tintoretto. See page 184.

I Carmini. Showcase for Tiepolo's artistry. See page 208.

Museo Correr. Superb museum on Venetian art and life. See page 104.

Fondaco dei Turchi. Turkish merchants' palace, now a museum of natural history. See page 144.

A gondola ride is a quintessential Venetian experience.

Tintoretto's The Fall of Man in San Rocco.

WATER EXPERIENCES

The Grand Canal. By vaporetto (line 1): leisurely palace-spotting along one of the world's greatest waterways. See page 125.

Gondola ride. Clichéd but memorable, particularly along the romantic back canals, rather than the bustling Grand Canal. See page 132.

***Traghetto* crossing.** Standing room only on the cheap but authentic gondola ferry across the Grand Canal. See page 248.

Water taxi trip. A private motor launch around the lagoon is wildly extravagant but worth it to travel in style to lesser-known Venice. See page 248.

The Brenta Canal. Ideally in summer, take a barge from Venice to Padua to see a clutch of historic Palladian villas. See page 240.

ONLY IN VENICE

The Ghetto. Many European cities concentrated their Jewish populations into a single district and Venice was one of them. The heart of Jewish Venice is home to the world's first ghetto, as the Venetians coined the phrase. See page 196.

The Rialto market. Once a crossroads of the world, this is still a fascinating warren of backstreets, from the fish and vegetable markets to the inns. See page 178.

Palazzo Grassi. Blockbuster art exhibitions are staged in this grand palace. See page 135.

Bacari (Traditional wine bars). Having cichetti e l'ombra, a snack and a glass of wine, is a Venetian tradition similar to Spanish tapas. See page 176.

Cichetti (Venetian tapas). These rustic tapas are the city's inexpensive signature snacks, and best eaten in a bacaro. See pages 85 and 176.

The Grand Canal by night. A line 1 vaporetto winds down the city's greatest water-way, illuminating opulent palaces. See page 137.

Masks and Murano glass. These are the two top city souvenirs, but only if bought from reputable outlets. See pages 77 and 225.

Legendary hotels. The Gritti, the Danieli and the Cipriani are world-renowned, but most of the luxury hotels have romantic waterside bars and roof-terrace restaurants that welcome non-residents. See pages 116 and 149.

Gondola serenade. Be a total tourist, once in your life. See pages 132 and 248.

Tranquil Castello.

BEST SQUARES

Piazza San Marco. The city's ceremonial stage-set of a square. See page 99.

Campo Santo Stefano. The most stylish square, with a top-notch gelateria. See page 116.

Campo Santa Margherita. The liveliest square for local nightlife and bars. See page 209.

Campo San Giacomo dell'Orio. Venice's most enchanting neighbourhood square. See page 180.

Campo Santa Maria Formosa. The quintessential canalside campo. See page 153.

The bustling Rialto fish market, or Pescheria, is set in an arcaded neo-Gothic hall by the quayside.

Lively bars line Campo Santa Margherita.

BEST WALKS AND TOURS

The Zattere. Follow the waterfront from La Salute around Punta della Dogana past the Gesuati church all the way to western Dorsoduro. See page 203.

The Ghetto. The official walking tour visits the synagogues and Jewish museum in off-the-beaten-track Cannaregio. See page 196.

Backwaters of Dorsoduro. From the Accademia, stroll to San Trovaso, San Sebastiano, Sant'Angelo, and Calle Lunga San Barnaba. See page 200.

The Arsenale. Follow Riva degli Schiavoni to the island of San Pietro, skirting the Arsenale shipyards and the Giardini. See Castello and Eastern Castello chapters.

Secret Itinerary. Dungeons and devilish plots on a tour of the Doge's Palace. See page 108.

The Tintoretto Trail. Visiting the Mannerist artist's masterpieces. See page 69.

Nature in the lagoon. Take an unusual nature tour with Natura Venezia. See page 219.

The baroque basilica of La Salute.

The island of San Giorgio Maggiore, with a belltower modelled on that of St Mark's.

BEST ISLANDS

San Giorgio Maggiore. A great first-day-in-Venice crossing to see the island closest to St Mark's. See page 218.

Murano, Burano and Torcello. Take a ferry to visit the three most diverse lagoon islands. See page 224.

Giudecca. Explore an island unscathed by tourism. See page 221.

San Lazzaro degli Armeni. An exotic Armenian island retreat. See page 242.

Sant'Erasmo. An escape to Venice's former market garden. See page 219.

BEST CHURCHES

La Salute. Landmark basilica. See page 201.

Il Redentore. Palladian masterpiece on Giudecca. See page 222.

Santi Giovanni e Paolo. (Zanipolo). Vast Gothic church dominating the square. See page 155.

Santa Maria dell'Assunta. Torcello's Veneto-Byzantine cathedral. See page 229.

I Frari. Franciscan church and canvas for Titian's masterpieces. See page 181.

San Sebastiano. Magnificent shrine to the art of Veronese. See page 206.

Madonna dell'Orto. Here you'll see Tintoretto's genius. See page 191.

San Giorgio degli Schiavoni. A remarkable cycle of paintings by Carpaccio. See page 159.

FESTIVALS AND EVENTS

Carnival. This masked extravaganza is a surreal 10-day party. See page 75.

La Festa della Sensa and La Vogalonga. May Ascension Day festival and regatta followed by a race around the city and lagoon. See page 80.

La Festa del Redentore. The July festival celebrates the city's salvation from plague with a picnic and procession. See page 81.

Il Biennale. The major six-month-long art extravaganza is staged in uneven years. See page 171.

Regata Storica. The September Historical Regatta is Venice's best water festival. See page 80.

Venice Film Festival. Hollywood comes to town in September for the movie awards. See page 232.

La Fenice. The opera season in the recon-structed opera house is unmissable. See pages 73 and 114.

Venezia Suona. Bands of all musical persuasions fill the air with their tunes in squares across the city on a June weekend. See page 252.

For more events, see page 251.

Festa del Redentore revellers.

Harry's Bar.

BEST BARS AND CAFÉS

Harry's Bar. Italy's most legendary bar, where the Bellini cocktail was invented. See page 114.

Caffè Florian. Founded in 1720, this is the oldest surviving café in Italy, home to a string quartet and a sumptuous interior. See page 87.

Caffè Quadri. Across Piazza San Marco is Florian's rival. See page 87.

Bancogiro. A cool waterfront Rialto bar popular with Venetians and visitors alike (www.osteriabancogiro.it).

Centrale. A slick Manhattan-style moment – with gondola waiting in the wings (www.caffecentralevenezia.com).

Cantina Do Mori. A *bacaro*, or traditional wine bar, for a taste of everyday Venice, including *cichetti* (savoury bar snacks). See page 176.

Muro Vino e Cucina. A hip bar by the Rialto markets where locals spill outside with cocktails in hand (www.murovenezia.com).

MONEY-SAVING TIPS

Several passes can save you money on sightseeing in Venice. A **Museum Pass** (www.visitmuve.it; adult/child €24/18) allows entry to the city's 11 civic museums (see page 109). A **Chorus Pass** (tel: 041-275 0462; www.chorusvenezia.org; child/adult/family €8/12/24) offers admission to 16 of the city's most interesting churches.

Venezia Unica (tel: 041-2424; www.veneziaunica.it) is an all-in-one city pass allowing unlimited use of public transport, free entry to Venice's museums, churches and various cultural events, as well as other services. The pass can be purchased online and collected from one of the sales kiosks or ticket booths throughout the city. The price varies according to the number of services chosen (from €27).

For €6, the **Rolling VENICE** card allows younger visitors (ages 14 to 29) to pay only €22 for a 72-hour transport pass worth €40 and offers discounted entry to many sights. Cards are available at Venezia Unica vaporetto (ferry) ticket booths and online.

A Venezia Unica card is a hefty investment, so weigh up your needs. Catching vaporetti is expensive, so walking is one way of saving cash. However, sooner or later you may want to take a ride. Single-ride vaporetto tickets are expensive, so opt for a multi-day pass. Passes are available for 1/2/3 or days (€20/30/40/60). If you don't plan to visit many museums, this is the cheaper option.

Venice, entirely built on water.

Two Venice icons: La Salute church and gondoliers.

Grand Canal view from the Gothic
Ca`d'Oro.

VENICE'S ALLURE

More like a stage set than a city, Venice has captivated visitors for centuries. It dazzles and mesmerises, although it can also overwhelm and confuse the unprepared.

Endlessly portrayed by writers, painters and philosophers, Venice is a canvas for every clichéd fantasy. Almost everyone who is anyone has been there. As a result, Venice can play cultural one-upmanship better than most cities. The Romantics were rewarded with a feeling of having come too late to a world too old. The Victorians saw Venice as dying, while contemporary doom-mongers now seek to bury the city anew. Although entombment by the sea would show symmetry, this resilient city rejects such neat scenarios.

Gondolas at sunset.

The only city in the world built entirely on water, Venice is no mere fantasy land, but a very real and extraordinary freeze-frame of glorious history that can uplift the spirit. The city offers a cradle-to-the-grave experience in the best possible taste. You can sleep in Tchaikovsky's bed or wake up in cavernous apartments that once welcomed princes and doges, Henry James and Hemingway. For romance, you can walk in Casanova's footsteps; for baroque passion, succumb to a Vivaldi concerto in Chiesa di Santa Maria Formosa, or savour the gondoliers' songs that inspired Verdi and Wagner. If you are feeling adventurous, bargain in the Rialto with latter-day merchants of Venice, or pick up the cobalt-blue cabbages that sent Elizabeth David into culinary raptures.

Carnival masks.

If you are feeling contemplative, you can ponder the passing of time with Proust's ghost in Caffè Florian. If fortunate, you can capture Canaletto's views with your camera, or see Titian's painting in the church it was designed for. If gregarious, you can savour the gossip and Martinis at Harry's Bar, Hemingway's favourite.

For more than a millennium, the Republic of Venice used all its strength to repel unwelcome invaders. Today one of the world's greatest maritime powers has become one of the world's greatest tourist attractions. Its sheer uniqueness makes it a wonder of the world.

Gondoliers waiting for customers.

THE VENETIANS

They're often characterised as being cold and contradictory, but the lagoon-dwellers do have a surprisingly hedonistic streak.

The character of Venice "is old, conservative and resistant to change. Here in the historic centre we lack the capacity for renewal, or even the numbers required to effect a change" said Massimo Cacciari, as lugubriously as ever, during his tenure as mayor (2005–2010). Certainly, the population is ageing, with the number of visitors greatly exceeding that of the resident population.

Yet the elusive Venetian spirit transcends such truisms, defies the simple arithmetic of the doom-mongers, and refuses to be confined by the straight-jacket of tourism. In a city defined by the sea, there can be no fortress mentality, only ebb and flow. In short, the slippery lagoon-dwellers retain their distinctiveness, or as much of it as they ever had.

> High rents have forced many Venetians to abandon the city at nightfall to return to their homes in Mestre, leaving Venice to *foresti* (outsiders), wealthier Venetians and staunch working-class residents.

Paolo Costa, Cacciari's predecessor, is worried little is being done to work on Venice's future. In his ideal city, Venetians would be involved in nebulous high-tech industries and be free from the yoke of tourism. By the same token, he also raised the occasionally repeated prospect of simply levying a day entry charge on tourists. Indeed, every few years, a new administration flirts with the idea of controlling access to the city by means of computerised

Ready for Carnival.

entry cards. Tourists have always been deplored but as the cliché runs: Venice without visitors would simply not be Venice.

Patrician Francesco da Mosto decries Venetian pageants as "pantomime on water", and worries that the few remaining schools will close before his children have finished their education. His barber's response is more pragmatic, admitting that "if tourism collapsed, we would too". Bartender Claudia Ruzzenenti concurs, while deploring the summer deluge: "Any Venetians who can, go away – we have to stay and work. Still, *non si sputa dove si mangia* – you don't spit where you eat, as we say, and tourism is all Venice has got."

The survival of the local dialect, Venexian, forms a strong bond with the Venetians who have moved to the mainland *al di là dall' acqua*. The impenetrable dialect is also a way of keeping in touch with Venetian values and of preserving privacy. Not that the Venetians wish to be unfriendly to visitors: they are naturally sociable, and happy to share their home with like-minded spirits. Nor do they wish to live in a museum, but in a living city.

> Even Marco Polo, the legendary explorer who wound up in the service of Kublai Khan, remained a home-town boy at heart: "Every time I describe a city, I am saying something about Venice."

To this end, they are courteous and tolerant, as befits a cosmopolitan people who have come to terms with the loss of empire. Their

There are almost three times as many pensioners as children under 14.

philosophical detachment is often mistaken for aloofness, with their calm and sanguine air likened to Anglo-Saxon aplomb.

Eternal outsiders

Italians from elsewhere still harbour a vague antipathy to the city, fuelled by historical grievances. The Republic was feared and respected but not much loved. Venetian justice was severe and far-reaching, with cruel deaths reserved for traitors to the Republic. Widespread fear was engendered by the Venetians' skill at spying. Within Venice, post-boxes for secret denunciations, known as *bocche di leoni* (lions' mouths), were placed along the walls of public buildings. But in marked contrast to modern-day Italian political ethics, the Republic was no respecter of rank – even a doge could be condemned. Moreover, the system was fair: if the charge was false, the accuser was punished as if he had been guilty of the very same crime. Venice was also the first state in Italy to abolish slavery and the death penalty. Even rivals grudgingly admired the Venetians' autonomous approach and the mercantile spirit of a great trading empire, as well as their shrewd mastery of foreign affairs and good governance of the Republic at home.

Today, the lingering image of the Venetians is that of a cool, closed people, cosmopolitan and conservative but concealing a sinister heart. There is a lighter side: a satirical, playful nature sustained by pageantry, carnivals and masked balls. The Venetians were always prone to social ostentation, lavish expenditure and a love of finery. This hedonistic reputation was acquired in the 18th century during a period of decadence, even if strict sumptuary laws and dress codes supposedly restricted the use of luxury fabrics.

City of Casanova and illicit liaisons

From medieval times onwards, Venice was famed for its courtesans and enjoyed a risqué image that persists to the present. Situated midway between seductiveness and salaciousness, Venice still relishes its reputation as a place for mistresses and illicit assignations. In the 15th century, prostitution in the Frezzeria quarter near San Marco was officially sanctioned,

A non-traditional way to cross the canal.

Labyrinthine Venice

Venice is a labyrinth, even with a map. The city is split into six *sestieri*, or districts, each with its main church and *campo* (square). Although the distinctiveness of individual parishes is fading, Cannaregio, in particular, retains its character as the last bastion for working-class Venetians who have not moved to the mainland. As in parts of Castello, washing-bedecked alleys are home to children and cats. Around the Rialto lies a humble slice of Venetian life, with a popular market, one of the few places where both Italian and the sing-song of Venetian dialect predominate. But throughout Venice, the *campo* is at the heart of community life. Away from San Marco, Sunday is still spent streaming from church to a trattoria for lunch.

As the slow exodus from the city continues (the number of Venice's inhabitants has fallen over the last decade to about 56,000 – the lowest ever), the Venetians are in a deadly vice, exacerbated by the cost of housing and lack of help for new businesses. The middle classes are the most vociferous, complaining that they are

supposedly to preserve the honour of Venetian ladies. Brothels also flourished in the banking district of the Rialto, the commercial hub of the Republic, which was soon to become equally famous for its fleshpots.

A 16th-century survey noted that the city had 3,000 noblewomen but more than 11,000 prostitutes. In a city graced by gondolas, dreamy mists and Casanova, the arch-seducer, seduction was raised to a fine art.

A well-deserved reputation for pleasure-seeking should not obscure the Venetians' more refined tastes. Their pronounced aesthetic sense is clearly evident in art and architecture. In painting they show a poetic sensibility and a penchant for colour and sensuality, rather than for more rational, monumental forms. As for architecture, while the Florentine palazzo is generally austere and unadorned, the Venetian equivalent is opulent and ostentatious, a showy symbol of prestige.

The Venetians are also noted for their curiosity and spirit of intellectual enquiry, a disposition that led to great empire-building. This lofty outlook is tempered by a profound indifference to matters beyond the lagoon.

Gondoliers in classic striped top and straw boater.

A typical bacaro.

too poor to buy property but deemed too rich to be eligible for subsidised housing. Venetian demographics also mean that there are almost three times as many pensioners as children under 14. Churches are under threat of closure, with an average of 30 parishioners who attend Mass, all elderly.

> Venetians, when asked the way, are known for always declaring: "sempre diritto, cinque minuti" (straight ahead, five minutes), no matter how misleading this may be.

By contrast, Venice's 4,000 children seem to lead a charmed life, despite the lack of facilities. Although they play in the Giardini Pubblici, the main park, most prefer their parish *campo*. San Giacomo dell'Orio, one of the city's most domesticated squares, is typical, home to daredevil children kicking footballs against the Byzantine apses while parents look on fondly. Although teenagers fare less well, there is a vibrant university quarter around Ca' Foscari and San Barnaba in Dorsoduro. To outsiders, the quirkiness of studious Venice, and especially of everyday Venice, holds a rarified, undeniable charm.

The Venetian philosophy

In Venice one walks, and there is always time to greet friends, gossip, choose between the grand Caffè Florian and a cosy neighbourhood bar in the Rialto market. Venetians love stretching out a social greeting into a leisurely chat. Standing at a bar counter, the locals sip an *ombretta*, a small glass of wine, and choose *cichetti*, savoury snacks of meatballs, baby squid or marinated sardines. If, on the other hand, two Venetians who have fallen out prefer not to talk as they pass one another, they have a way of acknowledging each other wordlessly and moving on without a fuss.

A Venetian élite may still meet to strains of Vivaldi at the fireside of a freshly gilded

Venetian street scene.

The seaside resort on the city's doorstep is the Lido, that elegant bathing beach which becomes a second home to Venetians in summer. On sweltering Sundays, the Lido's manicured beaches may be packed, but the more knowing choose to cycle along the Lido's Lungomare (Esplanade), from the quaysides to the Adriatic sea walls.

In a city where everything is conditioned by water, cool, independent Venetians are nothing if not survivors. Faced with Venice's mounting debt (due in part to the cost associated with frequent flooding but also to a series of corruption scandals), new mayor Luigi Brugnaro is considering selling some of the city's prestigious artworks. In 2015 Conservative and controversial Brugnaro caused public outcry when he banned all picture books with homosexuality content from Venice's public school libraries. He also announced that there would be no Gay Pride in Venice while he was mayor – though he retracted his statement only a few days later and allowed the event to go ahead. The mayor shows himself to be a contradictory character, and that is the mark of a true Venetian.

Fresh produce at the Erberia.

salon. However, most Venetians prefer a prosaic stroll and a meal out, knowing that a "prosaic" stroll around the canalsides can encompass more magic and drama than is on offer in any of the city's formal theatres. However, Venetian culture-vultures are well catered for. The Goldoni Theatre stages plays by the eponymous playwright (1707–93), author of delightful comedies in Venetian dialect. La Fenice and the Teatro Malibran stage fine opera. Gamblers will choose the Casino, in Palazzo Vendramin-Calergi, on the Grand Canal, formerly Wagner's home. The Film Festival, Biennale and Carnival are highlights of the Venetian social calendar.

At the first hint of summer, Venetian nobles fled the city for the Palladian villas of the Brenta Canal, a practice that still prevails on a small scale. Today's Venetians are vigorous outdoor folk, on the water in summer and on the ski slopes in winter. Thanks to its unique location, Venice has much to offer nature-lovers: the lagoon provides contemplation for fishermen and bird-watchers.

DECISIVE DATES

AD 337
First record of a lagoon settlement.

421
Legendary foundation of Venice on 25 March, conveniently the Feast Day of St Mark.

452
Attila the Hun plunders the Veneto.

453
Aquilea sacked by Attila, prompting an exodus of refugees towards Venetian lagoon.

568
Mass migrations take place from the mainland to Venice.

639
The island of Torcello is colonised and the cathedral founded.

697
According to Venetian legend, the election of

Paoluccio Anafesta, the first doge.

Paoluccio Anafesta, the first doge.

726
Election of Orso Ipato, the first recorded doge, who rules the lagoon from the now-vanished colony of Heraclea.

800
Charlemagne is crowned Holy Roman Emperor.

Gold and silver bust of Charlemagne from 1349.

814
The population of Venice moves to the Rivo Alto (Rialto), a more hospitable and easily defended island. Venetian coins first minted. Work begins on the first Palazzo Ducale (Doge's Palace).

828
Theft of St Mark's body; Venetian sailors said to have taken his remains from Alexandria to Venice.

832
First Basilica di San Marco completed.

840
Tacit independence from Byzantium.

1000
Venice controls the Adriatic coast. The Marriage to the Sea ceremony is inaugurated in honour of Doge Pietro Orseolo II's defeat of Dalmatian pirates in the Adriatic.

1095–9
Venice joins the Crusades, providing ships and supplies for the First Crusade to liberate the Holy Land.

1104
The foundation of the Arsenale.

1128
First street lighting in Venice.

1171
The six districts (*sestieri*) founded.

1173
First Rialto Bridge begun.

1202–4
The Fourth Crusade; the sack of Constantinople and the Venetian conquest of Byzantium provides the springboard for the growth of the Venetian empire.

1271–95
Marco Polo's epic journey to China. Later captured by the Genoese, he writes of his adventures in prison in Genoa.

1284
Gold ducats are first minted in Venice.

1297
Establishment of a patrician autocracy.

1309
Work begins on the present Palazzo Ducale.

1310
The Council of Ten is established as a check on individual power and as a monitor of security.

1325
The names of Venetian noble families are first inscribed in the *Libro d'Oro*, the Golden Book, or aristocratic register.

1348–9
An outbreak of plague kills half the population of Venice.

1355
Doge Faliero (Falier) is beheaded for treason

against the Venetian Republic.

1382
Jews permitted to operate as moneylenders.

1379–80
The Battle of Chioggia and decisive defeat of the Genoese takes place.

1403–5
The acquisition of Belluno, Padua, Verona.

1453
Constantinople falls to Turks.

1454
Acquisition of Treviso, Friuli, Bergamo and Ravenna – the zenith of Venetian power.

1457
The powerful Doge Foscari is deposed.

1489
Cyprus is ceded to Venice by Queen Caterina Cornaro (Corner).

1506
Names of Venetian ruling families are fixed in the Golden Book: no new entries allowed.

1508
League of Cambrai unites Europe against Venice. Titian's *Assumption* is hung in the Frari church, Venice. Birth of Palladio, architect from the Veneto.

1516
Jews confined to the Venetian Ghetto.

1518
Birth of Tintoretto, the celebrated Venetian Mannerist painter.

1528
Birth of Paolo Veronese.

1570
Loss of Cyprus to the Turks.

1571
Battle of Lepanto, decisive naval victory against the Turks.

Battle of Lepanto on 7 October 1571, where the Ottoman forces were defeated by the Christians under Don Juan of Austria.

The Grevenbroeck Manuscript depicts a doctor during the plague in Venice.

1577
The architect Palladio designs Il Redentore (The Redeemer) church.

1567
Birth of the composer Monteverdi.

1580
Birth of the baroque architect Baldassare Longhena.

1630
Venice is struck once again by an outbreak of plague.

1669
Loss of Crete – the last major Venetian colony – to the Turks.

1693
Birth of Tiepolo, the rococo artist.

1703
Antonio Vivaldi is appointed musical director of La Pietà church.

1708
A severe winter freezes the lagoon, allowing Venetians to walk to the mainland.

1718
Venice surrenders Morea (Peloponnese) to the Turks under the Treaty of Passarowitz; Venice left with its mainland empire, Istria, Dalmatia, coastal Albania, Corfu and some Ionian islands.

1720
The opening of Caffè Florian.

1752
Completion of the sea walls.

1755
Giovanni Giacomo Casanova is imprisoned in the Palazzo Ducale.

1757
Antonio Canova, neo-classical sculptor known for his realism, is born.

1790
Opening of La Fenice opera house.

1797
The fall of the 1,000-year-old Venetian Republic. Doge Lodovico Manin abdicates. Napoleon grants Venice and its territories to Austria in return for Lombardy.

1800
Papal conclave in Venice to elect pope.

1805–14
Venice under Napoleonic rule.

1815–66
Venice ceded to Austria under the terms of the Congress of Vienna.

1817
Accademia art collections opened to the public for the first time.

1846
Venice is finally joined to the mainland by a railway causeway.

1848
Venetian uprising against the Austrians takes place and a republic is set up. Austria retakes the city in 1849.

1861
Vittorio Emanuele crowned King of Italy.

Daniel Manin proclaiming Venice a republic in Piazza San Marco in 1848.

1866
Venice joins the Kingdom of Italy.

1885
First Biennale art exhibition.

1902
The Campanile (belltower) in Piazza San Marco collapses.

1918
Austrian air force bombs Venice.

How the MOSE will eventually look.

1926
The Porto Marghera industrial zone is built.

1932
First Venice Film Festival.

1933
A road causeway to the mainland is opened.

1945
British troops liberate the city from its Nazi occupiers.

1960
Construction of the Marco Polo airport.

1966
The worst flood in Venetian history hits the city, provoking a debate about restoration.

1979
The Venice Carnival is revived.

1985
Centenary of Biennale art exhibition.

1996
Burning down of La Fenice. The worst floods and *acqua alta* (high tides) since 1966.

1997
Radical separatists briefly capture the Campanile di San Marco.

2003
MOSE, the mobile dam project, gets the go-ahead and work begins.

2004
La Fenice opera house reopens after its reconstruction.

2005
Left-wing philosopher Massimo Cacciari elected mayor for second time; French magnate and collector of contemporary art, François Pinault, buys Palazzo Grassi and turns it into contemporary art gallery.

2008
Ponte di Calatrava, designed by Spanish architect Santiago Calatrava and the fourth bridge over the Grand Canal, opens after years of delays.

2009
The right-wing separatist Northern League wins the province of Venice in elections; Punta della Dogana contemporary art gallery, financed by François Pinault, opens.

2012
Serious flooding, with *acqua alta* (high water) of 149cm (5ft), the fifth highest in the last 150 years.

2013
The population of Venice falls to below 60,000.

2014
Venice's mayor Giorgio Orsoni and 35 others are accused of siphoning off millions of euros from the MOSE flood barrier project.

2015
Architect Luigi Brugnaro elected as the new mayor.

2018–2020
MOSE, the controversial and long overdue system of 78 mobile dams protecting the lagoon, is due to become fully operational.

CITY IN THE LAGOON

It had an unpromising start, founded by refugees among stagnant marshes on the shores of the Adriatic. Yet Venice became the most powerful city in the West.

Venice as a city "was a foundling, floating upon the waters like Moses in a basket among the bulrushes. It was therefore obliged to be inventive, to steal and to improvise." Writer Mary McCarthy sets the scene for the city's mythic status. The legendary foundation of Venice was in AD 421, on 25 March, a date conveniently coinciding with the feast of the city's patron saint, St Mark. Venice readily spun itself a romantic tapestry that has hoodwinked many a historian. Unlike its mainland rivals, Venice had been born free and Christian but without a golden Roman past.

> "Who in their senses would build more than a fishing hut on the malarial, malodorous shoals and sandbanks of the Venetian lagoon?" John Julius Norwich answers his own question: "Those who had no choice."

To make amends, the city claimed descent from ancient Troy and cultivated the mystique of Byzantium, its one and only master. Early settlers in Venice brought Roman souvenirs salvaged from their ruined homes on the mainland. This city without antiquity also looked east for its aesthetic identity, with Constantinople (modern Istanbul) the unwitting provider of purloined memorials to a fabricated golden age.

The barbarians swept through Italy in the 5th and 6th centuries, leaving a trail of devastation. The refugees, driven from the remnants of a glorious Roman past, found themselves washed up on these inhospitable islands.

Early settlements in the lagoon, a 16th-century drawing by Sabbadino.

Early settlements

Conventional wisdom has it that Venice was founded by migrants from the mainland fleeing to safety in the lagoon. However, it is conceivable the lagoon was already home to a fishing community. The first exodus was prompted by the arrival of Attila the Hun bearing down on northern Italy. Mass migrations began in AD 568 after a wave of Goths swept through the Veneto, terrorising the populations of Padua, Altino and Aquileia. The fugitives fled to the marshy coast and lagoon islands, settling in Chioggia, Malamocco, Torcello, Murano and

Detail from The Sack of the Byzantium by Tintoretto, whose gift for dramatic storytelling is evident.

Burano. The island of Torcello was colonised in AD 639 and remained the leading Venetian lagoon city, site of a magnificent cathedral, until the population's definitive move to the Rialto in AD 814.

As a vassal of Byzantium, the Eastern Roman Empire, Torcello acted as an effective trading post with Constantinople. Unlike many mainland cities, Venice was never feudal but born mercantile. A keen commercial spirit was bolstered by protectionism and monopolies. The shortage of land and the exposed position in the lagoon turned the island dwellers into skilful traders.

The medium of exchange was salt and salted fish, called "edible money" by the chronicler Cassiodorus. Yet even in the 8th century Venetian traders visited the Lombard capital of Pavia laden down with velvets and silks, peacock feathers and prized furs.

Trade brings wealth

Venice bordered two worlds: the Byzantine and Muslim East and the Latin-Germanic West. As the gateway to the East, the city traded Levantine incense, silks and spices for northern staples, including salt and wheat. Venice was helped by its command of the river mouths leading into northern Italy. The city conveniently lay at the crossing of rival trading routes: the Byzantine sway over Mediterranean trade was challenged by Muslim commercial routes, a consequence of the Arab conquest of Syria, North Africa and Spain.

When the population moved to the relative safety of the Rivo Alto (literally the "high bank", the site of today's Rialto markets), the Venice we know today was born. The election of the first doge in AD 726 paved the way for the oligarchy that founded Venice's fortune. Work on the doge's first fortress-palace commenced in AD 814, laying the foundations for the present palace. The institution of the doge was a marker in Venetian independence, a confident identity crowned by the patronage of St Mark. Venice was only nominally under Byzantine rule, and its independence was tacitly acknowledged in AD 840 when the city signed a treaty with the

Pile Drivers by Giovanni Grevembroch.

Holy Roman Emperor without seeking permission from Constantinople.

The theft of St Mark's relics from Alexandria in AD 828 showed the Venetian gift for improvisation and myth-making: the deed granted the city instant status, mystique and the presumed protection of St Mark. The Venetian triumph was marked by the decision to build Basilica di San Marco (St Mark's Basilica) the following year. Under the protection of St Mark, Venice could equate material gain with spiritual riches. Trade was turned into a means of glorifying the fledgling city; Christian duty later sanctioned the Crusades against the infidels (and entitled the victors to spoils). If Venice enjoyed a reputation as a virtuous state, it was a reflection of its perceived stability rather than its morals. Yet this continuity was the product of a singular government.

Conquests and crusades

By AD 1000, Venice controlled the Adriatic coast. The conquest of Dalmatia (Croatia) was achieved under Doge Pietro Orseolo (991–1009). His diplomatic skills were even greater than his military prowess, and he successfully juggled the powers of East and West. Ready supplies of timber, iron and hemp provided a stimulus to the burgeoning Venetian shipbuilding industry. The Venetians were soon the leading ship operators in the Mediterranean. Nonetheless, from the 11th century Venice faced naval challenges from the merchant republics of Pisa and Genoa. The Venetians defeated the Pisans off Rhodes in 1099, signalling the despatch of a former maritime power. From then on, the main threat was posed by the Genoese and the Turks.

The First Crusade was launched by Pope Urban II in 1095 to protect Byzantium and free the Holy Land. Jerusalem was captured in 1099 and a feudal kingdom established there. Venice participated eagerly, shamelessly exploiting both sides. Not only did the Venetian fleet return from the East laden with booty in 1100, but the episode acted as a spur to their maritime ambitions. Venice extended its foothold in the Aegean, Syria and the Black Sea. In 1122 the Venetians defeated the Egyptian fleet that was besieging Jaffa and then went on to sack Byzantine ports in the Aegean and the Adriatic. Trade in the Levant increased with ships sailing to Haifa, Jaffa and Tyre.

HOW TO BUILD ON WATER

Venice is built on mudflats and sandbanks divided by canals and swept by the ebb and flow of tides. To make marshy pockets suitable as building land, the early city government permitted the dumping of ballast and waste; this caused silting and the formation of mudbanks. However, the instability of the terrain – made up of layers of mud, clay, sand and peat – meant that the foundations needed to be very deep and very solid. Buildings were supported by a forest of timber piles *(pali)* driven deep into the subsoil. The oak piles came from the Lido and were later supplemented by oak, larch and pine from the Alps and Dalmatia (modern-day Croatia), a Venetian territory.

Working from the outside in, concentric circles of piles were driven through the unstable lagoon floor to the bedrock of compacted clay. The number and thickness of the piles depended on the weight of the building: La Salute church, for instance, is supported by over a million piles. The piles provided the base for a platform of horizontal beams, the *zatterone*, a raft-like structure made of larchwood, cemented in place with a mixture of stone and brick. The floor was then reinforced with Istrian stone; this stone, resistant to salt erosion, helped create damp-proof foundations. Oak beams and boards were placed on top, often finished by a traditional light marble floor.

The Fourth Crusade (1202–4) marked a turning point in Venetian history, the spur to its formation of a maritime empire, commanding the Adriatic and eastern Mediterranean. During the Crusades, the Venetians traded with both sides as well as profiting from the transport of pilgrims; since the Venetians supplied the fleet, pilgrims who failed to pay were sold as slaves. The Crusades reached a climax in the sack of Constantinople, led by the blind but charismatic 90-year-old Doge Enrico Dandolo. The Venetians were skilled at siege operations and returned in 1204 for a successful assault on a city that, as the seat of the Byzantine Eastern Empire, had never fallen. Venice was rewarded with the lion's share of the new Latin empire.

The Venetian victory is regarded as a shameful episode, with the invaders charged with wanton destruction and the deposing of the Greek emperor. In addition to receiving three-eighths of the empire, vital trading ports, Constantinople's arsenal and docks, the Venetians looted the city. Booty, now in the Basilica di San Marco, included the rearing Roman horses from the stadium in Constantinople.

Arrival of the relics of St Mark, a 13th-century mosaic on the west facade of Basilica di San Marco.

> *Machiavelli, the great political thinker, was impressed by the Venetians' imperialist ambitions, their skill at diplomacy, and their name which "spread terror over the seas".*

The Sea State

Dominion of the seas was paramount to Venetian policy and this led to repeated conflicts with rival maritime power, Genoa. This culminated in the 1379–80 Battle of Chioggia, which was sparked by the Venetian claim to control the Dardanelles. In response, the Genoese mounted a naval blockade at Chioggia. The Genoese penetrated the lagoon but failed to challenge the city of Venice. The result was a decisive Venetian victory and the once-great naval power of Genoa no longer posed a threat.

Much more troubling was the devastation caused by the Black Death. The plague of 1348 reduced the city's population by three-fifths. In the 14th century, Venice had 160,000 inhabitants at a time when a city of 20,000 was considered large. It took the city almost 200 years to return to the same size.

The State's reputation for ruthlessness was merited. When Doge Vitale Michiel was assassinated in 1172 his murderers sought refuge in San Zaccaria. As a punishment, neighbouring houses were razed to the ground and a ban imposed upon building in stone, one that survived until this century. Treason was always punishable by death. Antonio Foscarini, a 17th-century ambassador to France and England, was falsely condemned as a spy and hanged by his foot in the Piazzetta, a common Venetian end. This successful, if sinister, state was run by a closed circle, with its workings inscrutable, not merely to outsiders but to many of its participants as well.

Venetian grandeur was built on the bedrock of a unique system of government. The State was governed according to an extraordinary combination of monarchical, patrician and democratic principles. Its stability was guaranteed by a sophisticated system of checks and balances, which prevented any one family or individual from seizing power. Not that the system was immune to abuse, however. Before each major vote, members of the *Maggior Consiglio* (Great Council) used to gather in front of the

Fourteenth-century manuscript showing spoils of war being distributed.

Palazzo Ducale (Doge's Palace), where the richer members tried to buy the votes of the impoverished nobles, who were called the *barnabotti*. Named the *broglio*, after the area in front of the palace, this practice has also bequeathed us the term "imbroglio".

As the bedrock of the Republic, the Great Council confirmed political appointments and passed laws. Although it could not propose laws, it had the power of veto. One of its major functions was to elect the doge, the leader of the Republic. The Council sat in the Palazzo Ducale, with the doge in the centre, on the bench of St Mark, and the nobles ranged around him. Designed to represent the whole city, in time the Council became an élite corps of the Venetian nobility.

In 1297 a reform known as the "Closure of the Great Council" increased membership to 1,000, with all noblemen over the age of 26 obliged to serve; by 1323 membership was for life, and by the 16th century there were several thousand members, representing various branches of 150 families. In effect, every nobleman was a servant of the State. The onerous nature of this service is clear in the weekly

Marco Polo leaving Venice on his second trip to China (1271), from a 14th-century manuscript.

Marco Polo

Modern scholars are divided as to whether Marco Polo's epic journeys into Asia are wondrous fact or glorious fabrication.

Supporters of Marco Polo see him as the first explorer and chronicler of China, a talented merchant and administrator who found favour with the Great Mongol Kublai Khan.

Like many wealthy Venetian merchant families, the Polo clan maintained trad-

Woodcut of Marco Polo from the German edition of his book of travels.

ing houses abroad, at Constantinople and in the Crimea. The family home was in Cannaregio, where the atmospheric courtyard still stands (see page 195). Tradition has it that there were two journeys, the first in 1265 ending in the East,

and the second in 1271–95, which centred on an extended stay in China. It is this second expedition, involving Marco Polo and his uncles, which is controversial. After a three-year journey through Baghdad, Persia and central Asia, they reached Peking in 1275.

There have been attempts to debunk the Marco Polo story, but some facts are beyond dispute. He was imprisoned in 1298 by the Genoese, and he recorded his exploits in *Il Milione*, or *The Travels of Marco Polo*. Yet there are no references to him in Chinese records. Polo did not mention the custom of foot-binding, the Great Wall of China escaped his attention and he failed to notice tea ceremonies despite visiting such tea-growing centres as Hangzhou and Fujian.

The case for Marco Polo rests on the fact that he was a merchant, not a historian, primarily interested in the East for the purposes of trade. His defenders argue that women with bound feet would be closeted at home; that he probably had interpreters; and if Chinese records fail to mention the Venetian, he was mere wallpaper in the splendid court of the Kublai Khan at Shangdu.

Polo chronicled everything from the system of taxation and administration to the abundance of cotton and silk, sugar, spices and pepper. Chinese novelties Polo recorded include the practice of coal mining and the Chinese skill at making porcelain.

Critics claim that Marco Polo based his book on his uncles' genuine forays into the East, interwoven with extravagant tales told by other merchants and information plagiarised from Persian guidebooks. Even on Polo's return to Venice in 1295, contemporaries found his tales hard to believe, such as his description of Hangzhou, which, with a population of 2 million, was the biggest city in the world. Whatever the veracity of his accounts of the "lands of spices", Marco Polo fascinated and influenced generations of seafarers, including Christopher Columbus.

Sunday sittings and numerous unpaid duties. In session, secret notes were circulated with the common plea: "Don't elect me! Don't see me!"

The Senate proposed and debated legislation as well as providing the administrative class. Created *c.*1250, it comprised approximately 60 members chosen from the Grand Council and elected for a year, although this time limit could be extended by re-election. Senators had to be over the age of 40, although the age limit was eventually lowered to 30. They were helped by more than 100 *ex officio* members who had no voting rights. The Council of Ten, which was established in 1310, was designed to safeguard the constitutional institutions of the Republic. Presided over by the doge, the Council comprised 10 senators and six "sages". In time, it acquired a sinister reputation, thanks to the pervasiveness and the brutal efficiency of the revered Venetian secret police.

The Council also responded to the anonymous denunciations posted in *bocche di leoni* (lions' heads) placed outside public buildings. In addition, the Republic was underpinned by myriad other councils and consultative bodies.

Queen of the Seas

As the supreme naval power of the age, Venice was truly the Queen of the Seas. While Tuscan and Genoese wealth depended on banking and industry, the Venetian Republic prospered on foreign trade alone. Although patrician, the governing class were merchants rather than feudal barons or rentiers. From the start, Venice had imperial ambitions only in so far as they secured maritime trade; conquest was secondary.

The emerging empire never lost touch with its mercantile roots. Yet this quest for supremacy would never have been successful without the city's clear sense of identity, a self-confidence verging on vanity. The "soldiers of the seas" cultivated the spirit of a chosen island race, one set apart by its social cohesion and glorious constitution. The writer Jan Morris even compared Venice with England, "another maritime oligarchy", in which Venetians considered themselves "not rich men or poor men, privileged or powerless, but citizens of Venice".

At home, the State had a monopoly on salt and grain, which were stored in imposing warehouses on the Grand Canal. Local trades included tanning, silk-weaving, glass-blowing, shipbuilding and textiles. However, real wealth rested on international commerce. The great trade routes out of Turkestan, Persia, Arabia and Afghanistan all converged on the seaports of the Levant. These were the shipping lanes that kept the Republic rich.

Egypt, Beirut and Byzantium were trading partners, but Venetian outposts were strung along the shores of the Mediterranean and Middle East.

The empire was highly organised, with bonded warehouses and customs offices imposing levies on all goods that passed through its jurisdiction. The winged lion, the symbol of Venetian ascendancy, flew over countless territories and trading posts throughout the city's expanding empire.

The spice trade

Spices had been a valuable commodity since Roman times, but the Crusades marked the expansion of the trade, one the Venetians monopolised until the 16th century. Exotic seasonings were prized for their pungency, preservative powers and the flavour of distant fabled lands. Venetian

Bellini's painting of Doge Loredan, who ruled for 20 years from 1501.

The Doge in the Great College Doge's Palace, by Hainz.

warehouses were filled with pepper, cinnamon, cloves, ginger, nutmeg and cardamom.

Other luxury goods included silk, furs, velvets, precious stones, perfumes and pearls. The Venetians traded in wine and wheat from Apulia, and wax, honey, oil and wine from the Greek islands. Such Mediterranean goods were traded for Flemish cloth and English wool. Cotton and

Bocca di Leone letterbox.

sugar were shipped from plantations in Cyprus and Egypt while metalwork and precious cloth came from the Levant. From the late 15th century, Venetian State galleys were routed to the Catalan coast and to North Africa, where spices from either Alexandria or Syria could be bartered for local honey, wax and leather.

Maritime ventures

Oriental goods first reached Venice in Byzantine ships but soon the Venetians developed a large merchant-marine fleet. Ships were built in the Arsenale, medieval Europe's largest industrial complex. Sea voyages were nevertheless a dangerous undertaking, with the risk of pirate attacks, stormy weather and poor navigation. Not until the end of the 13th century did accurate charts and compasses assist navigation.

At the beginning of the 15th century, 3,000 trading vessels sailed under the Venetian flag. Most were in the coastal trade, delivering wood, stone or grain, or formed part of the fishing fleet. Overseas trade was carried out by 300 ships which sailed alone or in heavily armed State convoys, a system which survived until the mid-16th century. The costs of safe passage and cargo space acted as an incentive for private shipowners to travel at their own risk and reap the rewards. A way of offsetting the business risk of the perilous voyage was to form a partnership, or *colleganza*. This agreement stipulated that one party remained in Venice and provided three-quarters of the capital while the other, who went on the voyage, put up the remaining quarter. The profit was divided between the two.

The Venetians signed a treaty with the Turks and traded in "goods forbidden to Christians" such as arms, shipbuilding materials and even slaves. Although the slave trade had been forbidden since the 9th century, it was still a good source of income. The slaves were mostly obtained from the Black Sea, to where the convoys sailed on from Byzantium. Greek Orthodox Georgians, for instance, who were resold in Egypt and North Africa, could be traded in good faith as "non-Christians" because they were non-Catholics; nor was trade in heathen slaves forbidden. Pilgrimages represented a profitable sideline for the Venetians: pilgrims were offered a package tour, including the return fare, a donkey ride to Jerusalem and the various customs duties imposed upon Christians in the Holy Land.

The Portuguese voyages of exploration posed the greatest threat to the Republic's monopoly of the spice trade. In 1498 Vasco da Gama rounded the Cape of Good Hope to India, opening up the sea route to the East. The new route provided competition but transport costs were high and, by the mid-1560s, Venice was re-exporting even greater quantities of pepper and cotton than before.

A colonial power

The empire was divided into overseas dominions *(stato da mar)* and mainland territories *(stato da terrafirma)*, with the former originally more important. As early as the 14th century, the Adriatic was known as the Gulf of Venice, such was their trading monopoly. Venetian sway over the Adriatic led to treaties with Slav-controlled ports and then domination of Dalmatia (Croatia). The Greek islands were an attractive prize, yielding wine and corn from Crete, raisins from Zante, olive oil and wine from Corfu. Dominion over key Greek territories had been established in the 13th century, from Mykonos and Corfu (and, for several years, Athens) to Crete, the most valuable colony.

The Albanian coast also presented conquests, as did the Greek mainland: Morea (the

The Venetian Doge's State Galley, by Pieter Mortier (1693).

The Doge

The doge's income was strictly controlled and he was not allowed to accept any gifts except flowers and fragrant herbs – how times have changed.

Of the first 25 doges, three were murdered, one was executed for treason, three were judicially blinded, four were deposed, one was exiled, four abdicated, one became a saint and one was killed in a battle with pirates. Yet the institution of

The doge, like the pope, was elected for life, but bitter politics could make that life short.

electing a doge, the monopoly of old men, functioned well. As the mystical standard-bearer of St Mark and the symbol of republican Venice, the doge had no equal in grandeur among the Italian princes.

Resplendent in gold and white, the doge stood out from the red-clad senators and sombrely dressed patricians. Behind the pomp and ceremony lay the cornerstone of the Republic, an institution dating back to AD 726.

The doge was an elected office from the 9th century, with complicated balloting procedures coming into force in the 12th century. Although care was taken, the names of the same families had a habit of recurring: the Mocenigo clan alone furnished seven doges and the Contarini eight. "They kill not with blood but with ballots" was an outsider's sharp verdict on Venetian machinations.

Even so, the system of State paternalism served its purpose, producing stability and strong government without despotism. The last in a line of 120 doges was elected the year the French Revolution broke out: an oligarchy masquerading as a Republic was challenged by newly republican France.

The doge was elected for life by patrician members of the Great Council. The archetypal doge was a wealthy, 72-year-old elder statesman from a prominent family. To control family cliques, the doge's immediate relations were banned from high office and any commercial enterprise. The doge himself was watched closely; he was forbidden private contact with ambassadors and always accompanied by councillors on foreign missions. Such was the scrutiny that the doge's correspondence was censored. The Republic's myriad advisory bodies, and the complex rotation of offices, ensured that dictatorship was impossible and conspiracies nipped in the bud.

The doge was addressed as the "most serene prince"; unsurprisingly several doges succumbed to princely pomposity, an approach typified by Doge Agostino Barbarigo's addition of a princely staircase to the Palazzo Ducale. Yet despite the restrictions on his power, the doge should not be portrayed as a figurehead. In truth, he was a leading statesman who could work the checks and balances of the Constitution.

Seventeenth-century ship construction in the Arsenale.

Peloponnese) was prized for its wine and wheat. To secure the Gulf of Corinth, Lepanto was acquired in 1407, and Cyprus in 1489.

The 15th century saw a systematic pursuit of the *stato da terrafirma*, Italian mainland territories. By 1405, Vicenza, Verona and Padua had all come under Venetian sway. A century later, Venetian territory encompassed the modern regions of the Veneto and Friuli-Venezia Giulia, as well as the Istrian peninsula. The mainland territories were not a poor substitute for overseas dominions but part of the Venetians' plans for consolidation. Indeed, these Italian lands later compensated for losses in the East. Under Doge Francesco Foscari, Venice pursued an expansionist policy in mainland Italy: between 1432 and 1454, conquests around Brescia in Lombardy were followed by control of the entire area up to the river Adda, just east of Milan.

In 1453 Constantinople fell to the Turks, leaving Venice the leading Christian city in the Mediterranean. Ottoman expansion was initially a spur to Venice, since many dominions sought Venetian protection. Moreover, the Turks were more interested in slaves and tributes than in disrupting trade. For Venetians, religion was not allowed to interfere with commerce. Pope Pius II berated the Venetians: "Too much intercourse with the Turks has made you the friend of Mohammedans." But Venetian merchants had always traded as readily with Egyptian and Syrian Muslims as with Greek Christians in Byzantium.

> Two types of ship were used in international trade: the long galley, complete with sails and oars, which controlled the trade in luxury goods, and cogs – roomy sailing ships.

The Turkish threat

By the late 15th century the Turks were in a position to challenge the Republic's maritime empire, but relatively few Venetian possessions were lost. Venetian policy in the 16th century was designed to keep its possessions intact in the face of Turkish expansion and the ambitions of the European powers. The League of Cambrai in 1508 was an attempt by the European powers and the Italian city-states to

Painting of the Riva dei Schiavoni, by Leandro Bassano (1557–1622)

check Venetian expansion. However, by devious diplomacy Venice regained and consolidated its lost possessions. A policy of appeasement with Istanbul (Constantinople) was carried out to protect Venetian trade, helped by the fact that the Turks depended upon Venice for access to European markets. Yet Venice was ready to resist Ottoman expansion: to these ends, great fortresses were erected in Corfu, Crete, Cyprus, on the Greek mainland and in Dalmatia.

> When Famagosta, the last Venetian bastion on Cyprus, fell to the Turks in 1571, the Venetian commander was skinned alive and his stuffed skin was sent to Constantinople as a gift to the Sultan.

In 1570–1, the Turks brutally captured Cyprus, a Venetian possession, provoking the Christian world to respond to the "infidels". In 1571 the Holy League of Venice, Spain and the papacy engaged the enemy off Lepanto, a Hellenic port. Although outnumbered, the Christians inflicted a crushing defeat on the Turks in one of the greatest Mediterranean naval battles. Around 30,000 Turks were killed or captured, with 9,000 Christian casualties, but the Christians failed to follow up their famous victory.

Sunset on the serene society

The 17th century brought the Venetians little good fortune. The once flourishing maritime empire was on the wane. The Habsburgs developed the harbour of Trieste and encouraged piratical raids on Venetian ships. Long-running disputes with the papacy also came to a head. Venice had always taken a stand as an independent sovereign state: *Siamo veneziani, poi cristiani* (We are first Venetians, then Christians). While professing faith in the pope as supreme spiritual leader, the Venetians insisted that the doge and his officers were the masters of temporal affairs.

The papacy believed that the Republic treated Protestants too liberally and rejected the assumption that Rome should routinely rubber-stamp the Venetian candidate for Patriarch of Venice. After Venice refused to hand over two clerics to Roman ecclesiastical courts, the whole city was excommunicated. The Venetians were

Depiction of Turkish merchant from a 16th-century manuscript.

empire to the Ottomans. Yet the picture was less bleak than has often been painted. After a protracted struggle, Venice lost Crete in 1669, but this was mitigated by the preservation of Dalmatia and the gain of Morea (1684–8) in a campaign led by Doge Francesco Morosini. The decline was irreversible, but some trade and banking business survived and Venice remained a wealthy city.

A cosmopolitan city

Venice was termed "the metropolis of all Italy" by delighted visitors. The diarist John Evelyn (1620–1706) was surprised by the Venetian melting pot: "Jews, Turks, Armenians, Persians, Moors, Greeks, Dalmatians all in their native fashions, negotiating in this famous emporium." The far-flung empire in the Levant had turned Venice into the most cosmopolitan of cities, where East and West mingled. The Greeks, the longest-established foreign community, had their own church, school and liturgical centre. The Armenians, ensconced since the 12th century, enjoyed a similarly privileged position, first with their own church and later with a private island granted by the doge.

The Albanians and Dalmatians (Croatians) were established enough to have their own confraternity houses. There had been a significant Jewish community in Venice since the 14th century, acting as traditional moneylenders. The glittering emporium of Venice also attracted German and Turkish traders, who were granted magnificent warehouses and bases on the Grand Canal.

The end of an era

The 18th century was a time in which Venice withdrew from the world stage. The wars against

unbowed and the interdict was removed a year later, with much loss of face to the papacy.

The plague of 1630, however, confirmed the waning of Venice's powers, compounded by changing patterns of world trade. The commercial axis shifted towards the North Sea, favouring Dutch and English ports to the detriment of Venice. However, the eclipse of Venice was also hastened by Turkish naval supremacy in the eastern Mediterranean and by the loss of the colonial

A PATRICIAN AND PATRIOTIC SOCIETY

Venice was a city-state run along republican lines by an aristocracy. The Libro d'Oro (Golden Book), first formalised in 1506, was the register of the Venetian nobility, and only those included could seek high office. Exceptional services to the State could make a citizen eligible for membership. Occasionally wealthy commoners could buy their way in, but it took generations for the family to become accepted.

Patricians did not use titles and to curb the development of powerful clans, the Republic even forbade patricians from acting as godfathers to other nobles' children. There was no élite district; the nobility and populace lived cheek by jowl. In terms of finances and freedom of movement, the merchant classes often fared better than the patricians. Nobility entailed obligations: foreign visits required authorisation from the State; gifts to officials had to be declared and relinquished; even an ambassadorship had to be funded by the ambassador himself. The merchant classes were allowed to set up trading posts in the empire while the élite of the citizen class provided civil servants and even the Chancellor of the Republic.

The Opera Rehearsal by Mario Ricci provides a glimpse of salon life.

the Turks had cost the Republic dearly; armed neutrality became the new policy, with a refusal to become involved in the Wars of the French, Spanish and Austrian Succession. The Rialto was no longer a centre of overseas trade but, as commentator Francis Russell says: "Visible wealth, historic ceremonial and a lingering memory of the triumphal defence of Corfu against the Ottoman Turks in 1716 ensured that the city remained far more than a mere magnet for the tourist." But Morea and the Aegean possessions were finally lost in 1718 at the Peace of Passarowitz, a treaty concluded without Venetian participation. The loss signalled the end of the mighty maritime empire and the confirmation of Austrian power.

CULTURAL GHOSTS OF THE LAGOON

Tourism and Venice have been inextricably linked for hundreds of years. As an essential port of call on the Grand Tour, Venice attracted visitors drawn to the notion of slowly crumbling splendour. Henry James thought that "everyone interesting, appealing, melancholy, memorable or odd" gravitated towards Venice, and the city is awash with the ghosts of poets, novelists, philosophers, artists and musicians.

Charles Dickens was drawn to its seductive decline, Marcel Proust pondered the passing of time in Caffè Florian, while Ernest Hemingway propped up Harry's Bar. Contemporary accounts of Lord Byron have the Romantic poet swimming the length of the Grand Canal, conducting illicit affairs with a string of mistresses, writing or talking to Shelley long into the night. Thomas Mann used the city as a backdrop to his haunting novella *Death in Venice*.

Venice was equally beloved by artists, particularly the French Impressionists. Renoir chose to portray the city bathed in light, while the English Romantic painter, J.M.W. Turner, captured the city's iridescence in his marine studies. Tchaikovsky and Wagner tapped into the romantic emotions that Venice inspired. Even Nietzsche said that, if he searched for a synonym for music, he found "always and only Venice".

Bourbon ships arriving in the city

All that remained of Venice were its mainland possessions and republican dignity. According to critic Michael Levey, "Its grandeur and gravity, embodied by red-clad senators, were almost anachronistic, and there was some piquancy in a Europe of monarchs and princes in the tremendous, impersonal dignity of a state that continued to be a republic." Any attempts to democratise the archaic government were stifled by the conservative élite. For the patrician class, this was an inward-looking age of elegance, indulgence and *dolce vita*. The spectacle of Venice's demise held its own fascination, with the 18th century dying in a blaze of artistic glory. The illusionistic effects of Tiepolo (see page 205), Italy's last grand-scale imaginative painter, trumpeted the greatest illusion: that Venice still remained serene and splendid, gloriously in control of its own destiny.

In 1789, the French Revolution broke out. Napoleon, soon embroiled in conflict with Austria, was determined to destroy the Venetian oligarchy. He provoked a quarrel with the Venetians over a frigate and declared: "I want no more inquisitors, no more senate, I shall be an Attila to the Venetian State." In 1796 he marched into the Veneto without encountering any resistance. In 1797 the last in the line of 120 doges abdicated in recognition of the fait accompli of Napoleon's victories in northern Italy. In a tumultuous sitting, the Great Council dissolved the Republic. Laying down the *cufieta*, the linen cap worn under the doge's crown, Lodovico Manin turned to his valet and declared with great dignity: "Take it away; I shall not be needing it again."

A provisional government was soon installed, but Napoleon ceded Venice and the Veneto to Austria in 1798. With the exception of a French interlude between 1805 and 1814, Austrian rule lasted until 1866.

The actions of the French were far more destructive than Austrian rule. They whisked countless artworks to the Louvre in Paris and destroyed churches, convents, palaces, warehouses and shipyards. The monasteries were also suppressed and their treasures dispersed. The creation of the Giardini Pubblici (public gardens) entailed the demolition of a church, a cluster of historic buildings and medieval granaries next to the Mint. French building schemes were suitably grandiose: in Piazza San Marco (St Mark's Square), a wing was added to enclose the square.

Duplessis-Bertaux's depiction of the French entering Venice in 1797.

Revolution against Austria in the Arsenale.

Austrian rule

William Dean Howells, the American Consul in Venice, spoke of "a nation in mourning" under the Austrians, noting the disappearance

Eleanor Roosevelt visits Venice at the turn of the 20th century.

of "that public gaiety and private hospitality for which the city was once famous". He failed to note any meeting of minds between victors and vanquished. While the Venetians were a mercurial people, "like the tide, six hours up and six hours down", the Austrians were regarded as "slow and dull-witted".

Although resented for their burdensome bureaucracy, the Austrians governed justly and liberally, at least until the 1848 Revolution. The Austrians built bridges, funded questionable restoration projects and filled in insalubrious canals. In 1846 they built the historic rail causeway linking Venice to the mainland.

However, the city was virtually destitute during Austrian rule: there were no more government jobs, Trieste became the favoured Adriatic port, shipbuilding dwindled and tourism was negligible. Occupation rankled with the nobility but the loss of former glory may have saved the timeless fabric of Venice. The local aristocracy and bourgeoisie were reduced to poverty and could not indulge

Over 24 days in July–August 1849, Austrian siege guns pounded rebel Republican Venice into submission with bombardments that rained on to the starving and cholera-struck city.

in the ambitious building programmes that scarred many European cities.

Modern times

Although bombed on occasion in World War I and World War II, the city came out of the wars largely unscathed. Far greater damage was done by massive lagoon flooding in 1966. The flooding sparked endless and costly debate on how to protect the city and, in 2003, work on a series of mobile flood barriers (called MOSE) at the lagoon entrances began. Venetians are deeply divided over the barriers – former mayor Massimo Cacciari was decidedly against them. The Venice in Peril Fund (www.veniceinperil.org) supports the mobile barrier project, whilst admitting that it doesn't address the chronic issue of rising water levels and the degradation of the lagoon, exacerbated by the digging of deep navigation channels. The multi-billion-euro MOSE project has also been at the core of the biggest corruption scandal in the city's history. In 2014 former mayor Giorgio Orsoni (2010–14) and dozens of other officials were accused of embezzling the MOSE funds.

Independent candidate and entrepreneur Luigi Brugnaro has been mayor since 2015 – a tenure already marred by controversy. Decidedly conservative, Brugnaro banned all picture books with homosexual content in public school libraries and announced a ban on the Venice Gay Pride, before changing his mind on the latter after furore from the LGBT community, notably singer Elton John, who owns a property in Venice.

Perhaps more important than politics and flooding is the dwindling population. In 1951, the city (not including the mainland or other islands) reached a pinnacle in population, at more than 150,000. Today, the official number hovers around 56,000. If it drops much further, the city risks becoming a theme park.

Residents board a boat to safety during the 1963 flood.

Burano residents well-equipped for high tide.

SAVING THE CITY

The new flood barrier is a key factor in the future of Venice, as is the balance between the needs of the mainland and the "floating world".

In his epic *Childe Harold*, Lord Byron sounded the city's death knell. But in truth Venice has been in peril since the first foolhardy settlers sank the first stakes into the lagoon. Reports of the dowager's death may be exaggerated, but the politicians still need to protect the fragile ecological balance of the lagoon and solve the intractable problems between historic Venice and the modern mainland.

Venice's unique situation means that the city has myriad would-be saviours, from Unesco, Venice In Peril and Save Venice to the Green lobby and an interventionist Italian government. In 2003, Premier Silvio Berlusconi stepped into the breach to lend his support to a controversial new mobile flood barrier that is designed to safeguard Venice for centuries.

Murky waters

Venetian politics are rarely dull: a former foreign minister, the disco-loving local boy Gianni di Michelis left the political scene ignominiously after proposing a misguided plan to drain the lagoon for the site of Expo 2000. His nemesis was Massimo Cacciari, who presented himself as the antithesis of the proverbially corrupt politician. When first invited to enter politics in the 1980s, this future city mayor snubbed de Michelis with the quip; "No thanks, my family's got plenty of money already." Cacciari was succeeded by Paolo Costa only to be back in power again in 2005. In 2010 he was replaced by the centre-left Giorgio Orsoni, a professor of law who four years later was accused of embezzling MOSE funds and was forced to resign. The current mayor, architect and entrepreneur

The MOSE flood barrier takes shape.

Luigi Brugnaro, has envisaged selling some of Venice's masterpieces of art in order to alleviate the city's crippling debts. .

Preserving Venice as a viable living community is hardly straightforward. In recent years, the city has faced the burning down of its opera house, a separatist siege, the declaration of an independent toytown state, countless floods, the depositing of toxic waste in the lagoon, and gas exploration off the coast.

The most bizarre event of recent years was the independence bid to mark the 200th anniversary of the fall of the Republic. In 1997, separatist commandos unfurled the Lion of St

Mark, declaring: "The Most Serene Venetian government has occupied the belltower of St Mark's. Long live the Serenissima." This protest was foiled by *carabinieri* (armed police), who scaled the tower and caught the commandos by surprise. Separatist sentiment had been inflamed by corruption, and resentment of high taxes and Roman rule. It was a similar story a year earlier, when the separatist leader of the Lega Nord (Northern League), Umberto Bossi, launched his "march on the river Po" and proclaimed Venice capital of Padania, his make-believe kingdom. The mayor of Venice rejected Bossi's view of his city as a mythical northern Italian state, while Arrigo Cipriani, owner of Harry's Bar, was forthright: "Bossi belongs in an asylum with people who think they are Napoleon."

Divided city

The old city motto used to be: "Drink in the culture of Venice – find inner serenity in the Serenissima." Today's citizens are a little short of serenity. Venice is the capital of the Veneto, one of the richest regions in Italy, yet the city struggles to survive. Venice and its islands form the natural "floating world" of the lagoon, but over the causeway lies Mestre, another world. The two communities share a city council, but

Master glassmaker at his family's furnace on Murano.

that is all. While the mainland is industrial, entrepreneurial and left-wing, the historic centre is elderly, conservative, tourism-led and ecologically minded. In the last referendum, both parts of the city voted to remain together. However, the benefits of this are rather one-sided: the mainland gains from the lustre of historic Venice, while the lagoon city remains shackled to its bullying younger brother.

> *Aside from tidal floods, rain also causes flooding in Venice, pushing water up through drain pipes. Work to repair the pipes and seal the surface off from subterranean water has been ongoing for years.*

Since the 1950s, there has been a flight from the islands to the mainland. The population is little more than a third of its historic peak in 1951, down to just over 56,000 according to the city government. Some claim the real number is much lower, since the statistics are based on a count of those whose official residence is in Venice, not on those actually present. A little over 30,000 people live on the remaining islands around the lagoon and 178,000 on the mainland areas of the municipality. Some 30,000 commute from the mainland to Venice every day, mainly to service a tourism industry that caters to as many as 20 million visitors a year.

There is a premium to pay for living in Venice, with the cost and upkeep of city housing beyond many families. To stem the tide to the mainland, there are housing grants for the poorest, and plans for business and tax incentives.

Venice will always be a costly place, so added-value economics is a logical path to follow: this entails developing the high-tech sector, supporting the crafts tradition and competing for the conference trade. To this end, a Palladian convent has been converted into a conference centre, and the huge neo-Gothic flour mill, the Molino Stucky, has been turned into a luxurious Hilton hotel and conference centre with adjoining affordable housing. So far, however, these measures seem to have had a limited effect.

As for major job-creation schemes, the city is using the prestige and funds generated by the mobile-dam project as a means of reviving the Arsenale district. The reconversion of these sprawling historic shipyards, parts of which remain in naval hands, is the biggest urban challenge. The shipyard is now mainly used by the navy and as the assembly centre of MOSE, the new mobile barrier which is now due to become fully operational in 2018–2020. Some sections are used as art exhibition spaces during La Biennale as well as concert venues.

The endangered ecosystem

The economic challenges are dwarfed by even more pressing environmental concerns. If Venice is not to be doomed to a watery grave, the precarious lagoon world must be protected, both from the elements and from polluting human interference. The sight of oil tankers bearing down on the Palazzo Ducale (Doge's Palace) may be just a bad memory, but the sight of enormous cruise ships that dwarf the city skyline steaming down the Canale della Giudecca is not (a ban in 2015 on large cruise ships from entering the canal was revoked months later). Another threat is posed by gas extraction fields in the northern Adriatic. Such extraction poses the danger of subsidence along the entire Veneto coast, as well as in Venice proper.

The lagoon city has always faced the contradictory dangers of death by drowning and death by suffocation: the encroaching sea had to be tamed and the silting sands held at bay. The Venetians buttressed the mudbanks to protect the city and closed the gaps between the sandbars *(lidi)*, leaving only three entrances. Then as now, these served to strengthen the city defences and channel the cleansing tides. Breakwaters have always played a key role, notably the Murazzi sea walls, which were one of the Republic's greatest feats of civil engineering. After decades of neglect, the side canals are also benefiting from an ongoing dredging programme.

No matter how welcome these improvements, many of Venice's ecological problems can be traced back to the mainland. The industrial port of Marghera is blamed for many of the city's ills, from pollution to subsidence and flooding. Yet like historic Venice, it too was born from necessity. The Arsenale was closed during World War I, to the despair of the 8,000-strong workforce. To save the citizens from ruin, local benefactors created a modern industrial centre on the mainland. Porto

Anti-cruise ships demonstration.

Marghera was born, built over the mudflats, and served by the dormitory suburb of Mestre. After World War II, a second industrial zone was built over more reclaimed land and the exodus from historic Venice was unstoppable.

Over the years, the Mestre-Marghera industrial complex has dumped tons of pollutants into the lagoon. Closing the petrochemical complex is the obvious solution but too daring for politicians to contemplate. Much of the waste is now pumped out through purifier plants and

THE LIVING LAGOON

Sea water enters the lagoon through three inlets in the sandbars at the Porto di Chioggia, Malamocco and the Lido. While the "dead" lagoon is only fully covered at high tide, the "living" lagoon is fully navigable, with the tides coursing through the channels, cleansing it of debris and sediment. The marshes are criss-crossed with canals and sandbanks, with an outlying area of dyked lakes used for fish farms. Despite pollution, lagoon life survives, from kingfishers, cormorants and coots to grey herons and little egrets. Even so, the surest way of safeguarding the lagoon would be through the mooted creation of a marine park, stretching from the Lido to Chioggia.

An ocean liner sweeps into the fragile lagoon.

the overall amounts have been considerably reduced. Toxic fumes from the port are also damaging Venice's fragile buildings and statuary. Sulphur-based emissions are produced by industrial fumes as well as by the natural decay of vegetation on the lagoon mudflats. Sulphur dioxide combines with the salty air to form a toxic cocktail that damages the city's fabric. Emissions from the huge cruise ships moored in Venice also contribute to this problem.

No longer sinking

Venice officially stopped sinking in 1983, after the extraction of underground water was forbidden. The drawing of millions of gallons of water from artesian wells in Marghera had led to a sharp fall in the water table and threatened subsidence. In the 1970s aqueducts were built to pipe water from inland rivers to the industrial zone. However, Venetian subsidence is partly caused by the weight of the city, with many monuments under threat. Buildings are supported by wooden piles driven deep into the mudflats; change in the water levels means that at low tides the piles are exposed to the air, causing decay.

Nor is Venice itself blameless. While domestic sewage is treated, baths and sinks still drain into the canals. Phosphate-enriched household detergents have been banned as plant and marine life in the lagoon were being suffocated by the algae that thrive on these phosphates. As for the canals, the wash *(moto ondoso)* from cruise ships and other vessels (especially speeding water taxis that ignore city canal speed limits) causes erosion, eating away at the stonework of Grand Canal palaces.

> *Although much improved since the 1980s, water pollution in the lagoon remains an issue. It is estimated that 80 percent of lagoon flora has died since the Porto Marghera petrochemical plant opened.*

On a positive note, Venice has for some years been working on the consolidation of city foundations, from quaysides to canal banks and palaces, both in historic Venice and on the islands of Giudecca and the Lido. Piazza San Marco, for instance, has been raised to 1.1 metres (3.4ft). Salt marshes and wetlands are being reinstated on the edge of the lagoon. Aquatic extinction is still some way off.

Dams and Deadly Floods

Named MOSE after the prophet who parted the waves, a new tidal barrier looks set to save Venice from perilous floods.

The debate has raged for decades, but a dramatic increase in the frequency and severity of the floods forced the government to act. Despite protests and delays the mobile barriers are nearly complete and should be in action around 2018–2020.

wave breached the sea walls and the water level rose to 1.9 metres (6ft) above mean high tide. St Mark's Square, the lowest point in the city, was submerged under 1.2 metres (4ft) of water, with a filthy tide of debris seeping through the basilica doors and waves crashing against the Palazzo Ducale.

The MOSE tidal barrier, installed across the three lagoon inlets, will use 78 steel floodgates lying on the seabed to close the entrances to the lagoon by floating to the surface when floods of more than 1.1 metres (3.4ft) above sea level threaten. The barrier should operate three times a year, based on current sea levels, and could hold

Residents have their ways of coping with streets of water.

Acqua alta (high water) is one of the city's biggest problems, and occurs when southeasterly sirocco winds combine with tides to trap the high water in the lagoon. Global warming, human intervention and industrialisation are all culpable. The 20th century saw the delicate balance of the lagoon disturbed by land reclamation, the deepening of shipping channels (including one especially deep for oil tankers) and the enclosure of sections for fish farming.

Venice has always been threatened by floods, particularly between the months of September and April. However, the massive flood of 1966 mobilised the world. A tidal

out tides as high as 3 metres (9.9ft). The lagoon's 60km (40-mile) outer coastline has been reinforced with artificial reefs and new beaches backed by effective breakwaters.

The city has also gone part of the way down the environmental route, allowing some reclaimed land to be flooded and seeking to ban oil tankers. Venetian writer Damiano Rizzo is resigned to the change: "The city will go on fighting the high tides with traditional weaponry: wailing sirens, wooden duckboards, wellington boots and buckets of patience. Some day visitors might look back nostalgically at the quaint experience of high tide."

ARCHITECTURAL STYLE

Building here was never easy, but the unique setting inspired generations of architects to produce an eclectic blend of Byzantine, Gothic and Renaissance styles.

rchitects call Venice an artificial city, "a city born adult". It was never a blank slate, but built from remnants of ruined cities: Venice salvaged Roman bricks from Adriatic villas and recycled arches and statuary from churches and palaces in the romantic colony of Torcello. As the gateway to the East, Venice raided Byzantium for booty to adorn its noble facades. From marble to mosaics, the eastern colonies provided precious materials to transform the inhospitable lagoon islands into an imperial capital.

Oriental allure

Architecturally, the city succumbed to the spell of the East, with a Byzantine spirit poured into a Gothic mould; only reluctantly was Venice lured into the Renaissance. The palace (*palazzo*) is the classic unit of Venetian architecture, a form influenced by the Roman country villa and by Byzantine buildings in Ravenna and

Detail of the Palazzo Ducale, a glorious example of High Gothic style, overlooked by the Campanile.

Constantinople. Characterised by colour, decoration and eclecticism, the result is a synthesis of styles simply known as Venetian. Plaques and roundels created chiaroscuro effects and offset the flatness of the facade; the vivid marble also reflected the local love of colour.

The vernacular Venetian style is a hybrid. A typical cluster of buildings may show influences from East and West, sporting Moorish windows, a Gothic structure, Veneto-Byzantine decoration and Renaissance or baroque flourishes.

Materials were shipped to Venice with great difficulty: piling and timber came from the Lido, from alpine forests and from the Balkans; small, flat Roman bricks served as building blocks, salvaged from villas destroyed by the

WELL-HEADS

Carved well-heads are a familiar feature of Venice, from the drum-shaped Roman well-head outside the basilica in Torcello to a trio of delightful wells situated on Campo Santa Maria Formosa. The well-heads mask a complex and costly system below, acting as an outlet for an underground chain of storage tanks which often run the entire length of the *campo*. The rainwater used to be collected through apertures in the *campo* floor, purified through sand-filters and then channelled into cisterns. Since the late 19th century, however, the city's water has come from artesian wells on the mainland.

As you walk the streets, remember to look up for typical Venetian touches like this artistic balcony.

barbarian hordes; red Verona marble provided flooring; exotic marble came from Greece, with semi-precious stones from Constantinople; only glass was home-made in Murano, although brick was later made from local clay.

Venice is a city of brick rather than stone: it is at most a stone-clad city, where pink-hued bricks predominate, with cool stone restricted to finishings. According to Mary McCarthy, the city's beauty comes from "the thin marble veneers with which the brick surface is coated". Its sheer weight made stone unsuitable as the prime building material, at least until piling techniques became sophisticated enough to cope with such structures as La Salute church, supported by a million piles.

Since Venice began as a satellite of Byzantium, the oriental legacy is tangible. Craftsmen from Constantinople worked on the oldest buildings, as did Greek mosaicists. To appreciate the early city settlement, there is no substitute for visiting the remote island of Torcello. The basilica feels deeply Byzantine, founded in AD 639 and modified between the 9th and 11th centuries. Inspired by Ravenna,

its centrepiece is the Byzantine mosaic-studded apse, but it also displays Romanesque influences from Lombardy.

In central Venice, the majority of Byzantine buildings lie around the Rialto, the oldest section of the city, or close to San Marco. San Giacomo di Rialto is considered to be the oldest church, and displays the Byzantine Greek cross design. Austere San Nicolò dei Mendicoli, built for the poor, also retains its 7th-century basilican plan and small double-mullioned windows. However, San Marco remains the supreme example of Byzantine architecture, an elongated version of the five-domed Greek cross design, based on the Church of the Apostles in Constantinople.

Veneto-Byzantine style

Given the Venetian talent for fusion, the emergence of a unique Veneto-Byzantine style was a matter of course. Popular from the 11th to 13th centuries, this was an oriental, flowery form, with ornate capitals, pediments and niches and Byzantine arches. Slender columns (cushion or basket capitals) and stilted arches gave way to Moorish design, especially the horseshoe arch and the inflected arch, resembling a quivering flame.

Classic hotel interior.

Ca d'Oro courtyard, with its exquisite mosaic flooring.

The Byzantine legacy includes a love of voluptuous materials, from inlaid marble to porphyry and jasper. Facades were adorned with *paterae*, decorative stone or marble plaques, often bearing symbolic foliage and animal motifs – griffins, eagles, lions and peacocks symbolising eternal life through baptism, or vine leaves representing the "true vine" of St John's Gospel.

The Ca' da Mosto on the Grand Canal is one of the best-preserved of all the Veneto-Byzantine palaces. This 12th-century residence has an elegant loggia on the first floor, with arches adorned by fine *paterae*. The Ca' Loredan, which is also on the Grand Canal, retains ground-floor arcading surmounted by an open gallery. The original marble plaques and 12th-century capitals remain.

THE SQUARES OF VENICE

San Marco is the only square in Venice to be called a piazza; every other square is either a *campo* or a tinier *campiello*. Major *campi* contain a monastery or an oratory as well as a *scuola*, a confraternity which acted as the hub of social life for the bourgeoisie. But it's the homely neighbourhood square that encapsulates the distinctiveness of Venice. The quintessential *campo* is probably a lopsided space containing a church, a cluster of decrepit palaces, russet pantiled roofs, a bridge, a gondoliers' station, a carved well-head sprouting weeds, and an alley cat lurking in a smelly *sottoportego*. Beneath a facade with a chipped lion's head, a mangy dog suns himself by a flower stall while his master plays cards or chess with a friend from the news stand next door.

Each *campo* has its own individual charm, from stately Campo Santo Stefano to huge Campo San Polo, once the stage for popular fairs and bullfights but now a lively square overrun by boisterous children and used for an open-air cinema in summer. Particularly in summer, certain squares are taken over by students, notably Campo Santa Margarita, Campo San Luca, Campo San Barnaba and Campo San Bartolomeo. The tiny *campi* and *campielli* in the Castello district, representing the cheery underside of working-class Venice, are worth exploring.

> The Romanesque style, inspired by Roman-era basilicas, emerged in Lombardy around the 11th century. A lovely example in Venice is the cloister at the Museo Diocesano d'Arte Sacra.

In Cannaregio, Veneto-Byzantine friezes and roundels adorn the Corte del Milion courtyard, where Marco Polo's family reputedly lived.

This eclectic Venetian style has left its mark on palaces and warehouses (*fondaci*). The model was the *casa-fondaco*, combining the roles of commercial office and family home. The house followed a three-tiered plan that became the pattern for centuries to come. In the Veneto-Byzantine merchant's house an arcade ran along the ground floor with a loggia running across the floor above. Side turrets or parapets (*torreselle*) were a reminder of the days of defensive fortifications. The top floor could have a covered loggia (*liagò*), a feature of 13th- and 14th-century Venetian houses.

The Fondaco dei Tedeschi on the Grand Canal is a monumental square structure, previously a warehouse and residence for German merchants. The arcade at water level made for easy unloading; above is a bare facade which was frescoed by Giorgione and finished by Titian; poetic fragments remain in the Ca' d'Oro museum. The inner courtyard is framed by a loggia and porticoed facades, which were once frescoed by Titian.

You'd be hard pressed to see a 13th-century *palazzo* in the Fondaco dei Turchi, granted to Turkish merchants in 1621 and altered beyond recognition in a 19th-century renovation. Its structure and function were, in their day, similar to those of the Fondaco dei Tedeschi.

Gothic grandeur

Compared with its Byzantine predecessor, the Gothic palace was a nobler yet more ostentatious creation. The aesthete John Ruskin believed that Venetian post-Gothic architecture was a desecration. While this is blind prejudice, the Gothic palaces of the 13th to 15th centuries are one of the city's chief glories. The pure curve of a Byzantine arch progressed to a pointed Moorish arch and then to a Gothic ogival arch. The Byzantine continuous loggia evolved into

a fully-fledged loggia with cusped arches and quatrefoil (four-leaf) motifs. Glorious windows were framed by filigree stonework, with brick and stucco used in delicate two-tone colour combinations. Venetian Gothic is as idiosyncratic as the city: trade with the Levant in the period ensured palaces bore an Islamic and Byzantine stamp.

The Ca' d'Oro is arguably the finest Gothic palace, with detail as delicate as that on an oriental carpet. Decorated in a Venetian interpretation of the Flamboyant Gothic style, the palace's stone tracery becomes lighter and more fragile as it reaches the top, creating a giddy sensation of space.

> The popularity of the Lido as a summer holiday resort in the late 19th century coincided with the vogue of Liberty, Italy's Art Nouveau. Many of the island's hotels, in particular the Hungaria Palace, were built in this joyous style.

The church of San Zaccaria, a blend of Gothic and Renaissance styles.

Basilica of Santi Maria e Donato, on the island of Murano.

The Palazzo Ducale (Doge's Palace) began life as a 9th-century castle but it was transformed into a masterpiece of graceful High Gothic style. Seeming to float on air, the loggia and portico form a lacy lattice-work.

The Frari is the most glorious of Venetian-Gothic churches, based on a Latin cross plan with three aisles. It has a severe facade with a curved crowning and cross-vaulted roof with sturdy tie-beams. Santi Giovanni e Paolo, known as Zanipolo, is almost as grand, with a similar cross-vaulted roof. Exposed beams are a feature of many Gothic city churches, with the finest taking the form of ship's-keel ceilings, as can be seen in Santo Stefano, San Polo and San Giovanni in Bragora.

Renaissance splendour

The end of the 15th century was a golden age for all Venetian art forms. Although palaces acquired a classical air, native conservatism prevailed and a hybrid of Venetian Gothic survived well into the 15th century. Much was built in sandstone rather than brick, and supported by exceptionally strong foundations. Inspired by classical architecture, this was a symmetrical style using such motifs as Corinthian capitals, fluted columns, projecting roof cornices and rustication.

The 16th-century Scuola Grande di San Marco.

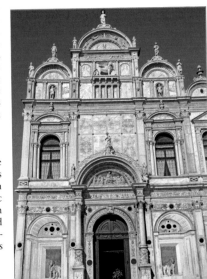

Palladio's San Giorgio Maggiore.

High Renaissance and baroque

The High Renaissance was led by Jacopo Sansovino (1486–1570), who quickly adapted to the Venetian sensibility despite his Tuscan background and Roman training. In his role as Superintendent of the Works, he had significant influence over Venetian architecture. Ca' Grande on the Grand Canal is a magnificent classical triumph. Here, as in other Venetian palaces, Sansovino established triple water-entrance arches and spandrels adorned with sculpture. He is also responsible for several of the grand buildings at San Marco, from the Zecca (Mint) to the Libreria Sansoviniana, his great library.

If the Renaissance was the apogee of refinement, baroque Venice belonged to a bold yet less-inspired age. By turns ponderous and whimsical, this was a relatively sober form of baroque, tempered by Palladianism. The style is characterised by stone rustication and heavy ornamentation. It revels in exuberant stucco-work and flamboyant friezes, with every surface studded with garlands, cherubs, coats of arms or grotesque masks.

The Arsenale, with its crenellations and ceremonial land gate, is considered to be the first flowering of Renaissance architecture. Built in 1460, the land gate leads to the armaments and shipbuilding complex. Other key structures were Antonio da Ponte's Ponte di Rialto and the Scala dei Giganti in the Palazzo Ducale.

The delightful church of Santa Maria dei Miracoli and Ca' Dario were designed by the Lombardi brothers, master-craftsmen. If the Venetian Renaissance was a compromise between classical precision and local convention, then Ca' Dario expresses its essence. The palace conveys an oriental richness with its coloured marble reliefs and interlacing design. The flowing arabesques were inspired by Byzantine mosaics in the Basilica di San Marco. Venice owes much to Mauro Coducci (1440–1504), an architect from Bergamo who was inspired by the city. He imposed symmetry on the Venetian model but did not dispense with Byzantine decorative reliefs. His designs were used for the Torre dell'Orologio by San Marco and the grandiose Palazzo Zorzi. In addition, he rebuilt the church of Santa Maria Formosa and created the graceful facade of San Zaccaria, his masterpiece.

> About one third of the buildings in Venice have been raised since the end of World War I. They range from the Soviet-style landward frontage of the elegant Bauer hotel to the Ponte di Calatrava, opened in 2008.

As the prime exponent of Venetian baroque, Baldassare Longhena (1598–1682) created the theatrical church of La Salute, with its grandiose plan indebted to Palladio's Il Redentore. In both churches and palaces, Longhena was noted for his sense of chiaroscuro, with dynamic and dramatic facades, heavily charged with rich carving. Ca' Pesaro has a theatrical inner courtyard and a rusticated Grand Canal facade rich in ornamentation and chiaroscuro effects. Ca' Rezzonico, also designed by Longhena, is more restrained.

Classical revival and beyond

In the 18th century there was a reaction against baroque and a return to Palladian values. Grandiose palaces were designed for

Campo Santa Maria Formosa.

wealthy *arrivistes*, with stateliness emphasised by monumental staircases. Palazzo Grassi, for example, was based on baroque plans by Longhena but completed by Massari (1686–1766), who was drawn to the new spirit of the classical revival. Massari also created the Palladian facade of the Gesuati church. The classical revival can also be seen in the design of La Fenice opera house. Completed in 1790, it was the last significant structure built under the Republic.

With Napoleon came a great deal of destruction and the building of the Ala Napoleonica. The Austrians contributed two bridges over the Grand Canal (Scalzi and Accademia) and little of significance has been added since.

ANDREA PALLADIO

Andrea Palladio (1508–80) was born in the Veneto and worked as a mason on mannerist monuments, but only fully formulated his classical philosophy after visiting Rome in the 1540s. He dedicated the end of his career to transforming the Venetian skyline with his bold buildings.

Although his sublime churches were consigned to the outskirts, with their creation Venice's waterfront vista was complete. His churches are there, framing the space where the sky meets the sea. This is true of San Francesco della Vigna, the church and hospice of Le Zitelle (now a luxury hotel) and Palladio's two masterpieces: San Giorgio Maggiore and Il Redentore.

San Giorgio, built in 1565, is a model of stylistic unity and classicism, a monastic stage-set with a cloister more fitting for a sumptuous palace than a place of prayer. Il Redentore, built in 1576, is a model of rigour and restraint, inspired by the Pantheon in Rome. An unwavering sense of proportion and perspective is reflected in the facades, the pedimented porticoes and the bold yet airy interiors. The subtle, spare designs are enhanced by broad domes, graceful columns and Corinthian capitals. Taken as a whole, Palladio's work on Venetian churches and patrician villas of the Veneto make him one of the most outstanding architects of all time.

The Venetian Palace

Designed for commercial and ceremonial purposes, the palace reflects both the city's mercantile character and an avowedly aesthetic sensibility.

The Venetian palace remains a cornerstone of city life. Compact and surrounded by water, it seems a hermetically sealed world. All palaces were built with both a land and a water entrance. The waterside entrance is the principal facade, decorated with Byzantine *paterae*, roundels or precious marbles. The flatness of the facade is relieved by balconies (*pergoli*) rather than loggias or colonnades. The water gate opens on to the great hall. Once lit by torches or heavy lanterns, this gallery runs the depth of the palace. Nowadays, canalside ground floors are rarely lived in due to the damp.

Some palaces had a mezzanine floor where the offices were situated. As the commercial function of the palace gave way to noble living, these quarters were transformed into libraries and treasure rooms. By the 17th century, the draughtiness of the main reception rooms caused nobles to convert these quarters into cosy sitting rooms. The *piano nobile*, the elegant first floor, which has the most elaborate windows in the palace, contains the *portego*, the main drawing room, and a series of reception rooms and bedrooms leading off it. Suitable for lavish banquets, this central gallery often runs the length of the house, culminating in a balcony. Later forming a loggia, this provided the ventilation necessary to survive both the winter humidity and the summer heat.

Despite ostentatiously frescoed ceilings, this was a spartan interior offset by the use of luxurious fabrics. From Gothic times, gilded leather lined the walls, with the *portego* hung with brocades, damask and silks. These products of trade with the Levant were preferred to tapestries. Although stuccowork and paintings became popular in the 17th century, objets d'art, Murano glass chandeliers, a chaise longue and oriental rugs still encapsulate the austere elegance of the grandest Venetian palaces.

The upper floors housed a warren of rooms for relatives and children. The attics tended to be used as servants' quarters and for the kitchens. The decorative chimney pots were also highly functional, the cone acting as a spark-trap.

The intricate lattice-work facade of the Ca' d'Oro on the Grand Canal.

Internal courtyards were introduced in the 17th century. These were reached by imposing land gates displaying the owner's coat of arms. Space constraints meant that many courtyards were swallowed up by encroaching buildings. However, delightful courtyards and secret, wisteria-clad gardens remain, often the preserve of cats.

IO·VNNES·BELLINVS
M·CCCCV·

ARTISTS OF COLOUR AND LIGHT

International trade brought the city into contact with varied artistic schools, but the Venetians adapted these new influences to suit their own taste.

Venetian sensibility reflected a shimmering, watery world. The constantly changing lagoon light created a fluid sense of space and contrast and an ambiguity that is absent from landlocked schools of art. Venice turned its back on the classicism and intellectual rigour of the Romans. To the Venetians, colour, light, texture and space were more important than form.

Venice's status as a great trading empire exposed it to new artistic influences, first from Byzantium and later from Flanders and the Italian schools of Padua, Mantua, Ferrara and Florence. However, Venetian insularity prevailed, with new ideas seeping in slowly and artistic developments transformed into a uniquely Venetian way of seeing things. Paradoxically, thanks to the inclusiveness of the Venetian vision and the varied sources of patronage, Venetian art was less formulaic than other schools, with the greatest painters free to form their own inimitable personal styles.

The Bellini family

Giovanni Bellini (c.1430–1516) was the leading exponent of Renaissance art in Venice. Although his brother, Gentile Bellini (1429–1507), rose to be official State painter, Giovanni ("Giambellino") was the unworldly genius. In later years, he succeeded his brother as State painter. Venice was slow to absorb Renaissance values but, largely thanks to Bellini, evolved its own expressive style.

With Bellini, oil paint displaced tempera (egg-based pigment). Its slow drying-time encouraged experimentation, with oils offering

Bellini's altarpiece, Madonna and Child (1488), in the Frari.

Partly in response to the extraordinary environment, the Venetian school embodied a poetic, painterly sensibility at odds with the rational, monumental and sculptural Florentine style.

more subtle tonal gradation and a greater simulation of textures. Influenced by Mantegna, his Paduan brother-in-law, Bellini had an understanding of perspective, and was one of the first Venetian artists to include landscapes in

Carpaccio's Meeting from his cycle of Scenes from the Life of St Ursula (1490–96), in the Accademia.

the background of his paintings. He revitalised Venetian painting, infusing his art with light, literally seen as a medium of grace.

Detail from Titian's Pesaro altarpiece.

Carpaccio

Vittore Carpaccio (c.1460–1525) is the most Venetian of painters, but not the greatest. The influence of Flemish art is apparent in his miniaturist precision, the details of faces and scenery. While no master of perspective, he captured the texture of Venetian life and mastered the minutiae without ever losing the unity of the scene.

There is a celebratory spirit in this artist, who offers an enticing vision of Venetian life: canalsides crowded with onlookers, pink-hued palaces, ceremonial galleys and gondolas; the noble profiles of confraternity worthies; cocky young blades in red hose and black Venetian caps; cool Venetian ladies at leisure. The sense of a cosmopolitan melting pot is achieved by background figures, from enigmatic Moors to Jewish merchants and turbaned Turks. Carpaccio's *The Lion of St Mark* in the Doge's Palace is a symbolic depiction of the Republic's might and an animated portrayal of the winged beast dominating Piazza San Marco and the Palazzo Ducale (Doge's Palace).

The Tempest by Giorgione (c.1508).

Giorgione

Giorgione (c.1478–1510) has been called "the first modern artist" thanks to the subjectivity of his vision. Few of his paintings remain and they are enigmatic. In Venice, he is noted for two works in the Accademia. *La Vecchia* is both a realistic portrait of an elderly woman and a meditation on old age. Poignantly, Giorgione died young, probably of the plague. *The Tempest* is a poetic and puzzling work that conveys a sense of enchantment disturbed by a mysterious inner tension. In a sense, Giorgione was a Romantic before his time. His understanding of *sfumato*, the soft gradations from light to dark, weaves a spellbinding atmosphere.

The best places to see Venetian art are the Accademia (see page 212), the Frari (see page 181) and the Scuola Grande di San Rocco (see page 184).

Titian

Titian (c.1487–1576), known as Tiziano Vecellio in Italian, was the polished master of the Venetian High Renaissance style. After Bellini's death, Titian became the undisputed leader of Venetian painting. Indeed, he was the complete Renaissance artist, with ineffable technique, varied subject matter and mastery of different media. His range remains unsurpassed in Western art, encompassing portraits, paintings, mythological poesy, allegories and altarpieces.

His style is characterised by a monumentality akin to Roman painting, by bold design, sweeping forms and sensuous modelling. Allied to this is his expressive style, gorgeous use of colour and the carnal confidence of his nudes. In spite of this enormous scope, he preferred the soft contours of the Venetian school to the sculptural monumentality of the Roman school.

At the height of his career, Titian received commissions from the pope, the emperor Charles V and Philip II of Spain. If he is not particularly well represented in his home town, it is partly because Napoleon commandeered a clutch of Titian paintings as the spoils of war – Venice's loss was the Louvre's gain.

Titian's greatest paintings in Venice are in the Frari, with the revolutionary nature of *The Assumption* vying with the secular opulence of

THE BYZANTINE TRADITION

The Byzantine tradition confirmed Venetian art in its conservatism and love of ornate decoration. One of the city's earliest known artists, Paolo Veneziano (c.1290–c.1360), created static symmetrical works set against a shimmering Byzantine gold background. His great work in the Accademia is the gloriously decorative *Coronation of the Virgin*, in which the central figures are rendered nearly invisible among the large amounts of decorative gold.

Veneziano is credited with introducing the taste for panel paintings to Venice, particularly into the churches. His methods also made sacred art more intimate, with panels placed at eye level to their admirers, by contrast

with the inaccessibility of mosaics and murals, which either decorated floors or were at the top of lofty domes.

Iconic Byzantine influences resurface in Venetian Renaissance art, in Bellini's decorative backgrounds or Veronese's shimmering surfaces. The Byzantine tradition was at one with the Venetians' painterly sensibility and love of surface colour. These are luminous, vibrant, harmonious colours: rich reds, glittering golds and warm sepias. Veronese added to this repertoire with his velvety greens and deep blues, while Tiepolo brought with him a palette of subtle pastels, including mauves and pinks, creams and pale greens.

View of the Church of the Redeemer and St James by Canaletto.

the Pesaro altarpiece. *The Assumption* echoes the vital confusion of life itself, reinforced by the image of mortals being swept up by the spiritual world. The Accademia possesses several of Titian's works, notably his powerful *Pietà*, which he had intended for his own tomb. Elsewhere, a luminous depiction of the Annunciation graces the Scuola Grande di San Rocco, while the Doge's Palace has several works by Titian, including a dramatic St Christopher, frescoed over a door of the Philosophers' Chamber.

Tintoretto

Tintoretto (1518–94) acquired his nickname ("the little dyer") after his father's trade as a silk-dyer. The artist boldly stated that his aim was to "reconcile the drawing of Michelangelo with the colours of Titian". Michelangelo's influence is clear in Tintoretto's virile compositions and battles with perspective: the bold foreshortening, the striking poses struck by his subjects, the passion for paint. Indeed, it is not fanciful to call the Scuola Grande di San Rocco Tintoretto's Sistine Chapel.

Tintoretto's debt to Titian is clear in his love of colour and mood, but these are from a bold, less subtle palette, dominated by virtuoso chiaroscuro effects. In short, Tintoretto's mannerist sensibility sacrifices luminosity for overwhelming contrasts and theatrical effects. But Tintoretto should not be underrated: he brought a new passion and religious fervour to Venetian painting. Although unworldly, he worked on sumptuous decorative schemes for the State, including mythological battles interpreted as allegories glorifying the Serene Republic.

Veronese

Paolo Veronese (1528–88) was nicknamed after his native city, Verona, but his concerns were utterly Venetian. As a colourist, he was the true successor to Bellini, while in his striving for splendour and decorative detail, his works echoed the Byzantine style. As a society painter, he portrayed the patrician ideal, a civilised life of leisure, a parade of sumptuous fabrics and Palladian decors. It is a fantasy world of formal and spiritual harmony, grace and Olympian perfection. These heroic, classical paintings are concerned with pictorial effects rather than narrative: on such dazzling stage-sets colour is used to convey mood, often one of

Emilio Vedova (1919–2006) was doubtless Venice's most important 20th century painter; mostly abstract in style, he is now honoured with a fine museum in Dorsoduro.

eternal spring. Veronese captured the taste of the times, and was chosen to work on the decoration of the Doge's Palace: *The Apotheosis of Venice* is one of his finest mythological scenes.

To great acclaim, he created the sumptuous painting in the church of San Sebastiano, where appropriately the artist is buried. After the death of Veronese, art in Venice declined, and more than a hundred years passed before La Serenissima was able to produce another great painter.

Tiepolo

Giambattista Tiepolo (1696–1770) is celebrated for his sublime artifice, heroic style and a virtuosity reminiscent of the Old Masters. Tiepolo was taken under the wing of the Venetian aristocracy: his heroic style, inventiveness and bravura display of skills struck a chord with his patrons, leading to commissions to decorate the finest palaces.

Tiepolo was a fresco painter with a love of grand designs. The art is decadent in that it is not life-assertive but bound by conventions, albeit forged by an unfettered imagination. Critics claim that Tiepolo lacked real passion, replacing it with bursts of motiveless intensity. Certainly, he was a master of elusive mood, excelling at languorous figures whose moods are not matched to the narrative reality.

Tiepolo's palette consisted of pastel tones; delicate, airy colours make the space within his pictures shine with an unearthly radiance. This earned him the epithet of "poet of light" and he was much in demand throughout the courts of Europe. Yet despite the ethereal settings, his figures have a fleshy, corporeal quality. His was a grandiose vision, but also one throbbing with sensuality.

Canaletto

Antonio Canal (1697–1768), known as Canaletto, was greatly admired for his limpid landscapes and photographic observations. In Venice he worked from nature, which was unusual for the period, creating detailed views that influenced generations of landscape painters.

Venice was beloved by Grand Tourists, notably the English, French and Germans. As the forerunners of modern souvenir-hunters, these acquisitive nobles became collectors of Venetian keepsakes, of which the most prized were paintings. Given that Canaletto's work was exported or copied by the crateful, little remains in Venice itself, apart from a few works in Ca'

> As the art critic John Steer says: "If colour is the most characteristic quality of Venetian art, then the most essentially Venetian artist of his period is Veronese."

Rezzonico and the Accademia. Although his depiction of San Giacomo di Rialto is better known, Canaletto's architectural whimsy in the Accademia was the work that won him membership of this august body.

The end of an era

Venetian painters followed in Canaletto's footsteps, focusing on picturesque, seemingly photographic views, pastiches custom-made for the collecting mania of the aristocracy. Francesco Guardi (1712–93) was an impressionistic painter whose views and caprices are, according to the art critic Michael Levey, an "intense response to Venice as a watery setting, its scattered islands, its sense of illimitable distance and silence amid crumbling fragments of ruin". Pietro Longhi (1733–1813) was most at home languishing in patrician palaces: as the leading genre painter, he mirrored Venetian high society with charm and intimacy.

The meeting of Anthony and Cleopatra, a fresco by Tiepolo inside Palazzo Labia.

ARTISTS' TRAILS

Tracking down the works of Venice's most prolific painters will take you all over the city, from Cannaregio to San Polo, Dorsoduro to the Doge's Palace.

Venice is awash with artists' trails, but Bellini and Tintoretto are the most representative, revealing different facets of Venetian art – the soft and the harsh, the rapt and the dramatic. Giovanni Bellini ("Giambellino") is considered the founder of the Venetian school. His contribution was expressiveness, conveying moods of grace, tenderness and poignancy. The **Accademia** is the natural place to appreciate his mystical work before moving on to the city churches. These are not all limpid, idealised Madonnas: in his poignant *Pietà*, the suffering Virgin cradles her son, her careworn face a testament to the painter's expressive powers.

Then take ferry line 1 two stops to San Tomà and head for the **Frari**, a barn-like church housing *The Madonna and Saints*, a Bellini masterpiece, graced by musical cherubs, reinforcing the notion of music as a symbol of order and harmony.

Ferry line 1 then whisks you to **San Zaccaria**, where the delightful church of the same name contains a superb Bellini altarpiece showing a beguiling interplay of colour and light in a rich blend of reds, golds and blues.

Next stop is the vast church of **Santi Giovanni e Paolo** for Bellini's St Vincent Ferrier altarpiece, showing the saint flanked by St Christopher and St Sebastian. Finally, stroll to the remote church of **San Francesco della Vigna** for *The Madonna and Saints*, set in a luminous landscape.

The dedicated can finish the day in style with a Bellini cocktail in Harry's Bar.

The Visitation in the Scuola Grande di San Rocco, Tintoretto's crowning glory.

The Palazzo Ducale is the place to view Tintoretto's splendid works for the Venetian State. The Sala del Senato contains grandiose works, while the Sala del Maggior Consiglio is decorated by his vast Paradise.

In the Accademia, Bellini's Pietà shows the city of Vicenza looming in the background.

Tintoretto's Assumption of the Virgin, in the Scuola Grande di San Rocco.

St Job altarpiece, in the Accademia, which illustrates Bellini's success in freeing Venetian painting from Byzantine formality and stiffness.

THE TINTORETTO TRAIL

Madonna dell'Orto in Cannaregio was Tintoretto's parish church.

The place to begin exploring the works of Venice's most prolific painter is **Madonna dell'Orto** (ferry line 42 from San Marco), where the artist lived and worked, assisted by his children. Despite becoming official painter to the doge in 1574, Tintoretto lived precariously and died penniless. However, his humble background gave him a sympathy for the poor, a theme which, combined with religious fervour, distinguishes him from his contemporaries. The parish church is a shrine to the artist, who is buried in a chapel to the right of the chancel. Here, *The Presentation of the Virgin* shows his characteristic traits of theatricality and grandiosity.

Cross the Rio Madonna dell'Orto canal to reach Rio della Sensa and **Tintoretto's house** (Fondamenta dei Mori 3399), a humble affair, where he lived until his death in 1594. Then walk up to Fondamente Nuove and the **Gesuiti**, a baroque church containing Tintoretto's *The Assumption of the Virgin*, influenced by Veronese's luminous colours.

From here, head south for the Rialto market district, where you could call into a *bacaro* for lunch. The rumbustious Do Mori on Calle do Mori has operated since 1462, so it's not inconceivable that Tintoretto was a patron. He would have approved of such mixing with the unwashed populace, and eating *crostini* with salt cod. After lunch, stroll to the church of **San Polo**, which displays Tintoretto's *The Assumption* and *The Last Supper*.

The church is a stepping stone to the **Scuola Grande di San Rocco**, Tintoretto's crowning glory. Mannerist works adorn every surface: they are larger than life, full of chiaroscuro effects and floating, plunging figures in dramatic poses. Next take line 1 from San Tomà to the Accademia, which holds some of his greatest works. Nearby, on **Rio di San Trovaso**, the church of the same name has many paintings. By the bridge is the Al Bottegon wine bar. You might find it hard to tear yourself away from delightful Dorsoduro, even for another work by Tintoretto.

Self-portrait by Tintoretto.

THE OPERATIC TRADITION

Venice's love of masks, romance and drama combine together beautifully in opera, which has long been a high point in the city's cultural life.

As one of the world's most operatic cities, Venice has a distinguished tradition in this field. A decisive factor in establishing the genre in the city was the opening of the first public opera house. Taken out of the private chamber, this complex and sophisticated music entered the public domain, and was no longer exclusively the preserve of the nobility. Venice's status as a state with a republican constitution, beyond the control of outside forces, also played an important role in making opera a popular national art form. The leading composers of their day wrote works for Venice, from Rossini to Verdi. Handel and Scarlatti both conducted their own operas in Venice.

Angelic musicians in a Bellini altarpiece in the Frari.

The golden age

Although opera first emerged in 16th-century Florence, the baton was quickly passed on to Venice. The 17th and 18th centuries were the golden age of Venetian music, celebrated by Monteverdi and Vivaldi, and, by the time opera had been defined as a special genre, the city had become its most important centre in Italy.

In the last 20 years of the 17th century, more than 150 operas were performed in the city, including 20 new ones. The operas of the early period perfectly reflected the tastes of Venetian society. Although classical mythology provided the colourful plots, the characterisation reflected the great scandals of the day. This

Giuseppe Verdi (1813–1901), one of the greatest composers of his age.

realism was one of the reasons for opera's success in the city, with Venetians only too familiar with the traditional operatic themes of intrigue, conspiracy and betrayal.

In time, it was Venetian composers who developed the sensuous melodies that have come to be considered the hallmark of all Italian opera. Cremona-born Claudio Monteverdi (1567–1643) is regarded as the founder of Venetian opera. Summoned to Venice after an early musical career at the Mantuan court, he was appointed choirmaster of San Marco and Master of Music for the Republic, remaining in his post for 30 years. He succeeded Andrea Gabrieli (1510–86) and his nephew Giovanni Gabrieli (1557–1612), early masters of massed choirs and baroque polyphonic music. Monteverdi wrote seven of his operas in Venice, proving his command of musical characterisation, especially in *Poppea*, a late work.

Teatro San Cassiano, founded in 1637, was the first of many grand public opera houses. By the 18th century, there were 19 such venues in Venice, including La Fenice (see page 73). These theatres were owned by prominent Venetian families who mounted short seasons, hence the constant renewal of the repertoire.

The Venetians were a demanding audience who expected strong librettos and elaborate staging. They got what they craved, and audiences were held spellbound by fantastic stage effects, which could convey dreams and ghostly visitations. Buildings were made to collapse, waves, thunder and lightning could all be simulated, and the clouds on which the gods were enthroned could divide into three as they sank, then re-form as they rose.

> Baldassare Galuppi (1706–84) was the father of a light new operatic genre, opera buffa (comic opera), which became all the rage in opera houses across 18th-century Europe.

In the 17th century the craze for opera swept the city, but the stage action often played second fiddle to the social aspects: the opera was the place to pick up the latest gossip, play cards, or simply to dine in the privacy of one's box. Outstanding vocal performances could provoke storms of applause. After the premiere of Rossini's *Semiramis*, an enthusiastic crowd escorted him home in a convoy of gondolas while an orchestra reprised melodies from the opera. Singers who did not live up to expectations, however, felt the public's wrath with a fusillade of rotten eggs and tomatoes, radishes or leeks.

Prima donnas and castrati

The 18th century saw the emergence of the concept of the star soloist, the female prima donnas and the castrati, their male counterparts. Their way was paved by the enrichment of operatic forms, the creation of fine arias and *coloratura*, or virtuoso, voice passages. Giving the *primo uomo* (leading man) a treble voice was a popular custom which started in the 16th century and was all the fashion in 18th-century Italy, finally dying out only in the 19th century. The custom of castrating young boys before puberty to preserve their clear soprano or contralto voices may have been linked to an earlier prohibition against women singing opera in public.

The castrato possessed a unique tone of voice, as well as the lung capacity necessary to sing with great power and the skill to scale the opera's most florid vocal passages. Castrati and prima donnas were so worshipped by their public that they became capricious divas. As overindulged soloists, they decided which arias to sing and which to leave out, as well as laying

Interior of the Teatro La Fenice, artist unknown.

down the *coloratura* passages which best suited their own vocal virtuosity, regardless of the composer's original intentions.

> Antonio Vivaldi (1678–1741) was a fine violinist and prolific writer, leaving behind more than 500 concertos. Easily his most popular work today is Le Quattro Stagioni (The Four Seasons).

Verdi in Venice

The appointment of Giuseppe Verdi (1813–1901) was a milestone in the history of La Fenice; here was the greatest composer of Italian *bel canto* creating works for Venice. Verdi was a patriot who found a responsive audience in republican-minded Venice. As one of the greatest composers of his age, Verdi inflamed Venetian passions with five of his finest dramatic works. After diplomatically announcing that Milan's La Scala needed a rest from him (with four of his operas in as many years), Verdi signed a contract with La Fenice. Milan's loss was Venice's gain, and *Hernani* was premiered there in 1844. The public were enchanted by Verdi's music and left humming the melodies.

The heroic composer gave his operas stirring undertones during Italy's struggle for national unity. From 1848, Verdi's name became a rallying cry for his countrymen in the fight for freedom from Austrian domination. The acronym **V**(ittorio) **E**(manuele) **R**(e) **D'I**(talia) was used as a reference to the first king of Italy, eventually crowned in 1861. In 1866 (the year the Veneto joined the newly created Kingdom of Italy), during a performance of *Il Trovatore*, the stage was bombarded by bouquets of red, white and green, the colours of the Italian tricolour flag.

La Fenice

The golden age passed, but La Fenice sustained its reputation, staging the Italian premiere of Wagner's *Rienzi* in 1873, and, after the composer's death in 1883, presenting the entire Ring cycle in German. While most European opera houses could only offer makeshift programmes during World War I, La Fenice presented no fewer than 68 premieres.

In 1930, the opera house created a festival of contemporary music, proof that Venice was committed to more than the classical canon. Its innovative approach reaped rewards: the world premieres of Gershwin's *Porgy and Bess* (1935), Stravinsky's *The Rake's Progress* (1951) and Britten's *The Turn of the Screw* (1954).

The resurrection of La Fenice was matched by the reopening of Teatro Malibran, a tiny jewel of an opera house dating to 1678.

The Return of La Fenice

The Phoenix opera house has risen from the ashes once again, its jewel-box intimacy intact. Yet not everyone's happy.

On 29 January 1996 fire raged through La Fenice opera house. Many Venetians sobbed as their beloved Phoenix burnt down before their eyes; the conflagration engulfed musical instruments, paintings, costumes and sets – 200 years of history up in smoke. Dame Joan Sutherland, the celebrated diva, was stunned: "It was probably the most beautiful opera house in the world; singing in the Fenice felt like being inside a diamond."

This was the third fire in its history. The first Fenice (Phoenix) replaced a 17th-century theatre which had burnt down in 1774. Inaugurated in 1792, the opera house lived to rue its name when, in 1836, fire razed it to the ground. However, just a year later, La Fenice rose from the ashes, rebuilt as before, in all its neoclassical splendour. The jinx appeared to have been broken until 1996, when the Phoenix again seemed doomed.

This third fire would resemble the plot of a comic opera if the consequences had not been so grave. Ironically, the draining of the canals left firefighters suffering from a water shortage. An electrical fault was soon ruled out and a more sinister story emerged. Conspiracy theorists made links with the Mafia-led cultural terrorism that struck Italy in the 1990s, but the truth was more banal: two electricians, behind schedule and due to face financial penalties, started a blaze to cover their tracks.

The decision was swiftly taken to rebuild the theatre and in 2004, eight years of scandals, lawsuits and delays ended in the flamboyant reopening of this tiny theatre. The curtain rose on the crowd-pleasing *La Traviata*, a symbolic opera that received its world premiere in the same theatre in 1853. Marcello Viot-ti, the musical director, declared his faith in the new Fenice: "We have always been in the vanguard ... I would like to see one new opera presented here every year." Since reopening, the opera house has hosted works by Rossini, Strauss and Wagner, supported by a world-class concert and ballet programme.

The critical response has been mixed. Supporters praise the state-of-the-art sets and the improved acoustics, while

La Fenice resurrected.

sentimentalists lament the brightness of the colours and the lack of finesse in the stuccowork. The fiercest art critics decry this as a kitsch imitation of the past – but to conservative Venetians and opera lovers the world over, the Phoenix has risen again.

CARNIVAL

The colourful pre-Lenten carnival, dating from pagan times, is an extravaganza of masked balls, pantomime and music.

Every year the city indulges in a 10-day masked ball – a Lententide "farewell to the flesh" – when a combination of poseurs and voyeurs come to wallow in the ghostly beauty of Venice as La Serenissima awakes to a whirl of colour, masks and costumes. Carnival has much to answer for: prices soar and the city has more mask shops than butchers; fashion shoots and foreign film crews swamp San Marco; cavorting crowds of motley Europeans dress as gondoliers and bosomy courtesans. Amidst air-kissing and cries of "*bellissimo*", there are displays of pan-European bad taste. These are all travesties of carnival, but carnival is a time for travesty. Despite the commercialism, this kitsch masquerade retains its magic.

A good place to do some Carnival planning is at the www.venice-carnival-italy.com website. Here you will find what's on when, the latest events news, and photo galleries.

Carnival lore

The Venetian carnival is the inheritor of a rich folk tradition, embracing pagan and Christian motifs. Linked to the winter solstice and fertility rites, such mid-winter folk festivals pre-date Christianity. According to pagan rites, winter was a force to be overcome, with the sun persuaded to return by a show of life at its most vital. Thus in Rome, the fertility rites of Saturnalia were celebrated with a riotous masquerade in which even slaves took part.

A masked ball in full swing.

Christianity gave the carnival new significance: the words *carne vale*, the Latin for 'farewell to meat', meant a last blow-out, particularly on Mardi Gras (Fat Tuesday), before the start of the long and rigorous Lenten period, marked by abstinence from the pleasures of the flesh and a focus on the spiritual.

In the past, the Venetian carnival was something of a moveable feast, beginning as early as October or Christmas and lasting until Lent. This long carnival season incorporated an element of "bread and circuses", with crowd-pleasing performances intended to curry favour with the populace. In addition to masquerades, there

The Carnival dates back to medieval times, but costumes are decidedly 18th century.

were rope dancers, acrobats and fire-eaters who routinely displayed their skills on Piazza San Marco. The diarist John Evelyn visited Venice in 1645–6 and reported on "the folly and madness of the carnival", from the bull-baiting and flinging of eggs to the superb opera, the singing eunuch and a shooting incident with an enraged nobleman and his courtesan, whose gondola canoodling he had disturbed. During the 1751 carnival, everyone gathered to admire an exotic beast, the rhinoceros, captured in a famous painting by Longhi, which is now displayed in the Ca' Rezzonico.

Carnival was not without barbaric flourishes, including spectacular blood sports with Venetian twists. As well as bear-baiting and Spanish-style bull chases, dogs were shot out of cannons for the crowd's amusement.

Another gory event commemorated the conquest of Aquileia in 1162, when the patriarch of Venice was captured along with 12 of his priests and ransomed for 12 pigs and a bull. After this incident, 12 pigs were flung from the campanile at every carnival, while a bull was beheaded.

When Napoleon conquered Venice in 1797, the carnival went the tragic way of the Venetian Republic. Although revived sporadically in the early part of the 20th century, it was only fully restored in 1979. The event was eagerly reclaimed by Venetians, with playful processions and masquerades.

The starting date for Carnival follows the vagaries of Easter's fluctuating dates; Carnival starts on 26 February in 2017 and 11 February in 2018.

It is fashionable to mock the carnival as a commercial fabrication, but its roots extend deep into the Venetian psyche. The city has an instinctive love of spectacle and dressing up, dating back to the glory days of the Republic. The carnival reaches back to medieval times and represents a cavalcade of Venetian history, tracing political and military events, factional rivalries and defeats. Today's carnival pays homage to the lavish lifestyles of 18th-century Venice. It is ironic that the carnival's heyday coincided with the terminal decline of the Republic. Costumes currently in vogue extol the voluptuous femininity of 18th-century dress for both sexes. It attracts people from all over the world, some of whom sport the most marvellous costumes in which to cavort at numerous private parties and public balls.

Devilish disguises

From Epiphany to Ash Wednesday Sior Maschera, the masked reveller, reigns supreme. During the Republic's official ceremonies a strict order of precedence had to be observed, but carnival was a time for the breaking of social taboos: the mask makes everyone equal.

The most traditional masks form a dramatic monochrome disguise, often harking back to periods of Venetian history or the dramatic tradition of the *commedia dell'arte*. Masks not based on traditional designs are generally known as fantasie, or fantasy masks. One of the finest is the *maschera nobile*, the white sculpted patrician mask. The head was covered with a *bauta*, a black silk hood and

lace cape, topped by a voluminous cloak (*tabarro*), in black silk for the nobility and in red or grey for ordinary citizens. The *volto*, the white half-mask, covered the face, with the finishing touch provided by a black tricorn hat adorned with feathers.

> If you need fancy dress for a return to the 18th century, drop by the Atelier Pietro Longhi (tel: 041 714 478, www.pietrolonghi.com, San Polo 2604/b), where you will find everything from powdered wigs to suits of armour.

Columbina (Columbine) is the name given to the elegant Venetian domino mask; more catlike and seductive is the mask commonly called *civetta* (flirt). Some masks are sinister, notably the menacing Plague Doctor, which features a distinctive beaked nose and black gown and was once worn as a protection against the plague.

The elegant *maschera nobile* and *commedia dell'arte* masks are not the only authentic disguises available. Masks representing or ridiculing the Republic's enemies, such as an exotic Moor or swarthy Turk, remain popular, as do more esoteric costumes associated with the carnival companies.

Revellers pose on a bridge, with San Maggiore as a backdrop.

A selection of handmade masks.

To buy a mask, visit a traditional made-to-measure mask shop, where they can whip you up anything from a brightly coloured Harlequin to a Medusa wreathed in snakes or even a sinister death mask. The most traditional masks are made of leather (*cuoio*) or papier mâché (*cartapesta*).

Festive calendar

"The finest drawing room in Europe" was Napoleon's overworked description of Piazza San Marco. Here the carnival opens in the presence of thousands of masqueraders, with a different theme each year. No theatre could provide a better setting. During the 10-day spectacle leading up to Shrove Tuesday, revellers come tumbling out of every alley, with the sound of Renaissance and baroque music echoing from every courtyard. Pantomime, operetta, concerts and literary readings are held in theatres and in the open-air spaces of the city *campi*. Campo San Polo, one of the largest squares, is a popular site for outdoor events, thus maintaining a role it has played since

medieval times. Many of the finest masked balls, fireworks and historical happenings are led by the Compagnie della Calza, the local carnival companies.

One high point of the festival is a grand masked ball, most recently held on the second Saturday of Carnival in La Fenice theatre. Revellers then move on to private parties or, in the case of celebrities, to the ball at the Cipriani, across the water.

Another big dance event takes place in Piazza San Marco (St Mark's Square) on Shrove Tuesday. In 2009, it was a Seventies night to mark the 30th anniversary of the relaunching of Carnival in 1979. Themes change each year. In the past, the midnight fasting bell would ring out from San Francesco della Vigna, signalling an end to licence and the onset of atonement. The end is signalled when the effigy of Carnival is burnt on Piazza San Marco.

Certainly, the Venetian love of disguise masks a desire to slip into a different skin. As Oscar Wilde said, "A man only reveals himself when wearing a mask."

Commedia dell'Arte

Many of the most distinctive carnival costumes are inspired by the comic genre *commedia dell'arte*.

The art of improvised theatre, or *commedia dell'arte*, emerged in 16th-century Italy and featured a fast pace and witty regional parodies. Given the physical nature of the comedy, the actors had to be skilled mime artists and acrobatic tumblers. In addition to stagecraft, the genre relied on stock characters who wore costumes and masks to differentiate their roles.

Characters spoke in regional dialects, leading to comic contrasts and misunderstandings. Thus, the classic pair of manservants, Harlequin *(Arlecchino)* and *Brighella*, come from Bergamo and speak the local dialect. The merchant *Pantalone* speaks Venetian while the Doctor (Dottore) favours Bolognese and the lovers Tuscan. The manservants, known as *zanni*, include *Brighella*, the wily servant: always plotting and intriguing, the bilious green colour of his mask shows his bitter nature, as does his broken nose and ugly face. He wears white livery, with green diagonal stripes. The acrobatic *Arlecchino* is often the butt of *Brighella's* jokes. Harlequin's costume of colourful rags is a symbol of his poverty, and later became his red, orange and green suit.

Harlequin's master is the miserly old Venetian merchant, *Pantalone*. Anglicised to "Pantaloons", this was a nickname for Venetians, derived from the name of a popular city saint. The image was reinforced by the character's trousers *(pantaloni)*, worn with a black cloak and red stockings. A brown mask with a bristling moustache and a long crooked nose complete the ensemble.

The foil to *Pantalone* is the pompous and lecherous *Dottore*. As a tedious doctor-at-law, his trademark is pedantry and tirades larded with Latin tags. His black half-mask features a bumpy forehead simulating an injury caused by a disgruntled student. The Captain *(Capitano)* is a braggart of Spanish extraction who has a huge ruff, plumed hat and a mask with a protruding nose.

Many other cartoon characters have sprung from these main types, including *Pulcinella*, the lovable clown, who in England turned into Mr Punch, half of the seaside Punch and Judy puppet

Pantalone (1550)

The miserly merchant Pantalone (1550), an old and often libidinous character.

show. As well as laying the foundations for puppet shows throughout Europe, the *commedia dell'arte* greatly enriched Continental comic drama, and led to the development of mime in France, and pantomime in England and Denmark.

REGATTAS AND WATER FESTIVALS

The doges have gone and the great navy is no more, but Venice still celebrates its festivals by staging spectacular water pageants.

Water festivals are the glory of Venice, with palaces on the Grand Canal festooned with streamers and silks, redolent of the pomp and pageantry of the Republic. From March to September, the lagoon is awash with regattas. All these events trace their origins back to naval exercises or military training for crossbowmen on the Lido. The most prestigious regatta honours Italy's four ancient maritime republics (Venice, Amalfi, Pisa and Genoa), with a different "republic" staging the event every year.

April's **Festa di San Marco**, honouring the patron saint of Venice, culminates in a gondola race across St Mark's Basin, and the eating of *risi e bisi*, thick rice-and-pea soup. **La Sensa**, the Ascension festival, celebrates Venice's Marriage with the Sea. Until the fall of the Republic, the doge would sail from San Marco to the Lido in the Bucintoro, the ceremonial State barge. With great pomp, a ring was cast into the Adriatic, symbolising Venice's sacred union with the sea.

Today's re-enactment is a pale imitation; the water marathon that follows is more memorable: **La Vogalonga** (Long Row) races from the Bacino di San Marco (St Mark's Basin) to Burano before returning via the Grand Canal. But the most magnificent water festival is September's **Regata Storica**, featuring participants in Renaissance costume. The water-borne parade down the Grand Canal is followed by rowing races best watched from a café by the Rialto Bridge.

The Regata Storica is the finest regatta in Venice.

The greatest Venetian boat of all was the State barge, the Bucintoro. It was lavishly decorated with gilded carvings and used for important state visits. On Ascension Day, it carried the doge to the Lido, where he would perform the ceremony of Venice's Marriage with the Sea, a tradition captured by Canaletto. The Bucintoro was destroyed by Napoleon's troops in 1798.

All classes of Venetian craft appear in regattas, from gondolas to sandoli, flat-bottomed boats good for skimming the shallow lagoon.

Musicians in the Regata Storica's parade.

THANKSGIVING FESTIVALS

The pontoon of boats during the Festa del Redentore.

Water festivals served to bind the patricians and people together to honour the State, both in times of triumph and disaster. **La Festa del Redentore**, the Feast of the Redeemer, takes place on the third weekend of July and is the most intimate of Venetian festivals. Begun under Doge Alvise Mocenigo, the festival focuses on Il Redentore, the Palladian church built as a token of thanks after salvation from the plague of 1575–7. A pontoon bridge of boats stretches across the Giudecca canal to the church, enabling people to walk across and attend Mass.

The real fun happens in the evening. Crowds line the Zattere and the Giudecca or take to boats of every description. From stately yachts to refuse barges and gondolas, the watercraft are bedecked in finery and glow like festive gazebos, most of them moored to one another to form one, giant floating party. Music is pumped out over loudspeakers and boisterous groups of families and friends enjoy on-board picnics of duck, lobster, mulberries, mandarins and sparkling prosecco. Boatless locals choose the more stable option of setting up trestle tables along the waterfront of La Giudecca and indulging in a community dinner prior to the spectacular midnight fireworks display, the breathtaking high point of the evening. Energetic souls carouse all night before rowing to the Lido for a dawn swim.

La Festa della Madonna della Salute, celebrated on 21 November, also commemorates the city's deliverance from the plague – of 1630. Here, too, there is a votive procession to the church, reached by a pontoon bridge from Santa Maria del Giglio. Venetians make the pilgrimage to La Salute to light candles in gratitude for the continuing good health of the city and its citizens.

The Festa del Redentore, with barges laden with fireworks and a parade of everyday and ceremonial craft, is the most moving night spectacle. Foghorns are sounded and the festival fireworks explode, turning Venice into a baroque dream.

EATING OUT

Venice is noted for top-quality seafood and for fine restaurants. But you shouldn't ignore the traditional bars and inns, known as *bacari*.

Food critics tend to damn Venetian food as overpriced and underachieving, but you can eat well if you choose wisely. Even so, the difficulty of transporting fresh produce adds 20 percent to restaurant prices. Mass tourism also means that the city can get away with grim tourist menus, indifferent service and inferior breakfasts. Yet for seafood lovers, the cuisine can be memorable, with soft-shelled crabs from the lagoon, plump red mullet, pasta heaped with lobster or black and pungent with cuttlefish ink.

Cichetti at Al Ponte, in the Castello district.

As the hub of a cosmopolitan trading empire, Venice was bristling with foreign communities – Arabs, Armenians, Greeks, Jews and Turks – each with its own distinctive culinary tradition.

According to Alastair Little, the British gourmet chef and Italophile, "the city's cosmopolitan past and superb produce imported from the Veneto have given rise to Italy's most eclectic and subtle style of cookery." Fine praise indeed. Like the Sicilians, the Venetians absorbed culinary ideas from the Arabs; they also raided Byzantium and, according to the Middle Eastern cookery writer, Claudia Roden, translated it into their own simple style: "If you could see the fish come in live at dawn in barges on the Grand Canal straight onto the market stalls, you would understand why all they want to do is lightly fry, poach or grill it."

Venetian trading posts in the Levant gave the city access to spices, the secret of subtle Venetian cookery. Pimiento, turmeric, ginger, cinnamon, cumin, cloves, nutmeg, saffron and vanilla show the oriental influences; pine-nuts, raisins, almonds and pistachios also play their part.

Reflecting the tastes of later masters of Venice, these exotic ingredients are enriched with a dash of French or Austrian cuisine. From the end of the 18th century, French influence meant that oriental spices were supplanted by Mediterranean herbs. The French brioche was added to the breakfast repertoire, as was the Turkish *crescente* (literally a crescent). The appearance of the croissant dates back to the Turkish defeat at the walls of Vienna in 1683.

The Venetian dish of fegato alla veneziana, made with calf's liver, and served with slices of grilled polenta.

Fish and seafood feature on menus more often than meat.

The Austrian conquest may have left Venice with a bitter taste in its mouth but it also left the city with an appetite for apple strudel and *krapfen* (doughnuts).

Eclectic tastes

A classic Middle-Eastern-inspired dish is *sarde in saor*, tart sardines marinated in standard Venetian sauce. *Melanzane in saor*, made with aubergines, is the vegetarian version. *Saor* means savoury or tasty, and is a spicy sauce made with onions, raisins, vinegar, pine-nuts and olive oil. *Riso* (rice), rather than pasta, predominates. Creamy Venetian risotto offers endless possibilities, flavoured with spring vegetables, meat, game or fish. *Risi e bisi* (rice and peas) is a thick soup blended with ham, celery and onion. Equally delicious are the seasonal risottos, cooked with asparagus tips, artichoke hearts, fennel, courgettes or pumpkins. An oriental variant involves sultanas and pine-nuts. To achieve the creamy consistency, the rice is fried with onions and ladled over with stock and wine. Venetians look for a rippling wave effect forming on the silky surface of the risotto; called *all'onda*, it is proof that the rice is cooked to perfection.

Fishy dinners

The fish on most local menus comes from the Adriatic. Inland fishing also occurs in *valli*, fenced-off sections of the lagoon, which is also

---

DINING TO ORDER

For visitors who spurn the tourist menu, there is often a choice between basking in the beauty of Venice over an exorbitantly priced dinner or hunting down an unpretentious trattoria in a malodorous back canal. It is hard to satisfy soul and stomach in one sitting. Yet, with perseverance, you can find that elusive table with a view and genuine home cooking.

The *antipasti* will feature fresh seafood, including *tartuffi di mare* (sea truffles) or *peoci saltati*, pan-fried mussels with parsley and garlic. Those who don't care for seafood should try *crostini* or roast-vegetable dishes. A typical *primo* (first course) is a *minestra* (soup) such as

pasta e fasioi, based on pasta and beans. If eating pasta, try *bigoli in salsa* (wholewheat spaghetti in a spicy sauce), *pappardelle alla granseola* (pasta with crab), or *spaghetti con astice* (with lobster). Expect a variety of seafood dishes using tiny sea snails (*garuzoli*), scallops (*capesante*) and cuttlefish (*seppie*). As a *secondo* (main dish), try *seppie alla veneziana*, cuttlefish cooked in its own ink, served with polenta. As for *dolci* (desserts), a typical one is *crema fritta alla veneziana*, squares of solid custard fried in egg and breadcrumbs. Those with a sweet tooth will like *tiramisù*, originally brought from Byzantium by the Venetians.

a source for a rich variety of seafood – anything from *folpeti* (tiny octopuses) through to the much prized *moeche* (small lagoon shore crabs). It is hard to better *antipasti di frutti di mare*, a feast of simply cooked shellfish and molluscs, dressed with olive oil and lemon juice; prawns and soft-shelled crabs vie with *peoci* (mussels) and squid. A trademark dish is cuttlefish risotto, served black and pungent with ink, or *granseola*, spider crab, boiled and then dressed simply in lemon and oil. Another staple is *baccalà*, dried salt cod, served in countless ways.

> In Venice, fish features more often than meat, but offal is favoured, particularly in *fegato alla veneziana*, calf's liver sliced into ribbons and cooked with parsley and onion.

Sweet treats

Biscuits, cakes and desserts are a forte, flavoured with exotic spices ever since the discovery of cinnamon and nutmeg. The Venetians introduced cane sugar to Europe, and have retained their sweet tooth. Spicy sweets are popular, including *fritelle di zucca*, sweet pumpkin doughnut served hot.

Where to eat

San Marco and Castello are home to some of the city's most prestigious restaurants. Further away from the bustle, dining experiences tend to be more varied, and prices lower. There is a handful of ethnic restaurants in Venice, ranging from Japanese to Indian, but most places are resolutely Italian or Venetian. Locals eat early. At dinner time, it is largely impossible to find a kitchen open after 10pm at the latest.

Venetian restaurants tend to opt for a timeless elegance or homely rustic setting, with exposed timber beams, tiny tables and copper pots hanging from the ceiling. Quite a few offer rear courtyard or pergola dining.

Reservations are required for the grander restaurants, which tend to be fairly dressy affairs. The opposite is true of the *bacari*, the traditional wine and snack bars, where you can dress as a market trader if you feel like it. More upmarket places are termed *ristoranti*, but may be called *osterie* (inns) if they focus on homely food in an intimate or rustic setting. Some inns have bars

that act like traditional *bacari*, so that one can opt for a quicker, cheaper snack at the bar or a full sit-down meal at a table.

The distinction between bars and restaurants is tricky in Venice, as most *bacari* also serve food, essentially Venetian tapas, known as *cichetti*, ranging from *polpette* (spicy meatballs) to *carciofini* (artichoke hearts), *tramezzini* (tiny sandwiches), *crostini* with grilled vegetables, *baccalà mantecato* (mashed cod prepared in garlic and parsley), *bovoleti* (little snails) and anchovy nibbles. For a taste of everyday Venice, especially near the Rialto market, little beats a *bacaro*.

Wine

The Veneto produces a number of superior (DOC) wines, from the fruity, garnet-red Bardolino to the popular wines of the Valpolicella region, led by the exquisite Amarone, made with dried grapes. Soave is the Veneto's best-known and one of Italy's best whites. It comes from vineyards around the eponymous castle and village, east of Verona. Dry whites from the Friuli Venezia Giulia region, to the northeast of Venice, such as Pinot Grigio, bring out the best in seafood dishes.

Regional wines can also be sampled in traditional wine bars: these *bacari* are a Venetian institution dating back to the Middle Ages. To eat *cichetti e l'ombra*, a snack and a glass of wine, is a

Seafood pasta.

A traditional bacaro.

> By far the most common tipple is prosecco, a lightly sparkling Veneto white that is popular at aperitivo hour. It is produced mostly around Conegliano, in the northeast of the Veneto region.

Venetian tradition. These snacks make an engaging choice for a light lunch or supper, and represent the Venetian equivalent of Spanish tapas.

Cocktail hour

Venice is noted for its cocktails, especially the Bellini, the delicious peach-and-prosecco aperitif invented in Harry's Bar.

But to look like a Venetian, risk the lurid orange cocktail known as *spritz* (pronounced "spriss" in Venetian dialect). The bright-orange drink was introduced under Austrian rule (named after the introduction of "selzer", fizzy soda water) and soon became a firm favourite. It consists of roughly equal parts of dry white wine or prosecco, soda water and an aperitif, usually Campari Bitter or Aperol (but also Amaro or Select), and garnished with a twist of lemon or an olive. The *spritz* may be an acquired taste, but once acquired, it's the clearest sign that you've fallen for Venice.

The cocktail hour between 7pm and 8pm is a Venetian ritual: locals can be seen sipping wine or classic cocktails in chic cafés, old-fashioned neighbourhood bars or *bacari*. Students hang out in a cluster of bars on Campo Santa Margherita and a more mellow crowd at several canalside bars in northern Cannaregio. A more sophisticated local crowd gathers in the several bars and *bacari* around the Rialto markets. The occasional new wine bar opens up here and there, including cool reinterpretations of the *bacaro*, where one can still request *un'ombra* (literally a shadow), a tiny glass of white Veneto wine, downed in one go. At the other end of the scale, several once staid hotel cocktail bars have been relaunched as cool lounge bars. As a result, Venetian bar culture is far broader than time-warp piano bars in sophisticated hotels.

Not that much changes in the historic cafés close to San Marco, where coffee has been drunk for centuries and post-prandial grappas downed since the days of the doges. Beyond Piazza San Marco are serious wine bars *(enoteche)*, where tastings rather than tapas are the main draw. Since 2000, a handful of designer gastro-bars has emerged that would be at home in Manhattan, apart from the gondola moored by the back door. For a city as small in terms of population, there is no shortage of pleasant drinking locations.

Enotecas will please wine connoisseurs.

Café Society

Venice was the first city to embrace the coffee society, ever since the Republic's trade with the Orient brought the Arabian stimulant to Europe.

After a morning spent enthusing in churches and museums, it is easy to while away the rest of the day in a chic Venetian café on Piazza San Marco. Like Paris and Vienna, Venice relishes its reputation as a café society, with all the spurious glamour this implies. Ever since the Republic's trade with the Orient brought the Arabian stimulant to Europe, caffeine has been the Venetian drug of choice. The first *bottega del caffè* (coffee bar) opened on Piazza San Marco in 1638.

With their string quartets, pirouetting waiters and pretentious airs, the coffee houses are part of the performance art that is Venice. Each café has its own particular charms: Quadri basks in the morning sun and an 18th-century ambience, while Florian, its celebrated rival, lies in the shade until noon; Lavena simply serves the best coffee without the beau-monde atmosphere.

Caffè Florian, considered the prince of coffee houses, was founded in 1720 and is the oldest surviving café in Italy. As an erstwhile literary haunt, it has welcomed Byron and Dickens, Goethe and Thomas Mann. Wagner kept away from Florian for fear of running into Verdi. Although trading on its past, Florian's air of *fin-de-siècle* Habsburg nostalgia is misplaced. After the Austrian army had quelled the 1848 Venetian uprising, Florian's became the meeting place for republican patriots. The Austrians preferred to survey their uncowed subjects from Caffè Quadri across the square.

Venetian coffee culture can be a complex thing. The cornerstone of any Italian breakfast is coffee, often in the form of a *caffè latte* (milky coffee) or *cappuccino* (also known as *cappuccio* for short), much the same thing but topped with hot froth and a dash of powdered chocolate. These are usually accompanied with a *brioche* (Italian version of the French croissant, a little dry and often with a whiff of marmalade about it).

Locals would never take these breakfast beverages at other times of the day. For that caffeine hit during the day, the *espresso* (strong and black) is the most common version, or a *macchiato* (liter-

Caffè Florian in Piazza San Marco.

ally "stained" with a shot of frothy milk à la cappuccino). A summer-time option is the *caffè freddo*, traditionally a cup of coffee poured into a glass with ice cubes. A trendier, modern version is the *caffè shakerato*, made as though it were a cocktail, sometimes with a hint of vanilla added, then served rather flamboyantly in a cocktail glass.

Basilica di San Marco in all its splendour.

Sleepy Cannaregio.

Time out in the Lido.

Gondolas at sunset.

INTRODUCTION

**A detailed guide to the city, with the principal sites
clearly cross-referenced by number to the maps.**

The first fleeting glimpse of Venice from the air is a foretaste of the watery puzzle that awaits below. At low tide, the lagoon reveals an expanse of mudflats, shifting sandbanks and brackish marsh; the sunlight momentarily withdraws from the glassy greyish-brown waters, showing the same desolation that failed to daunt the early settlers. Yet, as the plane circles the lagoon, the sinuous red-brick city floats into view, changing foreboding into fantasy.

Venice is traditionally divided into six *sestieri* (districts), a practice followed in this book. In addition, each main island is treated separately, as is the Grand Canal, which winds through the middle

Colourful Burano.

of the *sestieri*. Despite the watery insubstantiality of Venice, most time is spent walking rather than travelling by boat. However, a mastery of

The Bridge of Sighs.

key ferry routes can save unnecessary circling of the lagoon: an error can cost an hour on a short journey. (See the transport map inside the back cover, and page 247, for advice.)

To find an address, ask the name of the closest parish church; this is in fact more helpful than the postal address. Venetians will usually point you in the right direction. Despite the kindness of strangers, all visitors eventually lose themselves in this labyrinthine city.

The uniqueness of the city geography is captured in Venetian dialect, with the names of streets providing clues to the nature of the city. Familiarity with these terms will help in identifying places on your trails. Venetian spelling is variable, so expect alternative versions. (See page 101 for a brief lexicon.)

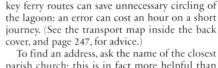

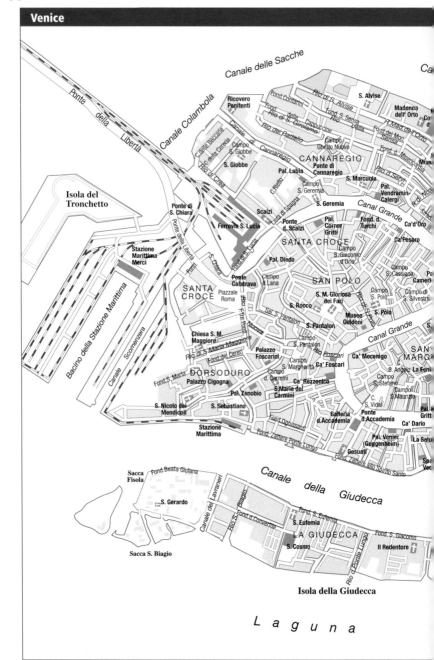

Isola del
Tronchetto

Canale delle Sacche

Canale Colombola

Ponte della Libertà

Ricovero
Penitenti

S. Alvise

Madonna
dell' Orto

Fond. Contarini

Rio di S. Alvise

Fond.ta delle Cappuccine

Rio di S. Girolamo

Rio dei Battello

Campo
Ghetto Nuovo

Fond. dei Mori

Rio Madonna dell'Orto

Fond. Sensa

Misericordia

CANNAREGIO

Calle della Racchetta

Rio della Cereria

Campo
S. Giobbe

Canale di Cannaregio

S. Giobbe

Pal. Labia

Ponte di
Cannaregio

S. Marcuola

Fond. d. Misericordia

Rio di Crea

Campo
S. Geremia

S. Geremia

Pal.
Vendramin-
Calergi

Ca'd'Oro

C. Rielto

Scalzi

Lista di Spagna

Canal Grande

Rio di Noale

Ponte di
S. Chiara

Ferrovia S. Lucia

Ponte
d. Scalzi

Pal.
Corner
Gritti

Fond. d.
Turchi

Ca'd'Oro

Stazione
Marittima
Merci

Ponte della Libertà

Fond. S. Lucia

SANTA CROCE

Campo
S.Giacomo
d'Orio

Ca'Pesaro

S. Chiara

Pal. Diedo

Campo
S.Cassiano

Campo
Camerle

Bacino della Stazione Marittima

SANTA
CROCE

Ponte
Calatrava

Piazzale
Roma

Campo
d. Lana

SAN POLO

S. M. Gloriosa
dei Frari

Campo
S. Polo

Campo di
S. Silvestro

Canale Scomenzera

Rio Fra' Pini

Sal. S. Pantalon

S. Rocco

Museo
Goldoni

S. Polo

Chiesa S. M.
Maggiore

Calle Nuova

S. Pantalon

Campo
S. Pantalon

Canal Grande

Rio di S. Maria Maggiore

Palazzo
Foscarini

Rio Foscari

Ca' Mocenigo

SAN
MARCO

Fond. dei Cereri

Campo
S. Margherita

Ca' Foscari

S. Angelo

La Fenice

DORSODURO

Fond.S. Marta

Palazzo Cigogna

Ca' Rezzonico

Campo
S. Stefano

Pal. Zenobio

S.Maria del
Carmini

Campo
S.Maurizio

S. Nicolo dei
Mendicoli

S. Sebastiano

Galleria
d.Accademia

Ponte
d.Accademia

C.
S. Vidal

Pal.
Gritti

Ca' Dario

La Salute

Stazione
Marittima

Fond. Ognissanti

Gesuati

Pal. Venier
(Guggenheim)

Fond. Zattere Ponte Lungo

Fond. Zattere allo Spirito Santo

Spirito
Santo

Sacca
Fisola

Fond Beata Giuliana

Canale dei Lavraneri

S. Gerardo

Canale
della
Giudecca

Sacca S. Biagio

Rio di Biagio

Fond.ta d.Convertite

Fond. S. Eufemia

S. Eufemia

LA GIUDECCA

Fond. S. Giacomo

Rio d.Ponte Lungo

S. Cosmo

Il Redentore

Isola della Giudecca

L a g u n a

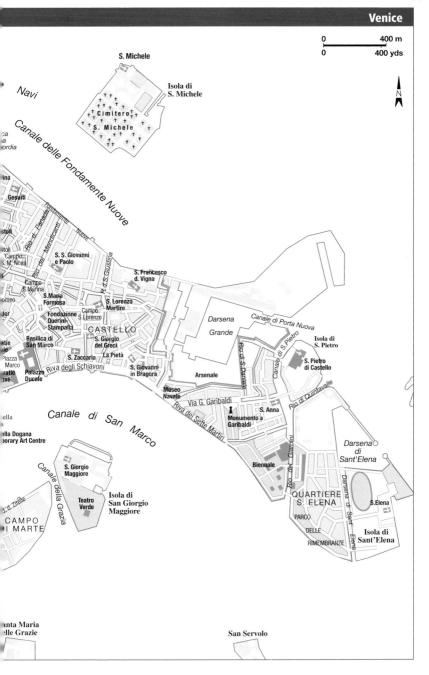

0   400 m

0   400 yds

N

Navi

Canale delle Fondamente Nuove

S. Michele

Isola di
S. Michele

Cimitero
S. Michele

ca
a
ordia

ina

Gesuiti

Fondamente Nuove

Rio di Mendicanti

Rio di S.Giustina

stoli

stoli
Campo
S. M. Nova

S. S. Giovanni
e Paolo

S. Francesco
d. Vigna

Campo
S. Marina

omeo

S.Maria
Formosa

S. Lorenzo
Martire

Darsena
Grande

Canale di Porta Nuova

Jor

Fondazione
Querini-
Stampalia

Campo
S.Lorenzo

CASTELLO

Isola di
S. Pietro

atie
ie

Basilica di
San Marco

S. Giorgio
del Greci

Rio di S.Daniele

Canale di S. Pietro

S. Pietro
di Castello

Piazza
Marco

S. Zaccaria

La Pietà

atie
ve

Palazzo
Ducale

Riva degli Schiavoni

S. Giovanni
in Bragora

Arsenale

Rio di Quintavalle

ella

Canale   di   San   Marco

Museo
Navale

Via G. Garibaldi

S. Anna

ella Dogana
porary Art Centre

Riva dei Sette Martiri

Monumento a
Garibaldi

Canale della Grazia

d. Zitelle

S. Giorgio
Maggiore

Rio dei Giardini

Darsena
di
Sant'Elena

CAMPO
I MARTE

Teatro
Verde

Isola di
San Giorgio
Maggiore

Biennale

QUARTIERE
S. ELENA

Darsena di Sant' Elena

S.Elena

PARCO

DELLE

RIMEMBRANZE

Isola di
Sant'Elena

nta Maria
lle Grazie

San Servolo

Piazza San Marco, one vast café terrace.

AROUND SAN MARCO

Piazza San Marco (St Mark's Square) is the heart of Venice: here are the famous basilica and belltower, the doges' fabulous palace, the Museo Correr, Harry's Bar and the best cafés in town.

Piazza San Marco was famously dubbed "the finest drawing room in Europe" by Napoleon. Like many visitors to Venice, he then proceeded to repaint it in his own image, even rearranging the furniture and moving the walls.

However, given the city's talent for fusing influences into an enchanting Venetian whole, the square has retained its essential character. Gentile Bellini's *Procession in Piazza San Marco* (1496) is the most reproduced view of Venice, a grand hierarchical affair of prelates and senators outside the Basilica di San Marco.

MODERN SAN MARCO

St Mark's belongs to the citizens as well as visitors. Venetians drink at the grand cafés, even if they often save money by standing up. Some attend Sunday Mass at the basilica or even dance at the open-air carnival.

For most of the day, though, St Mark's belongs to the pigeons, the crowds and the souvenir-sellers; only in early evening does it revert to a semblance of solitude.

Piazza San Marco acted as the heart of the Republic from the time the earliest settlement shifted from Torcello to central Venice. Its design was determined by the building of

the basilica and the Palazzo Ducale (Doge's Palace) in the 14th century. However, in the 16th century, the square was remodelled to reflect Venetian notions of glory. The basilica and palace were embellished, with a new library, mint and administrative buildings clustered around the square. The design remained intact until the bombastic Napoleonic era, when churches and monuments on the waterside were demolished to create a neoclassical wing, a ballroom and public gardens.

Main Attractions
Basilica di San Marco
Museo Correr
Palazzo Ducale
Torre d'Orologio
La Fenice
Santa Maria Zobenigo
Santo Stefano
Palazzo Fortuny
Palazzo Contarini del Bovolo

Map
Page 100

Tourist crowds on Piazza San Marco.

200 m
200 yds

0
0

Basilica di San Marco ❶

Address: Piazza San Marco,
www.basilicasanmarco.it
Tel: 041-522 5697
Opening Hrs: Mon–Sat 9.45am–
5pm, Sun 2–4pm, Easter–Nov till
5pm
Entrance Fee: free
Transport: Vallaresso, San Marco,
San Zaccaria

The Basilica di San Marco (St Mark's
Basilica) is the centrepiece of the
square, a place the aesthete John
Ruskin called "a treasure heap, a confusion of delight". Best visited in the
early morning, the basilica remains a
glorious mix of styles.

San Marco, modelled on Byzantine
churches in Constantinople, trans-
poses the essence of an eastern
basilica to the West. According to
the critic Mary McCarthy, it was
"an oriental pavilion, half pleasure house, half war tent, belonging
to some great satrap". The French
poet Théophile Gautier (1811–72)
declared San Marco "a pirate cathedral enriched with the spoils of the
universe", while Charles Dickens
(1812–70) was spellbound: "opium

couldn't build such a place... dim
with the smoke of incense; costly in
treasure of precious stones and metals; glittering through iron bars; holy
with the bodies of deceased saints".

The basilica was consecrated
in AD 832, intended as a mausoleum for St Mark's relics and as the
doge's ceremonial chapel. In AD
976 the church burnt down after a
riot but was rebuilt between 1063
and 1094, probably supervised by a
Greek architect. The basilica echoed
eastern models. At the same time,
Doge Selvo (1071–84) asked merchants to return with rare marble
and semi-precious stones to adorn
the basilica, from jasper to alabaster
and porphyry. John Ruskin admired
this "confused incrustation", which
incorporated Roman fragments and
looted Byzantine booty in an oriental basilica that professed to be a
Christian church. Yet for political
reasons, this majestic building was
technically designated the doge's
private chapel for most of the dura-
tion of the Republic. San Marco only
succeeded San Pietro as the cathedral
of Venice in 1807.

TIP

Stringent security
measures in the basilica
mean that all bags have
to be left in the Ateneo
San Basso on Piazzetta
dei Leoncini, a free left-
luggage service.

*The domes
of San Marco.*

A VENETIAN LEXICON

Ca' (from *casa*): house/palace
calle: street
campo: square; *campiello*: small
square
corte: external courtyard
cortile: internal courtyard
fondamenta: wide quayside
fontego or *fondaco:* historic warehouse
ramo: side street or dead end
rio (plural *rii*): canal lined by buildings
rio terrà: infilled canal
riva: promenade, quayside
ruga: broad shopping street
rughetta: small shopping street
sacca: inlet
salizzada: main street
sottoportico (or *sottoportego*): tiny
alleyway running under a building
stazio: gondoliers' station

TIP

Visitors to the basilica are channelled along set routes, so Catholics might consider visiting from 7 to 9.45am, when only worshippers are welcome.

The Treasury and Museo Marciano

The Greek-cross plan is inscribed in a square, and crowned by five domes, set over each arm of the cross. These are linked to one another by loggias and arcades. The bewildering contrast is between the oriental domes and rounded Byzantine arches, and the Gothic ornamentation of the central roofline. Gothic arches and pinnacles were grafted onto 12th-century facades and completed by a gallery overlooking the square. Most of the garish mosaics on the facade are 17th-century copies, with the only intact 13th-century mosaic depicting the arrival of St Mark's relics in the basilica (set above the doorway on the far left).

The basilica was controversially restored in the 1860s and 1870s, which led to the removal of the mosaics on the north and south facades. In a letter to his father, Ruskin, who helped mobilise international opinion, literally wept: "They appear to be destroying the mosaics. I cannot draw here for tears in my eyes." Although these mosaics were lost,

The basilica's glittering facade.

the international furore stirred up by Ruskin led to the reversal of other restoration blunders in St Mark's.

The exterior brickwork of the central apse is reminiscent of Santa Fosca in Torcello (see page 229). The southern side abuts the Palazzo Ducale. The baptistry doors are framed by the **Pilasters of Acre**, two ancient Syrian pillars plundered from Acre, in the Holy Land (modern Israel), after a victory over the Genoese in 1258. These sculpted, 6th-century marble columns stand beside a porphyry stump known as the *pietra del bando*, where the laws of the Republic were proclaimed.

In the corner are the **Tetrarchs**, often known as Moors because of their dress, a 4th-century Egyptian sculpture representing Diocletian and his fellow rulers who governed the Roman Empire.

From the inside, the 13th-century oriental domes seem much lower and smaller than they really are. The basilica pavement seems like an oriental carpet interweaving floral, animal and geometric motifs. The undulating mosaics of marble, porphyry and glass depict allegorical and naturalistic scenes. After the conquest of Constantinople in 1204, Venice celebrated its triumph with lavish cycles of mosaics and the display of Byzantine booty. Some of the greatest treasures in San Marco were plundered from Constantinople, including the **Madonna Nicopeia**, a sacred 10th-century icon, adorning the Altar of the Virgin.

The **Treasury** (Mon–Sat 9.45am–5pm, Nov–Easter till 4pm, Sun 2–4pm; charge) incorporates a 9th-century corner tower from the first Palazzo Ducale and displays Byzantine gold, silver and glassware. Since this collection began with the Venetian looting of Constantinople, it seems only poetic justice that French plundering should have depleted

The mosaics of St Mark's are symbolic rather than realistic.

The mosaics and altarpiece

Officially, St Mark's remains are encased in a sarcophagus under the altar, but sceptics believe that these were destroyed in the fire of AD 976. Behind the altar, often swamped by crowds, is the **Pala d'Oro** (charge), a superb medieval altarpiece studded with gems and covered in sacred scenes. The panels are enclosed in a gilded frame and encrusted with emeralds, rubies, sapphires and gleaming, translucent enamels bound by a filigree of gold; each tessera is a separate segment of colour. This 10th-century masterpiece was created by Byzantine goldsmiths but embellished in 1209 and 1345 by the Venetians and Sienese; panels from a sacked church in Constantinople also added to the lustre.

The interior is studded with mosaics, one of the chief glories of San Marco, but visitors are channelled along set routes, making lingering difficult. The mosaics date from 1071, first created by craftsmen from Constantinople; although the majority are from the 11th to 14th centuries, mosaics continued to be

the treasury. But much remains, despite a forced sale of jewels and the Napoleonic melting down of objets d'art.

The **Classical Horses** were also Byzantine booty. The rearing animals stood on top of a triumphal arch in Rome before gracing the hippodrome in Constantinople and finally adorning the facade of San Marco. Given that the horses symbolised the Venetian Republic's untrammelled independence, Napoleon had them harnessed to a chariot in Paris for 18 years. The humiliation ended with their return to Venice in 1815. They are now displayed in the **Museo Marciano**, the gallery above the entrance portal, allowing one to pause for a fine view of the interior before taking in views of the piazza and exterior mosaics from the loggia itself. Copies have taken their place on the basilica facade.

RESTORATION IN PIAZZA SAN MARCO

The buildings on St Mark's Square are often covered in scaffolding. Pollution, triggered by the combination of sulphur dioxide and the salty lagoon air, acts as a corrosive cocktail on the precious sculpted-marble reliefs on the facades. The British subsidised the cleaning of the capitals on the Palazzo Ducale, the restoration of the belltower's Loggetta and the Porta della Carta, the ceremonial gateway to the Palazzo Ducale. The facades of the basilica and the lovely clocktower at the landward end of the piazza have been restored, though some scaffolding remains. The grand gateway, Cappella Zen and the basilica crypt have been well restored, but Sansovino's Loggetta is posing a problem. The resins used to protect the restored marble have discoloured the facade, so work has been done to flush the resins out. Equally controversial was the Olivetti-funded restoration of the bronze horses of St Mark, with the originals placed within the basilica and copies left on the facade.

But much restoration work is aimed at combating the deadly flooding known as *acqua alta*, which invades the piazza, the lowest-lying area of the lagoon, 250 times a year. All around is evidence of one long-term solution, the consolidation of the quaysides, with the final verdict left to future generations (see page 52).

until the 18th century. The result is a bewildering tapestry, an illustrated Bible using 4,000 sq metres (4,780 sq yds) of mosaics. Even the windows of this oriental extravaganza were walled up to make more space for mosaics.

The mosaics are rich in geometric forms and symbolic meaning, part decorative, part naturalistic. Relatively naturalistic Old Testament scenes in the **narthex** (atrium) contrast with the more stylised figures of the central domes. As a rule of thumb, the lower walls depict saints, with the middle section featuring the Apostles, and the domes dedicated to Christ Pantocrator, the Creator of All. The atrium mosaics in the **Genesis Dome** show the Creation, unravelled in concentric circles. The **Pentecost Dome**, rising above the nave, depicts the descent of the Holy Ghost as a dove, and was perhaps the first to be adorned with mosaics. The paired figures between the windows represent the nations in whose languages the Apostles evangelised after Pentecost.

The central **Ascension Dome** shows Christ in Majesty, a 13th-century scene embracing the Apostles and the Virgin Mary. Now restored, the 14th-century **Baptistry** (same opening times as basilica) has some interesting mosaics, while the Zen Chapel houses the bronze 16th-century tomb of Cardinal Zen.

Museo Correr ❷

Address: Piazza San Marco 52, http://correr.visitmuve.it/
Tel: 041-240 5211
Opening Hrs: daily 10am–7pm, to 5pm in winter
Entrance Fee: charge
Transport: Vallaresso, San Marco, San Zaccaria

The piazza is bounded by the Procuratie, the offices and residences of the procurators of the Republic, the highest government officials. The **Procuratie Vecchie** is an elegant porticoed building stretching along the north side of the square. Dating from 1500, this functional affair was modelled on Coducci's designs but finished by Scarpagnino.

The Biblioteca Nazionale Marciana was a model for the **Procuratie Nuove**, the offices on the south side of the square. The long building

Palazzo Ducale.

was begun in 1586 but finished by Longhena in 1640. Although echoing the Marciana, it is more sober and less graceful than the earlier buildings. Napoleon converted it into a royal palace, creating a ballroom by demolishing a neighbouring church and replacing it with the **Ala Napoleonica** (the Napoleonic Wing), which closes off the west end of the piazza.

It is in the Ala Napoleonica that we find the entrance to the often overlooked **Museo Correr**, dedicated to Venetian civilisation, which extends around through Procuratie Nuove. The neoclassical rooms make a fitting setting for Canova's sculptures. The following section is a romp through Venetian history, featuring representations of the Lion of St Mark, and paintings of festivities and ceremonies. The final historical section covers the troubled times from the fall of the Republic to French and Austrian domination.

Those without a taste for coins and battle memorabilia can proceed to the more accessible picture gallery, which showcases Venetian art from the 13th to the 16th centuries. While no match for the splendours of the Accademia, the collection features fine Byzantine-influenced works by Paolo Veneziano and Bartolomeo Vivarini, and paintings by Giovanni Bellini, especially the poignant *Pietà*. However, the symbol of the museum is Carpaccio's *Two Venetian Ladies* (1507), depicted in a pleasure garden, surrounded by birds and dogs. Though often seen as courtesans, the "ladies" are probably noblewomen.

Next, you pass through the **Museo Archeologico** (daily 10am–7pm, till 5pm in winter), housed in part of the Procuratie Nuove and the adjoining Biblioteca Nazionale Marciana. The uninspiring core collection consists of Greek and Roman sculpture bequeathed by Cardinal Grimani in 1523, which influenced generations of Venetian artists who came to draw and study here. Among the Roman busts, medals, coins and cameos are Greek originals and Roman copies, including a 5th-century Hellenistic Persephone.

The **Biblioteca Nazionale Marciana** ❸ is a cool classical building

The porticoed buildings surrounding the square are known as the Procuratie.

set in an extended loggia around the corner and forms the last and most engaging stage of the visit to the Museo Correr. Designed by Sansovino in 1537, the library is also known as the Libreria Sansoviniana. This long, low building is lined with arches and expressive statues, and graced with a sumptuous stairway. Indeed, Palladio praised it as the richest building since classical times. The library was designed to house the precious collection of manuscripts bequeathed by Petrarch in the 14th century, and by Cardinal Bessarion, the Greek humanist, in 1468. The superb salon of the original library is covered with paintings by Veronese and Tintoretto, and is reward enough for trudging round the duller sections of the Museo Correr and the interconnected archaeology museum.

Palazzo Ducale ❶

Address: Piazza San Marco, www.visitmuve.it
Tel: 041-271 5911
Opening Hrs: daily 8.30am–7pm, to 5.30pm in winter
Entrance Fee: charge
Transport: Vallaresso, San Marco, San Zaccaria

The **Palazzo Ducale** vies with San Marco for attention and plaudits. The facade has been restored and the interior revamped to include a museum of sculpture and sections hitherto off-limits, as well as a bookshop and café. The best way of seeing the palace without the crowds is to pre-book the Secret Itinerary (see page 108), a special visit that explores behind the scenes; the same ticket allows access to the rest of the palace. (The intriguing 75-minute tour is available in English, French and Italian; tel: 041-4273 0892.)

The Palazzo Ducale was the seat of the Venetian government from the 9th century until the fall of the Republic in 1797. While rival mainland cities built grim fortresses, the Venetians indulged in a light and

Carpaccio's Two Venetian Ladies is the star of the Museo Correr.

airy structure, confident of the natural protection afforded by the lagoon. Apart from being the doge's official residence, it acted as the nerve centre of the Republic, containing administrative offices and armouries, council chambers and chancellery, courtrooms and dungeons, most of which are now visible.

The palace was a symbol of political stability and independence, as well as a testament to Venetian supremacy and a glorious showcase of Venetian art, sculpture and craftsmanship. Yet there was also a shadowy side to the palace, a secretive machine staffed by State inquisitors, spies and torturers-in-residence.

There is no trace of the original 9th-century building. The palace was essentially complete by 1438. However, sections were further embellished between the 14th and 16th centuries. Architecturally, the palace is a Venetian hybrid, a harmonious fusion of Moorish, Gothic and Renaissance.

Although often considered the symbol of Gothic Venice, the palace's distinctive facades were inspired by the Veneto-Byzantine succession of porticoes and loggias. The Gothic inversion of spaces and solids reached perfection in the floriated style of the southern corner, with a mass of masonry seemingly floating on air. The palace has two of the finest Gothic facades in existence, a vision of rosy Verona marble supported by Istrian stone arcades. With its noble loggia and arcading, the facade overlooking the piazzetta embodies the majesty of State.

Gothic tracery on the loggia became the model for other palaces throughout the city. The harmonious waterfront facade is a Venetian Gothic masterpiece, including the porticoes and ceremonial balcony overlooking the quays. The **Sala del Maggior Consiglio** was rebuilt in 1340, transforming this waterfront wing. The intricately sculpted capitals and statuary on the facade are a tribute to the superb skills of Venetian Gothic craftsmen (but some capitals are copies, with the originals on display inside).

The **Porta della Carta**, the main ceremonial gateway, a triumph of Flamboyant Gothic style, is named after resident archivists or clerks who copied petitions nearby. Above the portal is the sculpted figure of Doge Francesco Foscari, who commissioned the gateway, kneeling before the winged lion. Sadly, the sculpture is partly reconstructed, since the lions were obliterated during Napoleonic times. In the Renaissance, attention turned to the eastern wing, courtyard and interior. After a fire in 1483, this wing, tucked between the courtyard and the canal, was remodelled to improve the doge's apartments and provide grander magistrates' offices.

This transition is marked by the meeting of the two styles in the **Foscari Arch**, between the Porta della Carta and the Scala dei Giganti. This deep arch is adorned with the figures of Adam and Eve, copies of the 15th-century

Love them or loathe them, pigeons are very much part of the Piazza San Marco experience.

originals. Beyond lies an elegant courtyard with Renaissance wellheads. The **Scala dei Giganti**, the Giants' Stairway, was built in 1486 to provide access to the loggia on the first floor. In 1567, this triumphal staircase was lavishly sculpted with monumental figures of Mars and Neptune, symbolising Venetian supremacy on land and sea. Doges were crowned, with a ceremonial jewel-encrusted cap, at the top of the stairs.

Many of the carved capitals on the portico have been replaced by 19th-century copies, but the restored originals can now be seen in the **Museo dell'Opera** beside the entrance hall.

The palace interior

The interior reveals the inner workings of the Serene Republic, from the voting procedures to the courts of law. The profusion of wood panelling, coffered ceilings and paintings meant that fire was a constant hazard and destroyed many treasures on several occasions. For this reason,

Acqua alta – high water – on low-lying Piazza San Marco may soon be a thing of the past.

there are few paintings that predate the 1570s. Nonetheless, the interior is magnificent.

The **Scala d'Oro**, designed by Sansovino in 1555, is a ceremonial staircase linking the *piano nobile* with the ostentatious upper floors. Even in this most public setting is a *bocca della verità*, a secret box previously used for posting denunciations of one's fellow-citizens. The glittering, gilded setting is a prelude to the superb State rooms, intended to overawe visiting dignitaries. The **Sala del Collegio** was where the Signoria met and ambassadors were received.

Other highlights include the **Collegiate Rooms**, lavishly decorated with Tintoretto's mythological scenes. The **Sala del Consiglio dei Dieci** was the chamber of the feared Council of Ten, and has a ceiling decorated by Veronese. The **Sala del Maggior Consiglio**, the Grand Council Chamber, is a highlight of the tour, a grandiose affair studded with coffered ceilings, paintings and embossed surfaces. The paintings in the chamber both reassured Venetians of republican glory and reminded them of their boundless duties to serve the State.

An entire wall is covered by Domenico and Jacopo Tintoretto's *Paradise*. Veronese's *Apotheosis of Venice* is one of his finest mythological scenes: with his glowing colours, carefree and graceful pictures, Veronese captured the taste of the times. A frieze which runs around the upper walls features the first 76 doges, with the notable exception of the traitor, Marin Falier. The portraits continue in the adjoining **Ballot Chamber**, where votes were counted.

The Secret Itinerary

Few could fail to be enthralled by this exploration of the "shadow-palace", with its secret passageways and air of murk and mystery. The itinerary leads up the Scala d'Oro and then, via a secret door, disappears into a den of passageways, courtrooms and the chancellery, where all acts of state were drafted. En route, one sees the State inquisitors' rooms, torture chamber and prisons, including the stifling, timber-lined *Piombi* or Leads, under the eaves of the palace; it was from here that Casanova made his daring escape in 1755. (The *Pozzi* or wells, the harsher basement cells, cannot be visited.)

The final secret reveals the tricks of the roof space above the Sala del Maggior Consiglio, where a complex system of struts sustains a ceiling that, from below, has no visible means of support. Through portholes are surprising glimpses of the island of San Giorgio and the Venetian lagoon. Advance bookings for the Itinerari Segreti tour can be made up to two days before your visit (tel: 041-427 30892; www.visitmuve.it) or on the day depending on availability at the information desk.

Gondola depot

Just behind the Procuratie Vecchie is the **Bacino Orseolo ⑤**, the main gondola depot, too busy a spot for a romantic ride but ideal for watching water traffic.

Torre dell'Orologio ⑥

Address: Piazza San Marco, www.visitmuve.it
Tel: 848082000
Opening Hrs: Mon–Wed 10am and 11am, Thur–Sun 2pm and 3 pm
Entrance Fee: charge
Transport: Vallaresso, San Marco, San Zaccaria

At the east end of the Procuratie Vecchie stands the **Torre dell'Orologio**, the Clocktower. Based on designs by Coducci, this Renaissance tower (1496) has a large gilt and blue enamel clockface that displays the signs of the zodiac, position of the sun and the phases of the moon. Naturally, it also tells the time, with two bronze figures known as Moors (more because of the bronze patina than because of their aspect, which

TIP

A discounted combined ticket (valid for three months) allows access to all the museums on Piazza San Marco, including the Museo Correr. You can also acquire a Museum Pass for these Civic Museums and other Civic Museums around the city and lagoon. For details, see www.visitmuve.it.

Caffè Florian on Piazza San Marco: pricey, touristy but with a great view of the basilica.

is not overtly Oriental) striking the bell on the hour. A hammer strikes the bells 132 times at midday and midnight. On the Epiphany and Ascension, 18th-century wooden statues of the Three Wise Men preceded by an angel parade past a statue of the Virgin Mary and child on the level below the Moors. In 1646, the diarist John Evelyn records the death of the clock-keeper, hit by the hammer as it struck the hour: "and being stunned, he reeled over the battlements and broke his neck".

Visits are by guided tour only and you must reserve a spot in advance at the ticket desk of the Museo Correr. A maximum of 12 people can join the tours, which wind up four floors of narrow stairs. You see the complex clockwork mechanisms and the Moors up close. From the top, you have lovely views over Piazza San Marco and the alleys of the **Mercerie** (see page 120).

Campanile

Address: Piazza San Marco, www.basilicasanmarco.it
Opening Hrs: daily Apr–June and Oct 9.30am–7pm, July–Sept 9am–9pm, Nov–Mar 9.30am–3.45pm
Entrance Fee: charge

Golden winged lion above Porta San Clemente.

Transport: Vallaresso, San Marco, San Zaccaria

For a superb view across the city and lagoon take the lift or climb up to the top of the **Campanile**, St Mark's free-standing belltower. Curiously, one cannot see the canals, although on a clear day even the Dolomites are visible. Standing on the site of an earlier watchtower and lighthouse, the belltower was rebuilt in the 12th century and crowned by a pyramid-shaped spire. During the Republic, each of the bells played a different role, with one summoning senators to the Palazzo Ducale and another, the execution bell, literally sounding the death knell. As a symbol of the city, the belltower occupies a special place in Venetian memory: in 1902 it suddenly collapsed, but was rebuilt exactly as before.

THE LIONS OF VENICE

Venice "crawls with lions, winged lions and ordinary lions, great lions and petty lions… lions rampant, lions soporific, amiable lions [and] ferocious lions". The writer Jan Morris conveys a sense of a city under the wing of a triumphalist lion. For over a thousand years, the lion and the city were inseparable. The Venetians took the symbol in honour of St Mark, but were inspired by eastern models, converting chimeras and basilisks into Christian symbols.

Lions pose on flags unfurled over Grand Canal palaces, curl up in mosaics, fly as ensigns above ships, or crouch as statues in secret gardens. In the days of the Republic, the leonine standard was carried into battle, fires and plagues; it guarded palaces, prisons and citadels, fluttering over Venetian ships of war. A golden winged Lion of St Mark still adorns the city standard, and remains the symbol of the Veneto. Whereas the seated lion represents the majesty of State, the walking lion symbolises sovereignty – in times of war, carrying a closed book, or even clutching a sword in his paws.

The only casualties were the custodian's cat and the **Loggetta**, the classical loggia at the base of the tower, which was completely crushed. Originally a meeting place for the nobility, it was redesigned as a guardsroom by Sansovino in the 1540s. The Campanile was at the centre of controversy in 1997 when it was briefly captured by a separatist group before being retaken by police (see page 49).

Around the square

Clustered around San Marco are numerous official buildings, including **La Zecca** (the Mint), facing the island of San Giorgio. The severe 16th-century building is attributed to Sansovino. Venice minted silver and gold ducats from 1284, with the latter known as a *zecchino*, the accepted currency until the fall of the Republic. The mint and treasury functioned until 1870, but is now part of the Biblioteca Marciana, with

the courtyard covered over and used as a reading room.

Bounded by the mint, the basilica and the Palazzo Ducale is the **Piazzetta** (the Little Square), overlooking the Molo, or waterfront. This functioned as the former inner harbour, with ships unloading on the quays. Now a square, it is framed by the **Columns of San Marco and San Teodoro**, which marked the sea entrance to Venice. The columns were named after the city's two patron saints, with St Mark replacing St Theodore in AD 828. The granite columns, from the Levant, were reputedly erected in 1172, and the engineer's reward was the right to set up gambling tables between the two columns – a lucrative spot for business. This was also the site of public executions, and superstition has it that bad luck follows anyone walking between the columns.

While the statue of St Theodore is a modern copy (the original classical

WHERE

The Bacino Orseolo is the most central place to begin a gondola ride, but don't pay more than the official rate. Bargain beforehand if you want to book a musical serenade or to see anything outside the gondolier's set route.

Palazzo Ducale at dusk.

statue is in the Palazzo Ducale), the **Lion of St Mark** is genuine. This ancient winged beast with agate eyes may be a Middle Eastern hybrid or a Chinese chimera. After the lion was rescued from Napoleon's clutches in Paris, the damaged beast was restored and returned to his pedestal with a Bible placed under his paw. Thus was a beast "from the pagan east converted from a savage basilisk to a saint's companion", remarks the writer Jan Morris.

Grand café retreat

Before exploring the frenetic San Marco district, prepare for the assault by collapsing in one of the grand cafés on the piazza or in one of the modest bars situated off **Piazzetta dei Leoncini**, the tiny square beside the basilica. Named after the marble lions that guard it, the piazzetta is home to a long-suffering pair of lions used as play horses by countless generations of children. Michel Butor, the French novelist, is sanguine about those who despair of finding solitude or sanity in Piazza San Marco, saying: "The Basilica, like the city around it, has nothing

to fear from this fauna or from our own frivolity; it was born under the perpetual gaze of the visitor, and so it has continued."

THE SAN MARCO DISTRICT

Although overshadowed by the attractions of St Mark's Square, this *sestiere* (area) is noted for its bustling *campi* and the maze-like Mercerie, a fascinating shopping quarter. Some of the finest palaces also lie along this stretch of the Grand Canal. The loop in the canal occupied by San Marco is known as the "seven *campi* between the bridges", a succession of theatrical spaces, each with inviting bars. The noblest square is undoubtedly Campo Santo Stefano, one of the most prestigious addresses in Venice. This suggested circular route embraces the heart of the city before sweeping back to St Mark's.

Heading west along the waterfront you will pass the **Giardini Ex Reali** (Royal Gardens) ❼ and a **tourist office**, housed in a pavilion. These cool public gardens were

Ceiling of the Scala d'Oro, Sansovino's gilded staircase in the Palazzo Ducale.

KEEPING WATER AT BAY

Low-lying Piazza San Marco has long been especially exposed to the ravages of tidal lagoon flooding, known as *acqua alta* (high water). The ancient square is one of the lowest areas in the city and for years it has suffered floods of varying degrees around 250 days a year. The high water only needs to reach 60cm above normal sea level for water to start entering the basilica. The problems are multiple. Water arrives from the lagoon, but rain water also contributes, bubbling to the surface through the ancient and partly crumbling web of water-off pipes.

Work to remedy this began in 2003. The lagoonside quays have been raised and reinforced, ancient piping under the square has been restored or replaced, and new run-offs laid. A layer of bentonite has been spread below the surface of the square to further insulate it from rising waters. Similar work has been done on an adjoining stretch of Riva degli Schiavoni. The result should be that flooding should largely be a thing of the past for high tides of up to 1.1m (3.6 ft). If the MOSE mobile tide barriers work as planned, Piazza San Marco should be safe from any flooding from 2018–2020.

supposedly created by Napoleon's nephew, in pursuit of his desire for a sweeping view from his palace in the Procuratie Nuove.

Courtyard of the Palazzo Ducale.

On Calle Vallaresso, the next alley, awaits **Harry's Bar** ❽, the famous watering hole (see box). The *calle* is lined with smart designer boutiques and is the hub of a chic shopping district, embracing the **Ridotto**, once Venice's licentious casino for masked revellers, but now restored and part of the Monaco e Grand Hotel.

Just north is the **Frezzeria** ❾, a bustling shopping street, awash with tourist tat, masks and glass of dubious provenance. Named after the arrows it sold in medieval times, the street was also notorious for its prostitutes, who would "open their quivers to every arrow". Not that all clients were satisfied. John Evelyn, the diarist (1620–1706), was informed that Venetian women were *mezzo carne, mezzo legno* – half flesh, half wood.

Campo San Moisè ❿, which lies southwest of the Frezzeria, opens onto the most exclusive, but least-charming shopping quarter. The square is framed by the Soviet-style

Sala del Maggior Consiglio, Veronese and Palma il Giovane ceilings.

> **QUOTE**
>
> If a doge does anything against the Republic, he won't be tolerated, but in everything else, even in minor matters, he does as he pleases.
>
> Girolamo Priuli,
> 16th-century nobleman

frontage of an otherwise luxury hotel and the florid baroque facade of **San Moisè** (9.30am–noon), a church that is almost universally disliked. The novelist L.P. Hartley was one of the few to admire its exuberant architecture, with its "swags, cornucopias and swing boat forms whose lateral movement seemed to rock the church from side to side".

La Fenice ⑪

Address: Campo San Fantin 1965, www.teatrolafenice.it
Tel: 041- 786 675
Opening Hrs: 45-minute tours only, 9.30am–6pm
Entrance Fee: charge
Transport: Santa Maria del Giglio

From Calle Larga XXII Marzo, Calle delle Veste leads north to **La Fenice**, the famous opera house that was razed to the ground by a mysterious fire in 1996, but rose from the ashes (see page 73). The tour of the theatre (with audioguide) covers the foyer, Great Hall, Royal Box and Apollonian Halls.

The "Phoenix" officially reopened as an opera house in 2004, with a celebratory performance of *La Traviata*. The jury is still out on the quality of the restoration, with detractors pointing to a lack of finesse in the carvings and stuccowork. That

Set in a small converted storeroom, the resolutely un-glitzy Harry's Bar is all about food and fun, not romantic views.

The clock on the Torre dell'Orologio aided merchants and crews about to sail from the Bacino di San Marco (St Mark's Basin).

said, it is a painstaking reconstruction of the opera house raised in 1837. Hundreds of craftsmen were brought together to relearn traditional methods of plaster-making, creating chandeliers and spinning out gold leaf decoration.

HARRY'S BAR

On the basis that Harry's Bar is the best bar in the best city in the world, the famed Bellini cocktail is cheap at any price. This is a legendary watering hole, resolutely un-glitzy, apart from a clientele of visiting celebrities and celebrity-watchers. The lure of classic cocktails and a good gossip have drawn prominent personalities, from Churchill and Charlie Chaplin to Bogart and Bacall, Fellini and Mastroianni, Frank Sinatra and Madonna. Ernest Hemingway could always find inspiration or oblivion in his favourite bar; he slugged the Montgomery, a Martini made with 15 measures of gin to one of vermouth.

Founded by Giuseppe Cipriani in 1931 and still run by the family, Harry's is famous for the creation of the Bellini, a cocktail of crushed, puréed peach and sparkling prosecco. Clubby, crowded and cosmopolitan, Harry's, uniquely in Venice, has become accepted by the locals.

La Fenice was to many nobles a sort of club where they would gamble and laze around. This was frequently the case during performances too, which had to be especially good to reduce the chatty onlookers to admiring silence.

The area around Fenice remains an appealing district, dotted with cosy atmospheric wine bars.

Chiesa di Santa Maria Zobenigo ⑫

Address: Campo Santa Maria Zobenigo 2541, www.chorusvenezia.org
Tel: 041-275 0462
Opening Hrs: Mon–Sat 10am–5pm
Entrance Fee: charge
Transport: Santa Maria del Giglio

Just south of La Fenice, **Santa Maria Zobenigo** (Santa Maria del Giglio) is linked to Antonio Barbaro, a patron who rebuilt it in baroque style. The facade glorifies the Barbaro dynasty rather than God, with reliefs depicting the dominions governed by the Barbaros in the name of the Republic – Candia (Heraklion), Split and Corfu – as well as Rome and Padua, places in which the family held ambassadorial

Climb to the top of the Campanile for a sweeping view of the city and lagoon.

The seats can be removed for special occasions, like grand balls at Carnival time. In the 19th century,

The Molo and Columns of San Marco and San Teodoro.

Aerial view of the city.

posts. Inside is an interesting assortment of paintings, including the only work by Peter Paul Rubens in Venice *(Madonna and Child with St John)* and some Evangelists depicted by Tintoretto.

The adjoining square leads back to the waterfront and the **Gritti Palace** ⑬, a famous Venetian hotel. Ruskin, the art critic and aesthete, wrote his influential *Stones of Venice* while staying in both the Gritti and the Danieli. The Gritti terrace offers a grandstand view of the Grand Canal, lying diagonally opposite the church of La Salute.

Just west of Santa Maria Zobenigo is the **Campo San Maurizio**, of note mainly for the view of the curiously truncated Guggenheim Museum and the haunted Ca' Dario, visible by following Calle del Dose to the waterside and then looking across the canal. Four times a year, a popular week-long **antique market** (www.mercatinocamposan maurizio.it) takes over Campo San Maurizio, usually a week before Easter, the first weekend of June, in September and December.

Around Santo Stefano

From Campo San Maurizio, the lively Calle del Spezier leads to **Campo Santo Stefano**, a long, theatrical space lined with palaces and cafés. This spectacular square makes a seamless link with the Accademia, the great Venetian gallery on the far side of the bridge. Confusingly also known as Campo Morosini, after a famous doge, the wide square was a backdrop for bull-baiting until 1802, but is now more the setting for a chic evening *passeggiata*, with

The florid baroque facade of San Moisè.

the occasional baiting of music students by mischievous lawyers. A clutch of cafés occupies the space between the monumental palaces and the tilting belltower of Santo Stefano. The clientele changes with the time of day, but at cocktail hour these bars tend to be full of sleek Venetian professionals or mothers supervising toddlers enjoying the play centre by the church.

Few can resist **Paolin**, one of the most prized Venetian bars and ice-cream parlours.

Chiesa di Santo Stefano ⑭

Address: Campo Santo Stefano 2773, www.chorusvenezia.org
Tel: 041-275 0462
Opening Hrs: Mon–Sat 10am–5pm
Entrance Fee: charge
Transport: Accademia

At the far end of the square stands the Gothic church of **Santo Stefano**. This Augustinian monastic church has a Gothic main portal facing a café-lined alley. Unusually, a canal flows under the church, through which gondolas can pass if the tide is low. The interior boasts an entrancing ship's-keel ceiling, carved tie beams and notable paintings by Vivarini and Tintoretto. The tomb of Doge Francesco Morosini (1694) is also prominently

DRINK

In an alley off the main streams of pedestrian traffic, Teamo (Rio Terrà de la Mandola 3795, daily 8am–9.30pm; www.teamowinebar.com) is a relaxed and trendy place for a generous afternoon *spritz*, coffee or a few snacks.

La Fenice.

displayed in the nave. The cloisters, now appropriated by public offices, are accessible through a gateway in Campo Sant'Angelo to the north.

If you lack the energy to visit the Accademia (see page 212), then ignore the bridge over the Grand Canal in favour of an engaging quarter on the bend of the canal. **Campo San Samuele** ⓮ was Casanova's parish, with Lord Byron's former home nearby, in Ca' Mocenigo, overlooking the canal. San Samuele, Casanova's baptismal church, is graced with a Byzantine belltower.

Beside the San Samuele ferry landing stage looms the formidable **Palazzo Grassi**, now a major exhibition centre of contemporary art (see page 109).

From here, a circuitous route winds back to San Marco, beginning with **Campo Sant' Angelo**, a noble quarter lined with the very palaces where Casanova played his practical jokes.

Palazzo Fortuny ⓰

Address: Campo San Benedetto 3780, www.visitmuve.it
Tel: 041-520 0995
Opening Hrs: Wed–Mon 10am–6pm
Entrance Fee: charge
Transport: Sant'Angelo

From Campo Sant'Angelo, follow Calle Spezier and take the first turning left to **Palazzo Fortuny**, a fortress-like, late-Gothic palace and shrine to Mariano Fortuny y Madrazo, the Spanish painter and collector. Born in Granada in 1871, this eclectic artist bought the palace as his main home and studio in the early 20th century. Painter and stage-set creator, he also founded a high-quality textile factory on the Giudecca; Fortuny materials are still in demand in the best homes around the world. Fronted by two rows of *hectafores*, each a series of eight connected Venetian-style windows, the *palazzo* hosts temporary exhibitions as well as plenty of Fortuny's own works (including some 150 paintings spanning much of his life). Works range from portraits of his wife Henriette, through nudes and striking still lifes. A rich photography collection, some of them by the artist, covers a century

The grand nave of Santo Stefano.

The cost of taking a gondola is fixed, unless you want something extra like a serenade which you should bargain for.

concealed in a maze of alleys between Calle Vida and Calle Contarini, is **Palazzo Contarini del Bovolo**, a late-Gothic palace celebrated for its romantic arcaded staircase. *Bovolo*, meaning snail-shell in Venetian dialect, well describes the delightful spiral staircase that is linked to loggias of brick and smooth white stone. You can get a reasonable look at it from the grill outside, which is just as well because renovation work is still in progress.

From Campo San Luca to the Mercerie

Campo San Luca ⓲, the bustling square east of Campo Manin, is a popular student haunt, with several good bars. Its marble plinth supposedly marks the centre of the city.

Not far from the Rialto, on the far side of Rio di San Salvador, stands the **Chiesa di San Salvador** ⓳ (Mon–Sat 9am–noon, 4–6.30pm), a luminous Renaissance church adorned by Titian's impressionistic *Annunciation* and *Transfiguration*.

Overlooking the square is the Scuola di San Teodoro, one of the

EAT

Al Volto is one of the oldest wine bars in Venice, set on Calle Cavalli, close to Campo San Luca (tel: 041-522 8945, daily 10am–4pm and 6–10pm). This popular bar is a good place to sample an array of Venetian wines and snacks.

Sunday morning on Campo Santo Stefano.

from 1850 to World War II. Textile designs and clothing form a key part of the collection too, as does a fascinating collection of lamps (Fortuny devoted much time to the study of light).

Palazzo Contarini del Bovolo ⓱

Address: Corte del Bovolo 4299
Tel: 041-303 9211; www.scalacontarinidelbovolo.com/
Opening Hrs: Tue–Sun 10am–1.30pm and 4–6pm
Entrance Fee: charge
Transport: Rialto

From Palazzo Fortuny, cross Rio di San Luca into **Campo Manin**, named after a Venetian patriot who led the ill-fated revolt against the Austrians in 1848. Just south,

historic confraternity houses, now a venue for classical concerts.

Further north, just beyond the Rialto bridge, is the **Fondaco dei Tedeschi** ❷⓿, once an impressive trading centre for German merchants but now the city post office (see page 109). On warm evenings, **Campo San Bartolomeo** ❷❶, the adjoining square, resembles an open-air club: the statue of the playwright Goldoni, the half-hidden church and the basic bars are usually surrounded by chattering youngsters.

The Mercerie

Follow Via 2 Aprile to the **Mercerie** ❷❷ the shadowy maze of alleys running between the Rialto and San Marco. Named after the haberdashers' shops that once lined the route, these alleys were among the first paved city streets to be found anywhere in the world. In 1645, John Evelyn was entranced by "the most delicious street in the world", displaying "cloth of gold, rich damasks and other silks… perfumers and apothecaries' shops and the innumerable cages of nightingales".

Dining alfresco in Campo San Bartolomeo.

Terrace of the Gritti Palace.

Today, it remains an engaging bazaar, even if the perfumes of former times have been replaced by

Palazzo Contarini del Bovolo.

as marbled paper, Murano glass and carnival masks of every description. Here, designer leather goods and handcrafted jewellery also compete for space with kitsch glass gondolas.

For Venetians, the Mercerie has long been displaced by the district around **Calle Larga XXII Marzo** as the smartest shopping address in town. The Mercerie comes out under the **Torre dell'Orologio** on Piazza San Marco, but en route lies the church of **San Zulian** ㉓ (daily 8.30am–7pm), a refuge from commercialism. Dedicated to St Julian, the church was rebuilt in the 16th century.

The old Armenian quarter is just around the corner, based around **Santa Croce degli Armeni**, the well-hidden Armenian church. For the truest understanding of this ancient community, visit their monastery island of San Lazzaro degli Armeni (see page 242). This church can safely be missed in favour of a welcoming bar.

As the writer Jan Morris says, "There are 107 churches in Venice, and nearly every tourist feels he has seen at least 200 of them."

global clothing brands. Some of the goods are tawdry, but you can also buy such traditional souvenirs

The Gritti Palace, a well-known Venetian hotel.

THE WORLD'S GRANDEST PRIVATE CHAPEL

Everyone who comes to Venice visits San Marco – and with good reason. This golden, marbled pleasure pavilion is simply the city's greatest sight.

Although intended as the private chapel of the doges, San Marco soon became a symbol of republican splendour, set beside the Doge's Palace, the centre of Venetian power. The basilica has always been at the heart of city life, the focus for the greatest celebrations.

In recent years, San Marco has been a place of remembrance, with the city commemorating major anniversaries of the tragic 1966 floods through a series of spectacular concerts. After the burning down of La Fenice, the beloved opera house, similar fund-raising events followed, attracting famous politicians and foreign stars.

The eastern inspiration of the basilica is clear from its oriental domes and lustrous mosaics. French writer George Sand, visiting in 1844, found it "a grand and dreamy structure, of immense proportions; golden with old mosaics; redolent with perfumes; dim with the smoke of incense; costly in treasure of precious stones and metals; holy with the bodies of deceased saints".

Mosaic from the 13th-century in the main dome of the basilica.

The Essentials

Address: Piazza San Marco, www.basilica sanmarco.it
Tel: 041-522 5697
Opening Hrs: Nov–Mar Mon–Sat 9.45am–5pm, Sun 2–4pm (till 5pm Apr–Oct).
Entrance Fee: free
Transport: Vallaresso, San Marco, San Zaccaria

The interior is based on a Greek cross, with the branches divided into three naves, each crowned by a dome of its own.

Sculpted angels adorning the north facade of the basilica.

One of the finest examples of Byzantine craftsmanship, the basilica was known by the nickname Chiesa d'Oro (Church of Gold).

The Pala d'Oro, an exquisite medieval altarpiece studded with gems and covered in sacred scenes. The panels are enclosed in a gilded frame and encrusted with emeralds, rubies and sapphires.

THE FOUR HORSES OF SAN MARCO

The magnificent horses of San Marco are a clear statement of the supremacy of Venice in the 13th century.

"Below St Mark's still glow his steeds of brass, their gilded collars glittering in the sun." Byron was one of many travellers to admire the four bronze horses, 3rd- or 4th-century Hellenistic or Roman sculptures, which stood guard over the basilica's central doorway. Like the Lion of St Mark, these noble horses were a symbol of independence. Yet the tale of their travels is a story of imperial envy and an allegory of the Republic's rise and fall.

The horses, which had graced a triumphal arch in Rome, were standing guard over the stadium in Constantinople when the city was sacked by the Venetians in 1204 and they were transported to Venice. When Venice prostrated itself before Napoleon in 1797, the Corsican general removed the noble steeds to Paris, where they stood harnessed to a chariot for 18 years. After returning to Venice in 1815, the horses decorated the Loggia dei Cavalli on the basilica. The Venetians, never ones to look gift horses in the mouth, were delighted.

The originals are now displayed in the Museo Marciano (daily 9.45am–4.45pm; www.museo sanmarco.it) inside the basilica, with rather paltry replicas on the facade.

Many Venetians felt that the beasts should be left *in situ*, but conservationists thought the bronzes ought to be protected for posterity.

On the facade is the winged lion, symbol of St Mark.

Boat traffic along the Grand Canal.

THE GRAND CANAL

A trip on the Grand Canal, Venice's fabulous
high street, reveals a pageant of opulent
palaces, from the Guggenheim to Gothic
Ca' d'Oro and baroque Ca' Rezzonico and
Ca' Pesaro, all doubling as superb museums.

Venice is a place "where even the simplest coming and going assumes the form and charm of a visit to a museum and a trip to the sea". Marcel Proust captures the entertaining yet educational aspect of a trip along the Grand Canal. Known affectionately as the "Canalazzo", this "Big Canal" follows the course of an ancient river bed. It is nearly 4km (2.5 miles) long and up to 70 metres (230ft) wide. The surprisingly shallow high street is spanned by four bridges and lined by 10 churches and over 200 palaces. This great waterway sweeps through the six city districts *(sestieri)*, with its switchback shape providing changing vistas of palaces and warehouses, markets and merchant clubs, courts, prisons and even the city casino.

Once a waterway for merchant vessels and great galleys, the canal now welcomes simpler craft, from gondolas to garbage barges. However, the palaces remain as a testament to the city's imperial past. The Grand Canal was considered the register of the Venetian nobility, with the palaces symbolising their owners' status and success. Yet the lagoon is a great leveller, with low tide revealing the slimy underpinnings of the noblest palace. Venetian eclecticism and the habit of

recycling elements from various periods makes the dating of palaces difficult. Indeed, the writer Jan Morris wryly observes that guidebook writers are the only people who seem capable of distinguishing between the different styles.

A peculiarly Venetian phenomenon is the number of palaces with the same or very similar names. Palaces were often the seats of separate branches of one family, so their names bear witness to Venetian fortunes, feuds and intermarriages; a

Main Attractions
Guggenheim Collection
Ca' Dario
Accademia
Ca' Rezzonico
Palazzo Grassi
Ca' Foscari
Rialto Bridge
Ca' d'Oro
Ca' Pesaro
Palazzo Vendramin-Calergi
Fondaco dei Turchi
Calatrava Bridge

Map
Page 126

All dressed up for the Regata Storica.

The most heartfelt Venetian festival on the Grand Canal is the Festa della Madonna della Salute (21 November), when a pontoon bridge is slung across the waterway to the Salute church, in celebration of the city's salvation from the plague in 1630.

Palazzo Barbaro, which Henry James bought for a song at the turn of the 20th century.

family member sometimes added the name of the parish or new dynasty to avoid confusion. The city is littered with palaces linked to the patrician or Dogal dynasties of the Mocenigo, Corner, Giustiniani, Grimani, Pesaro and Pisani families.

Palatial homes

Thanks to inheritance laws, financial vicissitudes and the extinction of the old dogal families, few families inhabit their ancestral homes. Yet impoverished aristocrats may languish in part of a palace or live in one which, while not bearing their name, has been in the family for centuries.

Many palaces have become hotels or prestigious showcases for Venetian glass and textile manufacturers, while others belong to residents who relish the soft opulence of their second homes. Several of the grandest canalside art collections are housed in palazzi, notably the Guggenheim (modern art), the Ca' d'Oro (medieval and Renaissance art), Ca' Rezzonico (18th-century art) and Ca' Pesaro (oriental and modern art). The charm of these palaces lies in their variety. As

The Grand Canal

200 m
200 yds

Pal. Calbo Crotta
Scalzi 34
Pal. Fisca
Ponte degli Scalzi
35 i
Pal. Foscari Contarini
Ferrovia S. Lucia (Station)
36
S. Simeone Piccolo
Pal. Diedo
37
Ponte di Calatrava

The Grand Canal

al. Labia

S. Marcuola

Pal. Gritti **31**

Pal. Vendramin-Calergi

Pal. Erizzo **29**

Pal. Soranzo

Pal. Moin

Pal. Emo

Pal. Zulian

Pal. Barbarigo

Canal Grande

eremia

l. Donà
bi

Corner

Casa Correr

Pal. Giovanelli

Fond. d. Turchi (Museo Storia Nat.)

30

Deposito del Megio

Pal. Belloni-Battagià

Pal. Priuli

Pal. Tron

S. Stae **28**

International Gallery of Modern Art

Pal. Foscarini

Ca' Pesaro

Pal. Donà

Casa Favretto

27

Ca' Corner della Regina **26**

Pal. Gussoni

Pal. Boldù

Gall. Franchetti

Pal. Fontana

Pal. Sagredo **25**

Ca'd'Oro

Pal. Foscari

Pal. Michiel d. Colonne

Pal. Valmarana

Pal. Brandolin

Pal. Querini

Pescheria

Ca' da Mosto **24**

Fabbriche Nuove

Fabbriche Vecchie **23**

Pal. Civran

S. Giacomo di Rialto **21**

Pal. dei Camerlenghi

22 Fondaco dei Tedeschi

Pal. d. Dieci Savi

Ponte di Rialto

S. Silvestro

S. Bartolomeo

Pal. Papadopoli

Pal. Barzizza

Pal. Bernardo

Pal. Businello

Pal. Dolfin-Manin

Pal. Cappello Layard

Pal. Querini

Pal. Donà

Pal. Bembo Dandolo

Pal. Giustinian Persico

18 Pal. Barbaro d. Terrazza

Pal. Pisani Moretta

Pal. Corner Martinengo

20 Pal. Loredan

Pal. Corner Martinengo Farsetti

Marcello d.Leoni

Pal. Tiepolo

Pal. Grimani

Pal. Dandolo Paolucci

Pal. Martinengo Volpi

. Balbi

Pal. Contarini d. Figure **17**

Pal. Garzoni **19**

Pal. Corner Spinelli

Pal. Patriarcale

Foscari

Pal. Da Lezze

Pal. Corner Gheltof

Ca' Mocenigo

Torre dell' Orologio

16

15

Pal. Moro Lin

San Samuele

Procuratie Vecchie

Basilica di San Marco (St Mark's Basilica)

Campanile di S. Marco

P. dei Sospiri (Bridge of Sighs)

l. Nani

zzonica

14 Pal. Grassi

 isee del tecento niziano

Stern

Pal. Malipiero

Ca' d' Duca

Museo Correr

Piazza San Marco

Museo Archeologico

Procuratie Nuove

Palazzo Ducale (Doge's Palace)

13

Moro

Loredan

12 Pal. Falier

Pal. Giustinian

Bibl. Naz. Marciana

La Zecca

Pal. Contarini Scrigni

Pal. Cavalli Franchetti

Ca' Corner della Ca' Grande

Pal. Contarini

Pal. Tiepolo

Luna Baglioni

1

Ponte dell' Accademia

10

Pal. Pisani

7

Gritti Palace

4

3 Pal. Contarini Fasan

Ridotto

Galleria dell' Accademia

11

9

Pal. Barbaro

Casetta delle Rose

Canal Grande

Ca' Dario

Ca' Genovese

5

2 La Salute

Punta della Dogana

Pal. Contarini-Polignac

Pal. Loredan

Pal. Barbarigo

8 **6**

Pal. Venier (Guggenheim Collection)

Salviati

San Gregorio

Seminario Patriarcale

Punta della Dogana Contemporary Art Centre

Henry James remarked: "The fairest palaces are often cheek-by-jowl with the foulest, and there are few, alas, so fair as to have been completely protected by their beauty."

Grand Canal procession

Purchase a day pass and trail up and down the Canal to your heart's content, stopping at sights as the fancy takes you (vaporetto lines 1 and 82 both cover the route, but check the direction and be sure to get off before the boat sweeps away to the Lido). Ideally choose the slower, all-stops route No. 1 and take a return trip to appreciate both banks (it takes about 40 minutes each way).

From San Marco to the Accademia Bridge

Chugging westward along the Bacino di San Marco in a vaporetto, past the Palazzo Ducale, the mouth of the Grand Canal appears before you, its southern tip marked by the prow of the **Punta della Dogana** (the former customs station now turned into a grand contemporary art gallery, see page 202), and its north side marked

Looking down the Grand Canal to La Salute.

Romantic poet Lord Byron lived in various palaces along the Grand Canal.

by **Palazzo Giustinian** ❶, the first significant palace on the Grand Canal.

The Giustiniani were an illustrious dynasty tracing their origins to

Grand Canal gondolier.

the Roman Empire. Legend has it that, in the 12th century, the line was threatened with extinction, and the sole remaining heir was persuaded to leave his monastery for marriage to the doge's daughter. After saving the line by siring 12 offspring, he returned to a life of celibate seclusion. His sacrifice was a success: the Venetian branch only died out in 1962. In the 19th century, the palace was a hotel where Proust, Turner and Verdi stayed. The palace is now the headquarters of the Biennale exhibition organisation, the international art showcase staged every two years (see page 171).

On the left bank, the baroque church of **La Salute ❷** (see page 201) guards the entrance to the canal. Slightly further on, **Palazzo Contarini-Fasan ❸** appears on the right bank. This model of late-Gothic design in miniature has subtle carved cable moulding on the facade. It is nicknamed "Desdemona's House", since it supposedly inspired the setting for Desdemona's home in Shakespeare's *Othello*.

As soon as the boat stops at Santa Maria del Giglio, the **Hotel Gritti Palace ❹** can be seen. Built in 1525 as residence of the Doge Andrea Gritti, this is one of Venice's most sumptuous, linked to writers as diverse as Hemingway and Graham Greene. Ruskin and his wife stayed here rather than being tempted by the decadent notion of "hiring a house or palace – it sounds Byronish or Shelleyish".

Virtually opposite is **Ca' Genovese ❺**, a neo-Gothic palace, and **Palazzo Salviati**, with its vivid mosaics set in an ochre facade; these gaudy showrooms belong to wealthy Murano glassmakers. On the same side, several palaces further down, is the gently listing **Ca' Dario ❻**, one of the most delightful spots on the Grand Canal. Henry James adored this haunted palace, then let to motley foreigners, for its "little marble plates and sculptured circles".

On the right bank looms **Ca' Grande ❼** (or Ca' Corner della Ca' Grande), one of the greatest palaces, both in terms of importance and sheer size. Built by Sansovino for Jacopo Corner, a nephew of the queen of Cyprus, the palace is the

THE CURSE OF CA' DARIO

Five centuries of scandals, suicides and suspicious deaths have left Venetians wary of this sinister canalside palace. The Gothic palace belonged to Giovanni Dario. Dario's daughter died of a broken heart after marrying into the patrician Barbaro family. Although the Dario family retained ownership until the 19th century, tragedy regularly struck its members. In the 1840s, aesthete Rawdon Brown committed suicide in the drawing room. In 1936, French poet Henri de Régnier died shortly after moving in, while Charles Briggs, a colourful American who held homosexual orgies in the palace, was expelled from the city. In the 1970s the then owner, Kit Lambert, manager of The Who, was murdered over a drugs dispute. The most recent victim was industrialist Raul Gardini, who committed suicide in 1993 after being caught up in corruption scandals. Prospective purchasers have decided not to court disaster, but in 2006, an American millionaire bought it – so far, the curse seems to be lying dormant.

first confident High Renaissance building in Venice. The Corner dynasty had deep links with Venice and owned numerous palaces. The last of the line sold it to the Austrian administration in 1812, and the palace is now the seat of the Prefecture (the provincial government).

Palazzo Venier (Peggy Guggenheim Collection) ❽

Address: Palazzo Venier dei Leoni, Dorsoduro, www.guggenheim-venice.it
Tel: 041-240 5411
Opening Hrs: Wed–Mon 10am–6pm
Entrance Fee: charge
Transport: Accademia

Facing Ca' Grande is the **Palazzo Venier**, a white, truncated structure also known as "Nonfinito" (Unfinished). Legend has it that the owners of Ca' Grande forbade further building as it would block their view, but it is more likely that the project simply ran out of funds. Although now restricted to two storeys, the original palace was intended to rival the city's grandest. This 18th-century palace was built for one of the oldest Venetian dynasties, who produced three doges. The Veniers' lion

Palazzo Venier, home of the Peggy Guggenheim Collection.

Outdoor sculptures at the Peggy Guggenheim Collection.

nickname *(dei Leoni)* comes from their habit of having kept a pet lion chained in the courtyard. The building houses the **Peggy Guggenheim**

Ca' Dario, the bewitched palace where many have met a violent end.

Collection, named after the American millionairess, art collector and benefactor who lived here from 1949 until her death 30 years later.

It is appropriate that this startlingly modern-looking building should house a superb collection of modern art. This is a deservedly popular showcase for Chagall, Dalí, Klee, Braque, Giacometti, Kandinsky, Bacon and Sutherland. Most major movements are represented, from Picasso's cubist period to Severini's Futurism; from Mondrian's abstract works to Surrealist masterpieces by De Chirico, Delvaux and Magritte. Max Ernst, Guggenheim's second husband, is well represented. Other highlights include De Chirico's *Red Tower*, Magritte's *Empire of Light* and Pollock's *Alchemy*, forming a complement to the modern art collection in Ca' Pesaro (see page 141).

Although Peggy Guggenheim helped launch Jackson Pollock,

there is little expressionist work, since it did not find favour with the otherwise discerning collector. The sculpture-lined gardens feature works by Henry Moore and Marino Marini, and new pieces continue to be acquired. (Curiously, the water gates are often closed, to conceal the provocative erection sported by the rider in Marini's *Angel of the Citadel*.)

TO THE ACCADEMIA

Several palaces further along from Palazzo Venier is **Palazzo Barbarigo**, notable for its gaudy mosaics, and **Campo San Vio**, a pleasant spot from which to watch the water traffic.

On the same left bank, two palaces before the bridge, lies **Palazzo Contarini-Polignac** ❾, one of the first Renaissance palaces in Venice. In fact, a new facade, decorated with marble roundels, was added to the Gothic building. The Princesse de Polignac ran a sophisticated 19th-century salon here, and the palace remains in the same family.

On the right bank, virtually opposite, is **Palazzo Barbaro** ❿, a Gothic gem where Monet, Browning and

Interior of Ca' Pesaro.

Gondolas and Gondoliers

The gondola is uniquely adapted for the lagoon waters: it is streamlined yet sturdy, and able to navigate the shallowest waters and narrowest canals.

According to the writer Mary McCarthy, everything in Venice has an "inherent improbability, of which the gondola, floating, insubstantial, at once romantic and haunting, charming and absurd, is the symbol". To Thomas Mann, the gondola conjured up "visions of death itself, the bier and solemn rites and last soundless voyage". Although red was the traditional Venetian colour of mourning, funeral gondolas were eventually painted gold and black.

The gondola took its definitive form by the 17th century, made of eight different sorts of wood, finished off with 10 coats of black paint. The *ferro*, or metal prow, is the most distinctive feature, much admired by Mark Twain: "The bow is ornamented with a steel comb with a battleaxe attachment." The front of this projection supposedly symbolises the *corno*, the doge's cap, with the six forward prongs representing the six *sestieri* (districts) of Venice, and the seventh the Giudecca.

In the 18th century, Venice had about 10,000 gondoliers, but now the number has fallen to 425. The Gondoliers Association banned all "tasteless and tacky trappings" on gondolas, from garish cushions to statuettes on the prow. Threatened with losing their licence, gondoliers have reverted to restrained traditional style, which prescribes black seats and sober purple interiors.

The *gondolieri* are a breed apart: only native Venetians can apply for a licence, and the trade is often passed down from father to son. Attempts by outsiders, such as the one by German Alex Hai, to be accepted by the guild have come up against a brick wall. Ms Hai can work in the employ of hotels but not as a fully licensed gondolier to tout for tourist trade.

Until recently this was an all-male coterie – the first woman, Giorgia Boscolo, was accepted by the guild in 2010. *Gondolieri* are noted for their singing, but serenades are often spiced with lewd language, including lascivious appreciation of brides. (Since this is delivered in Venetian dialect, few visitors are likely to be offended.)

Spokesman Mario Ventin also defends fellow gondoliers against criticisms of colourful language: "Foreign visitors love to hear us shout at each other. If a water-taxi narrowly misses us, are we to bow and say politely, 'Sir, your keel was too near?' No! We dispatch the captain to hell!" Yet gondoliers do occasionally live up to their romantic image. Roberto Nardin met his Californian wife when she took a ride on his gondola. When Roberto described her eyes as "more beautiful than those September days when the sky dissolves into the lagoon", one more heart melted into the Venetian sunset.

For more information, see page 248.

Gondolas for hire.

Henry James were guests of the American Curtis family. James wrote *The Aspern Papers* here, and set *The Wings of a Dove* in his rooms: "part of a palace, historic and picturesque but strictly inodorous". The wheel came full circle with the making of the film of the same name in the palace. Next door is **Palazzo Cavalli-Franchetti**, a grandiose Gothic palace with an appealing garden.

Between the Accademia and Ca' Foscari

Beside the palatial bank is the distinctive wooden **Accademia Bridge**, a popular meeting place for Venetians. Beside it is the Accademia boat stop, with the world's greatest collection of Venetian paintings housed in the neighbouring **Accademia** ⓫ gallery (see page 212). Also on the right bank is **Palazzo Falier** ⓬, an early-Gothic palace with typical Venetian loggias *(liaghi)* facing the canal. This was supposedly the home of the infamous Doge Marin Falier, beheaded for treason in 1355.

Ca' Rezzonico ⓭

Address: Fondamenta Rezzonico, Dorsoduro, www.visitmuve.it
Tel: 041-241 0100

Opening Hrs: Wed–Mon Apr–Oct 10am–6pm, Nov–Mar 10am–5pm
Entrance Fee: charge
Transport: Ca' Rezzonico

Ca' Rezzonico lies on the left bank, by the boat stop of the same name. Henry James likened this bold building to "a rearing sea horse" because of its upward-thrusting cornices. This baroque masterpiece, designed according to Longhena's plans, is slightly more restrained than Ca' Pesaro. This is probably the most famous palace in the city, and one of the few on the Grand Canal open to the public. The newly ennobled Rezzonico banking family bought the unfinished palace in 1750 and supervised its completion in conservative baroque style. The effect is harmonious, if rather ponderous, with heavy rustication on the ground floor and a grand courtyard.

It was in this palace that the poet Robert Browning (1812–89) died. (His son, Pen, owned the palace in the 1880s and did much to restore it.) After lying in state in the ballroom, the poet was transferred to San Michele church and then to London's Westminster Abbey. A wall in the palace bears words taken from Browning's epitaph: "Open

Tiepolo fresco in the Ca' Rezzonico.

my heart and you will see/ Graved inside of it Italy".

Ca' Rezzonico is home of the **Museum of 18th-Century Life** (Museo del Settecento Veneziano). The rococo interior is sumptuous, with the re-hung picture gallery of superior genre artists on the second floor, and the eclectic art gallery on the top floor. In terms of Venetian art, Ca' Rezzonico takes up from where the Accademia leaves off.

In keeping with Venetian style, the rooms are sparsely but lavishly furnished, with the mirrored wall brackets, lacquered furniture and chinoiserie that characterised the period. A grand staircase leads to the **Piano Nobile**, the ceremonial first floor added by Massari. Here, the opulent setting makes a spectacular showcase for Tiepolo's *trompe l'œil* ceilings and Guardi's genre scenes. The **Sala da Ballo**, or ballroom, is daringly frescoed and embellished with glittering chandeliers and period pieces, including ebony vase-stands borne by Moors. Keep an eye on the schedule for various short concerts of chamber music here.

Off the ballroom is the **Sala dell'Allegoria Nuziale** (1758), raised

Entrance to Ca' Foscari, home to Venice University.

Contemporary art in a classical setting at Palazzo Grassi.

to great heights by Tiepolo's nuptial allegory on the ceiling, ostensibly depicting *The Marriage of Ludovico Rezzonico*. Accompanied by angels and cherubs, careering horses tumble through the billowing heavens, forging a link between the elevated residents and the gods. In the same year, a Rezzonico count was elected pope, thus putting the seal on the family's social acceptability.

Elsewhere there are lofty Tiepolo frescoes depicting *Nobility and Virtue* and *Fortitude and Wisdom*.

The second floor rivals the *piano nobile* in magnificence, with the huge *portego* used as a **Picture Gallery** for genre scenes by Canaletto, Guardi and Longhi. Genre painters seems a disparaging term for these great 18th-century salon artists at the peak of their powers.

Guardi's *Ridotto* (1748) captures the revelry of masked gamblers and revellers in the State casino, while his *Nuns' Parlour* (1768) depicts the spirited and worldly nuns whose reputation for lasciviousness made Venetian convents a byword for dissolute living. Longhi's superior salon pictures show patrician Venice at play, including the famous *Rhinoceros Show*, depicting masqueraders entranced by this exotic beast. Also on display is one of the few works by Canaletto in Venice: his view of *Rio dei Mendicanti* (1725). There are also subtle paintings and miniatures by Rosalba Carriera, the 18th-century portraitist.

Apart from these genre scenes and Tiepolo's frescoed ceilings, the highlights are the suite of rooms dedicated to frescoes salvaged from **Villa Zianigo**, the Tiepolo family home. Giandomenico Tiepolo's provocative yet playful frescoes reveal the mood of disenchantment in Venice towards the end of the 18th century. The greatest of these strange and unsettling pictures is *Mondo Nuovo* (New World), depicting a crowd staring out to sea, and suggesting the disorientation created by the fall of the Venetian Republic, with Venetians reduced to being mere bystanders.

If the second floor is a fond farewell to the Serenissima, the top floor is a tribute to the taste of one of Venice's most renowned art patrons, Egidio Martini. This well-displayed **Private Collection** spans four centuries of northern Italian art, including works by Tintoretto and Tiepolo. Its appeal lies in the collection's eclectic nature. Here, too, is a quaint period **Pharmacy**, complete with ceramic jars, glass bottles and wooden cabinets.

Palazzo Grassi ⑭

Address: Campo San Samuele, San Marco, www.palazzograssi.it
Tel: 041-271 9031
Opening Hrs: Wed–Sun 10am–7pm
Entrance Fee: charge
Transport: San Samuele

From Ca' Rezzonico, you gaze across the Grand Canal to the formidable **Palazzo Grassi**. Beside the San Samuele ferry landing stage, it was revitalised after a long period of closure to become a major exhibition centre of contemporary art. The building is an imposing patrician palace and model of neoclassical restraint. Although designed by Longhena, there is no trace of baroque exuberance; Massari completed the palace with due regard to classical orders. French magnate and contemporary art collector François Pinault bought the palace as a central base for his own private collection and commissioned architect Tadao Ando to give it a light-handed overhaul that respected the original ceilings and decoration. Some of Pinault's vast collection sometimes goes on display, although as often as not visiting exhibitions make up much of the programme. With his acquisition and renovation of the Punta della Dogana in Dorsoduro (see page 202), Pinault has single-handedly awarded Venice a major permanent stage for contemporary art, in harmony with the Biennale art show.

(see page 202)

Ca' Rezzonico.

The Rialto's lively fish market.

On the same bank lies a cluster of three palaces, commanding a sharp bend known as the Volta del Canal. **Palazzo Giustinian** is one of 15 palaces owned by the Giustiniani clan. This delightful Gothic show-piece is a double palace adorned with delicate tracery and linked by a water gate. Here, in 1857–9, Wagner composed *Tristan und Isolde*.

Between Ca' Foscari and the Rialto Bridge

Next door, **Ca' Foscari** presents similar Gothic coherence, with a waterside facade graced by the Foscari arms. Built at the height of Venetian power, this is a monument to the ambition of Doge Foscari, who ruled from 1423 to 1457. Tommaso Mocenigo, a previous doge, distrusted him: "He sweeps and soars more than a hawk or a falcon." Foscari survived to pursue expansionist goals until a conspiracy caused his downfall, and he died a broken man in this palace.

This Gothic stage-set witnessed countless extravagant pageants. During a state visit prior to being crowned,

Henri III of France stayed here and was fêted by the Venetians. The mosaic floor of his bedroom was remodelled to Veronese's designs; Titian painted his portrait and Palladio was commissioned to build a triumphal arch. Now the grandest part of Venice University, the palace has been tampered with down the years but has now been restored to former glory.

On the far (canal) side of the Rio, distinguished by twin pinnacles, is **Palazzo Balbi**, grandiose seat of the regional government.

Around the Rialto

Henry James found this middle stretch of the Canal evoked a "melancholy mood", likening it to "a flooded city". But there is an intriguing contrast between the bold palaces and the bustling quayside close to the Rialto market. As the boat stops at the **San Tomà** landing stage, look across to **Ca' Mocenigo** on the right bank. This cluster of palaces belonged to the influential Mocenigo family, who produced seven doges. Byron stayed here while writing his mock-heroic poem *Don Juan* (1819–24) and had an affair with the baker's wife, a woman "wild as a witch and fierce as a demon".

On the left bank a little further along is **Palazzo Pisani-Moretta** ⑱, with its Gothic tracery reminiscent of the Doge's Palace. Curiously, the palace has two *piani nobili* or patrician floors instead of the more common one. The palace is also exceptional in still belonging to descendants of the Pisani family.

On the right bank, beside the **Sant'Angelo** stop, is **Palazzo Corner-Spinelli** ⑲, the prototype of a Renaissance palace. Designed by Coducci, it has a rusticated ground floor as well as his trademark windows, two bold round-arched lights framed by a single round arch. Like Ca' Grande, the palace was owned by the Corner family, the royal Cypriot dynasty. The ownership passed to the Spinelli, important dealers in gold and silks, and still serves as the showrooms of noted Venetian textile merchants today.

As the boat stops at **San Silvestro** by the church, look across to the right bank to appreciate the **Palazzo Farsetti** and **Palazzo Loredan** ⑳, two of the finest Veneto-Byzantine palaces in Venice. Ca' Loredan, in particular, is graced with the

original capitals, arches and decorative plaques. The pair are occupied by the city council and the mayor. The banks between here and the **Rialto Bridge** are lined with deceptively appealing restaurants overrun by tourists rather than market traders.

Busy Rialto district at night.

From the Rialto Bridge to Ca' d'Oro

The **Rialto Bridge** was the only one to span the Grand Canal until 1854.

THE CANAL BY NIGHT

At night, after most tourists have returned to the mainland, is the time for a leisurely look at the Grand Canal. Pick up a No. 1 vaporetto and slip into one of the coveted seats on the prow. The palaces present a seductive face at night: the illuminated windows are an invitation to dream, revealing gleaming Murano glass chandeliers, red silk-clad walls and perhaps the odd summer party spilling onto the balconies.

On the water, you may catch a fleeting glimpse of a *sandolo*, a twin-oared rowing boat, scudding by, its prow lit by a rustic lamp. Afterwards, the tiny *campielli* near the banks of the canal provide a good vantage point for watching the water traffic: try the bench on Campo San Vio, between the Guggenheim and the

Accademia, or Campo della Pescaria, near the Rialto bridge. Writer Jonathan Keates revels in the elemental delight of walking in Venice after dark, with the city's ghostly stage-sets bathed in "muted brilliance, shadow and absolute murk".

Mark Twain, writing in 1878, was equally entranced by the city at night: "Under the mellow moonlight the Venice of poetry and romance stood revealed… ponderous stone bridges threw their shadows athwart the glittering waves… Music came floating over the waters – Venice was complete."

A conversational stroll or a boat ride are classic Venetian pastimes, activities that allow you to enter the contemplative rhythm of a timeless city without cars.

Rialto Bridge.

Today, the bridge provides the chance to watch the water traffic, from gondolas to garbage barges. The Rialto is also an ideal place for lunch in a *bacaro*, a rough and ready Venetian version of the Spanish tapas bar (see page 176).

On the left bank, just upstream, the severe **Palazzo dei Camerlenghi** ㉑ curves round the canal bend. Now a courthouse, it was built in 1525 as the seat of the exchequer, with the ground floor used as a debtors' prison. Like many multifunctional Venetian buildings, it also served as a merchants' emporium and administrative centre.

On the right bank, facing the *palazzo*, lies the **Fondaco dei Tedeschi** ㉒, named after the German merchants who leased the emporium. A healthy trade in precious metals from German mines meant that this privileged community created a cross between an emporium, commercial hotel and social club. The building was converted into the luxury department store T Galleria in 2016, comprising of three storeys of shops showcasing the best of Italian fashion and gastronomy. The fourth floor, with its amazing views over the city, is a public events space.

Set close to the Rialto commercial quarter, this self-contained haven even had its own chapel and casino. After a fire in 1505, it was rebuilt in traditional fashion, with a courtyard and towers that recall an earlier defensive function. The merchants left in 1812, abandoning the site to its banal fate as the city post office.

On the left bank stands the **Fabbriche Vecchie e Nuove** ㉓, an arcaded frontage concealing a key pair of mercantile institutions. The buildings around the Rialto were destroyed by fire in 1514 but rebuilt in classical style. The ground floors functioned as shops, while the upper floors were administrative offices and courts. The porticoes of the **Fabbriche Vecchie** housed sectors devoted to fruit and vegetables, fish, banking and cloth. Above were offices and tribunals to settle trading disputes. Sansovino's larger **Fabbriche Nuove**, built some 30 years later, echo the earlier design. Now the Court of Assizes, they formed the Republic's trading

The Lady of the Café, by Antonio Donghi (1897–1963), in Ca' Pesaro.

centre, with offices on the upper floors devoted to commerce, navigation and food distribution.

Virtually opposite the Fabbriche Nuove and the covered neo-Gothic fish market is **Ca' da Mosto** ㉔, a crumbling example of Veneto-Byzantine architecture thankfully now under renovation. This 13th-century palace was the birthplace of the explorer Alvise da Mosto (1432–88), credited with discovering the Cape Verde Islands and exploring coastal west Africa. His descendant, writer and television personality Francesco da Mosto, always gives the palace a rueful glance as he ponders on the loss of the ancestral pile by his careless forebears.

Ca' d'Oro ㉕

Address: Calle di Ca' d'Oro, Cannaregio, www.cadoro.org
Tel: 041-520 0345

Opening Hrs: Mon 8.15am–2pm, Tue–Sun 8.15am–7.15pm
Entrance Fee: charge
Transport: Ca' d'Oro

Further along on the right bank is the **Ca' d'Oro** (Golden House), one of the loveliest Gothic palaces in Venice, set beside the landing stage of the same name. Architecturally, this is a landmark building and a sumptuous version of a Venetian palace. On the facade, the friezes of interlaced foliage and mythological beasts were originally picked out in gold, leading to its popular name, the "Palace of Gold". The Veneto-Byzantine influence is clear in the design, from the oriental pinnacles to the ethereal tracery.

The palace has an arcade rather than the pointed watergate favoured by Gothic palaces. This was a single family courtyard, unlike palaces designed for several branches of the same family, which commanded twin water gates and double courtyards. As well as the water gate on the Grand Canal, the palace retains its original land gate in a brick courtyard.

In 1845 Ruskin wept while watching the brutal "restoration" of the

The Grand Canal by night.

TIP

For good views of the Regata Storica (see page 80), watch the start of the procession from the rooftop terrace of the Gabrielli Sandwirth Hotel. Alternatively, watch the races from the Rialto Bridge – reserve a canalside table if you can. The views, if not the food, will be memorable. Or join the street party after the races, when trestle tables are set up in the market for a communal dinner.

palace demanded by the owner, a famous ballerina. Fortunately, Baron Franchetti, a later owner, restored the Ca' d'Oro to its original glory, even tracking down the original staircases. While suffering from an incurable illness, the baron committed suicide in 1922, but not before bequeathing his beloved palace to the city.

The Ca' d'Oro houses the **Franchetti Gallery** (Mon 8.15am–2pm, Tue–Sun 8.15am–7.15pm), an idiosyncratic collection that reflects the refined taste of the owner. The courtyard contains the original Gothic well-head that Franchetti finally retrieved from a Parisian dealer. Although the interior is no longer recognisably Gothic, the coffered ceilings and fine marble floors make a splendid showcase for the medieval and Renaissance exhibits.

The gallery is adorned with Flemish tapestries as well as Gothic and Renaissance furniture. The highlights of the collection include a delightful *Annunciation* by Carpaccio, Guardi's views of Venice and Titian's *Venus*. Andrea Mantegna's *St Sebastian* is the most poignant of his paintings, with

Palazzo Vendramin-Calergi, home to Venice's Casino.

other versions existing in Paris and Vienna: this was Franchetti's favourite work. Yet the minor Venetian works give the greatest pleasure, ranging from 12th-century sculptures of interlaced peacocks to Vivarini's poetic Byzantine-style paintings.

The *portego*, or gallery, opens onto the Grand Canal. In fine weather, the loggia makes a delightful place to enjoy the sun and watch the comings and goings on the canal: looking towards the Rialto, there is a splendid view of the **Pescheria**, the fish market. A wooden Gothic staircase leads to the top floor and works by Guardi and Tintoretto.

From Ca' d'Oro to the railway station

Just upstream on the left bank is **Ca' Corner della Regina** ㉖, the birthplace of Caterina Corner, queen of Cyprus, who was the victim of a

The fine marble floors and sculptures of Ca' d'Oro.

cynical Venetian plot to gain control of the island. As a result of French conquests during the crusades, the island was ruled by King James of Lusignan, whom Corner married in 1468. When he died, leaving her queen of Cyprus, Venetian ambassadors persuaded her it was her patriotic duty to abdicate and grant Cyprus to the Republic. In return, she was given dominion over Asolo, a beautiful but minor town in the Veneto. In the 17th century, descendants of her family rebuilt the palace, which now houses the archives of the Biennale organisation as well as an exhibition place for the Prada Foundation.

Ca' Pesaro 27

Address: Fondamenta de Ca' Pesaro, Santa Croce, www.visitmuve.it
Tel: 041-721 127
Opening Hrs: Tue–Sun Apr–Oct 10am–6pm, Nov–Mar 10am–5pm
Entrance Fee: charge
Transport: San Stae

Ca' Pesaro, a stately baroque pile, bemused Henry James: "I even have a timid kindness for the huge Pesaro, whose main reproach, more even than the coarseness of its forms, is its swaggering size." In building Ca' Pesaro, Longhena was inspired by Ca' Corner.

The well-restored Grand Canal facade offers a play of chiaroscuro effects created by recessed windows and sharply delineated cornices. The rusticated ground-floor facade is interrupted by a triple-arched water entrance leading to a theatrical inner courtyard lined by balconies, loggias and a portico, with a grand well-head in the centre. In 1899, Duchess Bevilacqua La Masa bequeathed the palace to the city. It is now home to the International Gallery of Modern Art and the rather quirky Museum of Oriental Art.

The **International Gallery of Modern Art** could not be a slicker showcase for modern art, although the coffered or frescoed ceilings also merit admiration. The ground floor, or *androne*, is typical of noble Venetian palazzi, giving directly on to the Grand Canal. It is lined by a limited number of grand sculptures by 20th-century Italian artists.

Stairs lead to the first floor where a mix of landscapes by 19th-century

EAT

A delightful stop for an early evening snack and drink is Al Remer, set back on a little courtyard right on the Grand Canal. The all-you-can-eat buffet is great value and they sometimes have a little live music. It's a favourite with Venetians in the know.

Canal leading up to Ca' Pesaro.

in Pink and one of Rodin's quizzical Thinkers. Further highlights include works by Kandinsky, Picasso, Klee and Joan Miró. Other rooms focus on the Italians, from Morandi to De Chirico and Carlo Carra.

Italian and Oriental art

The huge second floor has been opened up for temporary exhibitions and a rotating display of some of the many large-scale works (Venetian and Italian art and sculpture from the mid-19th century to the 1970s) in the museum storerooms, hitherto tucked away out of public view.

Up on the top floor, as if half-hidden away in an attic, it feels like a trip back in time as you enter the fusty but fascinating **Museum of Oriental Art**. It draws on the eclectic 19th-century collection assembled by the Count di Bardi on his travels to the Far East. Japanese art of the Edo period (1614–1868) is mixed with oriental decorative screens and lacquerware. There are also precious fabrics, musical instruments, costumes and armour, plus masks and puppets.

On the same bank is the church of **San Stae** ㉘ (Campo San Stae, Santa Croce; Mon–Sat 10am–5pm), with its striking Palladian facade. Inside hangs Giambattista Tiepolo's *The Martyrdom of St Bartholomew*. A couple of palaces further on is **Palazzo Belloni-Battaglia**, which stands out for its stylish facade and highly distinctive pinnacles. It was designed by Longhena for the parvenu Belloni family, who bought their way into the local aristocracy.

Palazzo Vendramin-Calergi (Casino) ㉙

Address: Campiello Vendramin, Cannaregio
Tel: 041- 5297 111; www.vendramin calergi.com
Opening Hrs: Sat 10.30am
Entrance Fee: charge (donation)
Transport: San Marcuola

Fondamenta San Simeone Piccolo in San Croce.

Venetian artists, pastoral paintings by the Tuscan Impressionists and works by early winners of the Biennale are displayed. The most famous exhibits include Klimt's decadent *Salome*, Chagall's *Rabbi of Vitebsk*, Bonnard's *Nude in the Mirror*, Lavery's *Woman*

WORKING ON WATER

Venetians are well served by *vaporetti*, the work-horses of water buses, but on quieter canals, look out for the dredgers, refuse barges, and removals boats. Only the emergency services are allowed to break the speed limit of 8km (5 miles) an hour, rocking passing gondolas in their choppy wake. In practice, few respect the speed limit. The *gondolieri* demonstrate vociferously, but their complaints fall on deaf ears.

In Venetian dialect gondoliers are known as *"Pope"* which is what you shout when you want to cross the Grand Canal. The garbage men *(spazzin)* cry *"Pronti!"* as they collect the sacks heaped on the canal-bank, to be carried away by ship and incinerated. Major tidal flooding means the suspension of refuse collection as the boats cannot pass under bridges. When the stormy sirocco winds blow, the high-water siren sounds, provoking a chain reaction. Shopkeepers pile their wares on higher shelves; walkers don gumboots; duckboards are rapidly put down by the *spazzin*. Non-Venetians are distinguished by their inability to divine the different levels of pavements, to comical effect, by turn sinking leadenly into deep water and squelching like a duck on dry land.

A modern side of Venice, the Calatrava Bridge.

On the right bank, **Palazzo Vendramin-Calergi** is a testament to the changing fortunes of the Venetian nobility. It was built before 1500 by Coducci for the patrician Loredan dynasty, but later belonged to the Calergi, a Cretan family who bought their way into the Venetian nobility.

The Vendramin, scions of a banking and dogal family, then owned the palace until 1845, when it was sold to the French Bourbon Duchesse de Berry. Here she based her court in exile, a Versailles on the lagoon, with the interior hung with Renaissance paintings. Wagner rented the mezzanine wing from the family and, with his father-in-law Franz Liszt, gave a concert at La Fenice opera house. In 1883, Wagner suffered a stroke in his apartments and died in his wife's arms. The *palazzo* is now the city **Casino**.

Architecturally, the palace is a classical masterpiece, built in the familiar three-part design and faced with Istrian marble-like stone. It is notable for its horizontal line, Tuscan projecting cornices, sweeping balconies and a frieze studded with shields and heraldic eagles.

The palace still possesses a spectacular interior, despite the sale of the original furnishings by the de

TIP

To gamble in the impressive Casino (tel: 041-529 7111), dress smartly and bring your passport. It is open all year round daily 3.30pm–2.45am, till 3.15am on Sat (vaporetto lines 1 and 82 to San Marcuola).

Modern art on display at Ca' Pesaro.

EAT

Not far from the Fondaco dei Turchi you will find one of the best *gelato* joints in town. Alaska (Calle Larga dei Bari, Santa Croce 1159) offers rich, organic ice-cream and an unusual variety of flavours that will find favour with kids and grown-ups alike.

Berry heirs. The casino has coffered ceilings, chandeliers, marble fire-places and mannerist paintings, as well as a hall decorated with jasper columns from the fabulous Turkish ruins of Ephesus. A Wagner Society is housed in the composer's former quarters. Filled with period furniture, musical scores and other Wagneriana, they can be visited by guided tour on Saturday mornings. The best way to ensure a spot in a group is to book in person at the casino reception on Friday morning between 10am and midday.

Fondaco dei Turchi ㉚

Address: Salizzada del Fontego dei Turchi, Santa Croce, www.visitmuve.it
Tel: 041-275 0206
Opening Hrs: winter Tue–Fri 9am–5pm, Sat–Sun 10am–6pm, summer 10am–6pm.
Entrance Fee: free
Transport: San Stae

Built in 1227 for the noble Pesaro family, the Fondaco dei Turchi (Turks' Hotel) was leased to the Ottomans in 1621, partly as a means of supervision of Turkish traders and residents in the city. Bedrooms, shops and servants' quarters were created. In keeping with Muslim custom, doors and windows were sealed off, and the building included a mosque and Turkish baths. The Venetian State insisted that all weapons be surrendered on entry, and forbade Christian women and children from crossing the threshold.

The Fondaco only fell into disuse in 1838 and, after an insensitive restoration, became the **Museum of Natural History**. Henry James was stunned by "the glare of white marble without and a series of showy majestic halls within". The museum contains the sarcophagi of previous doges, but one bears no inscription since it belonged to the disgraced Marin Faliero, the doge decapitated for treason in 1355.

The museum has been thoroughly refurbished. On the ground florr you'll find a comprehensive scientific library, an aquarium and the Cetaceans gallery. The first floor is divided into three sections: 'On the tracks of life', dedicated to fossils and paleontology; 'Collecting to

Police patrol the canals.

A wine barge supplying neighbourhood bars and restaurants.

astonish', focusing on the evolution of naturalist collecting and scientific museology and 'The strategies of life', all about form and function in living things.

Next door stands the fortress-like **Deposito del Megio**, once the state granary. Now a school, the austere 15th-century granary is crenellated, in keeping with the Venetian approach to many public buildings.

On to the Calatrava Bridge

Near the Casino is the church of **San Marcuola 31**, and, upstream on the same bank, the square-towered **Palazzo Labia 32**. This eclectic palace, formerly the home of the RAI state broadcasting network, boasts superb Tiepolo frescoes (closed for restoration). Next door is the domed church of **San Geremia** and, just beyond, the severe **Palazzo**

Flangini 33 marks the last of the major palaces.

On the same bank stands the restored rococo **Scalzi 34** church, "all marble and malachite, a cold hard glitter and a costly, curly ugliness". Henry James thought little of the church, but Venetians have a soft spot for it as the sole monument to survive the building of the grim **Railway Station 35**. Across the canal, the church of **San Simeone Piccolo 36** was modelled on the Pantheon in Rome and created as a counterweight to La Salute, framing the Grand Canal with a baroque church at either end.

Linking the railway station and Piazzale Roma is the graceful 21st-century **Calatrava Bridge 37**, designed by Spanish architect Santiago Calatrava. Opened (after years of delays, cost over-runs and amid considerable controversy) in September 2008, the bridge is a low-slung arc of steel, stone and glass officially known as the Ponte della Costituzione (Constitution Bridge). A breath of modernity, the svelte walkway has something of the appearance of a rainbow.

Fondaco dei Turchi at night.

CASTELLO

Lying north and east of San Marco, Castello is a mix of sophistication and local charm. It has the city's best-known waterfront, one of its great Gothic churches and the seat of a mysterious confraternity.

Main Attractions

Bridge of Sighs
San Zaccaria
Querini-Stampalia
  Gallery
Santa Maria Formosa
Santi Giovanni e Paolo
Ospedaletto
San Francesco della
  Vigna
San Giorgio degli
  Schiavoni

Map
Page 148

The famous Bridge of Sighs.

Henry James's evocation of the essence of Venice easily applies to Castello: "a narrow canal in the heart of the city – a patch of green water and a surface of pink wall… a great shabby facade of Gothic windows and balconies". Yet this fails to do justice to the diversity of the district. As the most varied and the largest Venetian *sestiere*, Castello offers a spectrum of sights, from the sophisticated bustle along Riva degli Schiavoni to the quaint fishing-village ambience of San Pietro.

Castello's seafaring heritage may be strong but so are its cosmopolitan roots and mercantile spirit. Sailors, shipwrights and merchants came from Dalmatia, Eastern Europe, Greece and Egypt, attracted by the prospect of work at the Arsenale shipyards and great quaysides. The cosmopolitan legacy lingers on, with the district still home to sizeable Greek and Slav communities, as well as a small Armenian quarter.

Like Cannaregio, Castello offers a slice of everyday life, with Sundays ringing with church bells, and dark alleys opening into bright, bustling squares. Two of the most homely areas centre on Campo Santa Maria Formosa and San Giorgio dei Greci, the Greek church. Yet culturally the *sestiere* can compete with any in Venice. The district is home to

La Pietà, Vivaldi's church, and the Gothic majesty of San Giovanni e Paolo (San Zanipolo). The distinctive Venetian confraternities *(scuole)* are well represented, with San Giorgio degli Schiavoni the most intimate and San Marco the most prestigious. The Arsenale is the focal point of the eastern district, with its looming walls and defensive towers visible from afar.

While western Castello becomes increasingly gentrified, with boutique hotels and eclectic craft shops shunning carnival masks and Murano glass, the remoter parts of Castello are falling silent as workshops close. However, the eastern area is also the greenest in Venice, with shady gardens, wide waterfronts and the site of the Biennale exhibition. Castello's diversity is encapsulated by its bars: choose a drink in the Danieli, the haunt of the literati, or an *ombretta* of white wine in a secluded neighbourhood bar, under the sole gaze of a Venetian cat.

The Bridge of Sighs

Just beyond the Doge's Palace is the **Ponte dei Sospiri** (Bridge of Sighs) ❶, the most famous bridge in Venice. It crosses the canal to the "new" prisons, providing a link between the Doge's Palace, courtrooms and cells, allowing interrogators to slip back and forth. Built between 1595 and 1600, this covered stone bridge acquired its legendary name after the lamentation of prisoners as they crossed the bridge to their new and unpleasant lodgings. In reality, by the standards of the day, the prisons were relatively comfortable. The **New Prisons**, designed to hold the overspill from the "old" prisons in the Doge's Palace, occupy a sober, classical building. The **Old Prisons**, from which Casanova made his dramatic escape, were known as *I Piombi* (The Leads), because they were built right under the lead roofs

of the palace. A still more unpleasant set of cells were called *I Pozzi* (The Wells) because they were in the humid cellars.

The bridge marks the beginning of **Riva degli Schiavoni** ❷, the best-known stretch of Venetian waterfront. Now bustling with tourists and souvenir sellers, this sweeping quayside once thronged with slave dealers and merchants. Its name refers either to slaves or Slavs, who were often synonymous in Venetian minds. Certainly, the term came to embrace the Dalmatian merchants from Schiavonia, modern-day Croatia, who settled in Venice in great numbers during the 15th century. The quayside was widened and paved in 1782, and has been a popular Venetian promenade ever since.

Nor can visitors avoid the waterfront, since it is the focal point of ferry routes, and of the latter-day merchants of Venice who erect souvenir stalls along its length. As the hub of upmarket tourism, the Riva is lined with distinguished hotels, all vying for the cocktail clientele.

EAT

One of the best of Venice's traditional pastry shops, the Pasticceria da Bonifacio, is hidden away along Calle degli Albanesi, a street that takes its name from the Albanian community of immigrants from that territory when it was under Venetian control.

The story goes that lovers will be granted eternal love and bliss if they kiss on a gondola at sunset under the Bridge of Sighs…

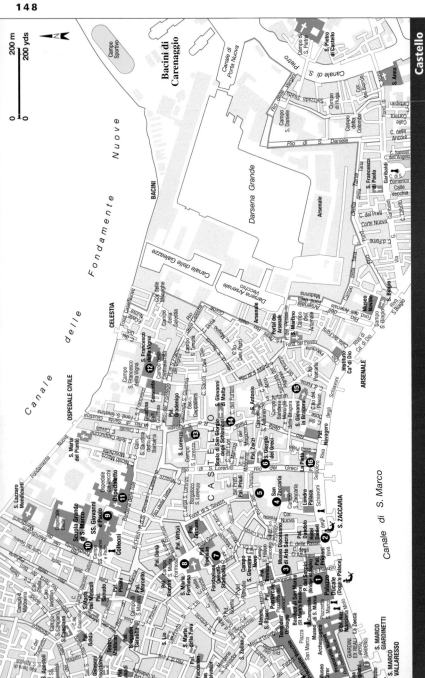

200 m
200 yds

N

Bacini di
Carenaggio

Campo
Sportivo

Campo di
S. Pietro

S. Pietro
di Castello

Canale di S. Pietro

Rio della Tana

S. Anna

Canale di S.

Campo
S. Daniele

Campo
di Ruga

Calle
Correra

C. delle
Ancore

Canale di Porta Nuova

BACINI

Darsena Grande

Rio di S. Daniele

Arsenale

S. Francesco
di Paola

Garibaldi

C. di S.
Domenico

Calle
Vecchia

Fondamente

Nuove

Canale delle Galeazze

Darsena Vecchio

C. del Preti

Corte Nuova

Via G. Garibaldi

Arsenale

C. del Forno

Fondamente

Canale

Ospedale Civile

delle

CELESTIA

S. Maria
del Pianto

S. Lazzaro
Mendicanti

Scuola Grande
di S. Marco

SS. Giovanni
e Paolo

Colleoni

Ospedale
dei Vecchi

Ospedaletto

S. Francesco
della Vigna

Convento

12

Pal.
Gradenigo

S. Lorenzo

Scuola di San Giorgio
degli Schiavoni

13

S. Giovanni
di Malta

S. Antonio

15

Museo delle
Navi

S. Martino

Portal des
Arsenale

ARSENALE

Instituto
Ca' di Dio

S. Biagio

CASTELLO

S. Giorgio
dei Greci

6

S. Giovanni
in Bragora

16

10

9

11

Pal. Dona

Pal. Grimani

S. Maria
Formosa

8

Fondazione
Querini
Stampalia

7

Museo Diocesano
di Arte Sacra

5

San
Zaccaria

4

Londra
Palace

Danieli

Riva degli Schiavoni

S. ZACCARIA

Pal. Vitturi

Teatro

S. Lio

S. Maria
della Fava

Campo
S. Giovanni
Nuovo

Pal.
Priuli

Museo Diocesano
di Arte Sacra

3

Dandolo
Hotel

2

Palazzo
Ducale

1

Basilica di
San Marco
(St Mark's Basilica)

Piazza
S. Marco

Museo
Correr

Bibl. Marciana
La Zecca

GIARDINETTI
REALI

S. MARCO
GIARDINETTI

S. MARCO
VALLARESSO

Canale di S. Marco

lights reflected in the lagoon waters. Henry James stayed further along the Riva (at 4145) while finishing *The Portrait of a Lady*. Here, "in the fruitless fidget of composition", he was distracted by "the waterside life, the wondrous lagoon spread before me, and the ceaseless human chatter at my windows".

Museo Diocesano di Arte Sacra ❸

Address: Fondamenta di Sant'Apollonia, www.veneziaupt.orgTel: 041-522 9166
Opening Hrs: Tue–Sun 10am–6pm
Entrance Fee: charge
Transport: San Zaccaria

This Museum of Sacred Art is tucked away on Ponte della Canonica, behind the Palazzo Ducale and Riva degli Schiavoni. The Romanesque cloisters of this canalside museum form an oasis of calm amidst the bustle of San Marco and are the star attraction here. Ranged around the cloisters are fragments of early medieval sculptures from San Marco, as well as Roman and Byzantine statuary. The museum displays

View towards St Mark's along Riva degli Schiavoni.

The Hotel Danieli

The **Danieli** is the most historic hotel in Venice, with even Proust enchanted by his room: "When I went to Venice I found that my dream had become – incredibly but quite simply – my address." The Danieli was also the scene of an unhappy love affair between George Sand and Alfred de Musset in 1883.

During the Liberation, in 1945, grand hotels were commandeered as officers' clubs, with the Danieli becoming the New Zealand headquarters. The terrace still remains a superb place to toast the ending of a war or the beginning of a romance.

Over the next bridge stands a well-known landmark, the horseback monument to Vittorio Emanuele, the first king of a united Italy. Behind lies the restrained **Londra Palace** hotel, with balconies looking across to the island of San Giorgio and

ROOMS WITH A VIEW

St Mark's Square was described by Napoleon as "the finest drawing room in Europe", which must make the Riva degli Schiavoni its sumptuous bedroom. Here the Danieli was favoured by Wagner, Dickens, Proust, Debussy, Cocteau and Balzac. Here, too, George Sand and Alfred de Musset famously fell in and out of love. Today the Danieli still attracts the rich and famous. Next door is the charming Londra Palace, with "a hundred windows on the lagoon". In splendid rooms overlooking San Giorgio, Tchaikovsky composed his Fourth Symphony. The grand Venetian hotels are still the place to strike a pose, perhaps starting with the Luna Baglioni, which claims to be the oldest hotel in Venice.

On the Grand Canal is the Gritti Palace, once favoured by Ruskin, Hemingway and Graham Greene. Over the water on the Giudecca is the Cipriani, the choice for guests who want luxurious seclusion. Yet even the most illustrious visitors once faced night-time horrors: "The great business before going to bed is the hunt for insects, vicious mosquitoes that particularly torment foreigners, on whom they hurl themselves with the sensual appetite of a gourmet." Fortunately, poet Théophile Gautier's experiences are lost to modern visitors.

The Londra Palace has "a hundred windows on the lagoon".

works salvaged from deconsecrated churches along with mannerist and baroque art, but is at its most interesting when temporary exhibitions are on show.

From here follow Salizzada San Provolo (which leads from Campo Santi Filippo e Giacomo) east to Campo San Zaccaria. En route are several simple inns, including Alla Rivetta, noted for its cuttlefish and polenta.

San Zaccaria ④

Address: Campo San Zaccaria
Tel: 041-522 1257
Opening Hrs: Mon–Sat 10am–noon and 4–6pm, Sun 4–6pm
Entrance Fee: charge
Transport: San Zaccaria

San Zaccaria is a delightful church graced by Coducci's curvilinear facade. Actually, the lower half betrays the church's Gothic beginnings. Inside, the mix of styles is clear. The first church on the site was founded in the 9th century, and acted as a Venetian pantheon, with eight early doges buried in the crypt. The original Byzantine basilica forms the crypt below San Tarasio chapel,

Mask-makers had their own guild in medieval times.

an atmospheric spot usually lying underwater. The chapel itself is decorated with Gothic frescoes and three lovely 15th-century altarpieces. The Sant'Anastasia chapel holds works by Tintoretto and Tiepolo, and mighty choir stalls.

In the north aisle of the main church is Bellini's glowing altarpiece of the *Madonna and Child*. The attractive square is completed by a Gothic belltower.

It is hard to associate this peaceful square with its sinister reputation for skulduggery and licence. Three doges were assassinated in the vicinity, while the adjoining Benedictine convent was a byword for lascivious living. Since noblewomen were frequently dispatched to nunneries to save money on dowries, tales of libertine nuns were rife. Venetian attempts to stem the scandals were half-hearted:

although chaplains and confessors had to be in their fifties or older, younger sons were made welcome at the convent's masked balls; the aristocracy encouraged such illicit liaisons as a means of keeping the family estate intact.

The nuns' parlour became a celebrated social salon, as portrayed in Guardi's famous painting in Ca' Rezzonico. Men are still made welcome in the former convent: the *carabinieri* barracks sacrilegiously occupy the Renaissance cloisters, linked to the church by a graceful open loggia.

A Gothic portal leads to bustling Campo San Provolo, which opens onto the charming quayside of **Fondamenta dell'Osmarin ❺**, notable for the **Palazzo Priuli**, a superb late-Gothic palace commanding the corner of Rio di San Severo and San Provolo and now home to a luxury hotel. From the bridge over Rio dei Greci is a view of the radically restored Gothic **Palazzo Zorzi** on the right, home to Unesco's European Bureau for Science and Culture.

San Giorgio dei Greci ❻

Address: Campiello dei Greci
Tel: 041-522 6581
Opening Hrs: Mon–Sat 9am–12.30pm and 2.30–4.30pm, Sun 9am–1pm
Entrance Fee: free
Transport: San Zaccaria

Across the bridge is the Greek Orthodox church, distinguished by its dome and tilting baroque tower. The Greeks represent one of the oldest ethnic communities in Venice, even if they have only been established within this enclosure since 1526.

After the Turkish conquest of Constantinople in 1453, the Venetian Greek community expanded greatly, working as merchants, scribes and scholars; in fact, only the Jews formed a larger ethnic group. The Greek contribution to Venetian culture can be seen in scholarship and printing, as well as in the production of icons and mosaics.

The 16th-century church has a tall, narrow facade and early-Renaissance purity. In keeping with Orthodox tradition, the interior has a *matroneo*, a

Ca' del Sol mask workshop on the Fondamenta dell'Osmarin.

women's gallery, and an iconostasis, an ornate 16th-century screen separating the sanctuary from the nave. This intimate church comes alive during the Easter festivals, when the golden interior and scent of incense create a heady exoticism. Wagner visited the church shortly before his death, and was disturbed by the oriental pomp and the mysterious mood created by the dark dome and flickering haloes of saints.

An elegant square encloses the church and a cluster of cultural buildings, including the Hellenic Institute, a museum of icons and a tiny Greek cemetery.

Museo di Pinti Sacri Bizantini

Address: Ponte dei Greci, www.istitutoellenico.org
Tel: 041-522 6581
Opening Hrs: daily 9am–5pm.
Entrance Fee: charge
Transport: San Zaccaria

Attached to San Giorgio dei Greci, the **Museum of Holy Byzantine Paintings**, or Icon Museum, is housed in the former Greek *scuola*, or

confraternity house, now run by the Hellenic Institute. The confraternity chapterhouse has kept its baroque decor, while the museum displays an outstanding collection of 16th- and 17th-century Cretan works, which illustrate the synthesis of Greek and Venetian art. Highlights are two 14th-century Byzantine icons, one representing Christ in glory and the other the Virgin Mary with the baby Jesus and Apostles.

Just around the corner is Da Remigio, a cosy trattoria noted for its gnocchi. From here, cross Rio dei Greci to Fondamenta dell'Osmarin, before taking the second bridge on the right into **Ruga Giuffa**, a narrow alley with overhanging roofs. This is both an everyday shopping street and Venice at its most insular. Although only a stone's-throw from San Marco, it feels like a private world, deeply Venetian yet historically linked to the Armenian community. The street, now noted for its food shops, was once populated by Armenian cloth merchants, and named after an Armenian enclave in Persia.

Querini-Stampalia gallery

Address: Campiello Querini Stampalia, www.querinistampalia.it
Tel: 041-271 1411
Opening Hrs: Tue–Sun 10am–6pm
Entrance Fee: charge
Transport: San Zaccaria

Overlooking the southern end of Campo Santa Maria Formosa is the **Fondazione Querini-Stampalia**. Intimate, eclectic and uncrowded, it offers a tranquil coffee shop as well a delightful small gallery and library brimming with over 350,000 books (open until late and at weekends). The Querini belonged to the ancient nobility, the families who elected the first doge. However, a foiled plot led to the dynasty's banishment to the Greek island of Stampalia, a title they later appended. The last count

The Geography Lesson, by Longhi, in the Querini-Stampalia gallery.

The baroque campanile of Santa Maria Formosa.

died in 1868 and bequeathed his home to the city.

Count Giovanni left his stamp on this Renaissance palace, from the new library to the gallery hung with family portraits and Venetian paintings, mainly 17th- and 18th-century genre scenes. Highlights include a poetic Bellini painting and the festive and domestic scenes of Gabriele Bella (1730–99). Several famous works by Longhi include *The Geography Lesson* and *The Ridotto*, depicting masqueraders at the Casino. The count's taste in furniture is typical of the refined yet relatively spartan interiors favoured by the nobility. Temporary exhibitions regularly beef up the interest.

Given such pared-down chic, it is fitting that the ground floor was remodelled by Carlo Scarpa, the Venetian modernist architect, in the 1960s, creating an airy atrium and a Japanese minimalist garden. Evening classical concerts are sometimes held in the frescoed main salon.

Santa Maria Formosa ❽

Address: Campo Santa Maria Formosa
Opening Hrs: Mon–Sat 10am–5pm
Entrance Fee: charge
Transport: San Zaccaria

Campo Santa Maria Formosa is a lovely asymmetrical space dotted with flower, fruit and junk stalls. Rivalled only by Campo Santa Margherita and Campo San Giacomo dell'Orio, this is the archetypal Venetian square. Set in the heart of Castello, this *campo* provided a backdrop for traditional festivities, from masked balls to bear-baiting. Today, the square rests on its laurels, sure of each Venetian element: the shadowy alleys running into a sunlit space, a striking Renaissance church, palaces from three different periods, a covered well-head surrounded by pigeons, unpretentious cafés filled with stallholders and visitors alike, a small market, and even a gondola station *(stazio)*.

The parish church of **Santa Maria Formosa** is especially endearing, with its eccentrically bulging apses. The foundations may date from the 9th century, but the church was redesigned by Coducci, the great Renaissance architect, and acquired a baroque belltower with a grotesque mask at its base. While the canalside facade is by Coducci, the *campo* facade was added in 1604. The cool grey-and-white marble interior contains a Vivarini *Madonna* (1473) and a chapel set aside for students "to pay a little visit on the way to school".

Palazzo Vitturi (at No. 5246) is a 13th-century affair decorated with Gothic and Moorish motifs – and now a boutique hotel (www.palazzo vitturi.com). The **Palazzo Trevisan** (5250) is a Renaissance palace

Antonio Vivaldi

Vivaldi, the Venetian composer of one of the world's best-known pieces of classical music, *The Four Seasons*, would have been delighted at its popularity.

To contemporary critics, Vivaldi (1678–1741) is one of the most important composers of late-baroque music. Although his work acted as a model for future followers, J.S. Bach among them, Vivaldi's music soon suffered a decline, and was only rescued from oblivion in 1926. It seems inconceivable that the works of such a celebrated composer could have been lost for nearly 200 years.

Vivaldi's great musical talent was encouraged by his father, Giovan Battista, a barber whose playing was good enough to gain him a place in the orchestra of St Mark's Basilica. His son was nurtured in the Venetian musical tradition and, as a budding violin virtuoso, allowed to stand in for his father. The young man entered the priesthood, which gave him time to devote to music, and he was widely known as *il prete rosso*, the red-haired priest.

Vivaldi devoted himself to composition and obtained a post as composer and violin teacher at the Ospedale della Pietà, a famous charitable institution. At once an exclusive girls' conservatoire and an orphanage, it was one of several schools where gifted orphans were elevated from poverty to follow careers in music.

It proved so popular that a plaque had to be erected threatening heaven's wrath on parents who passed off their young offspring as foundlings. Vivaldi spent 40 years here, coaxing fine performances from the choir and orchestra and introducing his compositions to a wide public.

Vivaldi's relationship with the Ospedale began superbly, with universal acclaim for his concertos, sonatas and sacred music, including oratorios. His gift for melody made him successful in most fields of music, but his favourite instrument was the violin. However, within 10 years the administration had become aggrieved by the maestro's new star status, his avoidance of Mass and his worldliness.

His reversal of fortune came with allegations of improper conduct with a pupil from Mantua, Anna Girò, a soprano who sang in his operas. The affair damaged his reputation as a teacher, priest and establishment figure. In his disappointment, Vivaldi turned his back on Venice and escaped to concert tours in Paris, Dresden, Prague and finally Vienna, where he died in poverty in 1741.

La Pietà church, Vivaldi's musical base in Venice, was remodelled shortly after his death. The church (open intermittently between April and October; see page 161) has a splendid Tiepolo ceiling. Next door, the composer's home has become the Vivaldi Hotel, an act of blatant commercialism that would probably have found favour with the maestro.

Il prete rosso, the musical red-haired priest whose downfall was caused by a soprano.

studded with slender columns and ornamentation. Opposite, the magnificent 16th-century **Palazzo Grimani** houses the **Museo Grimani** (Ramo Grimani; Tue–Sun 8.15–7.15pm, Mon 8.15am–2pm; free on the first Sun of each month) tel: 041-520 0345; www.palazzogrimani.org). To see inside is to get an idea of the wealth of Venice's leading families. On the Rialto end, above Ponte del Paradiso, stands a delicate Gothic archway.

Campo Santi Giovanni e Paolo (Zanipolo)

From the square, follow Calle Santa Maria Formosa north across Rio di San Giovanni to **Campo Santi Giovanni e Paolo**. This is one of the most monumental squares in Venice. While less intimate than Santa Maria Formosa, it is far more impressive architecturally. Occupying land given to the Dominicans by Doge Orseolo in 1234, the square encloses a great Gothic church and former Renaissance confraternity, as well as the finest equestrian statue in northern Italy.

This restless horse and rider commemorate **Bartolomeo Colleoni** (1400–76), a celebrated *condottiere* (mercenary soldier) whose bequest to the city came with a stipulation that a monument be erected to him on St Mark's Square. The rider has reason to be restless: the authorities cunningly relegated the idealised Renaissance statue to this lesser spot, outside St Mark's confraternity.

The *campo* possesses yet another Renaissance treasure, a sculpted wellhead attributed to Sansovino.

Santi Giovanni e Paolo (Zanipolo) ⑨

Address: Campo Santi Giovanni e Paolo
Tel: 041-523 5913
Opening Hrs: Mon–Fri 9am–6pm, Sat–Sun noon–6pm
Entrance Fee: charge
Transport: Ospedale

Dominating the square is the Dominicans' unique Gothic church, also known as **San Zanipolo**, a conflation of Saints John and Paul, to whom the church is dedicated.

Campo Santa Maria Formosa.

Sheer size and scale invite comparisons with the Frari, its fellow giant (see page 181). This, too, is an austere church, founded in the late 13th century but only consecrated in 1430. It peaks in a series of pinnacles, and the roofline displays statues of the Dominican saints. Close up, the plain brickwork of the church is enlivened by a 14th-century polygonal apse and a series of bulging chapels that potrude from its south flank into the square. The main portal incorporates Byzantine columns and ornamentation salvaged from Torcello. While characterised by a lofty nave and sparse decoration, the interior is initially more coherent and welcoming than that of the Frari. The cross-vaulted ceilings are supported by wooden tie beams and stone pillars.

The church is considered the Pantheon of Venice, honouring illustrious leaders, from admirals and noblemen to the occasional State artist, notably Bellini. Above all, this was the last resting place of the doges, with the pomp of State funerals matched by magnificent monuments

Lofty San Zanipolo.

The equestrian statue of Colleoni outside San Zanipolo.

to 25 doges. Among the profusion of funerary monuments is the sculpted Renaissance tomb of Doge Giovanni Mocenigo, close to the main portal. Made by the Lombardi family of master-craftsmen in 1500, it is one of many monuments to the powerful Mocenigo dynasty.

In the right aisle, also close to the main portal, is a memorial to Marcantonio Bragadin, the garrison commander flayed alive by the Turks in Cyprus in 1571. In the chancel, by the baroque high altar, lies the finest Renaissance funerary monument in Venice, dedicated to Doge Andrea Vendramin, who died in 1478. Diagonally opposite is the tomb of Doge Michele Morosini, a victim of the 1382 plague. This was the Gothic monument most admired by Ruskin.

The **Chapel of the Rosary**, at the end of the north transept, was

built to commemorate the Venetian victory over the Turks in 1571. Over the entrance is the funerary monument to Doge Sebastiano Venier, who commanded the fleet at Lepanto.

The chapel once contained works by Titian and Tintoretto but, after a fire, these were replaced with ceiling panels by Veronese, considered the most pagan and joyous of Venetian painters. The church interior is enriched by other works of art, including Vivarini's *Christ Bearing the Cross* (1474). A controversial Veronese *Last Supper* was painted for this church but is now in the Accademia (see page 212). In the right aisle, Bellini's gorgeous *St Vincent Ferrier* altarpiece survives, set in its original gilded frame. Tours in English are held every Thursday at 5.30pm (meeting point at the main entrance). For details see www.basilica santigiovanniepaolo.it.

The Scuola Grande di San Marco ⑩

Address: Rio dei Mendicanti
Tel: 041-529 4323
Opening Hrs: Tue–Sat 9.30am–1pm and 2–7pm
Entrance Fee: free
Transport: Ospedale

The unadorned facade of Zanipolo is flanked by the ornate **Scuola Grande di San Marco**, once the richest Venetian confraternity. Recently renovated, it is now part of the main city hospital. The second floor houses the Museum of the History of Medicine while the Sala dell'Albergo is the historic seat of the Medical Historical Library.

The confraternity retains its *trompe l'œil* Renaissance facade as well as its assembly rooms and chapterhouse. Coducci designed the curved crowning of the facade in 1490, conceivably inspired by the domes of St Mark's. The sumptuous

The Scuola Grande di San Marco at its most atmospheric.

Dining alfresco on Fondamenta San Lorenzo.

ideally for a concert. The ponderous baroque facade of the adjoining Ospedaletto church is attributed to Longhena. Ruskin dismissed these leering masks as "the most monstrous example of the Grotesque Renaissance… the sculptures on its facade representing masses of diseased figures and swollen fruit". The church interior is decorated with 17th- and 18th-century paintings, including an early work by Tiepolo.

San Francesco della Vigna  ⑫

Address: Campo San Francesco della Vigna
Tel: 041-520 6102
Opening Hrs: daily 8am–12.30pm and 3–7pm
Entrance Fee: free
Transport: Celestia

East of the Ospedaletto, the **San Francesco della Vigna** church is in an isolated, somewhat shabby area. However, this Franciscan church represents an architectural

To find a ferry or gondola, return to the Riva degli Schiavoni.

marble lower section was decorated by the Lombardi brothers.

A grand portal framed by illusionistic lions leads into the hushed hospital, with the foyer occupying the cloisters of the former Dominican foundation. To visit the former *scuola*, slip past reception and walk upstairs.

Ospedaletto ⑪

Address: Barbaria delle Tole
Tel: 041-924 933
Opening Hrs: Thur–Sat 3.30–6.30pm
Entrance Fee: charge
Transport: Ospedale

Barbaria delle Tole leads east off the square to the **Santa** Maria dei Derelitti **church, known as Ospedaletto**. This was one of four famous Ospedali, charitable institutions that acted as orphanages and prestigious music conservatoires. The frescoed Sala della Musica formed the main concert hall and can still be visited,

milestone, being Sansovino's first creation in Venice and the city's first flowering of the High Renaissance. The facade and crowning pediment were designed by Palladio, while the tall belltower is a familiar city landmark reminiscent of the Campanile in Piazza San Marco. San Francesco is a hallowed site, built on vineyards associated with a mysterious visit by St Mark. The present building was founded in 1534 by Doge Andrea Gritti, the Renaissance scholar and notorious womaniser. "We cannot make a doge of a man with three bastards in Turkey," declared one envious rival.

The church was built in accordance with neo-Platonic ideals, using the precision of proportional relationships based on the number three: even the width of the aisles corresponds to a third of their height. The cool but harmonious interior contains a monument to the doge (who died from a surfeit of grilled eels) and highlights include sculptures from the Lombardi school, Veronese's *Holy Family*, and a *Madonna and Child* by Negroponte

(1450). The lovely Gothic cloisters lead to the Cappella Santa (Holy Chapel), where a Bellini *Madonna* can be found.

Southwest lies the deconsecrated church of **San Lorenzo** ⓭, the presumed burial place of Marco Polo. Since the discovery of ancient foundations in 1987, the church has been undergoing seemingly eternal restoration work. San Lorenzo was, apparently, the site of a rather lax convent, so it is perhaps appropriate that the city's only (discreet) lap-dancing bar should be on this square.

Scuola di San Giorgio degli Schiavoni ⓮

Address: Campo San Francesco della Vigna
Tel: 041-520 6102
Opening Hrs: Mon 2.45–6pm, Tue–Sat 9.15am–1pm and 2.45–6pm, Sun 9.15am–1pm.
Entrance Fee: charge
Transport: Celestia

Tucked into Calle dei Furlani is one of the loveliest confraternity seats in Venice, **St George of the Slavs**. The *scuola* was intended to protect

Carpaccio's The Vision of St Jerome.

the interests of Slavs from Dalmatia (Schiavonia), which was the first Venetian colony. On the building's completion in 1501, the confraternity commissioned a painting cycle in honour of the Dalmatian patron saints, St George, St Tryphon and St Jerome. Carpaccio was chosen to decorate the upper gallery but, after the *scuola* was rebuilt in 1551, his masterpieces were moved downstairs.

Despite remodelling, the *scuola* retains its authentic atmosphere and boasts the only Venetian pictorial cycle to have survived in the building for which it was painted. Carpaccio's vibrant works are displayed in a mysterious, intimate setting, below a coffered ceiling. Unlike his superb cycle in the Accademia (see page 212), a portrayal of pomp, pageantry and everyday life, this cycle is characterised by dramatic storytelling. In particular, the *St George and the Dragon* paintings are bold chivalric scenes, with a captivating depiction of a veritable knight in shining armour, a dying dragon and a place of desolation, with the ground littered with skulls, vipers and vultures. Equally beguiling is the St Jerome trilogy, with *The Miracle of the Lion* showing the saint extracting a thorn from the lion's paw. Despite the scene's presumed eastern setting, Carpaccio has included San Giorgio and the Knights of Malta.

The Vision of St Jerome is both one of the most engaging works and his masterpiece, conveying a mood of contemplative calm and a Tuscan sense of space combined with Flemish realism. St Augustine is depicted in his study writing to St Jerome when a heavenly voice announces his imminent death. Carpaccio shows his customary accuracy in the depiction of a Renaissance humanist's study, from the bookspines to the astrolabes and musical scores. The perky Maltese dog by the saint's feet evokes the Knights of Malta, whose headquarters still lie next door. The upstairs room, hung with minor works and the confraternity pennant, is more memorable for the panelled ceiling.

Riva degli Schiavoni with the waterfront church of La Pietà on the right.

Behind San Giorgio stands **San Giovanni di Malta**, the secretive seat of the Knights of Malta. The members not only contributed to San Giorgio but continue to have close links with the confraternity.

To La Pietà

Fondamenta dei Furlani winds south to Salizzada Sant'Antonin and **San Giovanni in Bragora** ⓯ (Mon–Sat 9–noon, 3.30–5.30pm). This treasured parish church, set on a quiet *campo* beside a handsome Gothic palace, is essentially late Gothic, despite 9th-century foundations and a Renaissance presbytery. The interior is notable for its ship's-keel ceiling and Renaissance works of art, a style which reached Venice later than elsewhere. While Bartolomeo Vivarini's *Madonna and Saints* (1478) is a stiff, Byzantine-style work, his nephew Alvise shows humanist leanings in his *Resurrection* (1498), a dynamic High Renaissance altarpiece. Adorning the high altar is Cima da Conegliano's *Baptism of Christ* (1492), set against a mountain landscape.

Mouldering in a chapel on the right lies the mummified corpse of St John the Almsgiver. However, the church of St John is keener to proclaim birth than death: Vivaldi was baptised in the red marble font, as the proudly displayed copies of the baptismal register prove.

Calle del Dose leads back to bustling Riva degli Schiavoni and **La Pietà** ⓰ (Tue–Fri 10.15am–noon and 3–5pm, Sat–Sun 10.15am–1pm and 2–5pm; www.pietavenezia.org), a church with even stronger Vivaldi connections. The Ospedale della Pietà was the most famous of the Ospedali, institutions that combined the roles of orphanage and musical conservatoire. The church was the backdrop for the concerts given by the choir of orphan girls under Vivaldi's tutelage (see page 154).

The church was superbly remodelled by Massari shortly after Vivaldi's death in 1741, and transformed into the city's leading concert hall. The cool, oval interior was designed with acoustics in mind, enhanced by curving lines, low-vaulted ceilings, a vestibule that muffled the street noise, and the filigree-like choir galleries. Since Massari won the commission to rebuild the church in 1735, while Vivaldi was still in residence, it is perhaps not too fanciful to presume that the composer advised the architect on acoustic refinements.

The gleaming gold-and-white interior is crowned by Tiepolo's *The Triumph of Faith* (1775). In the dazzling fresco, the figures appear to come alive and billow into the church itself. The church is a venue for classical music concerts (see website for details).

La Pietà, once Vivaldi's musical base.

The gates of the Arsenale.

EASTERN CASTELLO

Dominated by the Arsenale shipyards, this elusive district has a scattering of important sites, including the rewarding Museo Storico Navale and the international exhibition pavilions of the Biennale.

Venetian romantics call this disparate district "real Venice", much of it like walking back into a 1950s time warp. Washing waves in the breeze and Venetian dialect is the lingua franca.

Outlying Eastern Castello is a complex blend of the homely and the international. The district embraces arty geranium-clad cottages on the San Marco side and gritty working-class tenements further east. If the remote island of San Pietro is home to an insular, boat-building community, bustling Via Garibaldi still feels like a forgotten Venice, barely grazed by tourism. Plonked beside all this cosy domesticity is the self-conscious internationalism of the Biennale pavilions. And, at its very centre, is the Arsenale, an amalgam of military base and shipyards turned into exhibition space and theatres. Unless your goal is the Biennale, this is a place for moods not monuments, and daydreams about Venetian naval might.

Napoleon's impact

The district around the naval complex contains a stretch of factory-like modular housing designed for

The area hosts the Biennale every odd-numbered year.

the former Arsenale workers, whose skills were greatly valued. One of the newest quarters lies further east, with the ancient island of San Pietro on the outskirts.

Napoleonic redevelopment and land-reclamation schemes created the streets and the public gardens that line the eastern waterfront. Following French demolition projects, the Austrians dutifully reclaimed swathes of the watery marsh off Sant'Elena. Intended as a military parade ground, this former island has now succumbed

Main Attractions
Arsenale
Museo Storico Navale
Biennale
San Pietro di Castello

Map
Page 165

to development, and is home to the city's lacklustre football club.

The Arsenale

Arsenal is a term that the Venetians have bequeathed to the Western world. Although the oldest dockyard of the Venetian **Arsenale ❶**, the Darsena Vecchio, still exists, the Darsena Nuovo and Nuovissimo now form a single basin, swallowed up by the Darsena Grande. Shipbuilding ceased many years ago. As a navy base, it was used to dispatch Nato warships to Albania and the former Yugoslavia in the late 1990s. Since 1999, most of the historical east and north sides of the Arsenale have been given over to the more peaceful activities of the Biennale, although only parts are ever used at any given time. Public access remains restricted to the west side of the shipyards, which is still navy property.

From the Arsenale vaporetto stop, on the Riva degli Schiavoni, wander along to the wooden bridge that stands opposite the main entrance. You can get a good view from the middle of the bridge, and, who knows, you

The gilded figurehead of a model replica of the Bucintoro at the Naval Museum.

may even meet a friendly naval officer who might let you take a peek inside.

Campo dell'Arsenale ❷ marks the entrance to the naval complex, with its impressive fortifications bounded by 16th-century walls and towers. Beyond the footbridge lies the water entrance, framed by crenellated brick towers. These picturesque waterside towers were rebuilt in the 17th century.

Beside the water gate stands the ceremonial **Porta Magna**, the majestic land entrance to the Arsenale. Built in 1460, this triumphal arch is celebrated as the first Renaissance monument in Venice. Yet, with typical Venetian eclecticism, the gateway recycles stolen statuary as well as four Greek marble columns and their Byzantine capitals.

Notwithstanding the Venetian victory at Lepanto in 1571, the Republic undertook defensive fortifications in response to fears of Turkish expansion.

One of the two towers framing Porta Magna.

As a sign of the warlike mood, the winged Lion of St Mark over the gateway holds a closed book, rather than displaying his traditional message of peace. The gateway was embellished with statues at the same time, with the allegorical figures added a century later. These are believed to have been carved from marble looted from the Parthenon during the 1687 Venetian bombardment of Athens. The land gateway is guarded by two lions pillaged from Piraeus during the same attack by Doge Morosini, admiral of the Venetian fleet. The lion sitting upright to the left of the gateway bears a runic inscription on his shoulder and haunches, probably carved by 11th-century Norse mercenaries who were defending the Byzantine emperor against Greek rebels. The smaller pair of lions on the far right may be Greek booty from Delos dating from the 6th century BC. In 1682, a terrace replaced the medieval drawbridge, setting the

seal on this ambitious modernisation programme.

This part of the Arsenale is still naval property and entry is not permitted – even the vaporetto that used to slip between the towers of the grand water entrance was scrapped years ago.

Exploring the mysteries of the Arsenale

Just east, along Rio della Tana, stands the hulking **Tana** (or **Corderie**), the former rope-and-cable factory that was founded as a hemp warehouse. Here, hemp plants were carded and spun before being passed to master cordwainers, who made the ropes and hawsers. This functional space was redesigned in the 1540s by Antonio da Ponte, the architect of the Rialto Bridge. Nearby, on **Campo della Tana** is the ticket office to the Biennale and the Teatro Piccolo dell'Arsenale, only occasionally open, usually for dance events related to the Biennale. Virtually next door is the Corderie

FACT

Venetian maritime traditions glorified the doge and the Republic, and no regatta was complete without the presence of the Bucintoro. This State barge resembled a gilded dragon, or some other mythical beast, with the winged Lion of St Mark on the prow. The doge occupied a throne by the figurehead. The last barge was destroyed by Napoleon in 1797, but a scale model made in 1828 is on display at the Naval Museum.

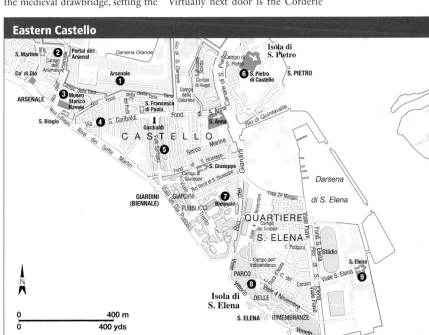

Eastern Castello

The Arsenale

The Arsenale was the symbol of Venetian maritime might. Founded in 1104, this secretive naval complex became Europe's largest medieval shipyard.

The term "arsenal" derives from the Arabic *darsina'a*, or house of industry, a most suitable description of this Venetian production line.

The Arsenale was a city within a city, bounded by 3km (2 miles) of walls, with wet and dry docks and ordnance depots that were envied abroad. It was also an armaments site. At its height, 16,000 people toiled in the foundries, gunpowder mills, munitions depots, sail factories, rope-works and grain stores. Industrial bakeries produced the dry Venetian bis-

cuits that were suited to preservation for consumption on long sea voyages but less acceptable to modern palates. The Arsenale's industrial caulkers' vats so impressed Dante that he described them in his *Inferno*, making immersion in the bubbling cauldrons of pitch a hellish punishment for corrupt officials.

Before the creation of the Arsenale, ship-building and repairs were often carried out in St Mark's Basin. Even at the height of its production capacity, the Arsenale was supported by numerous private repair yards, including some on neighbouring islands, especially Murano. As far as shipbuilding work was concerned, the state exercised a monopoly, with the Arsenale constructing fleets of ships.

The Arsenale acted as a medieval production line, manufacturing light galleys, ships of war and merchant vessels. Hulls constructed in the "new" Arsenale were towed past a series of openings in the "old" Arsenale, where they were rigged and fitted out with munitions and food supplies. Everything from oars and sails to barrels of biscuits was loaded by means of a pulley system; at the end, the galleys would be ready to sail. In its 16th-century heyday, the Arsenale could deliver a fully rigged galley in a day. In 1574, the Venetians clearly impressed Henri III of France by producing a seaworthy vessel complete with a 16,000-pound cannon in the time it took him to devour a state banquet.

Such pioneering methods of prefabricated construction were dependent on a highly skilled workforce. The *arsenalotti* comprised an artisans' élite of master shipbuilders, caulkers and carpenters. So greatly did the State value the experience and skill of these men, that workers were guaranteed jobs for life.

The 900th anniversary of the Arsenale, in 2004, was greeted with celebration and controversy, as part of the Arsenale was leased for 30 years to the management of the MOSE dam project. Major works to transform the area to allow the passage of transport vessels had some Venetian citizens up in arms.

Engraving of the Arsenale in 1797, before the Napoleonic occupation.

Cultural Centre and, along the east and north docks, exhibition space has been created in the former shipyards.

Much of this only opens during the Biennale. While viewing the avant-garde art, allow yourself to be sidetracked by the monumental 16th-century boathouse, designed by Sanmicheli, the noted civil and military engineer. Until Napoleon stripped it, the ceremonial State barge, the legendary Bucintoro, was housed here.

The central waterway of the Arsenale is the **Canale delle Galeazze**, named after the oar-propelled Venetian galleys, lined by 18th-century shipyards and the **Cantiere delle Gaggiandre** docks, with their dignified 16th-century arches. These were created after the 1571 Venetian victory at Lepanto, and were capable of dispatching a fleet of warships at a single moment's notice. The most significant building here is Sansovino's magnificently roofed boat-house, designed for the armed patrol craft that protected the lagoon ports.

A small detour takes you back to the waterfront via the site of the former Arsenale bakeries. These stand at the St Mark's Basin end of **Riva Ca' di Dio** (No. 2179–80). Set on the east bank of the canal, the **Forni Pubblici** date from 1473 and are distinguished by a marble frieze.

According to historian Pompeo Molmenti, one batch of long-lived Venetian navy biscuits was left in Crete in 1669 and discovered to be perfectly edible in 1821. Nearby stand workers' houses first designed for the *arsenalotti*, the Arsenale shipwrights and skilled craftsmen.

The Museo Storico Navale (Naval Museum) ❸

Address: Riva San Biagio
Tel: 041-2424
Opening Hrs: Mon–Fri 8.45am–1.30pm, Sat 8.45am–1pm (currently closed for renovation)

Entrance Fee: charge
Transport: Arsenale

Given the tantalising elusiveness of the Arsenale, the Naval Museum is the only place where you can fully appreciate the greatness of maritime Venice. Before its present incarnation, the 16th-century building was used as a naval granary and biscuit warehouse. The Austrians created the collection from the scant remnants to survive French depredations. (Many Venetian naval treasures are now displayed in the rival Parisian naval museum.)

The Venetian museum is spread out over four floors, full of interesting bits and pieces for those with an interest in Venetian and Italian naval history. On the ground floor, displays include giant lamps that used to light the way at night on Venetian galleys, a series of mortars used by the Venetian navy to fight pirates in the 18th century, weaponry from Venetian and Tuscan fortresses, model vessels of various eras and some weaponry from the two world wars, including a rather dodgy-looking manned torpedo used in the Mediterranean in World War II.

FACT

As Venetians grew wealthier, it became harder to find native oarsmen. By the 16th century, Dalmatian and Greek crews gave way to convicts who were dragooned into service.

A telltale anchor marks the entrance to the Naval Museum.

On the next floor, Venetian antiquarian maps depict the development of the Arsenale and the lagoon defences, while Venetian naval supremacy is illustrated by scenes of naval battles such as Lepanto, and by models of Mediterranean fortresses. Detailed models of vessels, including the last *Bucintoro*, the doge's ceremonial vessel, and the remains of a 17th-century flagship are also on show. Uniforms, mementoes, instruments and further models, mostly relating to the Italian navy since the Veneto joined a united Italy in 1866, dominate the second floor. The star of the third floor is Peggy Guggenheim's personal gondola, complete with the *felze*, or protective canopy. The fourth floor is, to say the least, odd, combining a sea shell collection with an exposition related to, of all things, the Swedish Navy.

The ticket gives you entry to the nearby Padiglione delle Nave, on Fondamenta della Madonna, near the canal entrance to the Arsenale. It is full of all sorts of historical vessels (no models here), including the ceremonial 18-oar Scalè Reale, used to transport kings and other dignitaries.

The former oars workshop is now the Ships Pavilion.

The Naval Museum runs along the Riva San Biagio.

The pavilion is the only part of the museum currently open to the public (daily 10am–5pm) while the main building is being renovated.

From the Naval Museum to Viale Garibaldi

From the Museo Storico Navale, a walk through one of the quietest and greenest parts of the city leads to the site of the Biennale exhibition and the island of San Pietro. Strolling east along **Riva San Biagio** takes you past the colonnaded San Biagio, a Greek church now used as the naval chapel.

On the left is **Via Garibaldi ❹**, the widest street in Venice, occupying a filled-in canal. As the commercial hub of Eastern Castello, this working-class street is lined with basic household shops and friendly bars. On the right is the former home of the Genoese-born navigator, John Cabot (Giovanni Caboto). After

A 6th-century BC lion guards the mighty Arsenale.

a stint in Venice, he wound up in England and, with his son Sebastian, explored Newfoundland in 1497.

Viale Garibaldi ❺, a tree-lined avenue further down, is a model of French rationality. Napoleon embellished this area, incidentally demolishing churches and monasteries. The avenue runs down to the Napoleonic gardens, a tree-lined promenade dotted with monuments. In 1834 the novelist George Sand found the park as deserted as most Venetian parks, populated only by "grumbling old men, some senseless smokers or some bilious melancholics".

From here, cross the gardens to the Biennale site, or retreat to an authentic canalside *trattoria* – a good choice is the Hostaria da Franz, which was opened in 1842 by an Austrian soldier who fell in love with a Venetian woman. Once refreshed, return to Via Garibaldi and cross the bridge to San Pietro, set in the far reaches of Castello. At the first quaint bridge at the end of the street is a distant view across to the Arsenale, with its cranes, walls and defensive towers. This endearingly shabby district is enlivened by the jaunty fishing boats, workshops and boatyards lining the Canale di San Pietro.

San Pietro and the Biennale

A wooden bridge leads to the island of **San Pietro**, the site of the original castle *(castello)* which gave its name to the district. **San Pietro di Castello ❻** (Mon–Sat 10am–5pm; www.chorusvenezia.org) rests on ancient foundations but is essentially Palladian, topped by a central dome. From the foundation of Venice until 1807, the church was the city cathedral, with the title only passing to St Mark's after the demise of the Republic. Ironically, this remote island church was the official seat of religious power while the splendid St Mark's Basilica was merely the doge's private chapel. This was the Venetian way of keeping the power of the papacy at one remove, with temporal power centred on the St Mark's district.

The disappointing interior contains a late work by Veronese and the Throne of St Peter, a marble seat decorated with Moorish motifs and Koranic inscriptions, cut from an Arab stela. The grassy *campo* beside the church is framed by Coducci's tilting Renaissance belltower and by the hulking might of the Arsenale shipyards across the water channel.

Retracing one's steps through the friendly but faded neighbourhood leads back to the Napoleonic gardens and the site of the **Biennale ❼**. The Biennale is based in the **Giardini Pubblici**, gardens lined by paths leading to designer pavilions. About 40 countries are housed in these permanent pavilions, with space set aside for international exhibitions.

FACT

Local supporters pour in from all over the Veneto to see the beleaguered F.C. Venezia (it went bankrupt three times in recent years, most recently in 2015) play in the Stadio Penzo in Sant'Elena. Special ferries are laid on between Sant'Elena and the Tronchetto car parks. For local atmosphere it makes for an original afternoon. Tickets can usually be bought at the stadium or at Venezia Unica outlets (tel: 041-2424; www.veneziaunica.it).

The pastoral nature of the site makes a pleasing contrast to the slick modernism of the exhibits.

The Biennale pavilions

A number of pavilions have been built by famous architects, notably Josef Hoffman's Austrian pavilion (1934), the Venetian architect Carlo Scarpa's Venezuelan pavilion (1954) and Alvar Aalto's Finnish creation (1956). The best spots are taken by the old-world powers. According to art critic Waldemar Januszczak, distortions of national rivalries are alive and well: "The British pavilion stares across at the German"; yet while the British space is vaguely Palladian, and looks as though it would do a nice line in teas, the German building is "one of the few bits of full-blown Nazi architecture to survive outside Germany".

The newest star is James Stirling's Book Pavilion (1994), facing the vast Italian pavilion. Inspired by naval design and intended to recall the neighbouring Arsenale, this spacious glass-and-copper structure resembles an overgrown vaporetto.

Biennale pavilion.

Cafés on Via Garibaldi, the widest street in Venice.

To make full use of the Giardini pavilions, a Biennale for architecture takes place in the intervening years and has already made its mark, attracting renowned international architects.

On the waterfront, the Giardini-Biennale boat stop returns you to the San Marco area. Energetic walkers can follow the shoreline east through **Parco delle Rimembranze** ❽ and the uninspiring island of **Sant'Elena**. The former Austrian parade grounds are now the stamping ground of Venice's football team, while the medieval monastery and seamen's hospital have succumbed to soulless urban sprawl. Dating from the 1920s, these streets bear the names of famous battlefields of World War I.

The goal is the Gothic church of **Sant' Elena** ❾, with its belltower, cloisters and Renaissance portal. Afterwards, the Sant'Elena vaporetto whisks you back to San Marco.

The Biennale

This glamorous summer forum for contemporary art, held in odd-numbered years, is a highlight of the international art calendar.

Every two years, the modern-art merchants of Venice bewilder the world with a display of artworks set in the city's historic naval yards and leafy gardens. It may be garish, sprawling and pretentious, but it is also chic, challenging and commercially successful. There is a place for everything, from postmodernist lampshades and erotic photography to a traditional boat installation from the Comores Islands moored in the Bacino di San Marco, a Finnish firefighting collection or ad hoc mural painting in various parts of the city.

The Biennale was designed to give Venice a fresh identity as a vital cultural metropolis within the new Italian nation. It aimed to attract leading artists, boost tourism and introduce an international audience to the wonders of Venice. Inaugurated in 1895 by King Umberto I, the show raised a furore because of Giacomo Grosso's symbolist work depicting women draped lasciviously over a corpse. The event has been controversial ever since.

In 1910 a work by Picasso was rejected for being too scandalous. In the early 1920s the Impressionists were well received, as were Degas and Toulouse-Lautrec. The Fascist period marked the lowest point, with Hitler declaring his "disgust" at the degeneracy of the art. Since World War II, however, the festival has paraded its avant-garde credentials. In 1948, the first post-war Biennale displayed works by Picasso, Klee, Schiele and Magritte, as well as by the Metaphysical painters Carrà, De Chirico and Giorgio Morandi. Here, too, the Impressionists vied with Otto Dix and other German Expressionists banished by Nazism.

In 1964, an American artistic invasion and the advent of pop art marked another great turning point. Robert Rauschenberg received the major prize, despite protests by staid French Academicians. In recent years, visitors have been scandalised by an Israeli pavilion overrun by a flock of sheep, only outdone by an Italian slaughterhouse. Recent exhibitions have seen the triumphant return of American artists, as well as successful showings by British artists Gilbert and George, Tracey Emin and Damien Hirst. The unofficial fringe still acts as a prestigious springboard for many a struggling artist.

The Biennale is tied in with events at the major galleries and at such curious exhibition spaces as a former leper colony, the salt warehouses on the Zattere, and even in the prisons on the St Mark's waterfront. Ca' Pesaro, the modern-art museum, now displays the best from the back catalogue.

The Biennale never fails to impress.

SAN POLO AND SANTA CROCE

These left-bank districts, centred on the Rialto, are a warren of alleys and markets that hide the great treasures of Bellini, Titian and Tintoretto in the Frari and Scuola Grande di San Rocco.

San Polo and Santa Croce form adjoining districts *(sestieri)* curved into the left bank of the Grand Canal. Together they encompass the bustling Rialto market and the picturesque backwaters towards the station, centred on the quintessential *campo* of San Giacomo dell' Orio. The hub of the left bank is the Rialto, "the marketplace of the morning and evening lands". Goethe's poetic evocation is fleshed out by the writer Jan Morris, who loved the Rialto's "smell of mud, incense, fish, age, filth and velvet".

The labyrinthine Rialto, with its dark alleys and tiny squares *(campielli)*, makes a sharp contrast to the more open spaces around Campo San Polo. In theory, this is lesser-known Venice, *Venezia minore*, implying a humility that does little justice to a district that contains two of the city's greatest sights: the Frari is a huge Franciscan church containing masterpieces by Titian and Bellini, while San Rocco is a shrine to Tintoretto. Nor is "minor" a fair summary of the stretch of Grand Canal from the Rialto Bridge to the station, a waterside lined by historic warehouses and palaces, including Veneto-Byzantine gems. (Best seen from the

water, this section is covered in the Grand Canal chapter, see page 125.)

The Rialto

"What's new on the Rialto?" was Antonio's cry in Shakespeare's *The Merchant of Venice*. Gossip remains a popular Venetian pastime in this city, and the **Rialto ❶**, with its market and mass of tiny bars, is still a talking shop. To Venetians, the Rialto is not restricted to the graceful bridge but embraces the district curved around the middle bend of the Grand Canal.

Main Attractions
Rialto
Erberia and Pescheria
Palazzo Mocenigo
San Giacomo dell'Orio
Frari
Scuola Grande di San Rocco
San Pantalon
Casa Goldoni
Campo San Polo

Map
Page 174

Gondolas by the Rialto Bridge.

Shops on the Rialto Bridge.

The Rialto (derived from *rivo alto* or high bank) also refers to the first settlement of central Venice, and became the capital from AD 814.

As the oldest district, the Rialto has the greatest number of Veneto-Byzantine palaces. From its earliest foundation, this was the powerhouse of the Venetian empire, a crossroads between East and West. As "Venice's kitchen, office and back parlour," it also acted as a commercial exchange and meeting place of wholesale and retail merchants.

Even outbreaks of fire failed to crush the city's mercantile spirit. In the past, the Rialto was as prone to fire as it is to flooding today. The fire of 1514 razed the Rialto to the ground in six hours, sparing only the stone church. However, the commercial district quickly recovered and was rebuilt much as before. Thanks to liberal laws and an entrepreneurial culture, the Rialto was a cosmopolitan centre, home to a mixture of races and a babble of tongues.

The Venetians were middlemen, making a profit from the sale of everything in this emporium. Long before Shakespeare's Shylock, the Venetians had a reputation for guile and business acumen. In this exotic marketplace, cargoes of spices and silks from the Levant were sold, along with Slav slaves. Here, northern Italian grain dealers and Flemish wool merchants rubbed shoulders with Jewish moneylenders, Arab spice traders and German silver traders, as well as with Florentine and Lombard cloth merchants.

Trading and banking centre

The district was also home to a cluster of highly functional mercantile buildings that supervised trade and administered justice. From the 13th century onwards, various magistracies governed the Rialto commercial centre, granting leases or supervising fiscal, financial and legal affairs. Foremost among these were the **Fabbriche Nuove** and **Fabbriche Vecchie ❷** trade offices and tribunals, which stand between the two main Rialto markets (see page 138).

Another key civic building was the **Palazzo dei Camerlenghi** ❸, the former State treasury and debtors' prison, housed in a Renaissance hulk built of Istrian stone.

Many guilds were located in the Rialto, including those for jewellers, woodcutters and goldsmiths.

The ancient market was a foreign-exchange and banking centre, with a cluster of private banks around the bridge. The Venetian ducat was a stable currency, and the Rialto dominated international exchanges. Private banks flourished from the 12th century onwards, with a fore-runner to the Banco di Giro, the earliest State deposit bank, opening in 1157. (The engaging Al Bancogiro wine bar now occupies this spot). The *giro* took the form of a writ-ten transfer from one account to another; no receipt was given, since the bank register was considered an official record. At night, the money was moved to the mint under an armed escort. With ready access to capital, the Rialto merchants funded fleets and made use of maritime insurance services and a commodity stock market.

The **Rialto Bridge** tradition-ally divides the city into two, with the right bank, the San Marco side, known as the *Rialto di quà* (this side) and the left bank known as the *Rialto di là* (that side). The Rialto Bridge spans the Grand Canal with a strong, elegantly curved arch of marble, a single-span bridge lined with shops. Henry James appreci-ated these "booths that abound in Venetian character", but also felt "the communication of insect life", a feel-ing shared by today's visitors as they run the gauntlet of stalls selling gon-doliers' garb and dodgy handbags.

The Rialto Bridge is merely the last in a series of bridges that began with simple pontoons and progressed to wooden bridges with a drawbridge section to allow the passage of tall ships. A new bridge was created in 1588–91 by Antonio da Ponte, who beat the greatest architects of the day, including Michelangelo and Palladio, to secure the commission.

The aptly named da Ponte sur-passed himself by designing a light,

Antico Dolo, a bacaro known for its tripe dishes.

BACARI: TRADITIONAL BARS

The Rialto market is the ideal place to indulge in a Venetian bar crawl, a *giro di ombre*, in the traditional wine and tapas bars known as *bacari*. On offer are an array of Venetian snacks *(cichetti)* and glasses of wine *(ombre)* in some of the oldest bars in Venice, dating back to the 15th century.

Some are mentioned in the Grand Canal chapter, but moving away from the canal and deeper into the maze, you'll find all sorts of places. Cantina Do Mori (Calle Do Mori, off Ruga Vecchia, Mon–Sat 8am–8pm) offers standing room only for its tiny sandwiches. The strong of stom-ach can visit Antico Dolo (Ruga Vecchia, daily 11am–11pm; www.anticodolo.it), which specialises in tripe, leaving the squeamish to seek out Ruga Rialto (Calle del Sturion, off Ruga Rialto, daily 11am–mid-night), a bohemian *bacaro* and inn with wooden benches, copper pots and simple but sound dishes. A local favourite nearby is Al Diavolo e l'Acquasanta (The Devil and the Holywater; Calle della Madonna, daily L and D), where stalwarts snack on *cichetti* at tiny cramped tables. Another very authentic stop for *cichetti* and wine is All'Arco (Calle dell'Arco, Mon–Sat 8am–2.30pm).

floating structure with shops nestling in the solid, closed arches. From the bridge one can admire the majestic sweep of palaces and warehouses swinging away to La Volta del Canal, the great elbow-like bend in the Grand Canal.

San Giacomo di Rialto, believed to be the oldest church in Venice.

The quayside

Henry James, who stayed in a palace nearby, admired "the old pink warehouses on the hot *fondamenta*". The Grand Canal palaces and warehouses are generally difficult to appreciate from the land, but on this stretch the waterside is lined with *fondamente* or *rive*, accessible quaysides. Here you can walk along both banks, weaving among the crowded terraces. The **Fondamenta del Vin ❹**, where barrels of wine used to be unloaded, is now a quayside overrun by tempting but touristy trattorias and souvenir stalls. Facing it is **Riva del Ferro ❺**, where German barges unloaded iron (*ferro*). Their trading house, the Fondaco dei Tedeschi, was close by (see page 138). Also on the right bank is Riva del Carbon, where coal merchants moored their barges.

San Giacomo di Rialto ❻, the church nestling comfortably among the fruit and vegetable stalls, is linked to St James, the patron saint of goldsmiths and pilgrims. Both were much in evidence in the Rialto, even if the pilgrims were often in search of gold rather than God. Affectionately known as San Giacometto, this

Cafés and gondolas line the Fondamenta del Vin by Rialto Bridge.

is reputedly the oldest church in Venice, founded in the 5th century but rebuilt in the 11th century.

Its most distinctive features, apart from the market bustle, are the Gothic portico, belltower and bold 24-hour clock. The 16th-century restoration respected the original domed Greek-cross plan, the ancient Greek columns and Veneto-Byzantine capitals. The cramped interior is disappointing but enlivened by the presence of resting market traders and dishevelled customers.

Campo San Giacomo ❼ preserves its mercantile atmosphere, an echo of republican times when money-changers and bankers set up their tables under the church portico.

Market life

Threading the labyrinthine alleys of the Rialto is an intoxicating experience, especially in the morning. The alleys and quays bear witness to the Rialto's mercantile past, with names such as *olio* (oil), *vino* (wine), *spezie* (spices), *polli* (poultry) and *beccarie* (meat). Ruga degli Orefici, Goldsmiths' Street, begins at the foot of the Rialto Bridge, while Ruga degli Speziali, Spice Traders' Street is nearby. Today, smelly alleys often triumph over spicy perfumes, but the market is rarely squalid and makes a refreshing change from the monumental Venice of St Mark's. Indeed, the market is one of the few places where Italian prevails, along with the guttural sing-song of Venetian dialect.

The Rialto remains a hive of commercial activity, with everything on sale between here and the Mercerie in the San Marco district. Ignore the tourist tat in favour of foodstuffs galore.

The **Erberia ❽** is the fruit-and-vegetable market overlooking the Grand Canal. Brightly painted boats from the lagoon supply the main markets with fish and fresh vegetables. Close by is the water gate, the "tradesmen's entrance" to the markets. Casanova spoke of the Erberia as a place for "innocent pleasure"; latter-day foodies find sensuous pleasure in the profusion of medicinal herbs, flowers and fruit, not to mention the asparagus, radicchio and baby artichokes.

The markets extend along the bank to the **Pescheria ❾**, the fish market,

Venice's main fish market.

Fresh produce from the Erberia.

set in an arcaded neo-Gothic hall by the quayside, a design inspired by Carpaccio's realistic paintings. Under the porticoes, fishermen set their catch on mountains of ice. Elizabeth David waxed lyrical about "ordinary sole and great ugly skate striped with delicate lilac lights, the sardines shining like newly minted silver coins". The sight of so much appetising food is an invitation to a casual lunch in a basic wine bar, probably in the alleys around **Campo delle Beccarie**, the former abattoir but still the beating heart of the market.

Just over the canal lies **San Cassiano** ❿ (Tue–Sat 9am–noon and 5–7pm), an oppressive church ruined by 17th-century remodelling, and not redeemed by an interior containing Tintoretto's eerie *Crucifixion* and a couple of 9th-century marble pilasters.

The district between here and Campo San Polo enjoyed a dubious reputation, with bare-breasted courtesans famed for leaning from their windows to attract clients. In 1608 the visitor Thomas Coryate was impressed by the profusion of prostitutes who "are said to open their quivers to any arrow".

From the former fleshpots, tiny alleys lead across the next canal to **Campo di Santa Maria Mater Domini** ⓫, a harmonious square with a Gothic well-head hemmed in by medieval palaces and a couple of bars. Set back from the square is the beguiling Renaissance church of **Santa Maria Mater Domini** (Mon–Sat 10am–noon). Often overlooked, the church has a well-restored interior, and a cool but distinctive atmosphere enhanced by clean Roman lines, a Byzantine cube shape and baroque cornices. There are fine 16th-century paintings, including one by Tintoretto.

Palazzo Mocenigo ⓬

Address: Salizzada di San Stae, http://mocenigo.visitmuve.it
Tel: 041-721 798
Opening Hrs: Tue–Sun 10am–5pm

Palazzo Mocenigo.

Entrance Fee: charge
Transport: San Stae

This palace-museum is linked to one of the greatest dogal families and to other Mocenigo status symbols on the Grand Canal. The ancestral home was so well preserved that, after Alvise Mocenigo bequeathed it to the city in 1954, it became a fitting showcase of gracious 18th-century living, from the lavishly decorated ballroom to the frescoed bedchamber. Defined by its Murano chandeliers, gilded furnishings and rococo frescoes, it makes a perfect setting for a display of Venetian period costumes, as well as for a family-portrait gallery worthy of a dynasty that produced seven doges. A new section added is dedicated to a lesser-known Venetian tradition: perfume.

To the Fondaco dei Turchi

A stone's-throw from the palace is the over-restored church of **San Stae** ⑬ (Mon–Sat 10am–5pm, Sun 1–5pm) overlooking the Grand Canal. The design is closer to Palladian than baroque, with Corinthian columns set on high plinths.

Just east is **Ca' Pesaro** ⑭, a sumptuous palace housing museums of modern and oriental art (see page 141).

Tiziano Vecelli, otherwise known as Titian.

To the west, also on the Grand Canal, lies the **Fondaco dei Turchi** ⑮, one of the greatest merchant's warehouses, now home to the Museum of Natural History (see page 144).

San Giacomo dell'Orio ⑯

Address: Campo San Giacomo dell'Orio, Santa Croce, www.chorus venezia.org
Opening Hrs: Mon–Sat 10am–5pm
Entrance Fee: charge
Transport: Riva de Biasio

Tucked into a corner of a leafy square of the same name, the church of **San Giacomo dell'Orio**, slightly off the beaten track, conveys an inviting Romanesque atmosphere lit by diffuse light. The coherence is particularly remarkable given the eclectic nature of the church, which spans many centuries since its 9th-century foundation. Behind the pulpit and in the right transept are several Byzantine capitals raided from

Campo San Giacomo dell'Orio.

The frescoed cupola inside San Giacomo dell'Orio church.

Constantinople, including one made of greenish Greek marble.

The poet Gabriele d'Annunzio likened it to "the fossilised compression of an immense verdant forest". Architectural eclecticism is apparent in the Veneto-Byzantine belltower and columns, wooden Gothic arches and classic Renaissance apses; the pièce de résistance is the Gothic ship's-keel roof.

The finest artworks here are a rare 14th-century wooden Tuscan crucifix, a rare altarpiece by Lorenzo Lotto and, in the **New Sacristy**, a Veronese ceiling. A stroll around the building reveals the characteristic bulbous apses, and is an invitation to linger in a bar on one of the city's most captivating squares.

Labyrinthine quarter

The church is part of a labyrinthine quarter of narrow *calli* and covered passageways *(sottoporteghi)*. A short

but confusing stroll south leads to the home of one of the surviving *scuole* or powerful lay confraternities. The **Scuola di San Giovanni Evangelista** ⑰ (concerts or by prior appointment, tel: 041-718 234, for visiting days see www.scuolasangiovanni.it) still serves its original purpose and, while difficult to gain access to, is worth seeing from outside.

The distinctive Renaissance marble portal and courtyard is watched over by an eagle, the symbol of St John, the confraternity's patron saint. The interior is graced by a monumental staircase, a barrel-vaulted, double-ramp affair, but most of the finest paintings are now in the Accademia (see page 212). Opposite is the deconsecrated 15th-century church of San Giovanni Evangelista, used for occasional exhibitions. From here, Calle del Magazzen leads to the greatest church on the left bank, the Frari.

Decorative gondola details.

Santa Maria Gloriosa dei Frari ⑱

Address: Campo dei Frari, San Polo, www.chorusvenezia.org
Opening Hrs: Mon–Sat 9am–6pm, Sun 1–6pm

TITIAN

Titian was the supreme artist. The Frari contains two of his masterpieces, including *The Assumption*, a work whose revolutionary nature caused it to be rejected initially by the friars; when they relented, the work made Titian's international reputation. The altar is dominated by this vibrant piece, completed in 1518. The Virgin floats heavenwards on a wreath of clouds borne aloft by cherubic angels. Unlike his rivals, Titian could make his illusionistic work command attention from afar. Vibrant colours helped: the counterpoint of the golden sky against the glowing red of the Virgin's robes. Titian aligned the work exactly with the opening of the rood screen, so that one's eye is drawn through the Gothic choir towards this magnificent altarpiece.

The Pesaro Altarpiece depicts members of the Pesaro family, Titian's patrons, with the steady gaze of the young heir to the family fortune looking out towards us. Titian was a shrewd businessman who flattered his many patrons. This is a Venetian *sacra conversazione* with a difference: worldliness. For the first time, the portraits of a patron and his family were made part of a devotional painting, thus breaking the previous strict division between sacred and secular.

The Scuole

Dating back to the Middle Ages, the *scuole* were charitable lay associations close to the heart of Venetian life.

Until the fall of the Republic at the end of the 18th century, the *scuole* acted as a state within a state, looking after members' spiritual, moral and material welfare. Anything could be provided, from a dowry or loan, to alms, free lodging and medical treatment.

Serving the citizen class, from lawyers and merchants to skilled artisans, the *scuole* were expected to support the State, play a part in processions and contribute to good causes. The richest foundations even recruited and financed military expeditions. For the merchant class, excluded from government, this was an opportunity to show their civic pride and communal spirit. In fact, these associations were the main focus of social life for citizens beneath the patrician class.

While there were great distinctions between the prestigious *scuole grandi* and the humble *scuole minori*, they were essentially democratic, with rich and poor able to join at different rates of subscription. Four of the *scuole grandi*, the major institutions, originated as flagellant societies in the 13th century. While the *scuole grandi* were more overtly religious, all the *scuole* were devotional associations: they prayed together and performed charitable works in the name of the patron saint.

Such confraternities appealed to the Venetians' puritanical streak as well as to their fondness for self-government. The *scuole* promoted pious living and forbade blasphemy, adultery, gambling, "frequenting taverns and lewd company".

The *scuole grandi* played a leading role in the ceremonial life of the city. Apart from San Rocco, these include the Scuole di San Giovanni Evangelista, I Carmini, San Marco and Santa Maria della Carità, now home to the Accademia gallery.

All *scuole* wished to glorify their patron saint and themselves by employing the great artists who had decorated the Doge's Palace. Corporate funds were lavished on the interiors of meeting houses, of which the grandest is San Rocco. Set on two floors and linked by a magnificent staircase, a typical headquarters had halls decorated by the finest artists of the age, rich in narrative scenes and in dazzling processions.

By the 18th century there were almost 500 confraternities. Although Napoleon sacked their headquarters and disbanded the confraternities themselves in 1806, several have since been revived and still more former meeting houses are now open to the public.

The *scuole* remain highly distinctive, whether used as living confraternities, permanent museums or concert halls. The Scuola Grande di San Marco one of the greatest, is now part of the city hospital, thus still serving the community in the broadest sense.

Tintoretto's Christ Carrying the Cross in San Rocco.

Entrance Fee: charge
Transport: San Tomà

Commonly known simply as the Frari and rivalled only by San Giovanni e Paolo, this is the greatest of all the Venetian Gothic churches. The hulking Franciscan complex, founded in the 13th century, was rebuilt in the 14th and 15th centuries.

The adjoining monastic cloisters house the state archives and a thousand years of Venetian history. Outside and in, the bare brick church is virtually devoid of decoration. The writer Jan Morris likens it to "a stooping high-browed monk, intellectual and medi-tative". Such simplicity stems from the dictates of Franciscan building rules: poverty was the guiding principle of the great mendicant orders.

Only the three Gothic turrets crowned with pointed gables act as a reminder of the richness of Venetian architecture. Yet inside, even the restricted colour range is used to great effect, with red-brick walls relieved by creamy Istrian stone, colours repeated in the red-and-white marble floor. The interior is a stark framework for the artwork, a pantheon of Venetian

glories. The choir chapels are lined with tombs of the doges, including the monument to Doge Francesco Foscari, deposed in 1457.

The nave is dominated by a Gothic choir screen and lovely choir stalls, the only such ensemble to survive in Venice. The high altar beyond is the focal point of the Frari, a space illu-minated by Titian's *The Assumption*, his masterpiece, flanked by dogal tombs. His other great work, the Pesaro Altarpiece, lies in the north aisle of the nave. Beside it is the Pesaro Monument to Doge Pesaro (1658), an overblown funerary piece honouring Titian's chief patron. Ruskin disliked the baroque, and this sculpture in particular, decrying it as "a huge accumulation of theatrical scenery in marble… [its] negro cary-atids grinning and horrible".

Titian's bombastic tomb, erected three centuries after his death, is set in the right-hand (south) aisle, close to the main portal. Directly opposite is the mausoleum of the neoclassical sculptor Canova, who died in Venice in 1822. Canova designed this as Titian's tomb, but it became a monument to

San Rocco, temple to Tintoretto.

Fumiani's The Martyrdom and Glory of St Pantalon adorns the ceiling of San Pantalon.

himself. Canova's sinister open-doored pyramid contains the sculptor's heart. The querulous Ruskin dismissed the work as "ridiculous in conception, null and void to the uttermost in invention and feeling".

To the right of the high altar lies the entrance to the Pesaro family chapel, dominated by Bellini's altarpiece, a radiant *Madonna and Child*. Henry James adored the triptych: "It is as solemn as it is gorgeous as it is simple as it is deep." Also delightful is an early-14th-century Byzantine-style *Madonna* by Paolo Veneziano. The writer Ian Littlewood recommends seeing the church in the evening when "the smoking candles and the softness of the light offer the giddy experience of slipping from one world to another".

The Scuola Grande di San Rocco ⓭

Address: Campo San Rocco, San Polo, www.scuolagrandesanrocco.it
Tel: 041-523 4864
Opening Hrs: daily 9.30am–5.30pm

Entrance Fee: charge
Transport: San Tomà

The apse of the Frari abuts Campo San Rocco, home to the **Scuola Grande di San Rocco**, one of the greatest city sights. San Rocco is the grandest of the *scuole* or charitable lay confraternities, and occasionally acts as a backdrop for baroque recitals. The society is dedicated to St Roch, the French saint of plague victims, who so impressed the Venetians that they stole his relics and canonised him. The confraternity's mission was the relief of the sick, a noble aim that soon became conflated with the prestige and social standing of the *scuola*.

The 16th-century building is also a shrine to Tintoretto, the great mannerist painter, whose pictorial cycle adorns the walls. Hand-held mirrors are provided to help view the ceiling paintings; even so, most visitors will find they suffer vertigo and sensory overload.

Tintoretto won the competition to decorate the interior, clinched by his cunning submission of a perfectly completed panel rather than the requested cartoon. The painter's overpowering Biblical scenes, executed between 1564 and 1587, provoke strong responses. Henry James found "the air thick with genius" yet palpably human: "It is not immortality that we breathe at San Rocco but conscious, reluctant mortality."

New Testament scenes are displayed in the **Sala Inferiore**, the Ground Floor Hall, including *The Annunciation*, a dramatic chiaroscuro composition. Such works show the painter's profound Biblical knowledge and skilful manipulation of mannerist iconography. Yet, according to art historian Bernard Berenson, "the poetry which quickens most of his works is almost entirely a matter of light and colour".

A gilded staircase leads to the **Sala Grande**, the Great Upper Hall, and the **Sala dell'Albergo**, the smaller assembly room. This upper floor is framed by an inlaid marble floor and by surfaces studded with one of the finest painting cycles imaginable. Tintoretto's genius is revealed in these dynamic orchestrations of colour and light, works marked by drama and strong composition.

Even the artist's faults, from a gaudy palette to the strenuous posturing of his figures, are a product of his visionary imagination, restless style and volatile changes of mood. The Sala Grande uses telling Biblical scenes to accentuate the confraternity's mission to heal. Stagily set on easels by the altar are Tiepolo's *Abraham and the Angels* and Titian's poetic *Annunciation*, matched by his *Christ Carrying the Cross*, previously attributed to Giorgione.

The Sala dell'Albergo contains allegories linked to the society's patron saint, including *St Roch in Glory*, the ceiling panel that won Tintoretto the entire commission. Facing it is *The Crucifixion*, both a vast masterpiece with a charged atmosphere and a poignant drama. Henry James contrasted the "portentous solemnity" of the paintings with "the bright light of the *campo*, the orange-vendors and gondolas". The orange-vendors have gone, but there are enough bars nearby to restore one's spirits.

The church of **San Rocco** (daily 9.30am–5.30pm), tucked into the tiny

The Frari, mother church of the Venetian Franciscans.

campo of the same name, is something of an anticlimax. The gloomy interior is lined with works by Tintoretto and Pordenone, another major mannerist artist. From here, follow Calle della Scuola across the next canal south to **Campo San Pantalon**.

San Pantalon ㉒

Address: Campo San Pantalon
Tel: 041-523 5893
Opening Hrs: Mon–Sat 10am–noon and 3–6pm
Entrance Fee: free
Transport: San Tomà

Set on a canalside *campo*, the church of **San Pantalon** (or Pantaleone) is dedicated to an obscure saint, who was both Emperor Diocletian's doctor and a miraculous healer. The church follows a common Venetian practice, whereby the interiors, with the exception of St Mark's or Palladian gems, are finer than the exteriors. The bare, unfinished 17th-century facade gives no indication of the splendours within. This is one of the most theatrical interiors in Venice, a tour de force of perspective which projects the nave high into the sky.

The ornate ceiling of the Scuola's Sala Grande.

The baroque ceiling paintings by Fumiani (1650–1710) depict *The Martyrdom and Glory of St Pantalon*. Unlike in San Rocco, there is no need for mirrors, since this majestic work was intended to be viewed from one single perspective, close to the entrance. This may be the largest painting on canvas ever completed, created on 60 panels and hoisted into place. The illusionistic ascent into heaven is populated by boldly foreshortened figures clambering, floating or ascending. On completion of the ceiling, the artist supposedly stood back to admire his work before slipping off the scaffolding to his death.

Veronese's last work, *The Miracle of St Pantalon*, is tucked away in a side chapel on the right, while one on the left houses several Byzantine-style paintings, including a delightful Paolo Veneziano *Madonna and Child* (1333).

Casa Goldoni ㉓

Address: Calle Nomboli, San Polo, http://carlogoldoni.visitmuve.it
Tel: 041-275 9325
Opening Hrs: daily Apr–Oct 10am–5pm, Nov–Mar 10am–4pm

Entrance Fee: charge
Transport: San Tomà

In this charming Gothic house was born Carlo Goldoni, the 18th-century Venetian dramatist, the city's finest. Even if you are indifferent to the playwright, glance at the attractive courtyard with its carved well-head and Gothic staircase. Upstairs, the 15th-century house contains all sorts of material and memorabilia linked to the playwright.

Campo San Polo ㉒

Campo San Polo, lying just across the canal of the same name, is the heart of a picturesque district. After San Marco, it is the largest Venetian square and lies at the heart of the San Polo quarter. Historically, this amphitheatre of a square was the scene of bull-baiting, tournaments and processions, even a great "bonfire of the vanities" in 1450. Today it is a popular venue for film screenings or carnival balls and, like Campo Santa Margherita, remains a classic Venetian space. At different times of day, the appealing square becomes a crèche, an impromptu football pitch or a place for a picnic lunch. At night, students converge on the square's historic *birreria*.

The lofty, rusticated **Palazzo Corner Mocenigo** is now the headquarters of the Guardia di Finanza, the financial police. However, in the past it was noted for having two doors so that the dead and the living would never pass through the same one. The Gothic **Palazzo Soranzo** (No. 2169–70), at the eastern end of the *campo*, was where Casanova's main patron lived. Here the humble violinist and future libertine was adopted by an ailing senator.

In the south-west corner the church of **San Polo** (Mon–Sat 10am–5pm) is hemmed in by houses. Essentially Gothic, the church features a rose window and ship's-keel ceiling, a frame for Tintoretto's *Assumption and Last Supper* and Tiepolo's *Apparition of the Virgin*.

An early 17th-century plaque outside the church forbids games, shopping and swearing "on pain of prison, the galleys or exile", but Venetians, then as now, paid little heed to such limitations on their pleasures.

DRINK

Linger for a drink in the friendly San Polo neighbourhood. Calle della Madonetta is a pleasant alley that runs over bridges and under buildings towards the Rialto. This is one of several adjoining streets with overhanging roofs, a rarity in Venice.

Campo San Polo is the largest square after San Marco.

Atmospheric passageway leading to La Maddalena church.

CANNAREGIO

This faded, northerly district, once the most fashionable in Venice, is a moody backwater and the site of one of the world's first Jewish ghettos.

Théophile Gautier, the sensitive French poet, wrote: "From alley to alley we had got deep into Cannaregio, into a Venice quite different from the pretty city of watercolours." Far from wanting to escape from this run-down quarter, he lapped up the deserted squares, desolate wharves and green, sluggish canals. Cannaregio is a district for those who have tired of the monumental sights around San Marco. Walks in the melancholic backwaters at the edge of the city trace a landscape of peeling facades and humble workshops, broad canals and wind-buffeted quays; the sense of abandonment creates a poetic atmosphere conducive to wistfulness.

Cannaregio is the most densely populated district and the closest both to the railway station and to the mainland. Before the advent of the causeway, the Canale di Cannaregio was the city's main entry point.

Former hotspot

This was once one of the city's most fashionable spots, dotted with foreign embassies and palatial gardens sloping down to the lagoon. Today, the palaces are faded and Cannaregio is one of the last bastions for working-class Venetians. In recent years, it

has become more cosmopolitan, with an influx of westernised Hassidic Jews, Middle Eastern immigrants, and a cluster of independent stores and chic boutique hotels.

The most northerly *sestiere*, it is bounded by the railway station, the northern quays and the Grand Canal. Within this arc are subtly diverse districts, from the Jewish quarter that gave the world the word *ghetto* to the quaint, remote quarter around Madonna dell'Orto. By contrast, the Grand Canal district contains palaces

Main Attractions
Madonna dell'Orto
Gesuiti Church
Oratorio dei Crociferi
Santa Maria dei Miracoli
San Giovanni Crisostomo
Ghetto
Museo Ebraico and the
  Synagogues
Palazzo Labia

Map
Page 190

Nuns heading to market.

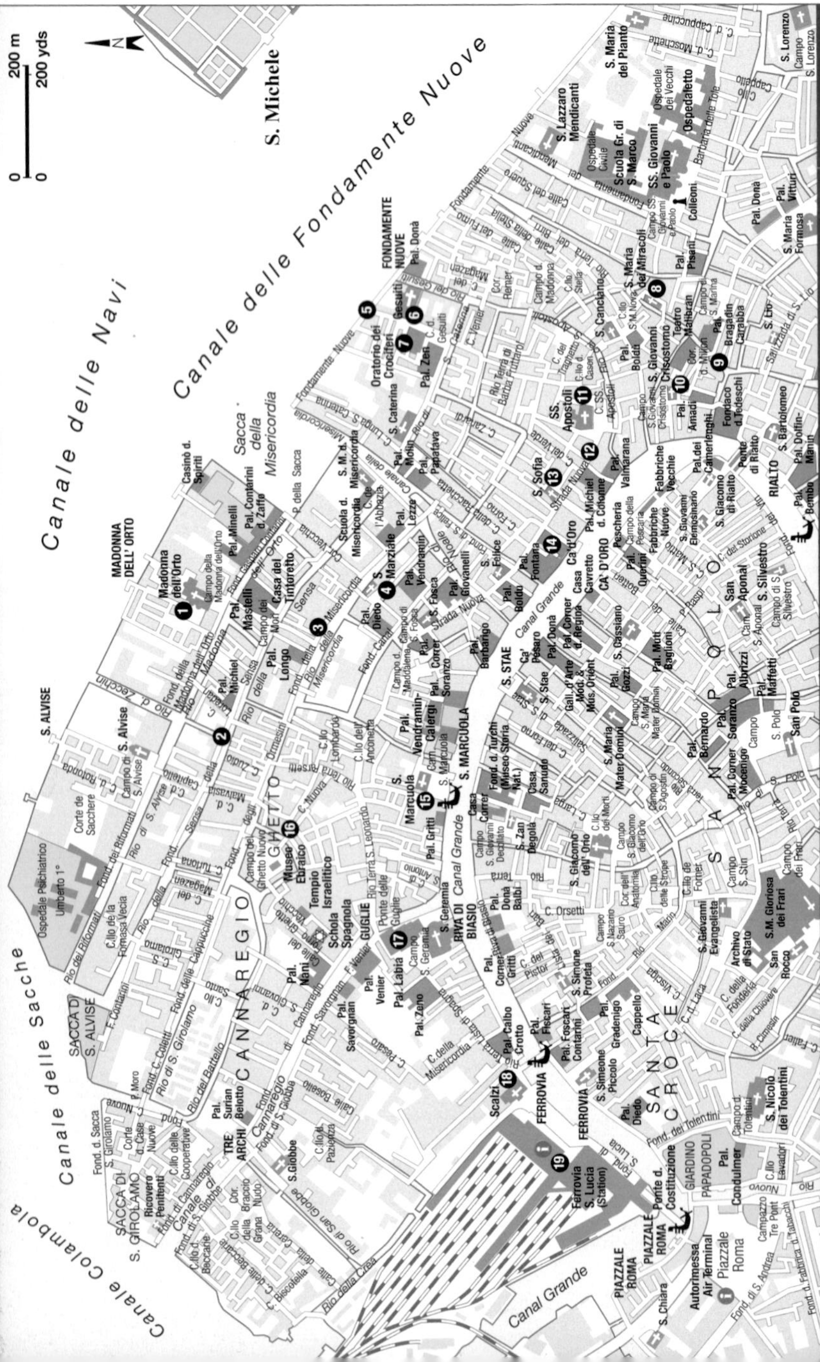

200 m
200 yds

N

S. Michele

Canale delle Navi

Canale delle Fondamente Nuove

FONDAMENTE NUOVE

Canale delle Sacche

Canale Colombola

Canal Grande

Sacca della Misericordia

MADONNA DELL'ORTO

S. ALVISE

GHETTO

CANNAREGIO

SACCA DI S. GIROLAMO

TRE ARCHI

PIAZZALE ROMA

FERROVIA

FERROVIA S. Lucia (Station)

SANTA CROCE

SAN POLO

RIALTO

Ospedale Civile

- 1 MADONNA DELL'ORTO
- 2 S. ALVISE
- 3 Casa del Tintoretto
- 4 S. Maria dell'Orto / S. Marziale
- 5 Oratorio dei Crociferi
- 6 Gesuiti
- 7 Pal. Zen
- 8 S. Maria dei Miracoli
- 9 Teatro Malibran
- 10 S. Giovanni Crisostomo
- 11 SS. Apostoli
- 12 Ca' d'Oro
- 13 S. Sofia
- 14 Ca' d'Oro
- 15 S. Marcuola
- 16 Museo Ebraico
- 17 Pal. Labia
- 18 Scalzi
- 19 Ferrovia

S. Lazzaro dei Mendicanti

Scuola Gr. di S. Marco

SS. Giovanni e Paolo

S. Maria del Pianto

S. Lorenzo

S. Maria Formosa

Pal. Grimani

S. Canciano

SS. Apostoli

S. Giacomo di Rialto

Ponte di Rialto

Fondaco dei Tedeschi

Pal. Bembo

SAN MARCO

Archivio di Stato

S.M. Gloriosa dei Frari

S. Rocco

S. Giovanni Evangelista

S. Nicolò dei Tolentini

GIARDINO PAPADOPOLI

Pal. Condulmer

Ponte della Costituzione

Piazzale Roma

Autorimessa

Air Terminal

S. Geremia

S. Simeone Piccolo

S. Simeone Profeta

S. Giobbe

Pal. Savorgnan

Pal. Manfrin

Pal. Venier

Schola Spagnola

Tempio Israelitico

Pal. Labia

GUGLIE

RIVA DI BIASIO

S. Marcuola

Pal. Vendramin Calergi

Casino d. Spiriti

Pal. Minelli

Pal. Contarini d. Zaffo

Scuola d. Misericordia

S. Marziale

S. Fosca

Cà Zen

Pal. Priuli

S. Felice

S. Stae

S. Maria Maddalena

Pal. Mocenigo

Pal. Corner della Regina

Pescheria

Fabbriche Nuove

Fabbriche Vecchie

as fine as any in Venice. Just inland, Strada Nuova is a bustling shopping district linking the railway station with the Rialto.

Cannaregio has a distinctly neighbourhood feel, with every parish possessing its own church and *campo*. It is alive with activity, with the space for chattering children and dozing cats. Glimpses of everyday life on secluded balconies or through half-shuttered blinds reveal elderly Venetians passing the time of day with their neighbours, or leaning out of windows hung with washing.

The tangle of alleys reveals the occasional *bottega* selling wood carvings, as well as earthy, hole-in-the-wall bars, *alimentari* (general food shops) and the odd place selling *vino sfuso* (draught wine). Far removed from San Marco, a Sunday in Cannaregio is still spent streaming from church to a trattoria for lunch.

The northern quays

Cannaregio has a cluster of different neighbourhoods rather than an obvious heart. The northernmost strip, centred on the church of Madonna dell'Orto, is one of the most curious quarters. (Despite its sense of remoteness, the district is easily reached by vaporetto 42 or 52 from the railway station.) Here parallel *fondamente* (quaysides) frame wide *rii* (canals) and are criss-crossed by smaller canals.

The three major *rii* were created from the Cannaregio marshes in medieval times, with Rio della Sensa arguably the most atmospheric. These faintly mournful waterways are flanked by houses and neglected palaces somewhat reminiscent of Amsterdam. In the 1890s, the de Goncourt brothers were moved to describe these quays as "a whole district in decay, like an antique sculpture eaten away by rain and sun".

Madonna dell'Orto ❶

Address: Campo della Madonna dell'Orto, www.madonnadellorto.org
Opening Hrs: Mon–Sat 10am–5pm, Sun noon–5pm
Entrance Fee: charge
Madonna dell'Orto

Set on a harmonious square of herringbone design, this church is named after a miracle-working

Canal life in Cannaregio.

TIP

If your time in Venice has awakened an unknown artistic bent, look into the printing, sculpture and design courses held by Roberto Mazzetto and his crew at the Bottega Tintoretto (Fondamenta dei Mori, tel: 9401 578 0276, www.tintorettovenezia.it), next door to where the grand master once lived.

statue of the Madonna found in a nearby vegetable garden (*orto*). The three-part composition of the facade, enlivened by a frieze of garlands, is reminiscent of the Frari, albeit on a smaller scale. The quirky campanile is topped by an onion-shaped cupola; this is the first belltower to greet visitors as they speed across the lagoon from the airport. Often bathed in a warm light, the church is a masterpiece of Venetian Gothic. The austere, brick-faced interior, graced by Greek marble columns and a fine wooden ceiling, was well restored by the British Venice in Peril fund after the 1966 floods.

The church also makes a good starting point for exploring Tintoretto's temperamental genius: the painter lived nearby and this, his parish church, is decorated with works he created *in situ*. His tender *Presentation of the Virgin* (1551) graces the Mauro Chapel, as does the over-restored statue of the "miraculous" Madonna. Two other Tintoretto works dominate the chancel.

The aesthete John Ruskin raved about *The Last Judgement*, seeing "the river of the wrath of God, roaring

Madonna dell'Orto.

down into the gulf where the world has melted"; his new bride ran out of the church, traumatised by "a death's head crowned with leaves". A memorial bust of the artist watches over his grave in a side chapel. Tintoretto aside, the church is a treasury of Venetian painting from the 15th to 17th centuries. The bridge in front of the church leads into Campo dei Mori, around the corner from which is Tintoretto's house, marked by a plaque and bas-relief of the painter.

Quayside atmosphere

For a fine view, follow **Fondamenta della Sensa ②** to **Corte Vecchia** and **Ponte della Sacca**. This bridge looks out over the northern lagoon and San Michele, island of the dead (see page 237). At twilight, especially when the boundary lights of the waterways are lit, this is the place for poignant thoughts. Another atmospheric spot is **Campo de l'Abbazia** at the end of **Rio della Sensa**. Here, the sculpted facade of the former confraternity of

TALES OF THE MOORS

The glowering mansion of Palazzo Mastelli, overlooking Rio della Madonna dell'Orto and Campo dei Mori, is a source of mystery and legend. To the right of the filigree balcony is an eastern-looking relief of a laden camel. One story suggests the owners of the camel and the house that stood here before this 15th-century *palazzo*, the Mastelli clan, were 12th-century merchants from the Morea, in Venetian-occupied Greece. Perhaps that was Eastern enough to make them seem like Moors (Mori) to Venetians, but other sources claim they were not Greeks at all, but Arabs.

Either way, the Mastelli were said to be ruthless, making their fortune on the misery of their neighbours. One tale says they overdid their avarice one day and were turned to stone – these are the turbaned figures embedded into the wall on Campo dei Mori. The one with the broken nose is known as Sior Rioba (Mr Rioba). His brothers were Afani and Sandi. The story goes that Rioba was cheating a woman out of a considerable sum in exchange for worthless cloth and used his favourite phrase: 'may my hand turn to stone if what I see isn't true'. Turns out the woman was St Madeleine, and all three brothers turned to stone.

The Campo dei Mori is named after the turbaned Moors that decorate the facade of the Palazzo Mastelli, near Tintoretto's house.

the **Scuola della Misericordia** overlooks a quaint well-head and a tiled, herringbone-style square.

The quaysides can feel rather exposed, but, if the weather is bleak, retreat to one of the bars and inns on **Fondamenta della Misericordia ❸** and **Fondamenta degli Ormesini**, the next quaysides south of Fondamenta della Sensa. This bustling section of quays overlooks **Rio della Misericordia**, with the middle section in particular lined by inns, bars and neighbourhood shops.

Fondamenta della Misericordia is bordered by austere former convents and the baroque church of **San Marziale ❹** (Mon–Sat 4–6.30pm, Sun 8.30–10am), with its boldly ornamented interior.

From here, head south to bustling **Strada Nuova** if the solitude of the quaysides has seeped into your bones, or stroll to **Fondamente Nuove ❺**, the quays bordering the northern lagoon, to see a baroque church, or set off for the islands. The windswept Fondamente Nuove, or New Quays, were created in the 1580s. Before then, this desolate stretch was a desirable residential district, with summer palaces and well-tended gardens lapped by the lagoon waters. These quays offer the fastest ferry times to the islands, as well as services to San Marco. On a clear day, the snowy Dolomite peaks are visible from here.

Gesuiti Church ❻

Address: Salizzada dei Specchieri
Tel: 041-528 6579
Opening Hrs: Mon–Fri 10am–noon, 4–6pm
Entrance Fee: free
Transport: Fondamente Nuove

The Jesuits were never very popular in Venice, a city that put patriotism before the papacy and declared: "Venetians first and Christians second". After their 50-year banishment was revoked, the Jesuits returned to Venice in 1657, and, in 1715, rebuilt this church. Set into a line of severe houses, the baroque, angel-bedecked

For glimpses of everyday life, lose yourself in the neighbourhood backstreets.

Campo Santa Maria Nova.

facade reveals a stage-set of an interior. The design is typical of a Roman Jesuit church, with a broad nave flanked by deep chapels and surmounted by a central dome. Gaudy stuccoes and frescoes set the tone for an interior decorator's delight, from the vaulted and domed ceiling to the lavish altars, including one encrusted with lapis lazuli.

The impression is of a wedding cake swathed in green-and-white damask, even if it is marble masquerading as drapery. The whimsical Théophile Gautier felt that the decor made "the Chapel of the Holy Virgin look like a chorus girl's boudoir". The highlights are Titian's stormy *Martyrdom of St Lawrence* and Tintoretto's joyous *Assumption of the Virgin*, the painting that most inspired Tiepolo. The flashes of lightning, the darting angels and the sheer creative passion had a lasting effect on the great rococo artist.

Oratorio dei Crociferi ❼

Address: Campo dei Gesuiti
Tel: 041-532 2920

Opening Hrs: Apr–Oct Fri 10am–12.30pm, Sat 3.30–7.30pm
Entrance Fee: charge
Transport: Fondamente Nuove

A few steps away from the Gesuiti, the **Oratorio dei Crociferi** is dedicated to the crusading mendicant Order of Crutched Friars, although it later passed into Jesuit control. It was once part of a medieval hospice, which housed pilgrims and the ill. The interior has a subtle pictorial cycle by Palma il Giovane (1548–1628) depicting, among other things, episodes in the history of the mendicant order and the hospice. Outside, Campo dei Gesuiti is dotted with houses associated with the guilds; on the walls are symbols or inscriptions referring to coopers, tailors and weavers.

Nearby is Palazzo Zen, a 16th-century palace with an eastern influence. If you do not wish to visit the islands, leave the quaysides of the Fondamente Nuove and head south.

From Campo dei Gesuiti, cross Rio di Santa Caterina and head south through a network of alleys, following signs for the Rialto. Well before the Rialto Bridge, take Calle Malvasia across the canal of Rio dei Santi Apostoli to **San Canciano** (8am–noon, 5.30–7.30pm), an ancient church decorated in bold baroque style.

Santa Maria dei Miracoli ❽

Address: Campo dei Miracoli, www.chorusvenezia.org
Opening Hrs: Mon–Sat 10am–5pm
Entrance Fee: charge
Transport: Fondamente Nuove

The lovely church of **Santa Maria dei Miracoli** seems to rise sheer from the water at the meeting point of several narrow canals, marooned like a marble siren awaiting the call of the sea. No wonder the church is a favourite with Venetian brides. Perfect proportions and seductive charm make this a Renaissance miracle in miniature, gleaming with a soft marble sheen.

The residential backstreets are full of delightful architectural details.

Its romantic setting invites such clichés as "Renaissance jewel-box", an image for once justified. The church is often compared with Ca' Dario, a palace also created by the Lombardi family of master-builders.

Certainly, this dazzling display of pastel marble is a far cry from the prosaic Venetian brick facade. Even Ruskin, no fan of the Renaissance, was forced to admit the Miracoli to be "the best possible example of a bad style". The interior has a *barco*, a nuns' choir gallery, and a barrel-vaulted and coffered ceiling, with the presbytery surmounted by a starry dome. The surfaces present a vision of pale pinks and silvery greys, and pilasters adorned with interlaced flowers, mythical creatures and cavorting mermaids.

Just south, sandwiched between the canals of **Rio Giovanni Crisostomo** and **Rio dei Tedeschi**, lie Marco Polo's former home and a historic church. **Corte del Milion ❾** is a quaint courtyard where the great explorer reputedly lived. While Marco Polo's house burnt down in 1596, the well-head remains, as does a courtyard and arch decorated by Veneto-Byzantine friezes.

San Giovanni Crisostomo ❿

Address: Salizzada San Giovanni Crisostomo
Tel: 041-523 5293
Opening Hrs: Mon – Sat 10am – 6.30pm, Sun 11.30am – 6.30pm
Entrance Fee: free
Transport: Rialto

Near the Corte del Milion stands the church of **San Giovanni Crisostomo**. Although founded in the 11th century, this restrained terracotta-coloured church owes more to the Renaissance. As the last work of Coducci, it boasts a tripartite facade reminiscent of San Zaccaria. The dome, supported by pillars and arches, is a model of classical coherence. The restrained marble interior contains a delightful altarpiece by Bellini (1515), possibly his last work.

Shopping district

Cannaregio's main shopping district begins at **Campo Santi Apostoli ⓫**, across the canal of the same name.

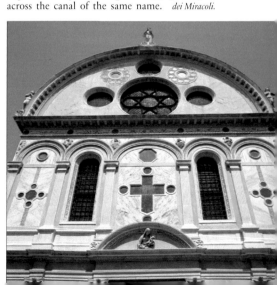

The gleaming marble facade of Santa Maria dei Miracoli.

The Jewish Ghetto

The attitude of Venetians towards the Jews was ambivalent, wavering between tolerance and persecution, protection and expulsion.

Shakespeare gave Jews a bad press in *The Merchant of Venice*, but they were already stigmatised. Jews were first mentioned in Venetian records in the 10th century, as passengers forbidden from travelling on Venetian ships. As an ambitious trading city, Venice feared competition from astute Levantine merchants.

Jews who practised as doctors or traders were tolerated, but pawnbrokers and moneylenders were resented. Jewish "banks for the poor" opened in 1366, and persecution reached its height in the 15th century, when the collapse of private banking institutions forced Venetians to use moneylenders – usuary was forbidden to Christians. Jews were forced to wear a distinguishing badge, yellow skullcap or red hat, while attempts to restrict Jews to the mainland resulted in the decree of 1423 forbidding Jewish property ownership.

In 1516, the fast expanding Jewish community was given its own closed living quarters. Ringed by canals, like a moated prison, this segregated, unhealthy area was within sight of the former foundry or *ghetto*, which came to mean a closed Jewish quarter. By day, many Jews worked outside the Ghetto, but night curfews prevailed. The locked gates were manned by Christian guards, whom the Jews were forced to pay. Ceilings were lowered in order to cram in seven floors.

The Venetian ambivalence to Jews was mirrored in the Ghetto itself. Jews often favoured splendid clothes and jewellery, the sole way of displaying status. While the synagogues were outwardly modest, the interiors were sumptuous, but real power was limited. Jews obeyed their contract with the Venetian state, collected taxes, settled legal problems and dealt with new immigrants. Even so, they had free schooling and a printing press in an age when few Christians were literate. Christians often patronised the Ghetto, visiting respected doctors or the banks.

While Venice's greatness declined during the 16th and 17th centuries, the Jewish community prospered on trade with Levantine Jews. Only in 1796 did the Napoleonic invasion cause the Ghetto gates to be flung open. Jews became full citizens in 1866, but found no peace in the 20th century: a bronze relief in the Ghetto Nuovo recalls the deportations and death of 200 Venetian Jews in World War II.

Grim though the Ghetto was, Venice was one of the few states to tolerate the Jews. The city was a liberal enclave compared with the brutality of 15th-century Spain, where pogroms in Jewish ghettos (the idea, if not the word, existed long before the creation of Venice's Ghetto) were common. The Ghetto remains at the heart of Jewish life, with fine synagogues and a cultural centre, a nursery, an old people's home, workshops and a kosher bakery and restaurant.

For more information contact: www.jewish venice.org or www.ghetto.it.

Ogival arches are typical of the architecture in the Ghetto.

The belltower of Santi Apostoli.

The sombre air of the church of **Santi Apostoli** (Mon–Sat 7.30–11.30am, 5–7pm) is offset by the liveliness of the surrounding square. The 16th-century church is built on ancient foundations but is undistinguished, apart from a prominent belltower and Tiepolo's *Communion of St Lucy*, set in the domed Renaissance Cappella Corner, a chapel designed for the family of the Caterina Corner (Cornaro), Queen of Cyprus (see page 140).

Campo Santi Apostoli marks the beginning of the **Strada Nuova ⑫**, which forms the main thoroughfare to the station, undergoing several name changes en route. Created under Austrian rule in the 1860s, the street represents an early piece of modern town-planning in Venice. Strada Nuova was carved through an ancient quarter, causing Campo Santa Sofia to be severed from its church. Running roughly parallel to the Grand Canal, the broad street offers tempting *bacari* and food shops

displaying juicy hams and home-made pasta. Side streets close to the Campo Santi Apostoli end of Strada Nuova conceal inviting inns such as Alla Vedova.

Despite the demolition of houses to make way for the Strada Nuova, the church of **Santa Sofia ⑬** survives, with its ungainly belltower seamlessly merging into the streetscape.

Campo Santa Sofia, with its Veneto-Byzantine palace and two pavement cafés, provides a sunny spot for a rest. The next left turn leads to the **Ca' d'Oro ⑭**, one of the finest palaces on the Grand Canal (see page 139). With several name changes, Strada Nuova continues westwards towards the station; at Campiello dell'Anconetta, either turn left to visit the Grand Canal or right to explore the Ghetto.

Turning left leads to the church of **San Marcuola ⑮** (Mon–Sat 9.30–11.30am), a Grand Canal landmark. The unfinished brick facade is a feature of many Venetian churches, as is the 18th-century remodelling of a medieval foundation, and even the presence of a fine Tintoretto work, *The Last Supper*.

EAT

Set at the entrance to the Ghetto, Gam Gam (Sottoportego del Ghetto Vecchio; tel: 366-250 4505, closed Fri and Sat) is the only kosher restaurant in Venice, and specialises in Italian-Jewish and Ashkenazi dishes.

Holocaust Memorial, Ghetto Nuovo.

Nearby is the San Marcuola stop and **Palazzo Vendramin-Calergi**, reborn as the Casino, and best visited in the evening (see page 142).

THE GHETTO ⓰

For now, turn your back on the waterfront and take Calle Farnese to Campo del Ghetto Nuovo, and the **Ghetto**. Nothing about the neglected facades of these drab tenements suggests that until the 17th century this was one of the major Jewish communities in Europe. The population density was three times greater than in the most crowded Christian suburbs. The Ghetto Nuovo, a fortified island, was turned into an enforced Jewish quarter in 1516. Its name (actually *getto nuovo*, but pronounced with the hard 'gh' by the Jews who were moved here) simply meant 'new foundry'. Later, the Ghetto was extended to include the Ghetto Vecchio (old foundry) in 1541 and Ghetto Nuovissimo in 1633. These concessions only provided temporary relief from the chronic overcrowding. **Campo del Ghetto Nuovo** (New Ghetto Square), a fortified island created in 1516, contains evocative

Campo del Ghetto Nuovo.

testaments to the deportation of Jews to the death camps, in the form of memorial plaques on several of the buildings around the irregularly shaped square.

Three of Venice's five remaining synagogues are set around the square, as unobtrusive as the Ghetto itself. Although hidden behind nondescript facades, the synagogues reveal lavish interiors, often with a Levantine feel. Gilt and stucco are used rather than marble, a material forbidden to Jews by the Venetians.

The synagogues, known as *schole*, were Jewish counterparts to the Venetian *scuole* (see page 182). The synagogues followed different rites and acted as community centres as well as places of worship.

Museo Ebraico and the Synagogues

Address: Campo del Ghetto Nuovo, www.museoebraico.it
Tel: 041-715 359
Opening Hrs: Sun–Fri June–Sept 10am–7pm, Oct–May 10am–5.30pm (closed Sat and Jewish holidays)
Entrance Fee: charge
Transport: Guglie

To visit the synagogues, head for the **Museo Ebraico** (Museum of Jewish History) which is interesting in itself but overshadowed by the guided tours of the synagogues that leave from here (the only way to see inside them).

The **Schola Grande Tedesca**, the German Synagogue, was built in 1528 and sits at the top of the building housing the museum, while its neighbour, the **Schola Canton**, possibly intended for Jews from Provence and also on the top floor, dates from 1532. Adjoining it is the **Schola Italiana**, founded for Italians in 1575. The hinges of the former Ghetto gates can be seen on **Sottoportego Ghetto Nuovo**, evoking a drawbridge leading to a mysterious world. Beyond the spacious square and bridge lies the **Ghetto Vecchio** (Old Ghetto), an overspill ghetto created

The baroque church of Scalzi.

in 1541, with two more synagogues. The **Schola Spagnola**, designed for Spanish and Portuguese Jews, was built in 1538 but gained a Baroque facade by Longhena. The hall is graced with a *matroneum*, or women's gallery, reminiscent of the grand circles of Venetian theatres.

The nearby **Schola Levantina**, linked to Sephardic Jews from the Middle East, dates from the 1530s and is a variant on the Schola Spagnola since it, too, was remodelled by Longhena. Inside, the highlight is the *tevà* or wooden canopied altar. As a rule, the guided tour will take in only one of these two, as only one is open at any given time. The lane from here to the Canale di Cannaregio takes you past a kosher bakery and **Gam Gam**, the kosher restaurant by the Ghetto Vecchio.

Palazzo Labia and the railway station

From the Ghetto, head for the station via **Ponte delle Guglie**, the charming bridge over the **Canale di Cannaregio**, an area lined with waterside stalls. Over the bridge awaits **Palazzo Labia** ⓱, a splendidly restored palace, with the ballroom frescoed by Tiepolo. The former owners, the noble Labia family, were renowned for their extravagance: once, after a riotous banquet, the gold plates were hurled into the canal as the host cried out: "*Le abbia o non le abbia sarò sempre Labia!*" ("Whether I have them or not, I'll always be a Labia!") The occasion for this extravagant pun had been carefully contrived, with precautionary nets placed in the water to catch the precious heirlooms.

From here, follow the masses along **Lista di Spagna**, the tawdry main thoroughfare redeemed by the occasional inn tucked into a tiny courtyard. Just beside the station looms the restored church of the **Scalzi** ⓲, a lavish baroque edifice ironically built for the barefoot *(scalzi)* order of Carmelites. The street bustle reaches fever pitch by **Ferrovia Santa Lucia** ⓳ and Calatrava's new bridge.

EAT

The Jewish bakery halfway along Calle del Ghetto Vecchio not only sells kosher products but some genuinely yummy pastries sought out by residents far and wide, Jewish or otherwise.

Night market along Rio Terà San Leonardo, one of Cannaregio's main arteries.

DORSODURO

The smartest area of Venice, and a haven for expatriates, Dorsoduro takes in the grand church of La Salute, and the Accademia, the city's most illustrious art gallery.

Main Attractions
La Salute
Punta Della Dogana
Zattere
Spazio Vedova
Gesuati
Squero di San Trovaso
San Sebastiano
Palazzo Zenobio
Scuola Grande di Santa
    Maria dei Carmini
Accademia

Map
Page 202

*La Salute dominates
Dorsoduro.*

Dorsoduro simply means "hard back", so called because the district occupies the largest area of firm land in Venice. This is upper-crust Venice, the grandest section defined by the Punta della Dogana, the Gesuati and the Accademia. This most fashionable residential district has long been favoured by foreigners, particularly the American and British communities. Dorsoduro remains a haven for wealthy expatriates, even if the southern flank, essentially on the left bank, contains poorer but picturesque areas towards the west. Yet, historically, Dorsoduro was a mixed district,

with the nobles and nouveaux riches ensconced in splendid Grand Canal palaces, the impoverished nobility living close to Campo San Barnaba, and sailors and fishermen confined to the scenically shabby west. Today, socially and geographically, there is considerable overlap: Campo Santa Margherita, the hub of Dorsoduro, is a cheerful district of shopkeepers, students and arty types.

The closeness of the university quarter, centred on Ca' Foscari, ensures that the bars are full and service is friendly. The parishes of San Trovaso and San Barnaba offer a similar mixture of youthful high

spirits and discreet privilege. In chic Dorsoduro, foreign bohemianism meets Venetian conservatism, resulting in understated good taste spiced with a touch of the cosmopolitan.

Dorsoduro is the most attractive quarter for idle wandering, with wisteria-clad walls, secret gardens and distinctive domestic architecture. Apart from the Accademia gallery, Peggy Guggenheim Collection and Salute church, the district is surprisingly free from visitors. The southern spur of the Zattere makes the most enchanting Venetian promenade, bracing in winter and refreshing in summer. These quaysides offer panoramic views, with the Punta della Dogana, an ex-Customs post now turned into a magnificent contemporary art gallery, at the most easterly point.

La Salute ❶

Address: Campo della Salute, www.marcianum.it/salute
Tel: 041-522 5558
Opening Hrs: daily 9am–noon and 3–5.30pm
Entrance Fee: charge
Transport: Salute

Eastern Dorsoduro is dominated by the baroque basilica of **Santa Maria della Salute**, a Venetian landmark guarding the entrance to the Grand Canal that is more commonly known as, simply, La Salute. Dedicated to Santa Maria della Salute (Our Lady of Good Health), the church was built as a thanksgiving for delivery from the 1630 plague. Longhena, the great baroque architect, wished it to be "strange, worthy and beautiful". Henry James's celebrated conceit springs to mind: "like some great lady on the threshold of her salon. She is more ample and serene… with her domes and scrolls, her scalloped buttresses and statues forming a pompous crown, and her wide steps disposed on the ground like the train of a robe."

However, Longhena's triumphal and grandiose church is also indebted to Palladio's Il Redentore. Although Longhena learnt from his classical forebear's choice of theatrical settings and magnificent use of space, lavish sculptural decoration was his own baroque contribution. Begun in 1631, the church took 50 years to complete.

La Salute marks the end of Venetian mannerism and heralds an era of bold baroque statements. Devised before Rome's Bernini and Borromini masterpieces, it became one of the few Italian churches to challenge the supremacy of Roman baroque. The interior boasts a spectacular central plan, with its revolutionary octagonal space surmounted by a huge dome. The octagonal structure alludes to the symbolic eight-pointed Marian star, while the theatrically raised high altar evokes the Virgin's rescue of Venice. The major works of art include Tintoretto's *Wedding at Cana*, paintings by Titian in the sacristy, and a small Byzantine Madonna, overawed by baroque splendour. While eminently praiseworthy, the interior is rather solemn and cold, clad in Istrian stone. The exterior is more

KIDS

Particularly suitable for children is La Salute *traghetto* (gondola ferry), which makes an enjoyable and inexpensive jaunt across the Grand Canal to Santa Maria del Giglio. It's standing room only, which can be tricky first time round!

Lining up for the traghetto.

WHERE

One of the most delightful walks in Venice stretches from the Accademia to La Salute and then rounding Punta della Dogana to the Zattere quays, which you can pursue west to the international boat station. Depending on the number of pauses, the walk could last the better part of a day, especially if you include art visits to the Accademia, Peggy Guggenheim Collection and Punta della Dogana.

joyous, with the majestic dome dominating the Venetian skyline.

Punta della Dogana ❷

Address: Campo della Salute, www.palazzograssi.it
Tel: 041 2001 057
Opening Hrs: Wed–Mon 10am–7pm
Entrance Fee: charge
Transport: Salute

For centuries, the triangular, prow-like eastern tip of Dorsoduro was occupied by the offices and warehouses of the **Dogana di Mar**, the customs house where ships and cargoes were inspected before being allowed to drop anchor in front of the Doge's Palace. Facing St Mark's Basin, a porticoed corner tower is crowned by a rich composition: bronze Atlases bear a golden globe, with a weathervane featuring the figure of Fortune glinting in the sun.

The complex was taken over by the French tycoon and contemporary art collector, François Pinault, who had his favourite architect, the Japanese Tadao Ando, undertake its restoration and conversion into one of the city's leading bastions of contemporary art in just 14 months – something of a record for slow-moving Venice

The result is **Punta della Dogana**, a lofty, light series of exposed brick exhibition halls and spaces. It works in tandem with Palazzo Grassi (which got the Pinault-Ando treatment in 2005–6; see page 135) as a permanent stage for the best in world contemporary art, filling what had long been something of a hole in Venice outside Biennale time.

More private galleries purveying contemporary art are springing up all the time and it would appear that Venice, whether as a matter of conscious policy or chance, is attempting to create a position for itself in the lucrative art trade. Pinault shocked the French art establishment when he chose Palazzo Grassi over a French site to display parts of his collection, said

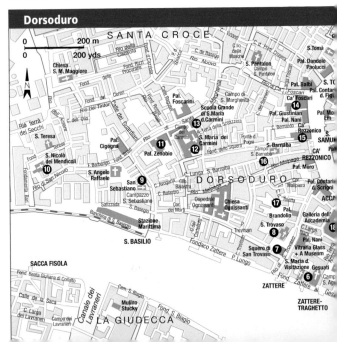

to consist of 12,000 pieces, stored in unknown locations. The commitment to Palazzo Grassi, and now Punta della Dogana, will help dispel the idea that Venice is a stick-in-the-mud in art terms, resting wholly on its laurels.

Combined with modern art collections, especially the Peggy Guggenheim Collection and Ca' Pesaro, Venice now has a formidable platform from which to sell itself as a truly modern art hub.

Zattere ❸

From the south flank of the Punta della Dogana gallery, the **Zattere** stretches all the way round Dorsoduro's southern shore, with its quaysides flanked by cafés, churches and warehouses. This promenade was created in 1516, and named after the cargoes of wood that were unloaded on these quaysides (*zattere* means "rafts"). This is a refreshing *fondamenta*, and the Venetians' favourite walking place; the residents prefer

vivid lagoon views to neat parks, which are usually deserted. At the first sign of spring sunshine, Venetian sun-worshippers flock to the landing stages and decks that line the shore. Summer *passeggiate* are also de rigueur, partly to combat the heat and city claustrophobia, partly to parade the latest fashions and sip drinks in one of several cafés.

Spazio Vedova ❹

Address: Fondamente delle Zattere, www.fondazionevedova.org
Tel: 041-522 6626
Opening Hrs: Tue–Sun 11.30–6.30pm
Entrance Fee: charge
Transport: Zattere

It's been a long time since salt was stored in the **Magazzini del Sale**, enormous warehouses near the Punta della Dogana. The low, regular neoclassical frontage conceals a 15th-century structure. For centuries, salt was a key product in the preservation

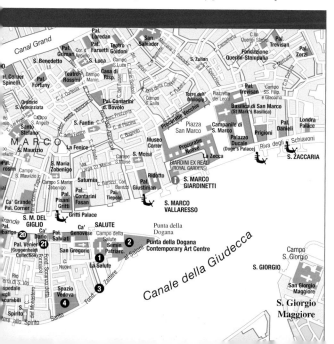

of foodstuffs, but the age of fridges brought an end to the need for salt storage and these warehouses have long been given over to other purposes. Now they are home to a permanently rotating collection of works by Venice's greatest 20th-century artist, Emilio Vedova (1919–2006).

Designed by star architect Renzo Piano, the site has retained its brick walls and timber roof trusses. Inside this historic shell, mechanical arms shuttle Vedova's works in and out of the exhibition space as required. Vedova, who started as an Expressionist, later veered to abstract painting.

Just before Rio delle Torresele lies the **Ospedale degli Incurabili ❺**, an austere former hospice for syphilitics, a medieval building redesigned by Sansovino in the 16th century. Now a children's home, in its time it has been an orphanage, a music conservatoire and a barracks.

Globe and weathervane figure on the customs house.

Gesuati ❻

Address: Fondamenta delle Zattere, www.chorusvenezia.org
Opening Hrs: Mon–Sat 10am–5pm
Entrance Fee: charge
Transport: Zattere

Gesuati church, Zattere.

Further along the Zattere stands the grandiose church of the Gesuati, a supreme example of 18th-century

Venetian architecture, not to be confused with the Gesuiti in Cannaregio. The facade, with its lofty Corinthian columns and Palladian motifs, was designed by Massari, an early rococo architect. The church is often seen as a counterpoint to Palladio's Il Redentore over the water (see page 222).

The Gesuati, dedicated to Santa Maria del Rosario, dates from 1726, and was commissioned by the Dominicans. The theatrical yet graceful interior holds Tiepolo masterpieces (1739) in their original setting. The master of the rococo adorned the vaulted ceiling with a heavenly vision, the air stirred by the beat of angels' wings. The central panel celebrates the *Institution of the Rosary*, showing the Madonna offering the rosary to St Dominic; the side panels illustrate the *Life of St Dominic*. Easier to see, in the first chapel on the right, is Tiepolo's exuberant altarpiece of the Madonna, accompanied by three venerated Dominican saints. Only a Tintoretto *Crucifixion* disturbs the Dominican orthodoxy and rococo mood.

Next door is **Santa Maria della Visitazione** (Tue–Thur 10.15am– noon and 3–5pm. Sat–Sun 10.15am– 1pm and 2–5pm), a Renaissance oratory attributed to the Coducci school. On the facade is a lion's-mouth letterbox for secret denunciations. Access to the oratory, with its 16th-century Umbrian coffered ceiling and cloisters, is through the gateway of a charitable institute.

TO SAN TROVASO

The **Zattere Boarding Stage** lies on this stretch of quays, with ferries to the Giudecca and San Marco. Towards the San Trovaso end of the Zattere are several cafés and pizzerias, with tables on pontoons jutting out over the water. Even if the views are finer than the food, few can complain.

From here, turn down **Rio di San Trovaso** to explore a privileged domestic district dotted with university buildings. Set on the corner of Rio Trovaso and Rio Ognissanti is the **Squero di San Trovaso ❼**, a picturesque gondola repair-yard best viewed from Fondamenta Nani on Rio di San Trovaso. Gondolas are overhauled at one of three *squeri*, the traditional boatyards of which this is the oldest in existence, dating from the 17th century. Naturally, the *squeri* are always set by a canal, with the yard sloping down to the canal. Beside the boatyard is a wooden galleried construction, a geranium-clad outhouse with living quarters above. The resemblance to an alpine chalet is not accidental: many of the early boatbuilders came from the Dolomites.

Nowadays, the main concern is boat maintenance. In summer, the upturned boats are scraped of weeds and retarred, but weeds are less of a problem since the council banned phosphate-rich detergents.

A shortage of skilled craftsmen and the labour-intensive nature of the work means that there is a waiting list for new gondolas: only a

THE TIEPOLO TRAIL

Dorsoduro is dotted with shrines to the greatest rococo artist, Giambattista Tiepolo (1692–1770). His credo was that "the mind of the painter should always aspire to the sublime, the heroic and perfection". This master of scenic illusion produced a riot of picturesque detail to seduce the most casual observer. Ca' Rezzonico is his chief canvas (see page 133). On the Zattere nearby, the Gesuati church has illusionistic frescoes and a joyous altarpiece (see page 204). From here, a stroll leads to the Scuola Grande dei Carmini and Tiepolo's sensuous *Madonna of the Scapular* (see page 208). His frescoes for the Scalzi church near the railway station can be admired in the Accademia too (see page 212).

Beyond Dorsoduro are other Tiepolo sites. San Rocco in the San Polo district shows Tiepolo in a softer light, as a painter of subtle portraits and altarpieces, notably *Abraham Praying before the Three Angels* (see page 184). Also worth discovery is his *Martyrdom of St Bartholomew*, in the San Stae church. In Cannaregio, the frescoes commissioned from him for Palazzo Labia are said to be his finest secular work. Other churches where you can admire his work include Sant'Alvise, in northern Cannaregio, San Zaccaria and La Pietà in Castello.

Tiepolo's Allegoria del Merito, in Ca' Rezzonico.

style. Curiously, there are two matching facades, one facing the canal, the other facing a raised stone *campo*. Tradition has it that two entrances were required to keep the warring clans of the Castellani and Nicoletti apart. The square and well-head conceal a rainwater cistern.

San Sebastiano ❼

Address: Campo San Sebastiano, www.chorusvenezia.org
Opening Hrs: Mon–Sat 10am–5pm
Entrance Fee: charge
Transport: San Basilio

Heading further west along the Zattere, you reach **San Sebastiano**, an early 16th-century church and classical canvas for Veronese's opulent masterpieces, painted between 1555 and 1565. The church is often praised as a perfect marriage of the arts, with architecture, painting and sculpture in complete accord. Veronese's works are enhanced by lavishly carved ceilings and a galleried choir which adds to the sense of spaciousness. This resplendent cycle of paintings shows Veronese in all his glory, exalting grace, harmony and serenity while indulging in occasional whimsy. Veronese's *trompe l'œil* interior is an architectural flight of fancy created by frescoed loggias, columns and statues. Blocks of pure colour adorn every surface, from the nave ceiling to the organ panels.

Although the paintings in the choir illustrating the martyrdom of St Sebastian look distinctly dark, the restored **Sacristy** reveals a vivid ceiling dedicated to the Virgin and the Evangelists.

TO SAN NICOLÒ DEI MENDICOLI

Behind Veronese's parish church lies a traditional working-class district once populated by fishermen, now home to port officials. On the next square west is the creamy-coloured **Angelo Raffaele** (Mon–Sat

handful are made each year, mostly destined for millionaires' pleasure lakes. Today, this asymmetric half-ton craft costs up to $80,000 to make.

Further along **Fondamenta Nani** lies a cluster of university buildings, including the sculpted Palazzo Nani Mocenigo. The scenic Rio di San Trovaso links the Grand Canal and the Giudecca Canal, with the Cantinone Già Schiavi (aka Al Bottegon), an old-fashioned wine bar, beside Ponte di San Trovaso.

Towards the Grand Canal end of the *rio* are several wisteria-clad palaces and a small bridge leading across the canal to the church of **San Trovaso** ❽ (Mon–Sat 8–11am and 3–6pm). Originally medieval, the church was remodelled in Palladian

The Dorsoduro gives you a taste of domestic Venice.

ancient foundations on the eponymous square.

The adjoining canal leads to the most remote waterside church in western Dorsoduro, **San Nicolò dei Mendicoli ⑩** (Mon–Sat 10am–noon, 4–6pm, Sun 4–6pm). Set in a dilapidated district, this former fishermen's and artisans' church is surprisingly sumptuous. San Nicolò presents a squat Romanesque belltower and a bare brick facade lit by mullioned windows and a rare Gothic portico graces the west facade.

The church, which was founded in the 7th century and then remodelled between the 12th and 14th centuries, is one of the oldest in Venice. It was sensitively restored by Venice in Peril in the 1970s. The endearing interior is one of the best-loved in the city, with a single nave ending in a Romanesque apse. Distinctive aspects include the Byzantine cornices and a nave graced by Romanesque columns, Gothic capitals and beamed ceilings. The interior is embellished with Renaissance panelling, gilded statues and school of Veronese paintings.

10am–noon and 3–5.30pm, Sun 9am–noon), a restored 17th-century church which stands on

Gondola yard on Rio San Trovaso.

Palazzo Zenobio ⓫

Address: Fondamente del Soccorso, www.palazzo-zenobio.com
Tel: 041-522 8770
Opening Hrs: limited
Entrance Fee: charge
Transport: San Basilio

From here, Rio di San Nicolò winds back to civilisation. Following the eastern bank of the canal, which changes its name to Rio Santa Margherita, brings you to the quayside of Fondamenta Briati. Overlooking the *rio* on the other side is **Palazzo Zenobio**, a rare example of Roman baroque in Venice. Although originally Gothic, the palace was remodelled in the 17th century and given a long, monotonous facade, softened by Italianate gardens at the back.

The grand interior leads from a *portego* (ceremonial hall) to the sumptuous, frescoed ballroom upstairs, adorned by a minstrels' gallery, gold-and-white stuccowork and *trompe l'œil* effects. The mirrors, chandeliers and door handles are all 17th-century. The palace has been an Armenian college since 1850, but the ballroom can be visited on request. Now that students' rooms have been opened to other guests, you may be able to get a good look at the *palazzo* if you decide to sleep here. The other way to get in without booking a tour is when exhibitions are held here.

Santa Maria dei Carmini ⓬

Address: Campo dei Carmini
Tel: 041-296 0630
Opening Hrs: 12.30–7pm
Entrance Fee: free
Transport: Ca' Rezzonico

A block away from Palazzo Zenobio is the church of Santa Maria dei Carmini. The baroque belltower is surmounted by a statue of the Virgin bearing the scapular (these two small white strips of cloth form the distinguishing badge of the Carmelites).

The church is often described as a display of Renaissance works in a Gothic setting, but the truth is more complex. The solemn nave has 17th-century arcades and a number of ponderous baroque paintings in honour of the Carmelite Order. Renaissance panelling covers a number of Gothic features, with the choir lofts decorated with 16th-century works. The finest Renaissance painting is a Cima da Conegliano *Nativity* in the second altar on the right, and there are also some rare contributions from Lorenzo Lotto. The Gothic cloisters now form part of an art institute.

Scuola Grande di Santa Maria dei Carmini ⓭

Address: Campo Santa Margherita; www.scuolagrandecarmini.it
Tel: 041-528 9420
Opening Hrs: daily 11am–4pm

The church of San Sebastiano.

Entrance Fee: charge
Transport: Ca' Rezzonico

Commonly known as I Carmini, the headquarters of the Carmelite confraternity is one of the city's grandest, at least in artistic terms. The uninspired facade, built by Longhena, conceals a lavish 18th-century interior. The ground floor comprises a frescoed great hall and sacristy. A monumental twin staircase, its barrel-vaulted ceilings encrusted with stuccowork, leads to a splendid showcase to Tiepolo.

On the left is the **Sala dell'Albergo**, which housed pilgrims, and the Sala dell'Archivio, where the confraternity archives were stored. The decoration of the **Salone** or assembly room on the right was entrusted to the artist Tiepolo. Since the wealthy Order prospered during the Counter-Reformation, with the cult of Mary acting as a counterweight to

Protestantism, the Carmelites could afford to summon the services of the greatest rococo painter.

Tiepolo repaid their confidence with a series of sensuous master-pieces, a floating world of pale skies and illusionistic effects. In the centre of the ceiling is a visionary work showing the Virgin with the Blessed Simon Stock. Tradition has it that Stock had a vision of the Virgin bestowing the Carmelites with their sacred badge, the scapular. As the order was re-established during the 13th century, Stock became one of the first Englishmen to join, leading the Carmelites during the time of their realignment to the Mendicant Friars. The corners of the ceiling are graced by four voluptuous Virtues, a radiant allegorical work.

Canal-boat vegetable stall, San Barnaba.

Campo Santa Margherita

From the doors of I Carmini spreads the broad **Campo Santa**

EAT

In the local inns, try *fegato alla veneziana*, tender calf's liver flavoured with parsley, onion and olive oil, or *bigoli*, dark skeins of wholewheat spaghetti, often served with an anchovy and onion sauce.

Caffè life on Campo Santa Margherita.

Margherita, the liveliest square in the district, and the archetypal Venetian meeting place for an evening's drinks. At one end of the sprawling square is the free-standing Scuola dei Varotari, formerly the tanners' guild. Just above several fish stalls stands an ancient stone sign prescribing the minimum size of fish permitted (eel must be over 25cm/10 ins long and sardines at least 7cm/3 ins).

One side of the square is bordered by dignified palaces with overhanging roofs, a style rare in Venice because of the fear of fire and a desire to let light into dark alleys. At the end of the square is the truncated belltower of Santa Margherita, with the deconsecrated church now a lecture hall. Students mingle around the market stalls and tiny but welcoming bars, all set amidst homely palaces. Given the contagiously upbeat mood, blue-rinse matrons from Milwaukee often join peace-protesting students in sipping a lurid orange *spritz* in one of the arty cafés.

AROUND CAMPO SANTA MARGHERITA

From the *campo*, the splendours of the Grand Canal beckon. Milling students may lead you to **Ca' Foscari** ⑭, the magnificent university palace (see page 136). Just south is **Ca' Rezzonico** ⑮ (see page 133). Don't miss the nearby **Palazzo Nani** with its impressive Vitraria Glass A + Museum (Dorsoduro 960, Tue–Sun 10.30am–6.30pm; www.vitraria.com), celebrating glass as both an item of everyday use and an artistic creation.

Alternatively, follow Rio Terrà across the canal to **Campo San Barnaba** ⑯. Bordering the scenic square is Rio San Barnaba, signalled by a colourful barge laden with fruit and vegetables. The square is reached by **Ponte dei Pugni** (Fists Bridge), the main bridge between San Barnaba and Santa Margherita. This was the scene of factional fisticuffs between rival clans until such brawls were banned in 1705. On and around the square, especially along **Calle Lunga San Barnaba**, are several attractive places to eat.

From here, Sottoportego Casin dei Nobili, once a refuge for ruined nobles, crosses Rio Malpaga to the quaysides of **Calle della Toletta** . This pretty, winding alley passes several neighbourhood bars and a good bookshop before returning to the delightful Rio di San Trovaso.

Around the Accademia

On the far side of the canal, Campiello Gambara leads to the **Accademia Bridge**, a prime spot for watching water traffic. The distinctive wooden bridge replaced a cast-iron one rebuilt under the Austrian occupation. Plans to replace the bridge with a transparent model were defeated by conservatives. It stands in front of the **Accademia**, the city's greatest repository of Venetian art (see page 212).

Between the Accademia and La Salute, the Grand Canal is lined with the finest palaces and museums (see page 128). Charming **Campo San Vio** is home to St George's Anglican Church, which serves the English-speaking community. Here, too, is **Palazzo Cini** (tel: 041-520 5558;

Wed–Mon 11am–7pm; www.palazzocini.it), former residence of Count Vittorio Cini (1884–1977), a noted industrialist. The count created the fine Cini Foundation at San Giorgio (see page 220), but lived here, filling his palace with period furniture, silver, ceramics and Tuscan Renaissance masterpieces. The Palazzo Cini Gallery on the second floor reopened in 2016; on display here are masterpieces from the Vittorio Cini Collection including works by Titian, Niebolo, Canaletto and Guardi previously never shown to the general public.

From here, Calle della Chiesa leads to the **Guggenheim**, the superb collection of modern art (see page 130). Virtually next door is the intriguing **Ca' Dario** (see page 129). Calle del Bastion slips back to La Salute, allowing you a last lingering look at the baroque church before taking the *traghetto* across to the right bank or a vaporetto along the Grand Canal.

Like Henry James, you may find it hard to leave the Salute steps, "with all the sweet bribery of association and recollection".

EAT

Sgropin, lemon sorbet, is made with vodka and prosecco, and traditionally served at the end of a fish course.

Bridge over Rio Malpaga.

THE ACCADEMIA

The world's finest collection of Venetian art is a showcase of ceremonial paintings and sumptuous religious art.

This treasury of Venetian art ranges from Renaissance works and Byzantine panel paintings to vibrant ceremonial paintings, Grand Tour caprices and portraiture. It is intimate rather than overwhelming, as memorable for its snapshots of everyday life as for its masterpieces.

The collection is housed in La Carità, a complex of church, convent, cloisters and charitable confraternity. The church was deconsecrated in Napoleonic times and became a repository of work created during the Venetian Republic, particularly paintings saved from suppressed monasteries.

However, the core collection was assembled by Venetian artists in the 18th century. Highlights include intimate works by Carpaccio and Bellini, High Renaissance art by Giorgione, Titian, Tintoretto and Veronese, and genre scenes by Tiepolo, Guardi and Canaletto. The Republic set great store by the State painter, with artists of the calibre of Bellini, Titian and Tintoretto expected to capture the glory of Venice.

The Essentials

Address: Campo della Carità, www.gallerie accademia.org
Tel: 041-520 0345
Opening Hrs: Mon 8.15am–2pm, Tue–Sun 8.15am–7pm
Entrance Fee: Charge
Transport: Accademia

The Pharmacist, by Pietro Longhi.

Fourteenth-century polyptych of the Annunciation with the Eternal Father and Saints, by Lorenzo Veneziano.

Paolo Veneziano is credited with introducing the taste for panel painting to Venice. His Coronation of the Virgin (1325) is symbolic rather than realistic, and is bathed in radiant colours.

Veronese's *Feast in the House of Levi* (1573) invoked the Inquisition's wrath, with its sacrilegious portrayal of buffoons, drunkards and dwarfs. Veronese side-stepped the issue by renaming his work in more secular vein.

The Ten Thousand Crucifixions on Mount Ararat by Vittore Carpaccio (*c.1460–1525*), a masterpiece of the High Renaissance.

THE COLLECTION

Detail from Carpaccio's Arrival of the English Ambassadors. Carpaccio is noted for a love of detail, narrative talent and sensitive use of colour. Carpaccio and Bellini were prime exponents of the narrative cycles known as istorie, a Venetian Renaissance phenomenon.

Room I occupies the Gothic chapter house, and is dedicated to Byzantine and Gothic artists, such as Paolo Veneziano and Antonio Vivarini (*c*.1419–76), noted for static yet rapt decorative works on gold backgrounds. **Rooms II to IV** display expressive early Renaissance altarpieces by Giovanni Bellini, brimming with poetic atmosphere.

Room V contains the most celebrated works: Giorgione's *The Tempest* (*c*.1507), a moody and enigmatic canvas, and his *Portrait of an Old Woman*, a meditation on time.

Rooms VI to X feature Renaissance and mannerist masters, from Titian to Veronese and Tintoretto. Titian's poignant *Pietà*, intended for his own tomb, is lit by a diffuse light and infused with an anguished questioning about the meaning of life; the troubled *Nicodemus* is Titian's last self-portrait. Veronese's *Feast in the House of Levi* (1573) covers an entire wall in **Room X** but was painted for the church of Santi Giovanni e Paolo. Intended as a *Last Supper*, the subject was a pretext for depicting a profane feast. Also here is Tintoretto's *Miracle of the Slave*, the work that made his reputation.

Works by Veronese and Tintoretto are in **Room XI**, as are rococo frescoes from ruined churches, culminating in Tiepolo's *Rape of Europa*, a triumph of pulsating light and shade. **Rooms XII to XVII** display 18th-century landscapes and genre paintings beloved by Grand Tour visitors. Guardi's caprices hang alongside Longhi's patrician homes and a rare Canaletto perspective painting, which uses a pastiche Venetian background.

The final section, from **Room XIX to the end**, returns to the Renaissance, with a showcase for the pomp and pageantry of the Venetian Republic, seen in vibrant ceremonial paintings by Carpaccio and Bellini. The last room retains its Gothic ceiling and displays Titian's *Presentation of the Virgin*. This work was painted for this very room, and so makes a fitting finale to any tour.

San Francesco del Deserto, dominated by the monastery of the same name.

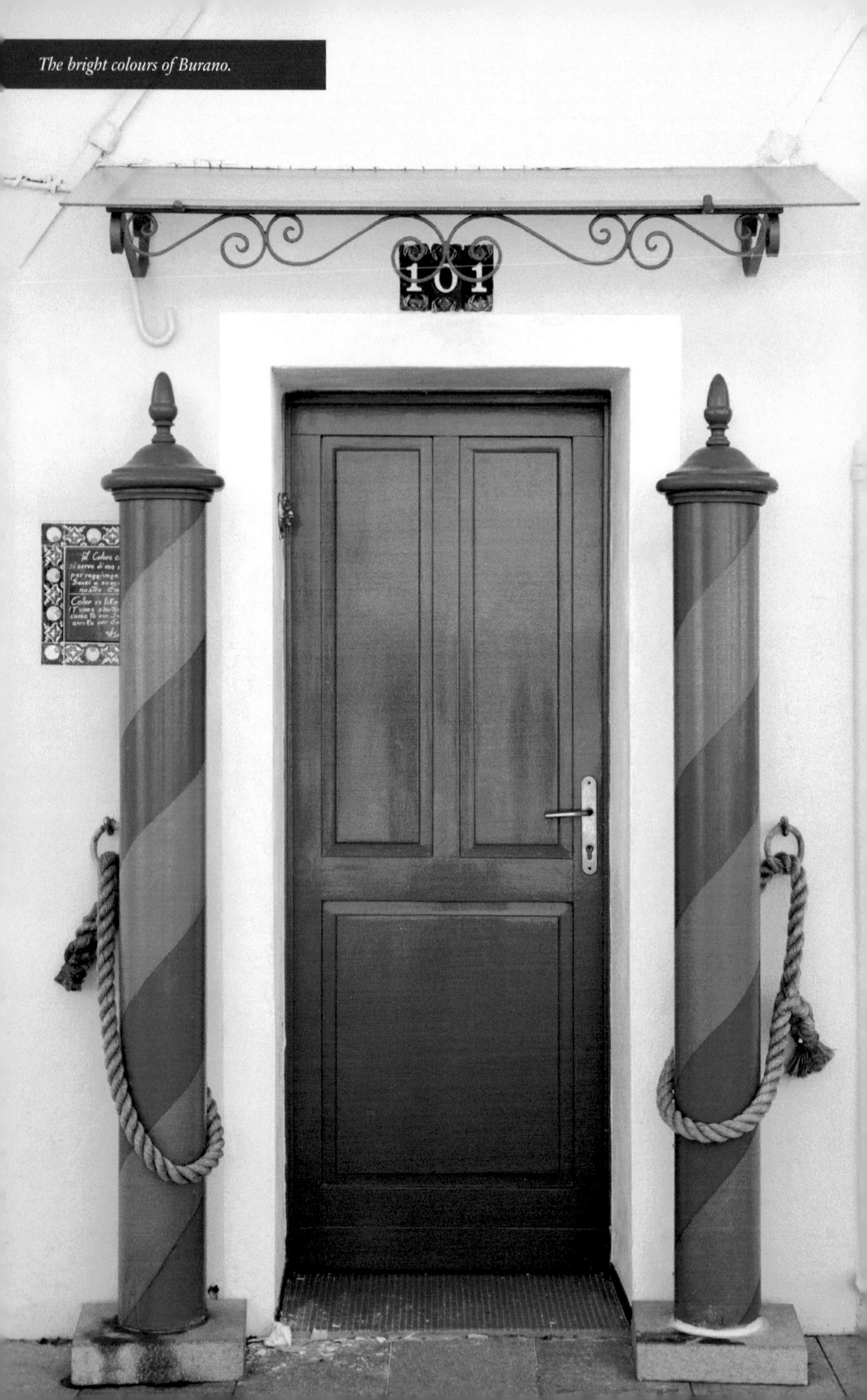

The bright colours of Burano.

ISLANDS OF THE LAGOON

Visit San Giorgio and Giudecca for the views and
churches, Torcello for mosaics, Murano for glass,
Burano for lace, and the Lido for its seaside air.

T he lagoon is a floating world
between the smoking oil refin-
eries on the mainland and the
fish slithering in the reeds. At times,
fumes intermingle with the cedar-
perfumed air of the islands and the
sound of cicadas. The desolation
of the lagoon waters is relieved by
sightings of wild ducks, mute swans
or the fragile-looking black-winged
stilt. Despite their proximity, the
lagoon islands are startlingly different, embracing marshland, orchards,
vineyards and even beaches.

Individual characteristics

These low-lying islands have a very
chequered past as monasteries or
munitions dumps, mental asylums
or market gardens, leper colonies
or crumbling fortifications. The
strangest places tend to be the
"minor" or outlying islands.

By comparison with these diverse
but dying communities, the main
islands survive on their location and
separate identities. Certain islands
are the preserve of fishermen, lace-
makers and glass-makers, while
others are home to boat-builders or
urban sophisticates.

Visitors with little time would do
well to make San Giorgio, Burano
and Torcello their priorities. San

Giorgio, facing San Marco, is the
closest to the city, and the only major
island untouched by commerce. The
belltower offers the most romantic
view of Venice. Torcello, the remot-
est of the islands, offers a stirring
impression of the earliest Venetian
settlement. The mood is set by the
surreal isolation of the site, the air
of stagnation, the scattered buildings
and the solitary red-brick belltower.

Out of season, Torcello is the
place for bathing in what the writer
Jan Morris calls "an ecstasy of

Main Attractions
San Giorgio Maggiore
Il Redentore
Murano
Burano
Torcello
Santa Maria dell'Assunta

Maps
Pages 220, 224 and 234

Fishing cages in the lagoon.

WHERE

Even if you have only a day in Venice, consider a trip to San Giorgio Maggiore – the view from the top of the belltower is an unmissable experience.

melancholia". By contrast, Burano is a splash of colour in a bleak lagoon, dispelling any mournfulness with its parade of colourful fishermen's cottages. Visitors tempted by gaudy Venetian glass or soft-shelled crabs will choose its neighbour, Murano. Giudecca, just off Dorsoduro, is celebrated for its Palladian church, but is a curious, quiet corner of 'real Venice', with an industrial past and few tourists. The Lido cannot compete historically, but its beaches and graceful Art-Nouveau architecture offer a semblance of escape from the summer heat.

THE ISLAND OF SAN GIORGIO MAGGIORE

The island of **San Giorgio Maggiore** was once known as *isola dei cipressi* because of the cypress-framed vistas. Seen from afar, the majestic monastery appears suspended in the inner lagoon, with its cool Palladian church matched by a belltower modelled on St Mark's. Together with the baroque beacon of La Salute, these two great symbols guard the inner harbour of Venice. San Giorgio is a hallowed spot, with its famous Benedictine monastery.

Despite the island's proximity to San Marco, the absence of distractions means that San Giorgio still has a secluded air. The monastery boldly looks out over St Mark's Basin, defying the conventional model of an inward-looking institution enclosed by cloisters. The medieval building was remodelled in the late-15th and early-16th centuries, but owes its classical grace to Palladio. Although the Napoleonic suppression of the monasteries in 1806 was accompanied by French plundering of San Giorgio, the monks refused to leave. The harbour was developed at the same time, with part of the monastery used to store munitions during World War II.

San Giorgio Maggiore ❶

Address: Isola San Giorgio Maggiore
Tel: 041-522 7827
Opening Hrs: Mon–Sat May–Sept 9.30am–6.30pm Sun 8.30–11am and 2.30–6.30pm, Mon–Sat Oct–Apr 9.30am–dusk, Sun 8.30–11am and 2.30–dusk.
Entrance Fee: charge (belltower only)
Transport: San Giorgio

View across to La Giudecca from San Giorgio Maggiore.

The vast Hilton Molino Stucky, a converted flour mill.

This is undoubtedly the finest monastic church in the lagoon. Only the churlish aesthete Ruskin found it "barbarous" and "childish in conception". Endowed by doges and favoured by humanist scholars, the monastery became a famous centre for learning.

Although most visitors restrict their visit to the church and belltower, to really appreciate the size and diversity of the monastic site, you need to tour the Cini Foundation. In 1565, Palladio was commissioned to rebuild the church, his finest Venetian legacy, rivalled only by Il Redentore. Here Palladio shows his mastery of the classical idiom, using the basic geometric volumes of cube, pyramid and sphere. Based on Alberti's precepts, this is a Christian church founded on classical principles and mathematical proportions.

The facade is composed of two overlapping temple fronts, with a central portico. The cool church is a model of perspective, with a domed interior which is bathed in white light. The overall sense of order is more impressive than the component parts: the vaulted ceiling, elegant choir and choir stalls, the striking marble floor and two minor works by Tintoretto.

A lift whisks visitors to the top of the **Belltower** for fabulous views over the city, whatever the weather. The angel on top of the tower fell off during a violent storm in 1993 but has been restored, with the original now displayed inside the church and a bronze copy on the roof. If the lift attendant is not too busy, he may be persuaded to unlock the **Sala del Conclave**, where the conclave met to elect Pope Pius VII in 1800, while Rome was occupied by French troops. Although it is now used as a private music room by the monks, members of the public can occasionally attend classical concerts here, as well as performances of Gregorian chant in the church.

TIP

Ferries for the main islands: for San Giorgio take line 2; for the Lido, take lines 1, 2, 5.1, 5.2, 6, 10 (seasonal), 14; for Murano 3, 4.2, 12, 13 Alilaguna; for Burano 12; for Torcello 12; for Giudecca 2, 41, 42. For information call 041-2424 or log onto www.actv.it.

EXPLORING THE LAGOON

It is often easy to be overwhelmed by this city of stone, and forget that La Serenissima is only a tiny portion of a vast lagoon that comprises hundreds of islands, archaeological sites, monasteries, farms, fortresses and wetlands, home to hundreds of species of birds.

The *vaporetti* operate a reasonable service through the lagoon, concentrating on tourist classics like the glass-blowers' island, Murano, and the brightly painted fishermen's houses on Burano and Torcello, where the earliest settlers arrived. Fortunately, you can now explore some of the lagoon on the public-ferry system. Moreover, thanks to enterprising ecologists, you can visit previously uncharted waters with the experts. Trips use public transport or a chartered boat to visit previously inaccessible islands, churches, excavation sites and the beautiful market-garden island of Sant' Erasmo. One trip uses a wooden *bragozzo*, a flat-bottomed boat capable of navigating the shallow channels of the shifting wetlands.

Here, you have the chance to see daily life out on the lagoon, from the giant nets belonging to squid fishermen to sightings of men in waders plunging their hands into the squelchy mud in search of lagoon fish.

Fondazione Giorgio Cini

Address: Isola San Giorgio Maggiore,
www.cini.it
Tel: 041-524 0119
Opening Hrs: Sat–Sun 10am–5pm,
till 4pm in winter
Entrance Fee: charge (belltower only)
Transport: San Giorgio

The **Fondazione Giorgio Cini** occupies much of the great former Benedictine monastery complex. The only way to see it is by one-hour guided visit on weekends. Count Vittorio Cini (1884–1977) bequeathed his home to the city and created the foundation as a memorial to his son, who died in a flying accident. The centre funds restoration projects and stages major exhibitions. The baroque architect Longhena designed the monastery's ceremonial double staircase and library, built on the site of Michelozzi's Renaissance library.

Other highlights are the huge Renaissance dormitory and the cross-vaulted Palladian refectory. More impressive still are the Renaissance **Cloister of the Laurels** (Chiostro degli Allori) and the Palladian

Ferry around San Giorgio Maggiore.

Cloister of the Cypresses (Chiostro dei Cipressi). Palladio also designed the ceremonial guest quarters

Giudecca and San Giorgio Maggiore

overlooking the lagoon. The sumptuous setting is more reminiscent of a palace courtyard than of a cloistered retreat. The Palladian cloisters lead to the monastic gardens and the **Teatro Verde** ❸, an open-air theatre that has been little used in the past few years. The foundation has also converted former navy warehouses on the island into a gallery for temporary exhibitions.

GIUDECCA

Giudecca is the most contradictory of Venetian islands, home to the city's most luxurious hotel and to its most raffish district. Until recently, this was a depressed island of decaying tenements and blind alleys, with a polarisation between the gentrified east and the postindustrialised west. It was easy to forget that the island was once celebrated for palatial villas, exotic gardens and risqué clubs. Giudecca probably began as a place of exile for punished nobles, but became a veritable pleasure garden.

From Renaissance times onwards, the island spelt indulgence for a nobility in search of the decadent *dolce far niente* (sweet idleness) typical of a Venetian summer. Giudecca was also noted for its convents, including one notorious for Casanova's amorous exploits. Industrialisation put an end to the patrician idyll: from the 19th century until the 1950s, the island became Venice's industrial inner suburb. The horizon was dotted with flour mills, fabric and clock factories, a brewery and boatyards. Decline set in with the growth of the industrial zone on the mainland, which left Giudecca an urban wasteland.

Today, this *popolare* or working-class district, is undergoing a rebirth, with the restoration of landmark buildings. While parts of Giudecca remain shabby, abandoned lofts are being bought by artists, giving the district a bohemian air. With property prices lower than in historic Venice, old flour mills and furniture factories are being converted into fashionable apartments. On the waterfront facing the city, the foundations are being restored, functional buildings have been put to

Wooden choirstalls inside San Giorgio Maggiore.

Murano glass.

Il Redentore comes alive during the Feast of the Redeemer, held on the third Sunday of July.

creative new uses, including a granary converted into a youth hostel and a brewery turned into flats, and contemporary art galleries are springing up.

Apart from the great Palladian church and the quayside facing the city, Giudecca feels immune to the effects of tourism. The churches may have been restored, but the women's prison is still in service, the boatyards remain active, and the waterfront bars are favoured by matronly locals sipping *spritzes*.

Il Redentore ❹

Address: Campo del SS Redentore, www.chorusvenezia.org
Opening Hrs: Mon–Sat 10am–5pm
Entrance Fee: charge
Transport: Redentore

Palladio's church is a Venetian landmark, visible from every side of St Mark's Basin, and a key reason for visiting the island. The church of the Redeemer was built in thanksgiving for the end of the 1576 plague.

Designed as a votive temple, this graceful church is still the scene of Venice's most beguiling summer festival. Architectural purists feel that this Palladian masterpiece, inspired by the Pantheon in Rome, surpasses even San Giorgio.

The facade is undoubtedly more subtle, resting on a rusticated pediment, with a sweeping flight of steps echoing the style of a gracious Palladian country villa. From here, the eye is inevitably led to the lantern surmounted by the figure of Christ the Redeemer.

However, compared with the lovely view of the floodlit facade, visible from the quaysides across the water, the interior can feel disappointing, despite its rigorous respect for classical principles, mastery of geometrical forms and effortless grandeur. Palladio was also influenced by contemporary Roman architecture, with the choir of Il Redentore echoing Bramante's central plan for St Peter's.

Elton John's Gothic palazzo on Giudecca.

East of Il Redentore

From the church, Ramo della Croce leads to the exotic **Garden of Eden** ❺, named after the Englishman who created it. Facing the garden is the former English Hospital, which cared for impecunious British expatriates during Edwardian times.

Retracing your steps leads you back to the waterfront and another Palladian gem. **Le Zitelle** ❻ bears all the Palladian hallmarks of stylistic unity, coherent classicism and an inspired sense of proportion. In keeping with Venetian tradition, the complex was originally designed as a convent but became a noted musical conservatoire. The complex is now home to the luxury Bauer Palladio Spa hotel.

The **Belmond Hotel Cipriani** ❼, set on the eastern spit of the island, enjoys sweeping views over the lagoon, especially from the summer terrace. Now one of the world's

most exclusive hotels, the Cipriani originally belonged to the founders of Harry's Bar. Cipriani's liveried motor boats regularly ferry guests across from San Marco to this oasis of peace. The hotel incorporates a Gothic palace and has gardens full of azaleas, rhododendrons and oleanders framing the wide expanse of the swimming pool.

West of Il Redentore

The section from Campo di San Cosmo to Rio Ponte Lungo runs through the area's old manufacturing district. Fans of industrial architecture can walk back along the waterfront past distinctive factories to the island's oldest church. **Sant' Eufemia** ❽ (Mon–Sat 8am–noon and 3–5pm; Sun 3–7pm) faces the great Gesuati church across the water on Dorsoduro (see page 204). Sant' Eufemia, marred by remodelling, survives as a bizarre mix of Veneto-Byzantine capitals, rococo stuccowork and 18th-century paintings.

The once industrial area around the church was long marked by decay but in recent years has undergone something of a resurrection. Abandoned buildings and land have been converted into apartments and the area considerably cleaned up. On the western edge of the island lies **Molino Stucky**, a neo-Gothic industrial relic. The novelist L.P. Hartley looked "almost with affection on the great bulk of Stucky's flour mill, battlemented, pinnacled, turreted, machicolated, a monument to the taste of 1870, that might have been built out of a child's box of bricks". Giovanni Stucky, the overbearing Swiss owner, was murdered by one of his workers in 1910. After decades of neglect, this fortress-like former grain silo, pasta factory and flour mill has been converted into the 380-room **Hilton Molino Stucky** ❾, with the largest hotel congress centre in Venice. Giudecca residents hope this grandiose monument to the Victorian age may yet come to symbolise an economic regeneration.

MURANO

"The most curmudgeonly of the Venetian communities, where it always feels like early closing day," moaned the writer Jan Morris. Yet Murano is proud of its past as a highly celebrated glassmaking centre and a summer resort for the nobility. In the 18th century, the island was noted for its villas, gambling clubs and literary salons. However, the closure of many churches and the rapaciousness of the glass factories has somewhat blunted its appeal.

On a sunny day, Murano can pass for a smaller version of Venice, but it can be very bleak in winter, with scruffiness and commercialism outweighing picturesque charm. Nonetheless, Murano makes a pleasant enough stopping-off point on the way to Torcello. The majority of visitors are enticed by the glassmaking, although an impressive Byzantine church and a cluster of bars also add to Murano's appeal.

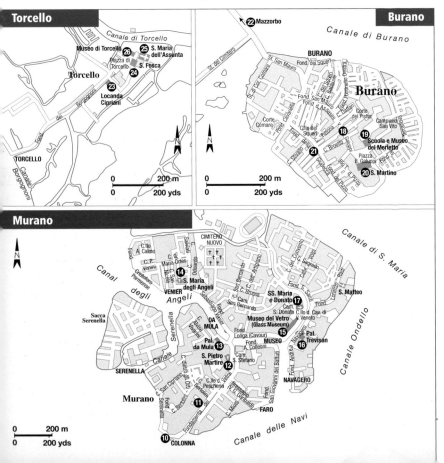

Burano laceworker.

Murano glass is an acquired taste, which many lifelong Venice fans fail to acquire. While few visitors would turn down an antique Murano mirror or an 18th-century chandelier, modern Murano glass is another matter. It errs on the side of virtuosity and garishness rather than refinement and elegance. Still, the skill of the glass-blowers makes an impressive display, while the crisis in the glass industry means that prices are competitive at the artistic end of the spectrum.

Visitors who only want a brief visit to Murano should stay on board the ferry until **Museo**, the third stop, close to the glass museum. However, serious shoppers will choose **Colonna** ⑩, the best stop for exploring the myriad glass factories.

The quayside opens onto **Fondamenta dei Vetrai** ⑪, the heart of the glassmaking district, with the 16th-century Palazzo Contarini on the left.

The showrooms along the quayside offer a chance to admire the glass-blowers' skills. You will find more glass-blowing workshops and showrooms along Calle Bressagio. Kitsch creations abound in Murano, from peacock-shaped glasses to gondola vases but there are also high quality showrooms, such as Berengo (www.berengo.com).

Towards the end of the quayside, by the bridge, is the church of **San Pietro Martire** ⑫ (9am–noon, 3–6pm, Sun 3–6pm). This Gothic church has a Renaissance portal and a restored altarpiece by Bellini (1488) depicting a "holy conversation" between Doge Barbarigo and the Virgin, the temporal and spiritual powers.

Further down the quayside, just before Ponte Vivarini, stands the **Palazzo da Mula** ⑬, a glassworks set in a Gothic palace and Byzantine walled garden. From here, there is a picturesque view looking west along Canale degli Angeli to the abandoned church of **Santa Maria degli Angeli** ⑭.

SHOP

Given the Far Eastern fakes flooding the Venetian market, buy "Murano" glass only where you see the trademark Vetro Artistico Murano (for details, see www.muranoglass.com or call tel: 041-527 5074).

THE SECRET ART OF GLASS

The Phoenicians discovered the art of glass-making by subjecting sand to extreme heat, thus forming a soft paste that could be moulded into objects before cooling. The first glassmaking centre on Roman territory was in the important city of Aquileia, northeast of Venice and there is evidence of glass being made in Torcello and Murano as early as the 7th century.

Later, Venetian glassmakers perfected their trade with masters in the Middle East – Venice's thick network of trade bases in places like Egypt and Syria was crucial in the cementing of these contacts, which led to Venetian glassmakers being among the best in Europe. At first, glassmakers could set up shop anywhere in Venice. By 1291, however, all glassmaking activity had been moved to Murano, because the kilns posed a fire hazard. By the Middle Ages, Venetian (ie Murano) glass was considered one of the best products of its kind in Europe and it was considered treason for glassworkers to leave the city. Venetian production declined from the 17th century in the face of stiff competition from French glassmakers and Bohemian and English crystal masters.

Many of Murano's masters emigrated but those that remained behind managed to overcome the crisis; many of the family names in modern Murano glass production are descendants of centuries of generations of glass masters.

Museo del Vetro

Address: Fondamenta Giustinian 8, www.visitmuve.it
Tel: 041-739 586
Opening Hrs: dailz 10am–6pm, till 5pm in winter
Entrance Fee: charge
Transport: Museo

From Palazzo da Mula, cross the main bridge over Canale Grande and turn to the right, following the quaysides of Fondamenta Cavour to the **Museo del Vetro**, the Glass Museum. This occupies the Gothic Palazzo Giustinian, originally the seat of the bishop of Torcello, which was transferred here after the earlier settlement on Torcello was abandoned. Although the palace retains a few original frescoes, it is essentially a showcase for Murano glass, from platters and beakers to crystal chalices and the finest chandeliers. Non-Venetian pieces include a Roman mosaic bowl, matched by mosaics from the local church of Santi Maria e Donato. As well as Renaissance enamelled glassware, there are satirical scenes mocking the Austrian rulers, Art-Nouveau objets d'art, and the glittering blue Coppa Barovier, a Gothic wedding chalice, adorned with allegorical love scenes. In short, the collection takes you on a chronological journey of the history of glass-making in Murano and beyond.

On the right bank, facing the museum, lies the classical **Palazzo Trevisan** ⑯, with its interior decorated with frescoes by Veronese.

Santi Maria e Donato ⑰

Address: Campo San Donato
Tel: 041-739 056, www.sandonato murano.it
Opening Hrs: Mon–Sat 9am–6pm, Sun from 12.30pm
Entrance Fee: free
Transport: Museo

On the left bank, just north of the glass museum is a beguiling church reflected in the water. **Santi Maria e Donato** is the finest church on Murano, despite a misguided 19th-century restoration. This 7th-century church, remodelled in Veneto-Byzantine style, boasts 12th-century apses, decorated with blind arches and loggias leaning over the canal. As in Santa Fosca on Torcello,

San Giorgio Maggiore at night.

the brick and terracotta apses are studded with zigzag friezes and dogtooth mouldings.

The charm of the interior has survived much tampering, with its Gothic ship's-keel ceiling, Greek marble columns and Veneto-Byzantine capitals. The apse is dominated by a luminous Byzantine-style mosaic of the Madonna and Child, rivalled by a beautiful altarpiece by Paolo Veneziano (c.1310). The highlight is the patterned mosaic floor, depicting interlaced foliage and allegorical animals. The pattern includes fragments of ancient glass mosaics, recalling the finest Murano craftsmanship.

BURANO

This most vibrant of Venetian islands makes a cheery stop en route to Torcello, its polar opposite. Hemingway mocked the islanders for having nothing better to do than make boats and babies. However, Burano is better known as the home of fishermen and lace-sellers. Weary visitors may be relieved to find that there are few cultural sights but atmosphere aplenty. To help preserve its character, the community regularly rejects applications for hotels.

Burano feels like an authentic old fishing village, with nets hung out to dry and boxes of crabs blocking the doorways. Burano romantics even portray lacemaking as an aesthetic extension of the net-mending tradition.

From the ferry stop, follow the flow to **Via Galuppi** ⓲, the main street, lined with fishermen's cottages.

When not ruining their eyesight poring over lace, the fishermen's wives painted the family homes in bold colours, often adding geometrical motifs over the doorways. By the same token, when ashore, the fishermen spent their time mending nets or boat-building. Burano remains the best place for boat-building, with craftsmen building by eye, not by design. The street is lined with lace shops and traditional trattorias, the place for the best crab and squid dishes.

Museo del Merletto ⓳

Address: Piazza Galuppi 187, http://museomerletto.visitmuve.it/

Arriving in Murano.

Tel: 041-730 034
Opening Hrs: Tue–Sun 10am–6pm
Entrance Fee: charge
Transport: Burano

Piazza Galuppi, the colourful town square, is home to the **Scuola e Museo del Merletto**, the lace museum and former school, housed in a Gothic palace. Given the difficulties of preserving lace, most samples on display tend to be from the 19th century, including a fine wedding train. Lace has been made in Venetian convents since medieval times, but the *punto in aria* method, using a needle and thread, only emerged in the 16th century. The art fell into decline with the Industrial Revolution, but was saved from extinction on Burano by the creation of a lacemaking school in 1872. By the turn of the century, the local industry sustained 5,000 people, but factory-made lace also fell out of fashion.

After a visit to the lace school, visitors learn to distinguish between cheap imported products and the increasingly rare genuine Burano lace, as light as tulle. Genuine handmade Burano-point lace is ridiculously expensive: but take into account the fact that it can take 10 women up to three years to make a single tablecloth.

From here, the leaning tower of **San Martino** ⓴ (8am–noon, 3–7pm) looms into view. The 16th-century church is best known for its paintings, especially a Tiepolo *Crucifixion*. A short walk leads to **Fondamenta della Giudecca** ㉑, and a stretch of colourful quaysides. The more adventurous should consider a water taxi ride to an atmospheric Franciscan retreat: Burano is the only sensible embarkation point for the lush island of **San Francesco del Deserto** (see page 237).

On the way back to the ferry, cross the footbridge to **Mazzorbo** ㉒, a former island for exiles. The verdant island is unremarkable, but there are evocative views towards Venice. The salt marshes and mudflats around Burano are being reinstated to restore the lagoon's ecological balance and act as a sea defence against high tides and storms.

TORCELLO

The long boat trip to Torcello helps one appreciate the remoteness of this evocative island, the earliest centre of Venetian civilisation. It is strange to think that Venice arose from these solemn marshes, a 7th-century settlement uprooted from its mainland home of Altinum. As an autonomous island and trading post, Torcello flourished, with 10,000 inhabitants in the 10th century. Decline set in with the rise of Venice, hastened by the silting up of this corner of the lagoon, which turned Torcello into a malarial swamp after the 14th century. Now only about 20 people live here permanently.

The novelist George Sand captured the pastoral mood of her visit in the 1830s: "Torcello is a reclaimed

Glassmaker at work in Murano.

wilderness. Through copses of water willow and hibiscus bushes run saltwater streams where petrel and teal delight to stalk." But where Sand celebrated life, other commentators have seen the haunting spirit of a ghost town. Ruskin mused on the scene, "this waste of wild sea moor, of a lurid ashen grey… the melancholy clearness of space in the warm sunset, oppressive, reaching to the horizon of its level gloom".

From the jetty, a canal towpath leads through the lush countryside to the Byzantine complex. **Locanda Cipriani** ㉓, a deceptively modest rural inn, lies just beyond the bridge. Film stars and royals have visited and feasted on the self-consciously simple seafood dishes.

Hemingway, who stayed here while working on his Venetian novel, has one of his characters give a simplified view of the creation of Venice: "Torcello boys were all great boatmen. So they took the stones off all their houses on barges… and they built Venice." Certainly, as the city declined, building materials were often recycled, first on Murano and Burano, and then in Venice itself.

At the end of the path stands the austerely lovely basilica of **Santa Fosca** ㉔ (10am–4.30pm). Built by Greeks, it was designed as a *martyrium*, housing the relics of a martyr. The church is a coherent masterpiece, a harmonious structure combining Romanesque with Byzantine elements. The basilica was built in the 11th century, at the same time as Santi Maria e Donato in Murano, and boasts the same blind arcading and geometrical motifs. The outer walls are girded by an octagonal portico resting on stilted arches, with sculpted columns. The central plan, a Greek cross inscribed within an octagon, is emblematic of Byzantine architecture, with the pentagonal apses echoing oriental forms.

Santa Maria dell'Assunta ㉕

Address: Piazza Torcello
Tel: 041-296 0630
Opening Hrs: daily 10.30am–5.30pm Apr–Oct, 10am–4.30pm Nov–Mar
Entrance Fee: charge
Transport: Torcello

Santi Maria e Donato church on Murano.

To Ruskin, the stark exterior of this ancient cathedral was reminiscent of a storm refuge. The cathedral is the oldest monument in the lagoon, founded in AD 639 as an episcopal seat. The basilica was modelled on those in Ravenna, but modified in the 9th and early 11th centuries to create a superb Veneto-Byzantine building. The church was first restored in 1008, with the raising of the floor and creation of a crypt: the lovely mosaic floor dates from this period.

The dignified interior is punctuated by slender Greek marble columns, bearing Byzantine capitals. Among the treasures included here are the original 7th-century altar, the pulpit, the ceremonial throne, and a Roman sarcophagus containing the relics of St Heliodorus, the first bishop of Altinum.

The solemnity of the architecture is counterpointed by the richness of the **mosaics**. These date from the 7th century, with some in the apse from the 9th century. A masterpiece of Byzantine design adorns the central apse: a slender, mysterious Madonna bathed in a cloth of gold. The frieze of the Twelve Apostles close by dates from the 12th century. Henry James admired these "grimly mystical mosaics", with the Apostles "ranged against their dead gold backgrounds as stiffly as grenadiers presenting arms". The 13th-century *Last Judgement* counterbalances the apse mosaics and is the most compelling narrative sequence. One should read it from top to bottom, with the *Crucifixion* leading to the *Descent into Limbo*, the *Day of Judgement* and the *Weighing of Souls*. Although sections of the work have been over-restored, it is still engrossing, with angels, devils and disembodied corpses competing for attention.

After climbing the newly restored belltower, glance at the vestiges of the 7th-century **baptistry**, built on a circular plan like the Roman baths. Also on the piazza is **Attila's Throne**, a Roman potentate's marble seat.

Museo di Torcello 🉖

Address: Piazza Torcello
Tel: 041-730 761
Opening Hrs: Tue–Sun 10.30am–5.30pm Mar–Oct, 10am–5pm Nov–Feb
Entrance Fee: charge
Transport: Torcello

Nearby stands the Torcello museum, a quiet complement to the site, spread over two buildings, the former town hall and city archives. Exhibits include mosaics from Ravenna and fragments from Torcello's *Last Judgement*, lost during a clumsy restoration in 1853. Compared with the largely intact and original buildings, these are the broken shards of a lost civilisation.

Like Ruskin, most writers strike an elegiac note when faced with the collapse of this early Venetian settlement: "The lament of human voices mixed with the fretting of the waves on the ridges of the sand." However, if

The ferry to Torcello.

you are fortunate, and the crowds are in abeyance, you may share George Sand's enchantment with Torcello: "The air was balmy and only the song of cicadas disturbed the religious hush of the morning."

After exploring this enchanted isle, it's hard to resist lunch at the delightful Locanda Cipriani.

THE LIDO

This long strip of land, sandwiched between the city of Venice and the Adriatic, belongs neither to Venice nor the mainland. This reflects the Lido's prime function, to protect Venice from the engulfing tides. In spirit, it is a place apart, not quite a traditional summer resort nor a residential suburb. After the time warp of historic Venice, the sight of cars, large villas and department stores can be disconcerting. Yet the island cannot be dismissed as soulless. There is a touch of unreality about the Lido, as there is about Venice itself, hence its role as a superior film-set. In this faded fantasy, neo-Gothic piles vie with Art-Nouveau villas and a mock-Moorish castle.

In the Romantic era, Byron and Shelley raced on horseback along the empty sands, but the advent of sea-bathing in the 1840s brought the fashionable élite and the world in its wake. The English and Germans were the chief culprits, but by the 1880s the Venetians had also succumbed

Basilica di Santa Maria Assunta Judgment Day mosaic.

Burano's brightly painted houses.

Venice Film Festival

The world's oldest film festival rivals Cannes in prestige and outshines the Côte d'Azur in terms of glamour and romance.

Founded as a showcase for Fascist Italy, the Venice film festival's success belies its unpromising origins. Recently, the 10-day jamboree has gone all out for Hollywood glitz, even if worthy art-house winners tend to triumph in the end.

Not that the festival failed to recognise talent at the very outset. Spencer Tracy was nominated for his role in *Dr Jekyll and Mr Hyde* in the first edition, and Venice has celebrated such vintage performances as Greta Garbo in *Anna Karenina* (1935) and Laurence Olivier's *Hamlet* (1948). Although early directors of the calibre of John Ford and Auguste Renoir brought glamour to the Lido, the festival has a checkered past, frequently beset by bureaucracy and political wrangling. The glory days coincided with

Brazilian model Alessandra Ambrosio at the Venice Film Festival.

New Wave cinema in the 1960s, a fame sealed by movies from Godard, Pasolini, Tarkovsky and Visconti. Since the 1980s, there have been constant charges of jury bias, and controversial directors have not always fared well in Venice. Nonetheless, there has been a revival in the festival's fortunes. The Golden Lion (Leon d'Oro) award may now mean more, particularly since the presentation ceremony is back in the Fenice opera house, resplendent after its restoration.

During the September festival, the Lido recovers a little of its turn-of-the-century lustre. Stars can be spotted sipping Bellinis on the terrace of the top hotels or parading along the seafront. The resort's *belle époque* Hôtel des Bains has both starred in *Death in Venice* and stood in for Cairo in *The English Patient*, while the Fascistic Palazzo del Cinema is still the heart of the festival.

The Venetian audiences enjoy basking in the presence of the stars, and then bringing them down to earth. Thwarted in his bid to pilot his plane onto the Lido beach, John Travolta had to settle for staying in Missoni's yacht, moored by St Mark's. In 2004, classic festival chaos meant that several stars were left standing at their own premieres, while delays led to Johnny Depp's and Kate Winslet's premiere finishing at 4am.

Big names continue to get top billing. In the 2008 festival, the opening film was the Coen Brothers' *Burn After Reading*, starring Brad Pitt, John Malkovich and George Clooney, all of whom turned up to bask in a little fevered adoration. In 2009 Sylvester Stallone got a prize for his life's work in film, and local director Giuseppe Tornatore's *Baarìa* was presented as the opening film – the first time in 20 years that an Italian film had the honour.

In 2015, a remastered version of Federico Fellini's Amarcord was screened, while the main competition was won by a Venezuelan film Desde allá by Lorenzo Vigas.

These are not easy times. Funding shortages and competition from other European festivals are putting on the pressure. That said, Palazzo Cinema's Sala Grande, the festival's main venue, was thoroughly restored and modernised for the 68th edition.

Travelling in style.

to the spell of sun, sand and sea. The island became the world's first lido, spawning a rash of brash or glitzy imitators across the globe. Ruskin railed against the crowds of uncouth smokers who filled "his" steamers: the populace "smokes and spits up and down the piazzetta all day, and gets itself dragged by a screaming kettle to the Lido next morning to sea-bathe itself into capacity for more tobacco". The once windswept dunes gave way to mass tourism in the 1920s, with D.H. Lawrence decrying the beach as "a strand where an endless heap of seals come up for mating".

However, the Lido is also Thomas Mann's Venice, a place of decadence and spiritual dislocation. Curiously, this does not dispel its staid reputation as an old-fashioned bourgeois retreat. The Lido has long been a bulwark of conservatism, residential rather than industrial, conventional yet cosmopolitan.

Since the Lido cannot compete with the historical riches of the rest of Venice, it remains the preserve of residents and visitors staying on the island. Although most day-trippers stray no further than the beaches and smart hotels, the Lido offers more subtle pleasures, from *belle époque* architecture to a gentle cycle ride along the sea walls to Malamocco.

The ferries from San Marco deposit visitors among the traffic at the edge of the shopping district. Close to the jetties stands the 16th-century church of **Santa Maria Elisabetta** ㉗, with the main shopping street beyond. **Gran Viale Santa Maria Elisabetta** ㉘ cuts across the island from the lagoon shore to the Adriatic. An air of gracious living still permeates the broad promenade, leading to the **Blue Moon complex**, the new beach playground and the **Lungomare**, the seafront promenade and the focus of the summer evening *passeggiata* (promenade). Beyond is a series of Adriatic beaches, private pockets of sand bedecked with colourful cabins.

TIP

For a bird's eye view of Venice, you can't beat a helicopter ride over the city from the fascinating, restored 1930s Aeroporto Nicelli airstrip in the north of the Lido. Contact Heliair Venice (tel: 041-526 0215; www.heliairvenice.it). A 10-minute jaunt costs €130.

Basilica di Santa Maria Assunta on the island of Torcello.

Sunset over San Giorgio Maggiore.

breath of flowers and shrubs from the nearby park."

Around the Island

Following the seafront east leads to the public beach and airstrip. **Nuovo Cimitero Israelitico** 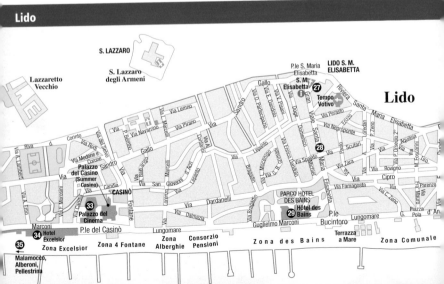, the Jewish cemetery, lies on Via Cipro, the street cutting across the island. The cemetery dates back to 1386 and reflects the special status of Jews in Venice (see page 196). You can arrange guided visits on Sundays through the Museo Ebraico in the Ghetto. Via Cipro leads to the lagoon shore and **San Nicolò**, a church and Benedictine monastery where the doge prayed after the Marriage of the Sea ceremony on Ascension Day. From here, there is a clear view of the **Fortezza di Sant'Andrea** on the island of Le Vignole, the impressive bastion that defended the lagoon (see page 239).

If beaches appeal, bear in mind that most are private and charge a fee, unlike the **Spiaggia Comunale**, the public beach at the northeast end of the island. Reports of pollution in the Adriatic do not deter the crowds. South of the Hôtel des Bains

The Lido is home to several of the city's most elegant hotels, including the **Hôtel des Bains** (Via Lungomare Marconi 17). Thomas Mann's stay in this eclectic Edwardian palace helped inspire *Death in Venice*. Even Mann's beach spelt foreboding: "Evening too was rarely lovely, balsamic with the

Lido

stands the **Palazzo del Cinema** ㉝, typical of the functionalist buildings of the Fascist era, and the focus of the Venice Film Festival. On Lungomare Marconi, along the seafront, stands the **Hotel Excelsior** ㉞, inspired by exotic Moorish models and Veneto-Byzantine traditions.

A cycle ride or leisurely walk lead south past the grand hotels and manicured beaches, following the sea walls into oblivion. The route passes **Malamocco** ㉟, a pleasant fishing village that has several seafood restaurants and a belltower recalling the campanile of San Marco. The original Malamocco is believed to have been an island off the Lido that has disappeared without a trace. The spit eventually peters out in the sand dunes of **Alberoni**, with the windswept views beloved by Goethe now only visible across golf courses. These are the Venetians' preferred beaches, where the sand and water are cleaner than further north, and anyone can lay out a towel free of charge. Buses run here from the ferry landing.

Beyond is the island of **Pellestrina**, a narrow strip of land bounded by

Aerial view of the Lido.

the *murazzi*, the great sea walls that protect the lagoon city. For the first time since the city's creation, the sea defences are being radically re-thought and a mobile dam is being built nearby: whether to save Venice from the sea, or as an act of political folly, only time will tell.

Sunbathing on Lido beach.

THE MINOR ISLANDS

The smaller islands of the lagoon show a
different face of Venice: among the delightful
backwaters are a famous cemetery, isolated
monasteries and a rural way of life.

Main Attractions
San Michele
San Francesco del
Deserto
Lazzaretto Nuovo
Sant'Erasmo
Le Vignole
Pellestrina

Map
Page 236

Adrift between the industrial and the rural world, the lesser-known islands of the Venetian lagoon are abandoned to birdsong, howling dogs and the prayers of monks. Apart from the religious communities who cherish their isolation, the minor islands are searching for a new identity. In the past, they served specific functions, with the

city defences bolstered by the islands close to the Lido, the monastic islands clustered around San Marco, and outlying islands used as hospitals or munitions stores. Remoteness rendered the islands suitable for such esoteric uses as quarantine centres and lunatic asylums, hermitages and monastic retreats – even cemeteries, leper colonies and dog sanctuaries.

About 20 of the 34 lagoon islands are virtually abandoned, although reclusive millionaires, cultural associations and hotel chains are waiting in the wings. At intervals, the Italian State, daunted by the future upkeep of the islands, auctions or leases certain minor treasures, usually on the understanding that any forts and monasteries are restored.

Although the fate of such islands as Lazzaretto Vecchio and Poveglia still hangs in the balance, success stories abound, from the university on San Servolo to the luxury resort on San Clemente and the opening up of the former quarantine island of Lazzaretto Nuovo and La Certosa.

Thanks to the shifting tides and the shallowness of the lagoon, the islands preserve a pastoral way of life, one that is rarely visible to visitors who stay close to the shore. At low tide, the shrimp fishermen leave their boats and seem to walk across water; families picnicking on remote

The Minor Islands

sandbanks appear from nowhere and then disappear again with the tide. With the blur of mainland pollution merging into a heat haze, you may catch sight of the vivid plumage of a migratory bird or two.

In the *valli* fisheries, locks are checked and the fish directed into different ponds while, to the east of Torcello, the salt pans continue to be worked. Children play in the vineyards of Le Vignole while their uncles tend to their market gardens on neighbouring Sant'Erasmo, and sun-worshippers stretch out on the sandbars of Pellestrina.

The autumn **Galuppi Festival** (www.festivalgaluppi.it) is a successful way of opening up unusual sites, with concerts staged in churches, forts and former leper colonies on San Francesco del Deserto, Sant'Erasmo and San Lazzaretto Nuovo.

San Michele ❶

Address: Isola San Michele
Tel: 041-729 811
Opening Hrs: daily Apr–Sept 7.30am–6pm, Oct–Mar 7.30am–4pm
Entrance Fee: free
Transport: Cimitero

San Michele, site of the city cemetery, is known as "the island of the dead". From afar, its silhouette is swathed in mist, floating as ethereally as a city in the afterlife. As the island closest to Venice, it is served by ferries from the Fondamente Nuove. The quayside and adjoining alleys serve the business of death: monumental masons vie with funeral florists, both doing their briskest business in winter. From the shore, one's eye is drawn to the contrast between the solemn cypress trees, black against the sky, and the high, rose-coloured brick walls.

Just by the landing-stage lies **San Michele in Isola**, a cool, austere Renaissance church by Coducci. As the first church faced in white Istrian stone, San Michele set a building trend throughout the Veneto. Beside the church is a domed Gothic chapel and cloisters leading to the cemetery.

This was where Napoleon decreed the dead should be despatched, away from the crowded city graves. Famous foreigners are allowed to rest in peace, but more modest souls tend to be evicted after 10 years. The rambling cemetery is lined with gardens stacked with simple memorials or domed family mausoleums awaiting further members. Here lie the tombs of several dogal families, obscure diplomats, and the victims of malaria or the plague. The grounds are studded with grotesque statuary, encompassing the monumental and the municipal, the cute and the kitsch.

In the eastern corner is the Protestant *(Evangelisti)* section, containing the grave of American poet Ezra Pound (1885–1972). Untended and overgrown, this is also the last resting place of obscure Swiss, German and British seamen. In the *Greci* or Orthodox section lie the tombs of the composer Igor Stravinsky (1882–1971) and the ballet impresario Diaghilev (1872–1929), along with the tombs of long-forgotten Russian and Greek aristocrats. The British architects David Chipperfield are creating an extension to the cemetery, including gardens, funerary chapels, footbridges and even a crematorium. The first courtyard has been completed and work started on a parallel island with tomb buildings and gardens.

San Francesco del Deserto ❷

Address: Isola San Francesco; www.sanfrancescodeldeserto.it
Tel: 041-528 6863
Opening Hrs: Tue–Sun 9–11am and 3–5pm
Entrance Fee: free (donations accepted)
Transport: boat hire (www.lagunafla.it)

TIP

For information on ferries, call 041-2424 as they can be infrequent. For San Lazzaro degli Armeni take line 20 (best at 3.10pm from San Zaccaria); for San Servolo line 20; for San Francesco del Deserto line N to Burano then water taxi; for San Michele, known as Cimitero, lines 4.1 or 4.2; for Sant'Erasmo and Lazzaretto Nuovo line 13.

San Michele, "island of the dead".

San Francesco del Deserto (St Francis of the Desert) is a fascinating Franciscan retreat. Since there are no ferry services, visitors will need to hire a water taxi or *sandolo*, a Venetian rowing boat, from Burano, the closest inhabited island. Legend has it that St Francis visited on his return from the Holy Land, symbolised by a tree that supposedly sprouted from the saint's staff. This early Franciscan community has been abandoned only twice, after an outbreak of malaria and military occupation, and was the only monastery to be spared desecration by Napoleonic troops.

The monastery exudes an air of self-sufficiency, from the serene friars to the cloisters, church and well-tended vegetable gardens. A contemplative mood is induced by the lofty cypresses and emblematic Franciscan paintings. Up to 10 friars live here, along with visiting novices and laymen on retreats.

Lazzaretto Nuovo ❸

Address: Lazzaretto Nuovo, www.lazzarettonuovo.com
Tel: 041-244 4011
Opening Hrs: Sat–Sun Apr–Oct 9.45am and 4.30pm
Entrance Fee: free
Transport: Lazzaretto Nuovo (Line 13 from Venezia-Fondamente Nuove).

Newly opened **Lazzaretto Nuovo** is a former monastery, quarantine island and military garrison (visits by prior arrangement only through the Archeoclub Venezia (www.archeove.com) who are carrying out archaeological excavations on the island, tel: 041-520 6713). This austere island was a Benedictine monastery until 1468, when it became a quarantine centre for Venetian ships suspected of harbouring contagion. Designed to combat the spread of diseases transported via oriental ports, the island became a model for quarantine centres all over the Mediterranean, from Malta to Marseille. It was dubbed "new" *(nuovo)* to distinguish it from **Lazzaretto Vecchio**, off the Lido, the "old" quarantine island for plague victims. In Austrian times, the island was converted into a military garrison, with a gunpowder-and-munitions factory.

The most impressive building is the **Tezon Grande**, a barn-like

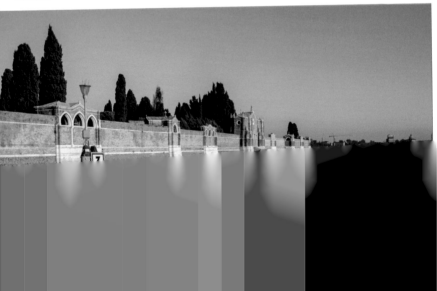

16th-century structure, complete with historical graffiti. The imposing bastions also make an atmospheric nature trail, with misty views over the lagoon. Guided visits on weekends are timed to coincide with discretionary stops by the number 13 ferry between Fondmente Nuove and Sant'Erasmo.

Sant'Erasmo

Facing Lazzaretto is **Sant' Erasmo** ❹, the large market garden in the heart of the lagoon. This little-visited island is home to just 800 people, many of them small-scale farmers, but the community now benefits from rural tourism. Venice's vegetable garden is famed for its production of radicchio, asparagus and artichokes, delivered to the Rialto market by boat. Yet Sant'Erasmo also attracts walkers, cyclists and canoeists in summer, when the small beach and simple restaurant at the southeast end become a magnet for Venetian families and teenage boat-boys.

There are several ferry stops on the island, but **Capannone** is the closest to Venice and is convenient for the beach, sole trattoria, fort and canoeing club. **Torre Massimiliana**, the Austrian fort once used as a barracks and munitions dump, has been well renovated and is used for temporary exhibitions.

Le Vignole and Isola La Certosa

Le Vignole ❺ lies just south of Sant' Erasmo but can also be viewed from the northern end of the **Lido**. Its sole claim to fame is that it served as the main plank in the Venetian defensive system. The Sant'Andrea fort, designed by Sanmicheli in 1543, guarded the lagoon, with chains stretching right across the water from here to a matching fortress on the Lido. The lagoon entrance was thus completely sealed off and reinforced by lines of cannons resting on rafts.

Although dilapidated, the fort is still visible, forming an arched

bastion with apertures at water level to accommodate more cannon. The island remains popular with Venetians, thanks to its patchwork of vineyards and smallholdings. In summer, the adults congregate in a makeshift café, while children dive off their parents' boats.

The neighbouring former monastic island of **La Certosa** has been

Church of San Michele cloisters.

Fishing near one of the lagoon's 34 islands.

Cruising the Brenta Canal

The area linking Venice and Padua is known as the Riviera del Brenta, reflecting its role as a summer retreat for the Venetian nobility.

The Brenta Canal is a showcase for Venice's rural treasures, over 50 sumptuous villas which are regularly open to visitors. In echoes of the Grand Tour, visitors can take a canal-boat along the Brenta to Padua. The route involves nine swing-bridges and five locks, a reminder that there is a 10-metre difference in water level between Venice and Padua.

The Veneto possesses the blueprint for the patrician villa, a harmonious rural retreat framed by waterside formal gardens and a working farm estate. Characterised by a classical portico, and modelled on a Graeco-Roman temple, these Palladian gems have influenced architectural styles the world over. From Renaissance times, the Venetian nobility commissioned these residences as retreats from the summer

Cruising past Villa Pisani.

heat. In summer, the villa became a society haunt, a setting for lavish festivities, notably gambling, a favourite Venetian vice. To this end, most villas have a *barchessa*, a colonnaded wing used as a summer house, banqueting hall or gambling pavilion.

From Venice, the first masterpiece is **Villa Foscari**, better known as La Malcontenta because of its troubled romantic past. This distinctive villa was designed for the Foscari family, and is still owned by their descendants. Raised on a pedestal to protect it from floods, it has a temple-like facade mirrored in the Brenta and a vaulted *piano nobile* modelled on the interiors of Roman baths.

Further along, set on a scenic bend in the canal, is the late-baroque **Villa Widmann**, decorated in fanciful French rococo style. The grounds are lined with cypresses, horse-chestnut and limes, and dotted with neoclassical statuary, centred on an ornamental lake. **Barchessa Valmarana**, which faces Villa Widmann across the water, is all that remains of a villa destroyed in the early 20th century to avoid death duties. This glorious relic has been restored and contains frescoes rivalling its more famous neighbours.

Closer to Padua is **Villa Pisani**, a palatial masterpiece which owes much to French classicism. A ballroom frescoed by Tiepolo is matched by grandiose grounds dotted with follies, an appropriate setting for Mussolini and Hitler's first meeting in 1934. At Stra, just beyond Villa Pisani, looms **Villa Foscarini Rossi**, a testament to the ambitions of the Foscarini dynasty, including Doge Foscarini, a past owner. The Palladian-inspired villa contains baroque *trompe l'œil* frescoes depicting allegories of war and peace, science and the arts. The heroic adventurer, Lord Byron, a previous resident, must have felt at home.

Several companies offer tours along the Brenta with visits to villas and optional lunch thrown in. The cruise is usually done one way from Venice or Padua, with a bus making the return trip. Try Il Burchiello (www.ilburchiello.it) and I Battelli del Brenta (www.battellidelbrenta.it). You can also visit most villas independently by car or bus.

converted into the base for Venice's main marina. Vento di Venezia (tel: 041-520 8588; www.ventodivenezia.it) offers moorings for more than 100 visiting yachts, repair shops, a hotel and restaurant-bar, sailing classes and boat charter. They also build and restore timber boats. Vaporetto lines 4.1 and 4.2 call here.

The southern lagoon

Known as **"The Hospital Islands"**, these former asylums and leper colonies are treated with disdain by Venetians, despite their newer incarnations as resorts or cultural centres. **San Clemente ⑥**, just south of Giudecca, began as a monastery, but, in the 19th century, became a lunatic asylum for women, later mutating into a psychiatric hospital until 1992. Since 2003, the island has been an austerely luxurious resort, playing up its past as a monastery rather than a madhouse. Despite insane prices, the island retreat is a lovely spot, with low-key restaurants and bars, open to visitors and guests.

Between Giudecca and the Lido lies **San Servolo** island, which rose to prominence as a Benedictine monastery, but then became a nunnery until 1615. After welcoming refugee nuns from Crete, a former Venetian colony, San Servolo started operating as a hospital. In 1725, it became an asylum for Venetian "maniacs of noble family", of whom there were many. The asylum was built within the monastic shell, with the church remodelled and new wards created. Byron often passed the island on his marathon swims from the Lido to the Grand Canal.

In recent years the restored complex has been given a new lease of life as a prestigious craft centre and as Venice International University, with English the medium of instruction. San Servolo has managed to preserve its 18th-century pharmacy and library as well as the cloisters and its lush grounds. In the **Museo della Follia** (Museum of Madness; tel: 041-276 5451/2; www.fondazionesanservolo.it), two chilling rooms explain asylum history, especially from the 19th century on. On show are instruments used for electro-shock therapy, chains and straight jackets. The guided tour of the island must be booked in advance. Take vaporetto 20 from San Zaccaria.

Santa Maria delle Grazie, immediately south of Giudecca, began as a medieval crusaders' staging post, but swiftly became a monastic site,

Sant'Erasmo, Venice's vegetable garden.

military base, munitions dump and hospital for infectious diseases.

San Lazzaro degli Armeni ❼

Address: San Lazzaro degli Armeni
Tel: 041-526 0104
Opening Hrs: tour 3.25–5pm
Entrance Fee: charge
Transport: San Lazzaro (Vaporetto no. 20 from San Zaccaria)

San Lazzaro degli Armeni, an island off the Lido, is one of the most intriguing monasteries in the lagoon, distinguished by its onion-shaped cupola. (This Armenian enclave is served by line 20 from San Zaccaria, with the 3.10pm ferry the only practicable option.)

The Armenians, along with the Greeks and Jews, form the oldest foreign community in Venice, having settled in the city from the 13th century onwards and remained on good terms with the Republic. The island was a leper colony until 1717, when the Armenians were granted asylum from Turkish persecution. Today, the island is a scholarly centre for Armenian culture, supported by the 5-million strong Armenian diaspora. The setting is idyllic, with the church and cloisters surrounded by orchards, gardens and strolling peacocks. The

San Clemente Palace service boat; the whole island is occupied by the luxurious resort.

remodelled Romanesque church is decorated with starry mosaics, the air laden with incense. The 18th-century refectory is where the courteous, trilingual monks and seminarians eat in silence while the Scriptures are intoned in classical Armenian.

The picture gallery contains fine Venetian and Armenian paintings, while the museum displays bizarre exhibits, from Phoenician artefacts to an Egyptian mummy. The library's priceless books and manuscripts are rivalled by the typesetting hall, which has an ancient printing press capable of reproducing 36 languages.

Although the printing centre closed in 1993, the Armenian press is still run from this nerve centre. One room is dedicated to Byron, because of his enthusiasm for Armenian culture and his contribution to an Armenian–English dictionary in 1816. Browning, Longfellow and Proust were equally impressed by this serene monastery.

Changing fortunes

Lazzaretto Vecchio, long abandoned to stray dogs, has been a pilgrims'

The island of San Servolo.

hostel, hospital and military site, but above all was Europe's first permanent quarantine hospital for plague victims during the 15th and 16th centuries. Hospital is a big word, as conditions during plague outbreaks were appalling. Mass graves with 1,500 victims were unearthed in 2007 and some of these remains could go on display in a long-mooted archaeological museum on the island.

Poveglia, a distinctive humpback island, hugs the southern shore of the Lido. It was once a powerful centre, but decline set in after the devastation of the Genoese war in 1380. Poveglia's chequered past includes a spell as a noble summer residence, a barracks and munitions depot and, until the 1960s, a hospice and retirement home. Despite its virtual abandonment, the island is coveted as a potential secluded holiday resort or marina.

Pellestrina ❽, a long sandy gash that helps protect Venice from the open sea, makes a relaxing summer excursion. (It is best reached from the Lido, by bus 11 to Alberoni connecting with the ferry for a five-minute boat ride to Pellestrina.) This ribbon of land forms a natural barrier strengthened by the *murazzi*, the great sea walls. The island is a haunt of

sunbathing Venetians or solitary walkers, with quaint fishing settlements, gossipy bars and jaunty cottages. You can take a bus down its length and a ferry to the mainland town of Chioggia. To explore, however, you might consider hiring a bicycle on the Lido rather than relying on buses.

As part of the newly reinforced dyke which helps preserve Venice for generations to come, Pellestrina makes a fitting end to an exploration of the lagoon.

The island of Pellestrina.

Mass at San Lazzaro degli Armeni church.

Sunrise in Piazza San Marco.

INSIGHT GUIDES TRAVEL TIPS
VENICE

Transport

Getting There **246**
    By Air **246**
    By Rail **246**
    By Sea **246**
    By Coach **246**
    By Road **246**
Getting Around **247**
    The Airports **247**
    Car Parks **247**
    City Ferries **247**
    Gondolas **248**
    Water Taxis **248**
    Boat Holidays **248**

A – Z

Accommodation **249**
Admission Charges **249**
Addresses **249**
Budgeting for Your Trip .. **250**
Children **250**
Climate **250**
Crime and Safety **251**
Customs Regulations **251**
Disabled Travellers **251**
Embassies/Consulates .. **251**
Etiquette **251**
Festivals and Events **251**
Gay and Lesbian
    Travellers **253**
Health and Medical
    Care **253**
Internet **253**
Maps **253**
Media **253**

Money **253**
Opening Hours **254**
Postal Services **254**
Religious Services **254**
Smoking **254**
Student Travellers **254**
Tax **254**
Telephones **255**
Time Zone **255**
Toilets **255**
Tourist Information **255**
Tourist Offices in
    Venice **255**
Travel Agents **255**
Visas and Passports **255**
Weights and Measures . **255**

Language

Communication **256**
Greetings **256**
In the Hotel **256**
At a Bar **257**
In a Restaurant **257**
Menu Decoder **258**
Sightseeing **259**
Shopping **259**
Transport **259**
Directions **259**

Further Reading

Literature and
    Biography **260**
Travel Memoirs **260**
Other Insight Guides **260**

TRANSPORT

GETTING THERE AND GETTING AROUND

GETTING THERE

Visitors from abroad are most likely to arrive by air. Although other modes of travel offer benefits, all require extra time.

By Air

The main airport for Venice is **Marco Polo** (tel: 041-260 9260; www.veniceairport.it) on the edge of the lagoon, 13km (8 miles) from the city centre. However, Ryanair and other budget airlines confusingly also refer to Treviso's **San Giuseppe** airport (tel: 0422 31 51 11; www.trevisoairport.it) as "Venice airport". This is, in fact, 30km (19 miles) to the north of Venice and far less convenient.

From Europe

There are direct flights to Marco Polo from the major European capitals. Among the airlines serving Venice and Treviso are:
Alitalia: tel: 06-2222, www.alitalia.it
British Airways: tel: 0870-850 9850, www.britishairways.com
EasyJet: tel: 0871-244 2366, www.easyjet.com
Germanwings: tel: 0900-191 9100, www.germanwings.com
Ryanair: tel: 0818-303 030, www.ryanair.com

Wizzair: tel: 895 895 4416, https://wizzair.com

From the US

There are direct flights from New York (JFK) and Philadelphia, but other flights to Venice are usually via London, Rome, Milan, Frankfurt or Amsterdam.
Delta: tel: 800-241 4141, www.delta.com
US Airways: tel: 800-622 1015, www.usairways.com

By Rail

International services converge on Venice from London, Barcelona, Paris, Geneva, Zurich and other major west European cities via Milan. Rail travel from abroad is longer and frequently more expensive than flying. However, train travel has a great deal more charm.

Once at Venice's Santa Lucia station, call in at the tourist office in the entrance hall and buy your vaporetto (ferry) ticket from the kiosk just outside the station, by the waterfront.

Within Italy, there are direct services to Venice from Bologna, Padua, Genoa, Rome, Florence, Ferrara, Milan, Turin and Verona.

Services range from high-speed Eurostar Italian (ES) trains that make limited stops to all-stops regional trains. The fastest

trains are the Alta Velocità (AV) trains that connect Venice with Milan, Rome, Napoli and Salerno.

You can buy train tickets for travel within Italy at machines in the train station, ticket windows (expect queues), travel agents and from Trenitalia (tel: 892 021; www.trenitalia.com).

By Sea

Greek Ferries (www.greekferries.gr) and **Anek** (www.anekitalia.com) has ferries between Venice and Greece. **Venezia Lines** (www.venezialines.com) runs summer boats to and from Croatia and Slovenia.

By Coach

Azienda Trasporti Veneto Orientale (ATVO; tel: 041-520 5530; www.atvo.it) buses run all over the eastern Veneto.
Eurolines (www.eurolines.com) runs international coach services to Venice from major cities all over Europe.

By Road

Travelling to Venice by car from abroad is not cheap. Costs include petrol, motorway tolls, hotels en route and the steep car-park fees in Venice. You will require a current driving licence (an EU licence or International

Driving Permit) and valid insurance.

GETTING AROUND

The best way to get around far-flung parts of the city is by boat – once you have mastered a few key ferry routes, water transport is quite straightforward, although most of the time you will probably be walking, which is often more practicable in the city centre.

The Airports

Both scheduled and charter flights arrive in Venice Marco Polo Airport (tel: 041-260 9260), on the edge of the lagoon. You can buy your bus or water travel pass from the special office in the arrivals hall, en route to the terminal exit. From here to the city centre, you have a choice of routes.

There are several options for reaching Venice from Marco Polo airport. Alilaguna (tel: 041 523-5775; www.alilaguna.com) offers fast ferries from Marco Polo airport to Venice (€27 return) or the islands (€18 return): Lido, Murano and Burano about once an hour. The blue line stops at Fondamente Nuove and Stazione Marittima. The red line stops at Murano (the Museo stop), Certosa, the Lido, Arsenale, Piazza San Marco and Giudecca Zitelle in that order. Travelling to the airport, you can pick up an Alilaguna ferry at several stops, including Zattere, San Marco, San Zaccaria and Arsenale. The orange line runs from San Marco via Rialto and Guglio to the airport. The trip to Piazza San Marco on the red line takes one hour and 10 minutes (a few minutes longer on the blue line). Check times with the booking office in the airport.

A water taxi requires greater outlay. A group of up to four people will pay about €100–160 to Piazza San Marco from the airport. Or pre-book a Venice

Shuttle for €27 per person (minimum 2 passengers) with **Bucintoro Viaggi** (tel: 041-521 0632; www.bucintoroviaggi.com).

Cheaper and more prosaic is the land approach from Marco Polo airport. **Azienda Trasporti Veneto Orientale** (tel: 041-383 672; www.atvo.it) Venice airport shuttle runs from Marco Polo airport to Piazzale Roma (€15 return, 20 minutes). **Azienda Consorzio Trasporti Veneziano** (tel: 041-2424; www.actv.it) bus No 5 (Aerobus) runs between Marco Polo airport and Piazzale Roma (€14 including a waterbus service for 90 minutes). Buses 15 and 45 run to Mestre city and the Mestrerailway station (€8 one way, €15 return).
Land taxis cost around €40 one way from Marco Polo airport to Piazzale Roma (15–20 minutes). From Treviso airport (€70–80) they can take an hour in traffic.

Car Parks

Visitors arriving in Venice by car will need to leave their vehicle at the entrance to the city. Venice is a traffic-free zone, and the closest you can get to the centre in a car is Piazzale Roma, where there are two large multi-storey car parks and good ferry services (http://avm.avmspa.it). There is also a huge multi-storey car park on the adjacent island of Tronchetto, the terminal for the car ferry to the Lido, where driving is allowed. Tronchetto (tel: 041-520 7555, www.veniceparking. it) is linked to Venice (Piazzale Roma) via the new monorail, called the People Mover. This modern elevated shuttle train runs to Venice's centre. It operates all-year round Mon–Sat 7am–11pm and 8am–10pm on Sun. A ticket costs €1,50.

City Ferries

Ferries or water buses are known as *vaporetti* (for timetable information tel: 041-2424) or, more colloquially, *batelli*. It is worth buy-

A Venetian water taxi.

ing an ACTV 1, 2, 3 or 7 day travel pass (respectively €20/30/40/60), which will allow you to travel on any city ferries during this period, including the islands. Those aged 6–29 years can also purchase a combined 3-day transport ticket plus Rolling Venice card offering many discounts and benefits for €28 (online only). The travel passes are expensive, but are cheaper and less fuss than buying individual trips (€7.50 and valid for 75 minutes from stamping on ACTV water bus). These passes do not include the Alilaguna airport water taxis.

You can buy tickets and travel passes online (www.veneziaunica. it) and collect them from vending machines or at one of the many sale and collection points throughout the city. Travel without a valid ticket or pass and you risk an on-the-spot fine.

Alilaguna waterbuses connect the airport with the city centre and the surrounding islands including Murano, Burano and Lido. The company offers passes in two versions: 24 hours for €30 and 72 hours for €65. A single journey costs from €8 to €10 (for timetables and fares see www. alilaguna.it).

The timetables displayed at stops are generally reliable, but double-check with a boatman. The most confusing landing-stages are at San Zaccaria (Riva degli Schiavoni), San Marco and

Public transport, Venice-style.

Fondamente Nuove, because they are spread out along the quaysides, with different services running from different jetties.

The *traghetto* is a useful commuter gondola that crosses the Grand Canal at certain strategic points (€0.70).

Main ferry routes

Line 1 is the most romantic and runs the length of the Grand Canal, stopping everywhere between Piazzale Roma and the Lido. Line 2 is a quicker, circular line with major stops at Piazzale Roma, the train station, Rialto, Accademia, San Zaccaria, along the Zattere and Giudecca, and, in summer, also the Lido. Note that some No. 1 and No. 2 services are limited (for instance, some No. 2s terminate at Rialto). This is usually indicated on the boat and announced by the boatman. Nos 41 (anticlockwise) and 42 (clockwise) describe Venice in a circular route, calling at San Zaccaria, Il Redentore, Piazzale Roma, Ferrovia (the railway station), Fondamente Nuove, San Michele, Murano and Sant'Elena. Vaporetti 51 and 52 also provide long, scenic, circular tours around the periphery, as well as stopping at Murano; in summer they go on to the Lido (change at

Fondamente Nuove to do the whole route). Note that the circular routes travel up the Cannaregio canal, stopping at Guglie, and then skirting the northern shores of Venice, including Fondamente Nuove and the Madonna dell'Orto (Tintoretto's church), the shipyards (Bacini stop), San Pietro di Castello and, eventually, the Lido. Nos 61 and 62 provide a fast route between Piazzale Roma and the Lido, going via the Zattere (Giudecca canal). For Burano, take the LN (Laguna Nord) line which departs from Fondamente Nuove and goes via Murano. Line T connects Burano with Torcello. Alternatively, hop on the lagoon lines (no. 12, 13, 14, 19) to get to the outer islands.

Ferries for minor islands

Double-check return times before setting out, as ferries can be infrequent. For San Servolo and San Lazzaro degli Armeni take line 20 from San Zaccaria; for San Francesco del Deserto, LN to Burano from Fondamente Nuove then a water taxi; for San Michele, known as Cimitero, 41 or 42; for Sant' Erasmo, 13 from Fondamente Nuove. For up-to-date information on ferries, call 041-2424.

Gondolas

The city authorities set official rates for gondola hire, often disregarded by the gondoliers. The official daytime rate is €80 for 40 mins (up to six people), then €40–50 for each subsequent 20 mins. The evening rate (from 8pm–8am) is €100. Agree a price and a route with the gondolier, but, for romance, stick to the back canals rather than the Grand Canal.

Water Taxis

Even if many islands are served by the ferry network, island-hopping is not always easy, so bargaining with fishermen is recommended for a rewarding view of Venice beyond the confines of St Mark's. To travel in style, pick up a pricey water taxi on the taxi stand on Riva degli Schiavoni, near San Marco (or call: 041-522 2303 or 041-240 6711).

Boat Holidays

For a houseboat holiday around the Venetian lagoon, contact **Boating Holidays** (tel: 1756 701 200, www.boatingholidays.com) in the UK or **Le Boat** in France (tel: 1-800-734-5491; www.leboat.com).

A – Z

TRANSPORT

AN ALPHABETICAL SUMMARY OF PRACTICAL INFORMATION

A

Accommodation

In theory, the closer you are to San Marco, the higher the price, but there are exceptions, with several pricey hotels on the Lido, Giudecca and San Clemente. The Castello district is an obvious choice, with lagoon views available from the hotels on Riva degli Schiavoni. Delightful, central and convenient though the San Marco area is, it feels resolutely touristy, so Venice fans or second-time visitors would do well to broaden their horizons. This can mean choosing an inn, B&B or a boutique hotel in Castello or San Polo, or even somewhere in the back lanes of Santa Croce and Cannaregio. The tranquil, romantic Dorsoduro district is charming, with small but sought-after mid-market hotels. For families with young children, the Lido makes a good summer choice, with its sandy beaches and bike rides, but remains the least Venetian area of Venice. The budget alternative is the station area, which is convenient rather than attractive.

A handful of options on other islands guarantee a different vision of the city. If forced to stay

outside the city, avoid soulless Mestre and opt for atmospheric Padua or Treviso, a 30-minute train ride from Venice.

Timing and booking

Since there is almost no offseason in Venice, hotels can easily be fully booked all year round, though the recent opening or refurbishment of so many luxury hotels means there is a wide choice at the top end of the market. In any case, make reservations well ahead of peak seasons such as Christmas, New Year, Carnival (February), Easter, May–June and September.

Cost and quality

Venice is the most costly city in Italy and its hotels are notoriously expensive. A simple, central hotel is often the same price as a midmarket hotel elsewhere in Italy.

The basic rules in Venice are: book early, and check where your room faces, and what the price differential is between poky rooms and palatial rooms. A typical hotel can offer a choice between an expensive large room overlooking the Grand Canal, and a poky back room overlooking a bleak courtyard. Even so, a room with a view can cost half as much again as one without a view.

Admission Charges

Among the most expensive sights are the Palazzo Ducale and Museo Correr, the Torre dell'Orologio, Palazzo Grassi and the Punta della Dogana galleries. Various combined tickets are available. A single one-entry combined ticket (Museum Pass) valid for the Doge's Palace, Museo Correr, Museo Archeologico Nazionale and Monumental Rooms of the Biblioteca Nazionale Marciana costs €24 (family and student discounts available). Meanwhile a visit to the Belltower (Torre dell'Orologio) will set you back €12. A combined ticket to the Palazzo Grassi and the Punta della Dogana galleries will cost another €20. For details about most museum opening hours and prices visit www.visitmuve.it. For more information on general passes, see Booking and Discount Cards.

Addresses

Finding your way around Venice can be tricky. Addresses in each *sestiere* (district) are numbered from 1 into the thousands. The numbering snakes in and around streets in a fashion that is not immediately logical, although once you get the hang of it, it's not so hard. Official addresses usually consist of this number and the

A – Z

LANGUAGE

sestiere. For newcomers, adding the street or *campo* name helps. Addresses in this book list street names and *sestiere* above all.

B

Budgeting for Your Trip

Given its unique location, Venice is the most expensive city in Italy. Make use of any travel passes and discounts on offer and use water taxis sparingly. Boat transport (see page 247) is expensive as it acts as an indirect city subsidy and tourism tax. But you will not need to use ferries every day, so plan island trips to run on the same or consecutive days and buy the right transport pass accordingly (for instance, plan to see Murano, Burano and Torcello on the same day).

Venezia Unica City Pass (www. veneziaunica.it) is an integrated, online-only booking system for key museums and transport, with discounts offered in quieter periods.

Museum Pass (www.veneziau-nica.com) covers 11 civic museums and the Chorus Pass includes the 16 Chorus Churches. All passes are integrated with the Venezia Unica City Pass and can be bought online (www. veneziaunica.it).

Rolling Venice is a youth pass is for those aged between 6 and 29. For €6 expect museum discounts, along with a discounted 72-hour vaporetto pass for only €22. A €34 version includes a return ticket from/to Marco Polo airport. Buy the pass online at www.veneziaunica.it.

As for meals, avoid bland "tourist menus"; instead choose a simple but atmospheric Venetian tapas bar (*bacaro*) as a budget option. In most places, there is a premium imposed on sitting down; even so, it is often worth it to appreciate the atmosphere of a grand San Marco café, for instance. For a full sitdown meal (three courses and house wine), you will rarely pay less than €30. Heading upscale, a more typical price might be around €60–80. At top-class restaurants, be prepared for bills well over €100.

For accommodation, reckon on a minimum of €100 per night for a double room. For a good mid-range hotel, you could pay up to €250. The sky's the limit at top-range hotels. A glass of wine at the bar can cost as little as €2–3, while a beer will usually be around €4–5.

C

Children

Venice can capture the imagination of children as much as adults. Simply watching the endless activity on the canals, jumping on a vaporetto or *traghetto* or climbing some of the viewpoints (like the Campanile in Piazza San Marco) will keep most kids engrossed. Throw in a good *gelato* every now and then and, in summer, a trip to the beaches on the Lido, and family union should be ensured.

Discounts are usually available for children under 12 on public transport, and at museums, galleries and other sights. *Viva*

CLIMATE CHART

Venice

- Maximum temperature
- Minimum temperature
- Rainfall

Venice, by Paola Scibilia and Paolo Zoffoli, and *Venice for Kids*, by Elisabetta Pasqualin are illustrated books aimed at children, full of tall tales and games about Venice. Some of the major hotels, especially those on the Lido di Venezia, offer a baby-sitting service.

Climate

The Venetian climate is notoriously capricious, with a spectrum of weather possible in one day. January can be bitterly cold, wet and windy and then illuminated by warm sunshine. Humidity affects the hottest and coldest days. Venice in the height of summer can be oppressively muggy, but there is always the Lido to escape to. The weather is hottest in August, with an average temperature of 24°C (75°F) but highs usually well into the 30s°C (90s°F).

Most rain falls in March to April and November to December, but *acqua alta*, which occurs between the autumn and spring, is the condition Venetians loathe: exceptionally high tides often flood the low-lying areas of the city, including San Marco. It rarely snows in Venice but the city is exposed to fog and two harsh winds: the *bora* blows from the steppes in winter and is linked with low atmospheric pressure, while the sirocco brings hot weather from the Middle East. That said, Venice experiences

TRANSPORT

A – Z

LANGUAGE

sunny days and limpid lagoon light in all seasons. The loveliest months of the year are probably May, June and September, but even the dark depths of winter, swathed in romantic mists, have their appeal. In spring, the city can be highly dramatic, viewed from the top of San Giorgio, with the wind buffeting the tower and the bobbing boats on the lagoon. Average temperatures are: January 3.8°C (38.8°F), April 12.6°C (54.6°F), July 23.6°C (74.4°F) and October 15.1°C (59.1°F).

Crime and Safety

Venice is an exceptionally safe city, no matter what thriller-writers would have one believe. Stringent security measures in St Mark's Basilica mean that all bags have to be left in the Ateneo San Basso on Piazzetta dei Leoncini, a free left-luggage service. That said, pickpockets are not uncommon, especially in the crowded areas around the Rialto and San Marco. Carry only what is absolutely necessary; leave the rest in the hotel safe.

Customs Regulations

Visitors arriving from non-European Union member countries may import, duty free: 1 litre of spirits (or 2 litres of wine), 50 grams perfume, 250ml eau de toilette, 200 cigarettes and other goods up to a total of €175. Anything over this limit must be declared on arrival and the appropriate duty paid.

D

Disabled Travellers

Venice presents considerable challenges, so careful pre-planning is required, especially for those with limited mobility: steps, queues, and getting on and off ferries and gondolas all present hazards; few museums and relatively few hotels have adequate access and facilities.

The official city website for the disabled, www.comune.venezia.it/handicap is useful. A map available from APT tourist offices indicates areas that can be explored without running into a bridge. Some bridges are equipped with lifts. Tourist offices should be able to provide keys to operate these lifts. A disabled assistance office is located in front of platform 4 at the railway station. Vaporetto lines 1 and 82 and the bigger lagoon ferries have wheelchair access.

Ca' Rezzonico and the Doge's Palace are fully accessible, apart from the prisons and the Secret Itinerary (see page 108); the Museo Correr is partially accessible. In the UK, contact **Holiday Care** (0845-124 9971; www.holidaycare.org.uk) for lists of accessible accommodation in Italy. In the US, contact **Access-Able** (www.access-able.com).

E

Embassies/Consulates

Venice has almost 40 consulates, but many foreign nationals will need to contact their embassies in Rome or consulates elsewhere. The British honorary consulate is in Mestre, mainland Venice (Piazza Donatori di Sange 2/5; tel: 041-505 5990). The nearest United States consulate is in Milan (Via Principe Amedeo 2/10; tel: 02-290 351), as is an Australian representative (Via Borgogna 2; tel: 02-776 741). The nearest Canadian Consulate is in Padua (Riviera Ruzzante 25; tel: 049-876 4833). Irish citizens will need to contact their embassy in Rome. Italian embassies abroad include:
Australia: 12 Grey St, Deakin ACT 2600, tel: 02-6273 3333, www.ambcanberra.esteri.it
Canada: 21st fl, 275 Slater St, Ottawa, Ontario, K1P 5H9, tel: 613-232 2401, www.ambottawa.esteri.it
Ireland: 63–5 Northumberland Rd, Dublin 4, tel: 01-660 1744, www.ambdublino.esteri.it

ELECTRICITY

220 volts. You will need an adaptor to operate British three-pin appliances and a transformer to use 100- to 120-volt appliances.

New Zealand: 34–8 Grant Rd, Thorndon, Wellington, tel: 04-4735 339, www.ambwellington.esteri.it
UK: 14 Three Kings Yard, London W1K 4EH, tel: 020-7312 2200, www.amblondra.esteri.it
USA: 3000 Whitehaven St, NW Washington, DC 20008, tel: 202-612 4400, www.ambwashingtondc.esteri.it

Etiquette

Visitors to churches should be modestly dressed. This means covering shoulders and knees. Venice's streets are narrow and locals become infuriated by slow-moving tourists blocking the way. More often than not, walking in single file along narrow lanes helps smooth ruffled feathers. Move inside and to the back when boarding vaporetti (water buses) – do not gather at boat entrances, blocking the way to others who wish to board or disembark. When meeting Italians for the first time, a handshake is the usual greeting. A kiss on each cheek is generally reserved for people who are already acquainted.

F

Festivals and Events

Venice is busy all year round, with the Lenten Carnival and the Film Festival flagged as the most popular events. While there are almost 100 regattas on the lagoon, the key one is in September. Most city water festivals are child-friendly and often accompanied by fireworks, while Carnival is the time for dressing up and parading around. For more on the main festivities, see Carnival (see page 75) and

Water Festivals (see page 80). Major art exhibitions take place throughout the year. For current events, pick up a copy of the free listings magazine, *La Rivista di Venezia*, from the tourist office or the magazines noted above. For upcoming events, check the official Venice websites (www.turismovenezia.it and www.culturaspettacolovenezia.it or www.veneziaunica.it).

January

Regata della Befana, 6 January, the Epiphany Regatta is the first race of the year.

February

Carnevale (Carnival) is the opening to the city's festive season. (See page 75)
So e Zo i Ponti, fourth Sunday of Lent. A non-competitive marathon crossing bridges and canals.

April

Festa di San Marco, 25 April, is the celebration of the city saint, with a ceremonial Mass in the basilica and the romantic presentation of a *bocolo* (rosebud) to women.

May

Festa della Sensa, Sunday after Ascension Day, is a re-enactment of the Marriage of Venice with the Sea, followed by a gondola regatta off the Lido.
La Vogalonga, the "long row", is a marathon rowing race (dates vary).
Il Palio Delle Quattro Antiche Repubbliche Marinare is a major regatta in honour of the four ancient maritime republics, which take turns to host it. Venice had the honour in 2015 (and will host it again in 2019).

June

Venezia Suona, the summer music festival, is held in the streets and squares of the city.
The **Sagra di San Pietro** on 29 June is dedicated to St Peter and centred on the church of the same name, with concerts in the city's first cathedral.
The **Art Biennale** contemporary

art show runs odd years only from June to November and is staged in the Giardini gardens, the Teatro Piccolo Arsenale, and in other locations around the city. The **Architecture Biennale** takes place in even years in the same locations. (Tel: 041-521 8711; www.labiennale.org.)
I Concerti di Piazza San Marco. A series of big-name concerts from June to August, with Italian and international stars filling St Mark's Square with the sound of music.

July

The **Murano Regatta** in early July is held off the island of Murano and is accompanied by feasts and music.
Festa del Redentore (Festival of the Redeemer), third weekend in July. This bridge of boats across the Giudecca canal is a celebration in thanksgiving for the city's survival from an outbreak of plague; an exceptional fireworks display takes place on the water.
The **San Pellegrino Regatta** near the end of the month celebrates racing and cooking.
D'Estate in Campo is when theatre, music and other events take place in Venice's squares and several mainland locations from July to September.

August

Ferragosto (the Assumption), 15 August, is celebrated with fireworks and concerts, including on Torcello.

September

The **Venice Film Festival** runs for 10 days in early September. Films are shown in their original versions

and, while art-house movies rather than blockbusters tend to win the awards, the festival attracts a glitzy Hollywood crowd. Nightlife is more cosmopolitan during the festival and centred on the Lido by day and San Marco by night.
The **Regata Storica (Historic Regatta)** on the first Sunday of the month is the finest regatta in Venice. It includes a procession up the Grand Canal led by craft and costumed Venetians, and is followed by gondola races. **The Sagra del Pesce**, the Burano fish festival and regatta, also includes a music festival held on the island of Burano.
Festival Galuppi (www.festivalgaluppi.it), named after a Burano composer, is a successful way of opening up curious sites, with concerts staged in Franciscan churches, forts and former leper colonies on the islands of San Francesco del Deserto, Sant'Erasmo, and San Lazzaretto Nuovo throughout September. There are also concerts and organ recitals in Ca' Rezzonico, La Pietà and in La Salute in central Venice (book on 041-522 1120). Burano's Sagra del Pesce festival is the last regatta of the season preceded by a feast of fried fish and white wine.

October

Festival del Mosto (Grape Harvest) takes place on the island of Sant'Erasmo; the small quantity of grapes is an excuse for a feast and party.

November

Festa della Madonna della Salute, 21 November. Procession

BOOKING AND DISCOUNT CARDS

Venezia Unica (www.veneziaunica.it) is the city's official tourist website where you can buy the useful **Venezia Unica** city pass. It offers access to public transportation (waterbuses), tourist attractions (museums, churches), cultural events, tours and much more at discount rates. You can find all

information about the pass at the Venezia Unica website. VeneziaSi is an organisation representing over 90 per cent of Venetian hoteliers, but it also accepts bookings for major exhibitions and concerts (from abroad call: +39-041-522 2264; in Italy call 199 173 309; www.veneziasi.it).

across the Grand Canal on floating pontoons to La Salute basilica in thanksgiving for the city's survival from the plague. November also marks the start of the **Venice Opera Season** at La Fenice (tel: 041-786 672).

December

Christmas concerts in the Basilica di San Marco and La Fenice. There are also displays of Murano glass cribs *(presepi)* in various churches.
New Year's Eve, celebrity rock concert in one venue, and a classical concert in La Fenice.

G

Gay and Lesbian Travellers

Homosexuality is legal in Italy and well tolerated in Venice. That said, there are no specifically gay or lesbian venues in the city. **ArciGay** (www.arcigay.it), the national gay organisation, has information on the gay and lesbian scene in Italy. The nearest gay organisation to Venice is ArciGay Tralaltro in Padua (Corso Garibaldi 41; tel: 049-876 2458; www.tralaltro.it), where you'll also find several gay nightlife options.

H

Health and Medical Care

EU citizens should carry a European Health Insurance Card (EHIC), which covers them for most medical care in public hospitals free of charge. In the UK, the card is available from post offices. Australia and Italy have a reciprocal arrangement for free medical care (Australians should carry their Medicare card). Even with these cards, travellers should take out appropriate insurance to cover emergency repatriation. Visitors of other nationalities should definitely take out travel insurance.

An Italian pharmacist is qualified to advise on minor health complaints. Night pharmacists *(farmacie di guardia)* operate on a rota system, so consult your hotel or check the sign posted on any pharmacy. If you are seriously ill, telephone 118 or go to the Pronto Soccorso (casualty department) of the nearest hospital. In central Venice, this is the Ospedale Civile, Campo Santi Giovanni e Paolo (San Zanipolo), tel: 041-529 4516 (casualty), beside the church of Santi Giovanni e Paolo and also accessible by water taxi. Take mosquito repellent in the summer, especially for lagoon trips.

I

Internet

WiFi has become increasingly common in bars and restaurants as well as in hotels. There is also a possibility to buy internet access (one- to seven-day packages) through the Venezia Unica Card scheme (www.veneziaunica.it). The city-wide **WiFi access network** costs €8 per day but check if the signal works properly in your chosen spots before buying a package. The number of internet cafés has dwindled recently with only a few still in operation, including Janata Internet and Telephone Centre (Via cappuccina,153/A) by the train station and Venetian Navigator 2srl (San Marco 5547; www.venetiannavigator.com) near the Rialto Bridge.

M

Maps

Insight Fleximap Venice is a water-resistant map with information on all top attractions in the city. A handy little map is the wine red-covered *Venezia* produced by the Touring Club Italiano (scale 1:5000). If you plan to stay for a long time, consider *Calli, Campielli*

e Canali (Edizioni Helvetica), the definitive street atlas. Or go online for the interactive map at www.ombra.net.

Media

International publications can be found in Venice. The main Italian papers *(Il Corriere della Sera* and *La Repubblica)* publish northern editions, but the most useful local daily is *Il Gazzettino*, which carries information on transport, entertainment and on duty chemists. This is presented clearly, so anyone with a smattering of Italian should understand it. To find out what's on, pick up a copy of *La Rivista di Venezia*, a monthly bi-lingual magazine with a listings insert, from the tourist office as well as the free booklet, *Un Ospite a Venezia/A Guest in Venice* from one of the grand hotels. Alternatively, go to http://events.veneziaunica.it.
In general, Italian television ranges from bad to appalling. Better hotels are fitted with satellite television, with channels in English, French, German and possibly Japanese.

Money

The unit of currency in Italy is the euro. There are 5, 10, 20, 50, 100, 200 and 500 euro notes, and 1, 2, 5, 10, 20 and 50 cent coins.
Banks are open Mon – Fri from 8.30am to 1.30pm and sometimes from 2.45 to 4pm. You will need your passport when changing money. Most of the time, you should be able to withdraw money from ATMs, the majority of which have instructions in foreign languages. Most hotels do not accept travellers' cheques. Major credit cards are accepted by most large stores and restaurants, but

LEFT LUGGAGE

There is a left luggage facility at the train station, which costs roughly €6 for the first five hours per piece of luggage.

TRANSPORT

A – Z

LANGUAGE

PUBLIC HOLIDAYS

Banks and most shops are closed on the following public holidays.

1 January New Year's Day *(Capodanno)*
6 January Epiphany *(Befana)*
March/April Easter Monday *(Lunedì di Pasqua)*
25 April Liberation Day *(Anniversario della Liberazione)*
1 May May Day *(Festa del Lavoro)*
2 June Republic Day *(Festa della Repubblica)*
15 August August holiday *(Ferragosto)*
1 November All Saints *(Ognissanti)*
8 December Immaculate Conception *(Immacolata Concezione)*
25 December Christmas Day *(Natale)*
26 December Boxing Day *(Santo Stefano)*

are less common than in North America or Northern Europe. Always check to avoid embarrassment. Foreign-exchange offices are plentiful around the San Marco and Rialto areas, but give a less-favourable rate of exchange than banks.

It is customary to tip for certain services, so it is worth carrying loose change (which also comes in handy for ensuring decent lighting in front of key treasures in city churches). Most restaurants impose a cover charge *(pane e coperto)* of €2–7. In addition, there is often a 10–12 percent service charge *(servizio)* added to the bill. If the menu says that service is included, then a small additional tip is discretionary. If service is not included, then leave between 12 and 15 percent of the bill. Gondoliers need not be tipped but water taxi drivers may expect a small tip. Tips to local guides depend on their ability and the length of the trip: €2.50–5 per person.

O

Opening Hours

Business hours are Monday to Saturday, 9 or 10am until 1pm, and 3 or 4pm until 7pm. Some shops are open all day and even on Sundays, particularly in peak season. Office hours are normally 7.30am–12.30pm and 3.30pm–6.30pm. Government

offices are usually only open to the public in the mornings. Churches tend to be open Mon–Sat from 10am to 5pm. The 16 churches included in the Chorus group (see Booking and Discount Cards box) are: Santa Maria del Giglio; Santo Stefano; Santa Maria Formosa; Santa Maria dei Miracoli; the Frari; San Polo; San Giacomo dell'Orio; San Giovanni Elemosinario; San Giobbe (closed for restoration); San Stae; Madonna dell'Orto; San Pietro di Castello; San Sebastiano; Il Redentore; Sant'Alvise and the Gesuati. The Frari opens Mon–Sat 9am–6pm and Sun 1–6pm while the Church of San Giobbe Mon–Sat 10am–1.30pm. Last entrance is 15 minutes before closing.

Museums tend to close on Monday (opening times are given in the main section of the book).

P

Postal Services

Post offices are generally open Mon–Fri 8.20am–1.30pm. In Venice, the main post office is at Fondachi dei Tedeschi on the St Mark's side of the Rialto (Mon–Sat 8.20am–12.35pm). Stamps *(francobolli)* are also available from tobacconists *(tabacchi)*. The postal service is not renowned for its speed, so if you need to send an urgent letter, ask for *posta prioritaria*.

R

Religious Services

Catholicism is the dominant religion in Venice and Italy. Visitors to St Mark's Basilica are channelled along set routes, so Catholics might consider visiting from 7 to 9.45am, when only worshippers are welcome. For a full list of church services, pick up the free *A Guest in Venice* from any of the grand hotels.

S

Smoking

Smoking is banned in all enclosed public spaces, except where properly ventilated smokers' areas have been set up. Many hotels offer non-smoking rooms.

Student Travellers

Students with a valid card often get discounts on tours, civic museums and other services. The Rolling VENICEcard, for young people age 6 to 29, is worth getting to ensure further discounts. The card (€6) is available with ACTV transport ticket (3 days) on line at www. veneziaunica.it.

The **Centro Turistico Studentesco e Giovanile** (Calle Foscari, Dorsoduro; tel: 041-520 5660; www.cts.it) is the Italian student and youth travel organisation.

T

Tax

On leaving the EU, non-EU citizens can reclaim any sales tax (IVA) on purchases of €155 or more. Fill out a form at the point of sale and have it stamped by Italian customs as you leave. At major airports you can obtain an immediate cash refund. Alternatively, the amount will be refunded to your credit card.

TRANSPORT

Telephones

Public telephones abound, although most only accept phone cards *(schede telefoniche)*, which are sold at news-stands and *tabacchi* for €5 and €10. If calling from a hotel, expect a steep mark-up.

To call Venice from abroad, dial +39-041 plus the number you require. If calling Venice from within Italy, including from within Venice itself, dial 041, plus the number.

Direct international calls can be made from public telephones. Dial 00 to get out of Italy, then the relevant country and area codes, followed by the telephone number. Country codes include: Australia (61), Canada (1), Ireland (353), New Zealand (64), South Africa (27), UK (44) and the US (1).

To save money, use your country's direct-dialling services paid for at home-country rates. Get their access numbers before you leave home.

Time Zone

Italy is one hour ahead of GMT/UTC during winter and two hours ahead during the daylight-saving period from the last Sunday in March to the last Sunday in October. Most other Western European countries are on the same time as Italy year round. The UK, Ireland and Portugal are one hour behind. The US East Coast is six hours behind Venice time, and the West Coast a further three hours behind.

Toilets

These are in comparatively short supply, so most visitors may need to resort to bars and museums. Several paying public facilities are sprinkled about strategic spots in the city, such as by the tourist office at the Giardini Ex-Reali on San Marco's waterfront, and outside the Accademia.

Tourist Information

The ENIT (Italian State Tourist Board) has several offices abroad: **Australia** Level 2, 140 William Street, Sydney; tel: 02-9357 2561; http://sydney.enit.it. **Canada** 69 Yonge Street, Suite 1404, Toronto, Ontario M5E 1K3; tel: 416-925 4882; http://toronto.enit.it. **UK/Ireland** 1 Princes Street, London W1B 2AY; tel: 020-7408 1254; http://london.enit.it. **US:** www.italiantourism.com. **Chicago:** 3800 Division Street, Stone Park, Chicago, IL 60165, tel: 312 644-0996; http://chicago.enit.it. **Los Angeles:** 10850 Wilshire Blvd., Suite 575, Los Angeles, CA 90024; tel: 310-820 1898; http://losangeles.enit.it. **New York:** 686 Park Avenue, New York, NY 10065, tel: 212 245 5618; http://newyork.enit.it.

Tourist Offices in Venice

The best tourist office (APT) is in the **Venice Pavilion** (tel: 041-529 8730) beside the Giardinetti Reali

(Public Gardens), with a good Venice bookshop. The hard-working but understaffed office is open daily 10am–6pm. There is another one on the western corner of **Piazza San Marco**, opposite the Museo Correr: San Marco 71/f, Calle dell'Ascensione/Procuratie Nuove; daily 9am–3.30pm. Both offices tend to charge for maps, events listings and other brochures. They also offer booking for tours and events. There are tourist offices at the railway station (**APT Venezia, Stazione Santa Lucia**), and at the airport: **APT Marco Polo**, which mostly deals with accommodation and transport tickets.

Travel Agents

Gran Canal Viaggi (Ponte del Lovo, San Marco; tel: 041-271 2111; www.grancanal.it) is a reliable travel agent.

A – Z

V

Visas and Passports

Citizens of European Union countries require no visa and may travel freely in Italy with a national ID card or passport. They should report to the police if they intend to reside in the country, as they will need local papers. Italy is one of 26 countries that makes up the Schengen area, within which all but spot border and passport checks have been abolished.

For visits up to three months, visas are not required by visitors from the US, Canada, Australia or New Zealand. Nationals of other countries should check with their nearest Italian consulate.

LANGUAGE

W

Weights and Measures

Italy uses the metric system. Note that 100 grams is the equivalent of an *etto* (a typical measure used in markets).

LANGUAGE

UNDERSTANDING THE LANGUAGE

It is well worth buying a good phrase book or dictionary, but the following will help you get started. Since this glossary is aimed at non-linguists, we have opted for the simplest options rather than the most elegant Italian.

COMMUNICATION

Yes *Sì*
No *No*
Thank you *Grazie*
Many thanks *Mille grazie/Tante grazie/Molte grazie*
You're welcome *Prego*
All right/That's fine *Va bene*
Please *Per favore* or *per cortesia*
Excuse me (to get attention) *Scusi (singular), Scusate (plural)*
Excuse me (in a crowd) *Permesso*
Excuse me (sorry) *Mi scusi*
Could you help me? (formal) *Potrebbe aiutarmi?*
Certainly *Ma certo/Certamente*
Can I help you? (formal) *Posso aiutarla?*
Can you show me...? *Può indicarmi...?*
Can you help me? *Può aiutarmi, per cortesia?*
I need... *Ho bisogno di...*
I'm lost *Mi sono perso/a*
I'm sorry *Mi dispiace*
I don't know *Non lo so*
I don't understand *Non capisco*

Do you speak English/French? *Parla inglese/francese?*
Could you speak more slowly? *Può parlare piu lentamente, per favore?*
Could you repeat that please? *Può ripetere, per piacere?*
here/there *qui/là*
yesterday/today/tomorrow *ieri/oggi/domani*
what/which *come/quale?*
when/why/where *quando/perchè/dove?*
Where is the lavatory? *Dov'è il bagno?*

GREETINGS

Hello (Good day) *Buon giorno*
Good afternoon/evening *Buona sera*
Good night *Buona notte*
Goodbye *Arrivederci*
Hello/Hi/'bye (familiar) *Ciao*
Mr/Mrs/Miss *Signore/Signora/Signorina*
Pleased to meet you (formal) *Piacere di conoscerla*
I am English/American *Sono inglese/americano*
Irish/Scottish *irlandese/scozzese*
Canadian/Australian *canadese/australiano*
How are you (formal/informal)? *Come sta (Come stai)?*
Fine, thanks *Bene, grazie*
See you later *A più tardi*

See you soon *A presto*
It's wonderful (a phrase that can equally be applied to food, beaches, the view) *È meraviglioso/a*

Telephone calls

May I use your telephone, please? *Posso usare il suo telefono?*
Hello (on the telephone) *Pronto*
My name is *Mi chiamo/Sono*
Could I speak to...? *Posso parlare con...?*
Sorry, he/she isn't in *Mi dispiace, è fuori*
Can he call you back? *Può richiamarla?*
Can I leave a message? *Posso lasciare un messaggio?*
Please tell him I called *Gli dica, per favore, che ho telefonato*
Hold on *Un attimo, per favore*
A local call *una telefonata urbana*

IN THE HOTEL

Do you have any vacant rooms? *Avete delle camere libere?*
I have a reservation *Ho una prenotazione*
I'd like... *Vorrei*
a single/double room (with a double bed) *una camera singola/doppia (con letto matrimoniale)*

a room with twin beds *una camera a due letti*
a room with a bath/shower *una camera con bagno/doccia*
for one night *per una notte*
for two nights *per due notti*
How much is it? *Quanto costa?*
Is breakfast included? *È compresa la prima colazione?*
half/full board *mezza pensione/pensione completa*
Do you have a room with a balcony/view of the sea? *Avete una camera con balcone/con vista mare?*
Is it a quiet room? *È una stanza tranquilla?*
The room is too hot/cold/noisy/small *La camera è troppo calda/fredda/rumorosa/piccola*
Can I see the room? *Posso vedere la camera?*
Could you show me another room please? *Potrebbe mostrarmi un'altra camera?*
What time does the hotel close? *A che ora chiude l'albergo?*
big/small *grande/piccola*
What time is breakfast? *A che ora è la prima colazione?*
Please give me a call at... *Mi può chiamare alle...*
Come in? *Avanti!*
Can I have the bill, please? *Posso avere il conto, per favore?*
Can you call me a taxi please? *Può chiamarmi un taxi, per favore?*
key *la chiave*

AT A BAR

I'd like... *Vorrei...*
coffee *un caffè*
small, strong and black *un espresso*
with hot, frothy milk *un cappuccino*
with warm milk *un caffelatte*
weak *un caffè lungo*
tea *un tè*
lemon tea *un tè al limone*
herbal tea *una tisana*
hot chocolate *una cioccolata calda*

(bottled) orange/lemon juice *un succo d'arancia/di limone*
orange squash *l'aranciata*
fresh orange/lemon juice *una spremuta di arancia/di limone*
a glass/bottle of *un bicchiere/una bottiglia di*
fizzy/still mineral water *acqua minerale gasata/naturale*
with/without ice *con/senza ghiaccio*
red/white wine *vino rosso/bianco*
beer *una birra*
a gin and tonic *un gin tonic*
an aperitif (vermouth, cinzano, etc) *un aperitivo*
milk *latte*
(half) a litre *un (mezzo) litro*
ice cream *un gelato*
pastry/brioche *una pasta*
sandwich *un tramezzino*
roll *un panino*
Anything else? *Desidera qualcos'altro?*
Cheers *Salute*

IN A RESTAURANT

I'd like to book a table *Vorrei riservare un tavolo*

Have you got a table for... *Avete un tavolo per...*
I have a reservation *Ho fatto una prenotazione*
lunch/supper *il pranzo/la cena*
I'm a vegetarian *Sono vegetariano/a*
Is there a vegetarian dish? *C'è un piatto vegetariano?*
May we have the menu? *Ci dia la carta?*
wine list *la lista dei vini*
What would you like? *Che cosa prende?*
What would you recommend? *Che cosa ci raccomanda?*
What would you like to drink? *Che cosa desidera da bere?*
a carafe of red/white wine *una caraffa di vino rosso/bianco*
the dish of the day *il piatto del giorno*
home-made *fatto in casa*
cover charge *il coperto/pane e coperto*
The bill, please *Il conto, per favore*
Is service included? *Il servizio è incluso?*
Keep the change *Va bene così*
I've enjoyed the meal *Mi è piaciuto molto*

PRONUNCIATION TIPS

Italians claim that pronunciation is straightforward: you pronounce it as it is written. This is approximately true, but there are a couple of important rules for English speakers to bear in mind:
c before **e** or **i** is pronounced ch, eg. *ciao, mi dispiace, la coincidenza.* **Ch** before **i** or **e** is pronounced as **k**, eg *la chiesa.* Likewise, **sci** or **sce** are pronounced as in sheep or shed respectively. **Gn** in Italian is rather like the sound in onion, while **gl** is softened to resemble the sound in bullion.
Nouns are either masculine (*il*, plural *i*) or feminine (*la*, plural *le*). Plurals of nouns are most often formed by changing an **o** to an **i** and an **a** to an **e**, eg *il panino: i panini; la chiesa:*

le chiese. As a general rule, words are always stressed on the penultimate syllable unless an accent indicates that you should do otherwise.
Like many languages, Italian has formal and informal words for "you". In the singular, *tu* is informal while *lei* is more polite. In general *voi* is reserved for you plural, though in some places it is also used as a singular polite form. For visitors, it is simplest – and probably safest to avoid offending anyone – to use the formal form unless invited to do otherwise. There is, of course, rather more to the language than that, but you can get a surprisingly long way in making friends by mastering a few basic phrases.

MENU DECODER

Antipasti – starters

antipasto misto **mixed hors d'œuvres; cold cuts of meat, cheeses, roast vegetables (ask for details)**
caponata aubergine, **olives, tomatoes**
insalata caprese **tomato, basil and mozzarella salad**
insalata di mare **seafood salad**
insalata mista/verde **mixed/ green salad**
melanzane alla parmigiana **fried or baked aubergine with parmesan and tomato**
mortadella/salame **similar to salami**
peperonata **grilled peppers drenched in olive oil**

Primi – first courses

gli asparagi **asparagus**
il brodetto **fish soup**
il brodo **broth**
crespolini **savoury pancakes**
gnocchi **potato-and-dough dumplings**
la minestra **soup**
il minestrone **thick vegetable soup**
pasta e fagioli **pasta and bean soup**
il prosciutto (cotto/crudo) **(cooked/cured) ham**
i suppli **rice croquettes**
i tartufi **truffles**
la zuppa **soup**

Secondi – main courses

arrosto **roast meat**
ai ferri **grilled without oil**
al forno **baked**
alla griglia **grilled**
involtini **skewered veal, ham, etc**
stagionato **hung, well-aged**
ben cotto **well-done (steak, etc)**
al puntino **medium (steak, etc)**
al sangue **rare (steak, etc)**
l'agnello **lamb**
la bresaola **dried salted beef**
la bistecca **steak**
il capriolo/cervo **venison**
il carpaccio **wafer-thin raw beef**
il cinghiale **wild boar**
il controfiletto **sirloin steak**
le cotolette **cutlets**
il maiale **pork**
il fagiano **pheasant**
il fegato **liver**
il filetto **fillet**
il manzo **beef**
l'ossobuco **shin of veal**
la porchetta **roast suckling pig**
il pollo **chicken**
polpette **meatballs**
la salsiccia **sausage**
le scaloppine **escalopes**
lo stufato **braised, stewed**
il sugo **sauce**
il vitello **veal**

Frutti di mare – seafood

affumicato **smoked**
alla brace **charcoal grilled**
ai ferri **grilled without oil**
alla griglia **grilled**
fritto **fried**
acciughe **anchovies**
l'anguilla **eel**
l'aragosta **lobster**
il baccalà **dried salt cod**
i bianchetti **whitebait**
il branzino **sea bass**
i calamari **squid**
i crostacei **shellfish**
le cozze **mussels**
il fritto misto **mixed fried fish**
i gamberi **prawns**
il granchio **crab**
il merluzzo **cod**
le molecche **soft-shelled crabs**
le ostriche **oysters**
il pesce **fish**
il pesce spada **swordfish**
le sarde **sardines**
la sogliola **sole**
le seppie **cuttlefish**
la triglia **red mullet**
la trota **trout**
il tonno **tuna**
le vongole **clams**

I legumi/la verdura – vegetables

gli asparagi **asparagus**
il carciofo **artichoke**
le carote **carrots**
il cavolo **cabbage**
la cipolla **onion**
i contorni **side dishes**
i funghi **mushrooms**
i fagioli **beans**
l'insalata mista **mixed salad**
l'insalata verde **green salad**
la melanzana **aubergine**
le patate **potatoes**
le patatine fritte **French fries**
i peperoni **peppers**
i piselli **peas**
i pomodori **tomatoes**
rucola **rocket**
spinaci **spinach**
la zucca **pumpkin/squash**

La frutta – fruit

le arance **oranges**
le banane **bananas**
il cocomero **watermelon**
le ciliege **cherries**
i fichi **figs**
le fragole **strawberries**
i lamponi **raspberries**
le mele **apples**
le pesche **peaches**
le pere **pears**
l'uva **grapes**

I dolci – desserts

il dolce **dessert/sweet**
un gelato **ice cream**
una granita **water ice**
una macedonia di frutta **fruit salad**
un semifreddo **semi-frozen dessert (many varieties)**
il tartufo (nero) **(chocolate) ice-cream dessert**
il tiramisù **cold, creamy rum-and-coffee dessert**
la torta **cake/tart**
zabaglione **sweet dessert made with eggs and Marsala**
la zuppa inglese **trifle**

Basic foods

l'aceto **vinegar**
l'aglio **garlic**
il burro **butter**
il formaggio **cheese**
la frittata **omelette**
i grissini **bread sticks**
l'olio **oil**
la marmellata **jam**
il pane **bread**
il parmigiano **parmesan cheese**
il pepe **pepper**
il riso **rice**

il sale **salt**
le uova **eggs**
il yoghurt **yoghurt**
lo zucchero **sugar**

SIGHTSEEING

la basilica **basilica**
il belvedere **viewpoint**
la biblioteca **library**
la chiesa **church**
il duomo/la cattedrale **cathedral**
il fiume **river**
il giardino **garden**
il lago **lake**
il mercato **market**
il museo **museum**
il parco **park**
la pinacoteca **art gallery**
il ponte **bridge**
la spiaggia **beach**
la torre **tower**
l'ufficio turistico **tourist office**
aperto/a **open**
chiuso/a **closed**

SHOPPING

bakery/cake shop *la panetteria/ pasticceria*
bank *la banca*
bookshop *la libreria*
boutique/clothes shop *il negozio di moda*
butcher's *la macelleria*
chemist's *la farmacia*
delicatessen *la salumeria*
fishmonger *la pescheria*
florist *il fioraio*
grocer *l'alimentari*
greengrocer *l'ortolano/il fruttivendolo*
ice-cream parlour *la gelateria*
jeweller *il gioielliere*
market *il mercato*
news-stand *l'edicola*
post office *l'ufficio postale*
shoe shop *il negozio di scarpe*
stationer's *la cartoleria*
supermarket *il supermercato*
tobacconist *il tabaccaio (also sells travel tickets, stamps, phone cards)*
Can I help you? (formal) *Posso aiutarla?*
How much does it cost? *Quant'è, per favore?*
Do you take credit cards

NUMBERS

0 *zero*	**18** *diciotto*
1 *uno*	**19** *diciannove*
2 *due*	**20** *venti*
3 *tre*	**30** *trenta*
4 *quattro*	**40** *quaranta*
5 *cinque*	**50** *cinquanta*
6 *sei*	**60** *sessanta*
7 *sette*	**70** *settanta*
8 *otto*	**80** *ottanta*
9 *nove*	**90** *novanta*
10 *dieci*	**100** *cento*
11 *undici*	**200** *duecento*
12 *dodici*	**500** *cinquecento*
13 *tredici*	**1,000** *mille*
14 *quattordici*	**2,000** *duemila*
15 *quindici*	**5,000** *cinquemila*
16 *sedici*	**50,000** *cinquantamila*
17 *diciassette*	**1 million** *un milione*

Accettate carte di credito?
I'd like... *Vorrei...*
this one/that one *questo/quello*
Have you got...? *Avete...?*
Can I try it on? *Posso provare?*
the size (for clothes) *la taglia*
the size (for shoes) *il numero*
It's too expensive/cheap *È troppo caro/economico*
It's too small/big *È troppo piccolo/grande*
Give me some of those *Mi dia alcuni di quelli lì*
(half) a kilo *un (mezzo) kilo*
100 grams *un'etto*
200 grams *due etti*
More/less *Più/meno*
A little *Un pochino*
That's enough *Basta così*

TRANSPORT

aeroplane *l'aereo*
arrivals/departures *arrivi/ partenze*
boat *la barca*
bus *l'autobus/il pullman*
bus station *l'autostazione*
coach *il pullman*
connection *la coincidenza*
ferry *il traghetto*
first/second class *prima/ seconda classe*
flight *il volo*
left luggage *il deposito bagagli*
platform *il binario*

railway station *ferrovia (la stazione ferroviaria)*
return ticket *un biglietto di andata e ritorno*
single ticket *un biglietto di solo andata*
taxi *il taxi*
ticket office *la biglietteria*
train *il treno*

DIRECTIONS

right/left *a destra/a sinistra*
first left/second right *la prima a sinistra/la seconda a destra*
Turn to the right/left *Giri a destra/sinistra*
Go straight on *Vada sempre diritto*
Is it far away/nearby? *È lontano/vicino?*
It's 5 minutes' walk *Cinque minuti a piedi*
opposite/next to *di fronte/ accanto a*
Where is ....? *Dov'è ....?*
Where are ....? *Dove sono ....?*
Where is the nearest bank/bus stop/hotel/garage? *Dov'è la banca/la fermata di autobus/ l'albergo/l'officina più vicino?*
How long does it take to get to...? *Quanto tempo ci vuole per andare a...?*
Can you show me where I am on the map? *Può indicarmi sulla cartina dove mi trovo?*

FURTHER READING

LITERATURE AND BIOGRAPHY

Memoirs, by Giacomo Casanova. The arch-seductor was also a spy, soldier and traveller. How much can be believed of his ripping yarns, which take him well beyond Venice, we will never know, but they are entertaining.

Across the River and into the Trees, by Ernest Hemingway. Colonel Cantwell's Venice is a melancholy place.

The Wings of the Dove and **The Aspern Papers**, by Henry James. One of the greatest observers of Venice flexes his fiction in two novels set in the city. In the first, a researcher tries anything to extract a poet's love letters from their aged recipient, while in the latter, an heiress comes under siege.

Friends in High Places, by Donna Leon. Leon's local detective solves another mystery in this one of a long, gritty detective series set in Venice.

Death in Venice, by Thomas Mann. Haunting and atmospheric tale in which Gustav von Aschenbach is slowly consumed by a Venice riven with illness.

The Comfort of Strangers, by Ian McEwan. An eerie novel in which a stranger comes between a married couple in an unnamed city but it is clearly Venice.

A Venetian Affair, by Andrea di Robilant. Based on 18th-century love letters, this story of an romance in the latter years of the Republic is captivating.

Miss Garnet's Angel, by Sally Vickers. Whimsical tale of an art trail, in which a retired school teacher decides to head off and live in Venice for six months.

HISTORY, ART AND ARCHITECTURE

The City of Falling Angels, by John Berendt. Berendt digs up the dirt on scandals past and present in a city that has always lent itself to intrigue.

Venice, Biography of a City, by Christopher Hibbert. A delightfully written journey through the city's history and art.

Venice, a Maritime Republic, by Frederick C. Lane. A core (if dry) historical account that lays out the economic foundations of the mercantile empire's success.

Painting in 18th-Century Venice, by Michael Levey. Far more than a disquisition on artists from Canaletto to Tiepolo, art historian Levey reveals much about Venetian society in its final century of independence.

Francesco's Venice, by Francesco da Mosto. Lavish romp through Venetian culture by an aristocratic Venetian architect.

A History of Venice, The Rise to Empire, The Greatness and Fall, by John Julius Norwich. Possibly the best foreign historian of all things Venetian, Norwich manages to maintain an engaging, narrative pace.

The Stones of Venice, by John Ruskin. Ruskin let himself go in his apology for Gothic Venice in what is part art manual, part tirade.

The Thief Lord, by Cornelia Funke. An international best seller about orphaned brothers joining a band of street children who live in an abandoned movie theatre in Venice.

Venice: History of the Floating City, by Joanne M. Ferraro. Arguably the best book on the history of the Venetian Republic.

TRAVEL MEMOIRS

Venice, a Portable Reader, by Toby Cole (Ed.). Literary extracts by celebrated visitors.

Venice: a Literary Companion, by Ian Littlewood. Informed, literary presentation of lesser-known Venice.

Venice Observed, by Mary McCarthy. Acerbic look at Venice from an intelligent observer.

Venice, by Jan Morris. A personal account by award-winning travel writer and former Venice correspondent, this is one of the most elegant paeans to the city. Jan Morris followed with **The Venetian Empire: A Sea Voyage**, recounting the turbulent history of the city's foreign possessions.

Venice Rediscovered, by John Pemble. A look at Venice as it was seen from the 19th century, emerging from a century of neglect and capturing the imaginations of its wealthy foreign visitors.

My Venice and Other Essays, by Donna Leon. Leon shares in a humorous and sometimes poignant way episodes from her life in Venice.

OTHER INSIGHT GUIDES

Other books in the series covering Italy are **Insight Guides** Italy, Rome, Florence, Tuscany, Sicily and Sardinia.

The **Explore Guides** to Florence, Italian Lakes, Naples, Rome and Venice highlight the best walks and tours, with itineraries for all tastes.

The **Experience Guide** to Rome offers a collection of around 100 inspiring ideas for your stay in the city, with plenty of secret gems and offbeat haunts in the mix.

VENICE STREET ATLAS

The key map shows the area of Venice covered by the atlas section. An index of street names and places of interest shown on the maps can be found on the following pages. For each entry there is a page number and grid reference

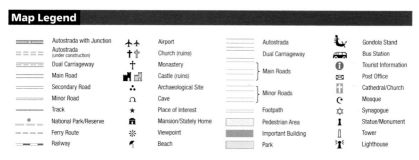

Map Legend

▭	Autostrada with Junction	✈✈	Airport	▭	Autostrada	🚣	Gondola Stand
▭	Autostrada (under construction)	†✝	Church (ruins)	▭	Dual Carriageway	🚌	Bus Station
▭	Dual Carriageway	†	Monastery	▭	Main Roads	❶	Tourist Information
▭	Main Road	▮▮	Castle (ruins)			✉	Post Office
▭	Secondary Road	∴	Archaeological Site			♱	Cathedral/Church
▭	Minor Road	∩	Cave	▭	Minor Roads	☾	Mosque
▬	Track	★	Place of Interest	▭	Footpath	✡	Synagogue
•	National Park/Reserve	⌂	Mansion/Stately Home	▭	Pedestrian Area	⚡	Statue/Monument
▭	Ferry Route	⁂	Viewpoint	▭	Important Building	▯	Tower
▭	Railway	☙	Beach	▭	Park	⌖	Lighthouse

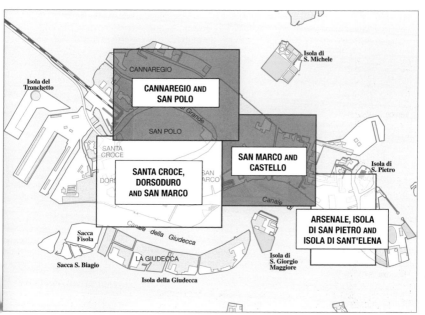

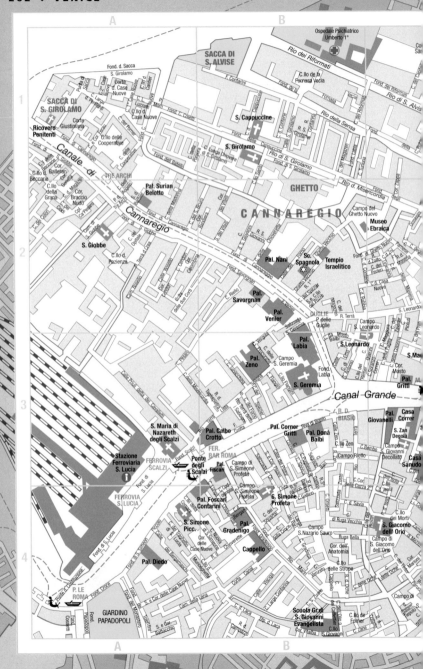

S. ALVISE

ECCHIERE

MADONNA
DELL'ORTO

vise

Rio d'Zecchini

Fond. della Madonna dell'Orto

Pal. Michiel

Madonna
dell' Orto

Campo della
Madonna dell'Orto

Pal. Minelli

Pal.
Mastelli

Pal. Contarini
d. Zaffo

Casa del
Tintoretto

Pal.
Longo

P. de
istraterr

Rio della Misericordia

P. della
Sacca

*Sacca
della
Misericordia*

Ex Conv. S.M.
d. Servi

S.Marziale

Rio della Sensa

S. M.
Valverde

Pal.
Diedo

Cam.
dell'Abbazia

S. Caterina

Pal. Lezze

Pal.
Molin

Campo di
Maddalena

Pal.
Vendramin

S.Fosca

Pal.
Papafava

S. Antonio

Orat.
d. Crociferi

S. Maria
Assunta
dei Gesuiti

Pal.
Correr

Pal. Campo dei
Zen Gesuiti

S. Maddalena

Pal.
Soranzo

Pal.
Giovanelli

Noale

lergi

Pal.
Erizzo

Pal.
Emo

Pal.
Molin

di

Canale della Misericordia

Rio dei Gesuiti

tagia

Pal.
Barbarigo

Pal.
Zulian

Cor.
Remer

al.
ron

Pal.
Priuli

Pal.
Gussoni

S. Felice

Cam.
S. Felice

S. Stae

Pal.
Foscarini

Ca'
Pesaro

(Grand Canal)

International
Gallery of
Modern Art

Pal.
Bonà

Pal.Corner
d.Reg.

Pal.
Fontana

Gall.
Franchetti

S. Sofia

SS. Apostoli

Agnus Dio

Gall.d'Arte
Mod. &
Mus.Orient.

Casa
Favretto

Pal.
Giusti

Ca'd'Oro

Campo dei
SS. Apostoli

Cor.
S.Canciano

Campo

Pal.
Sagredo

igo

Pal.
Brandolin

CA'
D'ORO

Pal.
Foscari

Pal.
Michiel
d. Colonne

Scuola d.
Ang. Custode

S.Canciano

Pal.
Boldù

S. M.
Mater
Dom.

Pal.
Gozzi

S. Cassiano

Pescheria

Pal.
Valmarana

Cor. de
Leon Bianco

S.Maria
dei Miracoli

Pal.
Sanudo

Campo
Mater Mater
Domini

Pal.
Querini

Campo della
Pescaria

Cat da
Mosto

Fabbriche
Nuove

Campo
S.Giovanni
Crisostomo

S. Giov.
Cristosomo

Teatro
Malibran

Pal.
Bragadin
Carabba

Pal. Muti
Baglioni

Fabbriche
Vecchie

Cam.
Cesare
Battisti-Erba

Pal.
Civran

Pal.dei
Camer-
lenghi

Pal.
Amadi

Casa di
B. Cappello

ardo

S. Giovanni
Elemosinario

S. Giacomo
di Rialto

0 ──── 200 m
0 ──── 200 yds

Cam. di S. Andrea

S. Andrea

Autorimessa
Air Terminal

Piazzale
Roma

P.LE ROMA
R. NUOVO

GIARDINO
PAPADOPOLI

Pal.
Condulmer

Fond. di S. Andrea

Rio Terra di S. Andrea

R. Cossetti

R. Cossetti

Campazzo Tre Ponti

S. e Cor. Battocchio

S. e Cor. dei Amai

Campo
d. Tolentini

S. Nicolò
dei Tolentini

Scuola
S. Giov.
Evange

S. Giov
Evange

Archivio
di

San
Rocco

SANTA CROCE

Fond. d. Fabbrica

d. Tabacchi

Burchielle

Fond. delle
Pensieri

R. Bernardo

C. delle
Subbiola

Rio Terra dei Pensieri

Fond. Bernardo

Fond. dei
Pagan

C. Correra

Fond. dei Magazen

Fond. Minotto

Fond. del Gaffaro

Cor.
del Gatto

Fond. del Rio Nuovo

Rio
Nuovo

C. de Basego

Rio
Nuovo

Fond. del Rio Nuovo

C.llo delle
Mosche

Campo di
Castelforte
S. Rocco

Scuola
Grande
di S.Rocco

S. M. Maggiore

Fond. di S. Maria

Maggiore
delle

Cor. S. Marco

Sestiere di
S. Croce

Fond. Rizzi

Cor. Contarini

S. Pantaleon

Campo
S. Pantalon

C. della Madonna

Fond. Procuratie

C. Sporca

Ceren

Cor.
Bonazzo

Calle

Fond. Rossa

Calle Larga Bernardi

C. dei
Renieri

C.d.
Pistor

C. dei
Carfenter

Campo
di
S. Margherita

C. dei
Tagia
Fabri

Calle
Lunga

C. Camerini

Calle dei Guardiani

Fond. dei

Pal.
Foscarini

F. Foscarini

Scuola Grand
di S.Maria
d.Carmini

Campo dei
Carmini

C. della
Scuola

C. d'l
Forno

C. S.ta
Chiara

C. Brocchetta

Fond. di MaIcanton

Fond. del Magazen

C. del
Forno

Fond. del
Soccorso

Ist. Sup.
d'Arte
Applicate

S. Maria dei
Carmini

Rio Terra della Scoazzera

Cor. del
Forno

Cor.
S. Margherita

Fond.
Alberti

S. Barnal

C. di Cristo

C.d. Pazienza

Calle Briati

C. Rossi

Cor.
Zappa

C.llo
Avogaria

C.llo
Balastro

Cor. Lunga S. Barnaba

Campo
S.Barnaba

Ariani Cicogna
Palace

Fond. di D. Lorenzo

Fondamenta Barbarigo

Fondamenta Pescheria

Salita S. Chiesa

Chiesa San
Sebastiano

Angelo
Raffaele

Chiesa di San
Sebastiano

Cor. dei
Vecchi

C. Avogaria

C. Batastro

Fond. dello Squero

Fond. Gerardini

C. Nicoletti

Piazza
S. Barnaba

Cor. del
Borgo

Fond. Lombardo

S. Trov

Salita San Baseglio

Cor.
dei Morti

C. della Ch.

Fond.Ognissanti

Ospedale
Ognissanti

Chiesa
Ognissanti

Cam.
Ognissanti

Cor.
Bontadina

Cor. dei
Pram

Fond. delle
Eremite

C.llo Occhialera

Bra

CAM. di
S. Basilio

C. del
Vento

C. dei Morti

C. della Masena

C. dei Cordaroli

Cor. Zattere

Trevisan

Fond. Bornini

S. Trov
Camp

ZATTERE

S. BASILIO

Fondaco
Zattere

P.
Lungo

ZATTERE

d. V

Canale della Giudecca

Fond. S. Biagio

S. Giovanni Elemosinario
S. Giacomo di Rialto
Pal.dei Camerlenghi

Pal. Bernardo
Casa di B. Cappello
Pal. Albrizzi
Pal. Aponal
Pal. d. Dieci Savi
Fondaco d.Tedeschi
Ponte di Rialto

Pal. Corner Mocenigo
Pal. Soranzo

San Polo
Pal. M. Olivio

Campo di S. Polo

S. Bartolomeo

N POLO

RIALTO

Campo di S. Silvestro
S. Silvestro

Pal. Papadopoli
Pal. Barzizza

Pal. Dolfin-Manin
Pal. Bembo

Casa di C.Goldoni
Pal. Businello
Pal. Donà

Pal. Corner Martinego
Pal. Farsetti

Pal. Loredan
Pal. Dandolo

San Salvador

Pal. Cappello Layard
Pal. Bernardo Querini

S. SILVESTRO

Teatro Goldoni

Pal. Barbarigo d. Terrazza
Pal. Pisani Moretta

Canal Grande

Pal. Martinengo Volpi

Pal. Grimani

Pal. Marcello d'Leoni
Pal. Giustinian Persico

S. ANGELO

S. Luca

S. TOMÀ

Pal. Garzoni

S. Benedetto

Teatro Rossini

Pal. Dandolo Paolucci

Pal. Corner Spinelli

Campo Manin

Pal. Contarini d. Figure
Ca' Mocenigo
Pal. Gheltof

Pal. Pesaro

C. d. Forno Vecchio

al. Contarini d. Figure
Pal. Lezze
Pal. Moro Lin
Pal. Grassi

Fortuny

Pal. Cont. d. Bovolo

Campo S. Gallo

Oratorio S. Annunziata

San Samuele
Campo S. Samuele

Santo Stefano

Campo S. Angelo

S MARCO

SAN MARCO

Teatro La Fenice

S. Fantin

Bocca di Piazza

Campo San Stefano/ F. Morosini

S. Maurizio

Pal. Malipiero

Ca'd'Duca

Pal. Loredan
Pal. Bellavite

Campo S. Maurizio

S. Maria d. Giglio

S. Moisè
Campo S. Moisè

Pal. Falier
Pal. Contarini d. Zaffo

S. Vidal

Pal. Morosini

Pal. Pisani

Ca' Grande
Pal. Corner

Pal. Pisani Gritti

Pal. Contarini

Pal. Tiepolo

Ridotto

Pal. Giustinian

ACCADEMIA

Pal. Cavalli Franchetti

Pal. Barbaro

Pal. Contarini Fasan

Galleria dell' Accademia

Ponte dell' Accademia

(Grand Canal)

S. M. DEL GIGLIO

Scuola della Carità

Pal. Contarini Polignac
Pal. Loredan
Pal. Barbarigo

Pal. Venier dei Leoni
Pal. Dario
Pal. Salviati

SALUTE

Fond. della Dogana alla Salute

Punta della Dogana

Campo d. Carità

Campo S. Vio

Pal. Centanni

Coll. Peggy Guggenheim

San Gregorio

Campo della Salute

Punta della Dogana

S. Agnese

Fond. Ospedaleto

Seminario Patriarcale

Basilica di S. Maria della Salute

Campo di S. Agnese

Rio Terra dei Catecumeni

S. Spirito

Fond. Zattere allo Spirito Santo

0   200 m
0   200 yds

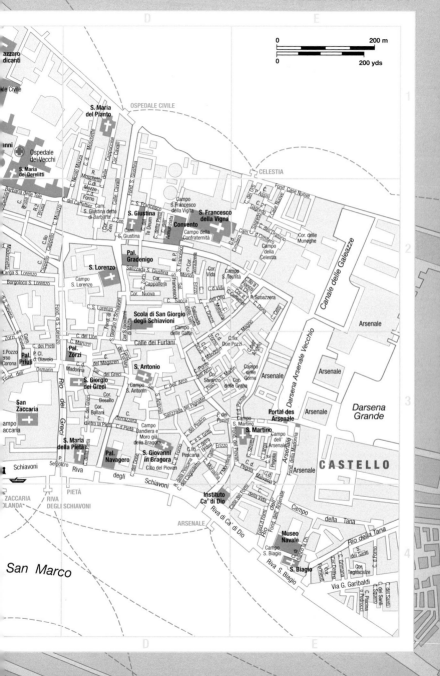

0   200 m
0   200 yds

azzaro
dicanti

ale Civile

anni
   Ospedale
   dei Vecchi
S. Maria
dei Derelitti

S. Maria
del Pianto

OSPEDALE CIVILE

CELESTIA

Barbaria delle Tole

Larga S. Lorenzo

Borgoloco S. Lorenzo

S. Giustina detto
di Barbaria

S. Giustina

S. Lorenzo

Campo
S. Lorenzo

Pal.
Gradenigo

Campo
S. Francesco
della Vigna

S. Francesco
della Vigna

Convento

Campo della
Confraternità

Campo
della
Celestia

Cor.
Cappalleri

Cor.
Vida

Campo
S. Ternita

Scola di San Giorgio
degli Schiavoni

Campo
delle Gatte

Cor.
Nuova

Calle dei Furlani

C.flor.
Due Pozzi

Pal.
Zorzi

S. Antonio

Campo
S. Antonin

San
Zaccaria

S. Giorgio
dei Greci

Campo
delle Gorne

Cor.
della Grana

Arsenale

Arsenale

Arsenale

Darsena
Grande

ampo
accaria

S. Maria
della Pietà

Pal.
Navagero

Campo
Bandiera e
Moro già
della Bragora

S. Giovanni
in Bragora

Portal des
Arsenale

S. Martino

Campo
dell'
Arsenale

CASTELLO

Schiavoni

Riva

degli

Schiavoni

ZACCARIA
OLANDA

RIVA
DEGLI SCHIAVONI

PIETÀ

Instituto
Ca' di Dio

ARSENALE

Riva di Ca' di Dio

Campo
della Tana

San Marco

Museo
Navale

Campo
S. Biagio

S. Biagio

Riva S. Biagio

Via G. Garibaldi

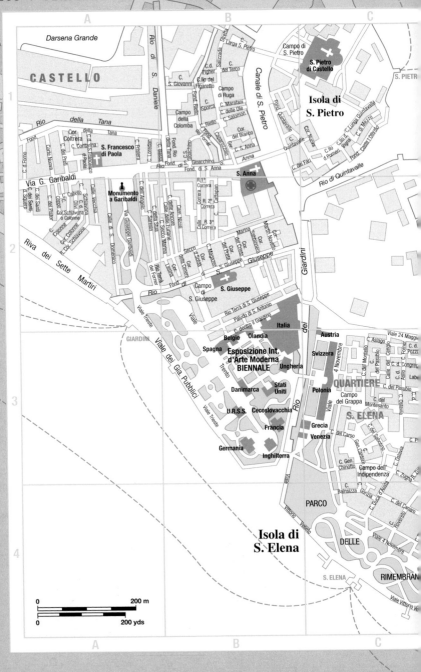

Darsena Grande

CASTELLO

Rio di S. Daniele

Rio della Tana

Fond.

Cor. Coltrera
C. Contarina
S. Francesco
di Paola

Via G. Garibaldi

Monumento
a Garibaldi

Campo
della
Colomba

Strada

C. Larga S. Pietro
C. del Terco

C. Figher
C.lo del Figaretto
C. S. Giovanni

Campo
di Ruga

C. Marafani
C. delle Olie
C. Salomon

C. Sporca

Cor. del Bianco

C. S. Anna

Fond. Rio della Tana
Fond. Gioacchino
Rio di S. Anna

Campo di S. Pietro

S. Pietro
di Castello

Isola di
S. Pietro

S. PIETR

C. Quintavalle

Rio di Quintavalle

S. Anna

Canale di S. Pietro

Riva dei Sette Martiri

Calle di S. Domenico

Via Giuseppe Garibaldi

C. del Forni

Sec co d. Forni
Rio Terra del Forner

Rio
Fond.

Campo
di
S. Giuseppe

S. Giuseppe

Giardini

Giardini

Viale Trieste

Viale dei Gia. Pubblici

Viale Trieste

Rio Terra di S. Giuseppe
Paludo il Giardino
detto il Giardino

Italia

Belgio   Olandia

Spagna

Esposizione Int.
d'Arte Moderna
BIENNALE

Ungheria

Danimarca

Stati
Uniti

U.R.S.S.

Cecoslovacchia

Francia

Germania

Inghilterra

Austria

Svizzera

Polonia

Grecia

Venezia

Viale 24 Maggi

4 Novembre

QUARTIERE

Campo
del Grappa

S. ELENA

C. del Carso

Campo dell'
Indipendenza

PARCO

DELLE

Isola di
S. Elena

RIMEMBRAN

S. ELENA

Viale Vittorio Ve

Viale 4 Novembre

Vittorio Veneto

0   200 m
0   200 yds

STREET INDEX

A

Accademia, Ponte dell'
264 C3
Acque, C d. 266 B2
Agnello, C. dell' 262
C4
Albanesi, C. degli 262
C3, D3, 264 C1, 264
C1
Alberagno, C. 262 C2
Albero, Fond. dell' 264
D2
Alberti, Fond. 264 C2
Albrizzi, C. 262 C4
Amai, S. e Cor. dei 264
B1
Amor degli Amici, C.
264 C1
Anatomia, Cor. dell'
262 B4
Anconetta, C.llo dell'
262 C2
Ancore, C. delle 268 B2
Ancore, C. 266 B3
Angelo Raffaele, Cam.
dell' 264 A3
Angelo, C. dell' 262 A2,
262 D4, 266 B3, C1,
266 E3
Annunziata, C. dell'
266 D2
Antonio Foscarini, Rio
Terrà 264 C4
Appello, Cor. d' 264 E2
Archivio di Stato 264 C1
Arco, C. Ponte dell' 266
D3
Arrigoni, C. 262 C2
Arsenale 266 E3
Arsenale, Cam. dell'
266 E3
Arsenale, Fond. dell'
266 E4
Artidi già Guerra, Cam.
d 266 B3
Arzere, Fond. d' 264 A2
Ascensione, C. dell'
266 B3–B4
Aseo, C. dell' 262 C2,
E4, 264 C2
Asiago, C. 268 C3
Asilo, C. d. 268 C3
Assassini, Rio Terrà
degli 264 E2
Ateneo S. Basso 266 B3
Avogaria, C. 264 B3
Avvocati, C. degli 264
D2

B

Bagatin, C. 262 E4
Baiamonte Tiepolo, C.
262 C4
Bainsizza, C. 268 C4
Balastro, C.llo 264 B3
Balbi, C. 266 B2
Balleran, Cor. 262 A1
Ballotte, C. d. 264 E2
Banco Salviati, C. d.
264 D1
Bande, C. delle 266 B2
Bandiera e Moro già
della Bragora, Cam.
266 D3

Bandiera, Cor. 262 A2
Barba Fruttarol, Rio
Terrà di 262 E3
Barbaria delle Tole 266
C2
Barbarigo, Fond. 264
A3
Barbaro, C. 262 E3
Barbaro, Fond. 264 D3
Barbier, S. d. 262 A2
Barcaroli Frezzeria, C. d.
264 E2
Bari, C. Larga dei 262
C4
Barizza, C. 264 D1
Barozzi, C. 264 E3
Barzizza, Cor. 264 D1
Basilica di S. Maria della
Salute 264 E4
Basilica di San Marco
266 B3
Basilio, C. de 264 B2
Bassa, C. 268 A1
Bastion, C. 264 D4
Batello, Fond. dell 262
A1
Battocchio, S. e Cor.
262 A4
Beccarie, C.llo d. 262
A1
Beccarie, Cam. delle
262 D4
Beccher, C. d. 262 D3
Bembo, C. 262 B3,
264 E1
Bergamaschi, C. 264
E3
Bergamaschi, C. dei
262 A4
Bergami, C. d. 262 B4
Bernardo, C. 264 A1,
C2, 264 D1
Bevilacqua, C. 266 A3
Bezzo, C. 264 B1
Bianco, Cor. de Léon
262 E4
Bianco, Cor. del 268 B1
Biblioteca Marciana
266 B4
Biennale, Esposizione
Int. d'Arte Moderna
268 B3
Birri, Rio Terrà de 266
C1
Bisatti, S. d. 264 C4
Bissa, C. della 266 B2
Bocca di Piazza 264 E2
Bognolo, C. 264 E2
Boldù, C. 262 E2
Bollani, Cor. 266 D3
Bollani, Fond. 264 C3
Bombaseri, C. dei 264
E1
Bonazzo, Cor. 264 B2
Bondi, C. d. 262 E4
Bonfadina, Cor. 264
B3
Bontini, Fond. 264 C4
Borgato, Sal. 262 E3
Borgo, Fond. di 264 C3
Borgoloco S. Lorenzo
266 C2
Bosello, Cam. 262 A2
Bosello, Cor. 266 D3

Botta, C. d. 262 D4
Botta, C. della 266 A1
Botteghe, C. delle 264
C3
Botteri, C. dei 262 D4
Braccio Nudo, Cor.
262 A2
Bragadin, Fond. 264 D4
Brazzo, C. 262 D2
Brentana, C. 264 E2
Bressana, C. 266 C2
Briani, C. 264 A2
Briani, C. e C. 262 C2
Briati, Fond. 264 A3
Brocchetta, C. 264 B2
Brusa, C. 266 C2
Brusa, C. Larga 264 D4
Buccari, C. 268 C4
Burchielle, Fond. delle
264 A1

C

Ca' Bala, Fond. di 264
D4
Ca' d'Duca 264 C3
Ca' d'Oro 262 D4
Ca' da Mosto 262 E4
Ca' Dario 264 D4
Ca' Foscari 264 C2
Ca' Genovese 264 E4
Ca' Grande Pal. Corner
264 D3
Ca' Lin 264 C2
Ca' Mocenigo 264 C2
Ca' Pesaro 262 D3
Ca' Pesaro, Cpl. 262 A2
Ca' Rezzonico 264 C3
Caboto, C. 268 A2
Cadene, C. d. 262 E2
Caffettier, C. del 264
B2, 264 D2, 266 B2,
266 C2
Cagnoletto, C. del 266
D3
Calderer, C. del 262 D2
Calegheri, C.llo dei
264 D3
Caliari, C. 262 C2
Calice, C. d. 262 C4
Camerini, C. 264 A2
Campaniel, C. del 264
C2
Campanile, C. del 262
D4
Campanile dei Preti,
C. del 262 C3
Campazzo, R. d. 262
B4, 264 B1
Canal, Cor. 262 B4,
264 B3
Canal, Fond. 262 D2
Canaro, C. del 268 C4
Candele, Cor. d. 262 E3
Cannaregio, Fond. di
262 A1–B2
Cononica, Fondamenta
266 C3
Cantier, C.llo d. 262
A1
Cantore, C. Gen. 268
C3
Catorta, C. 264 D2
Caparozzolo, Cor. 268
B1
Capitaneria di Porto
266 B4
Capitello, C. del 262
C1

Cappallera, Cor. 266
D2
Cappeller, C. del 264
C2
Cappello 262 B4
Cappello, P. 266 C3
Cappello, R. 264 B2
Cappuccine, C. delle
266 D2
Cappuccine, Fond. della
262 B1
Capuzzi, C. 264 D4
Carbon, C. d. 264 E1
Carità, Cam. d. 264 C3
Carità, Rio Terrà d. 264
C4
Carlo Goldoni, C. 264
E2
Carminati, C. 266 B2
Carmini, Cam. dei 264
B2
Carozze, C. delle 264
C2, 266 C2
Carro, C. d. 264 E2
Carso, C. del 268 C3
Cartellotti, C. dei 264
B4
Casa Correr 262 C3
Casa del Tintoretto
262 D2
Casa di B. Cappello
262 D4
Casa di C. Goldoni 264
C2
Casa Favretto 262 D4
Casa Sanudo 262 C3
Case Nuove, C.llo d.
262 A1
Case Nuove, Cor. della
262 A4
Case Nuove, Corte d.
262 A1
Case Nuove, Fond. 266
E2
Casetta delle Rose 264
D3
Casin, S. d. 264 C3
Cason, C.llo d. 262 E4
Cassellaria, C. 266 B2
Cassetti, R. 264 C1
Caste l Olivolo, Fond.
268 C1
Castelforte S. Rocco,
Cam. di 264 C1
Castelli, C. 262 E4
Catecumeni, Rio Terrà
dei 264 E4
Cattapan, C. 268 B2
Cavalli, C. 264 D1,
266 D2
Cavalli, Cor. 266 D1
Cavallo, C. d. 266 C2–
C1
Cavallo, Cor. 262 C1
Cazziola, Fond. d. 264
B1
Celestia, Cam. della
266 E2
Celsi, C. 266 E2
Cendon, Cor. 262 A2
Cenere, Cor. della 268
B2
Cengio, C. del 268 C3
Centanni, S. e Cor. 264
D4
Centoplere, C. 264 C3
Cerchieri, C. dei 264
C3

Cereri, Fond. dei 264
A2
Cesare Battisti, Cam.
262 D4
Chiesa e del Teatro, Sal.
della 264 D2
Chiesa Ognissanti 264
B3
Chiesa S. Maria
Gloriosa dei Frari
264 C1
Chiesa S. Maria
Maggiore 264 A2
Chiesa, C. d. 264 D4
Chiesa, C. dietro la 264
E2
Chiesa, C.llo d. 262
D3, E4
Chiesa, Sal. della 262
B3
Chinotto, C. Gen 268
C3
Chiovere, C. delle 264
B1
Chioverette, C. della
262 B2
Chioverette, R. d. 262
B4
Cimesin, R. 264 B1
Cimitero, C. d. 266 D2
Cimitero, Cam. dietro il
264 A3
Cinque, C. dei 264 E1
Ciodi, C. dei 262 A2
Clero, C. del 264 B1
Clero, C. Larga del 264
D3
Cocco d. Renier, C. d.
266 C2
Codognola, C. 262 B4
Coletti, Fond. C. 262
A1
Coll. Peggy Guggen-
heim 264 D4
Collalto, C. d. 262
C4
Colomba, Cam. della
268 B1
Colombina, C. 262 C3
Colombina, Cor. 262
A2
Colombo, C. 262 C4
Colonna, C. della 262
C3
Colonne, C. 264 E2,
268 A2
Colonne, Cor. 268 A2
Colonne, Rio Terrà
della 266 B3
Colonnello, C. 264 A3
Colori, C. d. 264 C3
Colori, C. dei 262 A2
Coltrera, Cor. 268 A1
Comare, C.llo della
262 A4
Comello, C. 262 E4
Condulmer, Fond. 264
B1
Confraternità, Cam.
della 266 D2
Congregazione, C. d.
268 C3
Console, C. d. 266 C2
Consorti, C. d. 262 E3
Consorzi, P. dei 266 B3
Constantini, C. 264 D4
Contarina, C. Larga
262 B4

Contarina, C. 268 A1
Contarina, R. 262 B1
Contarini Corfù, C. 264 C3
Contarini e Benzon, C. 264 D2
Contarini, Cor. 262 E3, 264 B2
Contarini, Fond. 262 B1, 264 C1
Conterie, C. d. 262 B1, B2
Cooperative, C.llo delle 262 A1
Coppo, C. 268 A2
Cordellina, C. 262 C2
Corona, C. d. 266 C3, 266 C3
Correggio, Cor. 262 D4
Corrente, C. 262 D3
Correra, C. 262 B3, 268 B2
Correra, Cor. 264 A1
Cortese, Cor. 266 C1
Cortesia, C. d. 264 E2
Corti, C. dei 264 C1
Cossetti, Fond. 262 A4, 264 A1
Cossetti, R. 264 A1
Crea, C. della 264 D4
Crea, R. Terrà d. 262 A2
Cremonese, C. d. 264 A1
Cristi, C. del 262 D4
Cristo, C. del 262 C4, D3, 264 A2, 264 C2, D2
Cristo, Cor. del 262 E3, 264 E3, 266 A3, 268 B2
Croce, C. della 262 B4
Croce, Fond. 262 A4
Crociferi, Orat. d. 262 E3
Crosera, C. 264 D2
Crotta, Fond. 262 B3

D
Dandolo, Fond. 266 C1
Degolin, C. del 264 B3
Delfina, Cor. 266 E4
Dell' Olio, C. 266 D2
Dentro il Giardino, C. 268 B2
Dep. d. Megio 262 C3
Diavolo, Cor. del 262 C4
Diavolo, P. Cl. d. 266 C3
Doanetta, C. 264 C1
Doberdo, C. 268 C3
Dogana alla Salute, Fond. della 264 E4
Dogana di Terrà, C. 264 E1
Doge Priuli, C. Larga 262 D3
Dolera, C. e S. 264 D1
Dona, C. 266 E2
Donna Onesta, C. di 264 C2
Donzella, C. della 264 E1
Dose da Ponte, C. del 264 D3
Dose, C. del 266 B2, 266 D3

Dragan, C. 262 E4
Dragen, R. 266 A1
Drazzi, C. 266 D2
Duca d'Aosta, C. 268 C4
Due Corti, C. delle 262 D2
Due Pozzi, C.llo 266 D3

E
Emo, C. 262 B3
Erbarol, C. dell' 262 D4
Erberia 262 D4
Eremite, Fond. delle 264 B3
Erizzo C. detro 266 D3
Ex Conv. S. M. d. Servi 262 C2

F
Fabbri, C. dei 264 E2, 266 B3
Fabbrica, Fond. d. 264 A1
Fabbriche Nuove 262 D4
Fabbriche Vecchie 262 D4
Fabbro, R. d. 262 C4
Falier, C. 264 B1
Fari, C. dei 268 B1
Farnese, C. 262 C2
Farsetti, Rio Terrà 262 C2
Fava, C. delle 266 B2
Feltrina, C.llo d. 264 D3
Felzi, Fond. d. 262 D3, 266 C2
Fenice, C. della 264 E2
Ferau, C. e Cor. 262 A1
Fianco la Chiesa, C.llo a 266 E2
Figaretto, C.llo d. 268 B1
Figher, C. del 266 C3
Filosi, C. 262 C4
Finetti, R. 262 E3
Fiori, R. dei 262 D3
Fiubera, C. 266 B3
Flaminio Corner, C.llo 262 E4
Flangini, C.llo 262 B3
Fondaco d. Tedeschi 264 E1
Fondazione Querini Stamp. 266 C2
Fondego, C. del 264 B2
Fonderia, C. delle 264 B1
Fontego d. Tedeschi, C. d. 264 E1
Formenti, Cor. 266 E4
Fornasa Vecia, Fond. de la 262 B1
Forner, Fond. del 264 C2, 268 B1
Forner, Rio Terrà del 268 A2
Forni, Fond. d. 266 E4
Forno Vecchio, Cor. d. 264 E2
Forno, C. d. 264 E1, 266 D2–E4
Forno, C. del 262 B2, B3, 262 C2–E3, 264 B1

Forno, Cor. d. 264 D4
Forno, Cor. del 264 B2
Foscari, C. Larga 264 C2
Foscarini, F. 264 B2
Franceschi, Rio Terrà dei 262 E3
Franchi, C. 264 D4
Francia 268 B3
Frari, Cam. dei 264 C1
Frari, Fond. dei 264 C1
Frezzeria 264 E2
Frisiera, C. 268 A1
Fruttarol Lanza, C. del 264 D4
Fruttarola d. Banco Salviati, Fond. 264 D1
Furlane, C. delle 268 B2
Furlani, Fond. dei 266 D3
Furlanis, Cor. 264 C3
Fuseri, C. dei 264 E2

G
Gabriella, C. 266 C1
Gaffaro, Fond. del 264 B1
Galeazza, C. 266 B2
Galizzi, C. 264 E1
Galleria d'Arte Mod. & Mus. Orient. 262 C4
Galleria dell' Accademia 264 C3
Galleria Franchetti 262 D3
Gallion, C. 262 B4
Gallo, Cor. del 264 B1
Gambara, C. 264 C3
Gasparo Contarini, Fond. 262 D2
Gatte, Cam. della 266 D2
Gerardi, Cor. 262 E4
Gerardini, Fond. 264 B3
Gesuiti, Cam. dei 262 E3
Ghetto Nuovo, Cam. del 262 B2
Ghetto Vecchio 262 B2
Giacinto Gallina, C. Larga 266 C1
Giardini Pubblici, V. dei 268 A3–B3
Gioacchina, C. 262 B3
Giuffa, Ruga 266 C2
Giuseppe Garibaldi, V. 266 E4
Giustiniana, Cor. 262 A1
Gonella, Cor. 262 A1
Gorizia, C. 268 C4
Gorne, Cam. della 266 D2
Gradenigo, Fond. 262 B4
Gradisca, C. 262 B4, 262 C1
Grana, C.llo della 262 A2
Grappa, Cam. del 268 C3
Grassi, C. 264 C2
Greci, C. dei 266 D3
Gregolina, C. 262 D2
Gregolino, C. d. 266 B3

Grimana, C. 266 E4
Gritti o del Campanile, C. 264 D3
Gritti, C. e S. 266 D3
Groppi, C. 262 D2
Grue, Fond. delle 266 C4
Guardiani, C. dei 264 A2
Guerra, P. d. 266 B2
Guglie, P. della 262 B2
Gustavo Modena, C. 262 E4

I
Incurabili, C.llo 264 D4
Indipendenza, Cam. dell' 268 C3
Indorador, C. d. 264 B3
Instituto Ca' di Dio 266 D4
Isola, C.llo d' 262 C3
Istituto Superiore d'Arte Applicate 264 B2

L
Labia, Fond. 262 B1, B3
Laboratorio, C. d. 268 C3
Laca, C. d. 262 B4
Lana, Cam. della 262 A4
Lardona, Cor. 264 A3
Larga Canossiane, C. 262 C1
Larga d. Legname, C. 262 C1
Larga, C. 262 C1, C4, 262 D2, 266 E3
Lavadori, C.llo 264 B1
Legname, d. 262 C1
Legnami, C. dei 262 E2
Léon Bianco, Cor. de 266 B1
Leoni, Piazzetta dei 266 B3
Lesina, Cor. 268 B2
Lezze, C. 262 C2, 264 C2
Librer, Fond. Rio Terrà 264 D1
Lion, C. del 266 D3
Lista di Spagna, Rio Terrà 262 B3
Lizzò Fusina, Fond. 264 A3
Locanda, C. della 264 E2
Locchi, C. 268 C3
Lombardo, C. 262 A1
Lombardo, Fond. 264 C3
Longo, C. 262 C2
Loredan, C. 262 C2, 264 E1, 268 A1
Lotto, C. d. 264 C3
Lustraferri, P. de 262 C2

M
Maddalena, Cam. d. 262 C3
Maddalena, Rio Terrà della 262 C2–D3
Madonna dell' Orto 262 D1

Madonna dell' Orto, Fond. della 262 C1
Madonna, C. d. 262 E3, 264 B1, 264 D2, 266 C2–C3
Madonna, C. della 262 A2, 262 E4, 264 A2, C2, 264 D1, E1
Madonna, Cam. d. 266 B1
Madonna, Fond. delle 264 A2, 266 E3
Madonna, R. d. 262 E4
Madonnetta, C. d. 266 C2
Madonnetta, C. della 264 D1
Magazen, C. d. 262 A2, 264 C1, 264 D1, 266 C3
Magazen, C. del 262 B1, B2, 262 E4, 264 B2, 264 D1 266 D3
Magazen, Fond. del 264 B1
Maggioni, C. 262 E4
Maggiore, C. 262 C3–C2
Magno, C. 266 E3
Malatina, C. 266 D2
Malcanton, Fond. del 264 B1
Malipiero, Saliz. 264 D2
Malvasia Vecchia, C. d. 266 E3
Malvasia, C. d. 262 C2
Malvasia, Fond. d. 264 D3
Mandola, C. d. 264 D2
Mandolin, C. 266 D3
Manin, Cam. 264 E2
Manzani, C. V. 262 E4
Marafani, C. 268 B1
Marangon, C. del 264 D4
Maravegie, Fond. 264 C4
Marco Foscarini, C. 262 E3
Marconi, Cor. 264 C2
Marioni, Cor. 262 C4
Martin Novello, Cor. 268 B2
Martinengo della Palle, C. 266 B2
Martiri, C.del 13 264 E3
Maruzzi, C. 266 D3
Masena, C. della 262 C2, 262 E2, 264 B4
Mazzini, C. Larga 264 E1
Megio, Fond. d. 262 C3
Meloni, C.llo d. 266 D1
Mende, Cor. d. 264 D4
Mendicanti, Fond. dei 266 C1
Mercanti, C. 266 C3
Mercerceria d'Orologio 266 B3
Mezzo, C. d. 262 C4, 264 A3, 264 D1, 268 C1
Miani, C. 262 D4
Michiel, Cor. 262 D4, 264 E3

Milion, Cor. d. 262 E4
Minelli, C. 264 E2
Minotto, Fond. 264 B1,
Miracoli, C. dei 266 B1
Misericordia, C. della
262 A3, 264 B1
Mocenigo Casa Nova,
C. 264 D2
Mocenigo, C. 264 C2
Modena, C. del 262 C4
Molin, C. 264 B1, 264
D4
Molo 266 B4
Monastero, C. del 264
D4
Monastero, Fond. del
262 A4
Mondo Nuovo, C. del
266 B2
Montello, C. del 268
C3
Montesanto, C. del 268
C3
Monti, C. d. 264 E2
Mori, C. dei 264 E4
Mori, Cam. dei 262 D2
Morion, C. 266 D2
Moro, C. 264 C1, D4
Moro, Fond. 262 D2
Moro, P. 262 A1
Morosina, F. 266 D3–
E3
Morosini, C. 264 D3
Morosini, Cor. 262 E4
Morti, C. dei 262 D4
Morti, C.llo dei 262 C4
Morti, Cor. dei 264 B3
Mosche, C.llo delle
264 B2
Moschette, C. d. 266
D2
Mosto Balbi, C. da 262
B3
Mosto, C. da 262 B3
Muazzo, C. 266 C2
Muneghe, C. delle 262
C1, 264 D2
Muneghe, Cor. delle
266 E2
Munoéghette, C.llo d.
262 A4
Murer, Cor. d. 264 D4
Museo Archeológico
266 B3
Museo Civico Correr
266 B3
Museo d. Settecento
Veniziano 264 C2
Museo Ebraica 262 C2
Museo Fortuny 264 D2
Museo Guidi 266 C3
Museo Navale 266 E4
Mussata o Tosca, C. d.
266 B2
Muti, Cor. dei 262 D2

N

Nami, Fond. 264 C4
Nani, C. Larga 264 C4
Navagero, F. 266 D3
Navaro, C. 264 D4
Nave, C. d. 264 A3
Nicoli, Lun. 268 B2
Nicoló Mazza, C. 266
D2
Nicolosi, C. 264 B3
Nomboli, Rio Terrà dei
264 C1

Nuova dei Tabacchi, C.
264 A1
Nuova, C. 262 C2, 262
E3, 264 A3
Nuove, Fond. C. 262
A1
Nuovo, C. 264 E4

O

Oca, C. dell' 266 A1–B1
Occhialera, C. 264 C3
Oche, C. della 262 C4,
B4.
Ognissanti, Fond. 264
B3
Ole, C. delle 268 B1
Olio o del Caffettier, C.
dell' 262 B4
Olio, C. dell' 262 D3,
D4, E4, 264 A2
Olivi, C. d. 268 A2
Onesta, Fond. d. D. 264
C1
Opitale, C. del 262 A2
Oratorio S. Annunziata
264 D2
Oratorio, C. dell' 266
B2, 266 E2
Orbi, C. dei 264 D2
Ormesini, C. 262 C2
Ormesini, Fond. degli
262 C2
Orseolo, Fond. 264 E2
Orsetti, C. 262 B4
Orso, C. dell' 266 B2
Orti, C. dei 266 E2
Oslavia, C. 268 C3
Ospedale Civile 266
C1
Ospedale dei Vecchi
266 C1
Ospedale Ognissanti
264 B3
Ospedale, C. dell' 266
C2
Ospedaleto, Fond. 264
D4
Osteria Campana, C. d.
262 D4
Ostreghe, Fond. 264 E3
Ovo Marzarietta, C. d.
264 E1

P

Padiglioni, C. del 262
E3
Pagan, Fond. del 264
A1
Paglia, C. della 262 C3
Pal. Agnus Dio 262 C3
Pal. Albrizzi 264 D1
Pal. Amadi 262 E4
Pal. Balbi 264 C2
Pal. Barbarigo d. Ter-
razza 264 D2
Pal. Barbarigo 262 C3,
264 B3
Pal. Barbaro 264 C3
Pal. Barzizza 264 D1
Pal. Battagià 262 C3
Pal. Bellavite 264 D2
Pal. Bembo 264 E1
Pal. Bernardo 262 C4
Pal. Boldù 262 E4
Pal. Bragadin Carabba
262 E4
Pal. Brandolin 262 D4
Pal. Businello 264 D1

Pal. Calbo Crotto 262
B3
Pal. Cappello Layard
264 D1
Pal. Cavalli Franchetti
264 D3
Pal. Centanni 264 D4
Pal. Cigogna 264 A3
Pal. Civran 262 E4
Pal. Condulmer 264
B1
Pal. Cont. d. Bovolo
264 E2
Pal. Contarini 264 E3
Pal. Contarini d. Figure
264 C2
Pal. Contarini d. Zaffo
262 D2, 264 C3
Pal. Contarini Fasan
264 E3
Pal. Contarini-Polignac
264 D3
Pal. Cor. Gritti 262 B3
Pal. Cor. Martinego
266 A2
Pal. Corner d. Reg. 262
D4
Pal. Corner Gheltof
264 D2
Pal. Corner Martinego
264 E1
Pal. Corner Mocenigo
264 D1
Pal. Corner Spinelli
264 D2
Pal. Correr 262 D3
Pal. d. Dieci Savi 264
E1
Pal. da Lezze 264 C2
Pal. Dandolo 266 A2
Pal. Dandolo Palucci
264 C2
Pal. dei Camerlenghi
262 E4
Pal. Diedo 262 A4
Pal. Dolfin-Manin 264
E1
Pal. Donà Balbi 262 B3
Pal. Donà 262 D3, 264
D1, 266 C2
Pal. Ducale 266 B3
Pal. Emo 262 C3
Pal. Erizzo 262 C3
Pal. Falcaon 266 B2
Pal. Falier 264 C3
Pal. Fiscari 262 B3
Pal. Fontana 262 D3
Pal. Foscari Contarini
262 A4
Pal. Foscari 262 D4
Pal. Foscarini 262 C3,
264 B2
Pal. Garzoni 264 D2
Pal. Giovanelli 262 C3,
262 D3
Pal. Giusti 262 D3
Pal. Giustinian 264 C2,
E3
Pal. Giustinian Persico
264 C2
Pal. Gozzi 262 C4
Pal. Gradenigo 262 B4,
266 D2
Pal. Grassi 264 C3
Pal. Grimari 264 D1,
266 C2
Pal. Gritti 262 C3

Pal. Gussoni 262 D3
Pal. Labia 262 B3
Pal. Lezze 262 D3
Pal. Longo 262 D2
Pal. Loredan 264 C3,
D3, E1
Pal. Marcello d. Leoni
264 C2
Pal. Marcello 266 B2
Pal. Martinengo Volpi
264 D2
Pal. Mastelli 262 D2
Pal. Michiel d. Colonne
262 D4
Pal. Michiel Olivio 264
D1
Pal. Michiel 262 C2
Pal. Minelli 262 D2
Pal. Mocenigo 262 C4
Pal. Molin 262 D3, E3
Pal. Moro Lin 264 C2
Pal. Moro 264 C3
Pal. Morosini 264 D3
Pal. Muti Baglioni 262
D4
Pal. Nani 262 B2, 264
C2
Pal. Papadopoli 264
D1
Pal. Papafava 262 D3
Pal. Patriarcale 266 B3
Pal. Pesaro 264 D2
Pal. Pisani Gritti 264
E3
Pal. Pisani Moretta 264
D2
Pal. Pisani 264 D3
Pal. Priuli 264 C3, 266
C2, 266 C3
Pal. Querini 262 D4
Pal. Reale 266 B4
Pal. Sagredo 262 D4
Pal. Salviati 264 D3
Pal. Sanudo 262 E4
Pal. Savorgnan 262 B2
Pal. Soranzo 262 C3,
264 D1
Pal. Stern 264 C3
Pal. Surian Belotto 262
A2
Pal. Tiepolo 264 D2,
E3
Pal. Trevisan 264 C3
Pal. Trevisan 266 C3
Pal. Tron 262 C3
Pal. Valmarana 262 D4
Pal. Vendramin 262 B3
Pal. Vendramin-Calergi
262 C3
Pal. Venier dei Leoni
264 D3
Pal. Venier 262 B2
Pal. Zecca 266 B4
Pal. Zen 262 E3
Pal. Zeno 262 B3
Pal. Zorzi 266 C2
Pal. Zulian 262 D3
Paludo, Cor. del 266
C1
Panada, P. d. 266 B1
Papadopoli, Fond. 262
A4
Paradiso, C. 264 E1
Paradiso, Cor. d. 266
C2
Pasqualigo, C. 264 D3
Passion, C. delle 264
C1

Passione, C. d. 266 B3
Pasubio, C. del 268 C3
Paternian, Rio Terrà
264 E2
Pazienza, C.llo d. 262
A2
Pazienzea, C. d. 264 B2
Pedrocchi, C. 264 C3,
264 E3
Pegola, C. delle 262
D4, 266 E3
Pegolotto, S. del 262
C2
Penini, P. del 266 D3
Penitenti, C. Larga d.
262 A1
Pensieri, C. dei 264 A1
Perdon, C. del 264 D1
Perleri, C. dei 262 C2
Pesaro, C. 262 A3, 262
C3, 264 D2
Pescaria, C.llo 266 D3
Pescaria, Cam. della
262 D4
Pescaria, R. della 266
D3
Pescheria, Fond. di 264
A3
Pestrin, C. del 264 D2,
E3, 266 D3
Pezzana o Tasso, C. 264
D1
Piave, C. Larga 262 D1
Piccuti, C. 262 C2
Pietà, C. della 266 D2,
D3
Pignate, C. delle 262
D2
Pignater o del Tabacco,
C. del 262 C2
Pignater, Sal. del 266
D3
Pignoli, C. dei 266 B3
Pinelli, C. 266 C2
Pio X., Sal. 264 E1
Piombo, C. 266 B2
Piova, P. d. 264 A3
Piovan, C.llo del 262
B4
Piovan, Fond. del 266
E3
Pisani o Barbarigo, R.
264 C3
Pisani, C. 262 C1
Pisani, Cam. 264 D3
Pisani, S. e Cor. 262 B3
Piscina o Pedrocci, C.
266 E4
Piscina, C. di 264 E2
Pistor, C. del 262 B3,
262 D3, 264 C3,
268 A2
Pistor, C.llo di Sal. 262
E4
Pizzochere, C. 264 D2
Podgora, C. 268 C3
Pomeri, C.llo d. 268
C1
Pompea, C. 264 C4
Ponte degli Scalzi 262
A3
Ponte dei Sospiri/Bridge
of Sighs 266 C2
Ponte della Costituzi-
one 262 A4
Ponte Storto, C. del
262 C4
Ponte, C. d. 264 C4

Porpora, C. della 262 A1
Portal des Arsenale 266 E3
Posta, C. della 262 E3, E4
Pozzo Roverso, Cor. d. 266 C3
Pozzo, C. d. 268 C3
Prete, Cor. del 268 B2
Preti Crosera, C. d. 264 C2
Preti, C. 268 A1
Preti, C. dei 262 C3–C2, 262 E4, 266 C3
Prigioni 266 C3
Prima, C. Larga 264 C1, C4
Priuli detta dei Cavalletti, C. 262 A3
Priuli, Fond. 262 E3, 264 C3
Privata, C. 262 C4
Procuratie Nuove 266 B4
Procuratie Vecchie 266 B3
Procuratie, C. della 262 B3, 264 A2
Procuratie, Fond. delle 264 A2
Proverbi, C. Larga dei 262 E3
Pugliese, C. 262 B3
Punta della Dogana 264 E4
Punta di Sacca 262 A1
Puti, C. dei 264 B3

Q

Querini Stamp., C.llo 266 C2
Querini, C. 262 B3, 264 D4
Questura 266 D2
Quintavalle, C. Lunga 268 C1
Quintavalle, Fond. 268 B1

R

Rabbia, C. d. 262 C2
Racchetta, C. delle 262 D3
Ragusei, C. Larga 264 B2
Ramo Dragen 262 D4–E4
Rampani, C. selle 262 D4
Rampani, Rio Terrà 264 D1
Raspi, P. 262 D4
Rasse, C. delle 266 C3
Ravano, C. d. 262 E4
Regina, C. della 262 D4
Remer, C.llo d. 266 B1
Remer, C.llo del 262 B3, 262 E4
Renier o del Pistor, C. 264 B2
Rialto Nuova, Cam. di 264 E1
Rialto, Ponte di 264 E1
Riccardo Selvatico, C. llo 262 E4
Ricovero Penitenti 262 A1

Ridotto 264 E3
Riello, C. 262 B2, 268 B1
Riello, Fond. di 264 A3
Riformati, Fond. dei 262 C1
Rimedio, C. d. 266 C3
Rimpetto Mocenigo, Fond. 262 C4
Rio della Tana, Fond. 268 B1
Rio Marin, R. 262 B4
Rio Nuovo, Fond. del 264 B1–B2
Rio Terrà del Cristo 262 C3–C2
Rio Terrà d. Carampane xxx C4
Rio Terrà detto i Sabbioni 262 B3
Rio Terrà Primo del Parucchetta 262 C4
Rio Terrà Secondo 262 C4
Riva degli Schiavoni 266 C3–D3
Riva dell'Olio, Fond. 262 D4
Riva di Ca' di Dio 266 D4
Rizzi, Fond. 264 A2
Roma, Piazzale 264 A1
Rombiasio, C. 264 D3
Rosa, C. della 262 D4
Rossa, Fond. 264 B2
Rossi, C. 264 A3
Rosso, P. 264 A2
Rotonda, C. d. 262 C1
Rotta, Cor. 262 C4
Roveretto, C. 268 C4
Rubini, C. 262 C1
Ruga Bella 262 B4
Ruga degli Speziali 262 D4
Ruga Vecchia, C. di 262 B4
Ruga, Cam. di 268 B1
Rughetta, Fond. 264 A2

S

S. Agnese 264 C4
S. Agnese, C. Nuova 264 C3
S. Agostin, Cam. di 262 C4
S. Alvise 262 C1
S. Alvise, Cam. di 262 C1
S. Andréa 264 A1
S. Andrea, C. 266 A3
S. Andrea, Fond. 262 E3
S. Angelo Raffaele 264 A3
S. Angelo, Cam. 264 D2
S. Anna 268 B1
S. Anna, Fond. di 268 B1
S. Antonio 266 D3
S. Antonio, C.llo 262 E3
S. Antonio, C. 264 E2, 266 B2
S. Antonio, Paludo di 268 B2
S. Aponal 264 D1

S. Aponal, Cam. 264 D1
S. Apostoli, Terrà di 262 E4
S. Barnaba 264 C3
S. Barnaba, C. Lunga 264 B3
S. Bartolomeo 264 E1
S. Bartolomeo, Cam. 266 B2
S. Basegio, Cam. di 264 B3
S. Basegio, Sal. 264 A3
S. Basilio, Fond. 264 B3
S. Benedetto 264 D2
S. Biagio 266 E4
S. Biagio, Fond. 264 D4
S. Biagio, Riva 266 E4
S. Boldo, C. 262 C4
S. Canciano 262 E4
S. Canciano, Cam. 262 E4
S. Cappuccine 262 B1
S. Cassiano 262 D4
S. Caterina 262 E3
S. Caterina, C. Lunga 262 E2
S. Cristoforo, C. 264 D4
S. Domenico, C. di 264 D4, 268 A2
S. Fantin 264 E2
S. Felice 262 D3
S. Felice, Fond. di 262 D3
S. Fosca 262 D3
S. Francesco d. Paola, C. d. 268 A1
S. Francesco della Vigna 266 D2
S. Francesco di Paola 268 A1
S. Francesco, Sal. 266 D2
S. Gallo, C. 264 E2
S. Geremia 262 B3
S. Giacomo dell' Orio 262 C4
S. Giacomo di Rialto 264 E1
S. Giacomo di Rialto, C. 262 D4
S. Gioachino, C. 268 B1
S. Giobbe 262 A2
S. Giobbe, Fond. di 262 A1–A2
S. Giorgio d. Schiavoni, Fond. di 266 D2
S. Giorgio degli Schiavoni 266 D2
S. Giorgio dei Greci 266 D3
S. Giovanni Cristosomo 262 E4
S. Giovanni Decollato, Cam. 262 C3
S. Giovanni di Malta, Cor. 266 D3
S. Giovanni Elemosinario 262 D4
S. Giovanni Elemosinario, Ruga Vecchia 262 D4
S. Giovanni Evangelista 264 C1
S. Giovanni in Bragora 266 D3

S. Giovanni Novo 266 C3
S. Giovanni, C. d. 262 B2
S. Giovanni, C. 264 D4, 268 B1
S. Girolamo 262 B1
S. Girolamo, C. Lunga Chiovere di 262 B1
S. Girolamo, Fond. di 262 B1
S. Giuseppe 268 B2
S. Giustina detto di Barbaria, Cam. 266 D2
S. Giustina 266 D2
S. Gregorio 264 E4
S. Lazzaro Mendicanti 266 C1
S. Leonardo 262 C2
S. Leonardo, Cam. 262 B2
S. Lio 266 B2
S. Lio, Sal. di 266 B2
S. Lorenzo 266 D2
S. Lorenzo, C. 264 A3, 266 D2
S. Lorenzo, Fond. di 266 C2
S. Luca 264 E2
S. Lucia, Fond. di 262 A4
S. Maddalena 262 C3
S. Marco 266 B3
S. Marco, Campanile di 266 B3
S. Marco, Cor. 264 A2
S. Marco, Fond. di 264 B2
S. Marco, Piazzetta 266 B3
S. Marcuola 262 C3
S. Margherita, Cor. 264 B2
S. Maria Assunta dei Gesuiti 262 E3
S. Maria d. Zobenigo 264 D3
S. Maria dei Carmini 264 B3
S. Maria dei Derelitti 266 C1
S. Maria dei Miracoli 262 E4
S. Maria del Pianto 266 D1
S. Maria del Rosario dei Gesuiti 264 C4
S. Maria della Fava 266 B2
S. Maria della Pietà 266 D3
S. Maria di Nazareth degli Scalzi 262 A3
S. Maria Formosa 266 C2
S. Maria Maggiore, Cam. di 264 A2
S. Maria Mater Domini 262 C4
S. Maria Nova, Cam. 262 E4
S. Maria Valverde 262 D2
S. Maria Zobenigo, Cam. 264 D3
S. Marina, Cam. di 266 B2

S. Martino 266 E3
S. Marziale 262 D2
S. Mattio, C. 262 D4
S. Maurizio 264 D3
S. Michèle, C. d. 268 C3
S. Moisè 264 E3
S. Nazario Sauro, Cam. 262 B4
S. Nicoletto, R. 264 C1
S. Nicolò dei Tolentini 264 B1
S. Pantalon 264 C2
S. Pantalon, C. 264 C2
S. Pantalon, Cam. 264 B2
S. Pietro di Castello 268 C1
S. Pietro, C. Larga 268 B1
S. Polo 264 D1
S. Provolo, Cam. 266 C3
S. Provolo, Salizzada 266 C3
S. Revendin e S. Paternian, C. 264 E2
S. Rocco 264 C1
S. Rocco, Scuola Grande d. 264 C1
S. Salvadego, C. 264 E2
S. Salvador 264 E1
S. Salvador, Mercerie 264 E1
S. Samuele 264 C2
S. Scuro, C. del 262 A2
S. Sebastiano 264 A3
S. Sebastiano, Campazzo 264 A3
S. Severo, Cam. 266 C2
S. Silvestro 264 E1
S. Silvestro, Cam. 266 A2
S. Simone Piccolo 262 A4
S. Simone Profeta 262 B4
S. Simeone, C. Nuova di 262 B4
S. Sofia 262 D3
S. Sofia, Cam. 262 D4
S. Spirito 264 D4
S. Stae 262 C3
S. Stefano, C.llo 264 D2
S. Stefano/F. Morosini, Cam. 264 D3
S. Stin, Cam. 264 C1
S. Teresa 264 A2
S. Ternità, Cam. 266 D2
S. Tiossi 262 C4
S. Tomà 264 C2
S. Tomà, Cam. 264 C1
S. Trovaso 264 C3
S. Trovaso, Cam. 264 C4
S. Vidal 264 D3
S. Vio, Cam. 264 D4
S. Vio, Rio Terrà di 264 D4
S. Zaccaria, Cam. 266 C3
S. Zan Degolà 262 C3
S. Zorzi, C. 264 E2
S. Zuane, C. 262 B4
S. Zulian 266 B3
Sabbion, Cor. d. 264 D4

Sabbionera, Cor. 268 B2
Sabotino, C. del 268 C3
Sacca S. Girolamo, Fond. d. 262 A1
Sacca, C. 266 D2
Sacca, P. della 262 D2
Sacchere, C. d. 264 B1
Sacchere, Cor. de 262 C1
Sagredo, C. 262 B3, 266 E2
Sagrestia, C. della 266 C3
Sale, C.llo del 262 D4
Salomon, C. 262 D3, 268 B1
Salute, Cam. della 264 E4
Salute, Fond. della 264 E3
San Aponal 266 A2
San Marco, Piazza 266 B3
San Salvadore 266 B2
San Zaccaria 266 C3
Sangiatoffetti, Fond. 264 C3
Sansoni, C.llo dei 262 D4
Santi d. Squero, C. del 266 E4
Santi, C. dei 266 E4
Santi, Cor. dei 264 B4
Santi, S. del 266 E4
Santo Stefano 264 D2
Santo, C.llo 262 B2
Sanudo, Fond. 266 B1
Saoneri, C. dei 264 C2, 264 C1–D1
Saoneria, C. dei 264 C2
Saresin, C. 268 A2
Sartori, Fond. dei 262 E3
Savia, C. d. 262 B4
Savorgnan, Fond. 262 B2
Sbiacca, C. d. 264 B1
Sbianchesini, C. d. 264 D1
Scaco, C. 264 A3
Scalater, C. del 264 C2
Scale, Cor. delle 264 C1
Scaleter, C. d. 262 C4
Scaletta, C. 266 B2
Scalzi, Fond. 262 A3
Schiavine, C. 264 E2
Schiavona o Colonne, Cor. 268 A2
Schiavona, C. 268 A2
Schiavoncina, C. 266 C2
Schiavone, R. Cor. 268 A2
Schola Spagnola 262 B2

Scimia, C. d. 262 D4
Scoacamini, C. dei 264 E2
Scoazzera, Rio Terrà della 264 B2, 264 D1–E1
Scrimia, C. d. 262 D4
Scudi, C. d. 266 D3
Scuola d. Ang. Custode 262 E4
Scuola Gr. di S. Giovanni Evangelista 262 B4
Scuola Gr. di S. Marco 266 C1
Scuola Gr. di S. Maria d. Carmini 264 B2
Scuola, C. d. 264 C1
Scuola, C. della 264 E4
Scuole, C. dietro le 266 C1
Secco Marina, C. 268 B2
Seconda d. Saoneri, C. 264 C1
Selpolcro, P. 266 C3
Sensa, Fond. della 262 C1, 262 C1
Seriman, Sal. 262 E3
Sernagiotto, C. 262 E4
Sesriere di S. Croce 264 A2
Sette Martiri, Riva dei 268 A2
Silvestro, S. 266 A2
Soccorso, Fond. del 264 A3–B2
Soldà, Cor. d. 268 B2
Soranzo detta Formace, Fond. 264 D4
Soranzo, C. 264 C1
Soranzo, Cor. 266 D3
Soranzo-Correr, C. 262 B3
Sottoportego Oresi 262 D4
Specchieri, C. d. 266 B3
Specchieri, Sal. dei 262 B3
Spezier, C. del 262 B2, C3, 264 D2
Spezier, C.llo del 262 C4
Spezier, C. 266 B2
Spiaccio, C. 266 B2
Spiriti, Casinò d. 262 D1
Sporca, C. 262 B3, 264 A2, 268 B1
Squartai, C. dei 262 B4
Squellini, C.llo dei 264 C2
Squero Vecchio, R. e C. 266 C1
Squero Vecchio, R. 262 E3

Squero, C. d. 264 D4, E3
Squero, Fond. dello 264 B3
SS. Apostoli 262 E4
SS. Apostoli, Cam. dei 262 E4, 266 B1
SS. Filip. e Giacomo, Cam. 266 C3
SS. Giovanni e Paolo 266 C1
SS. Giovanni e Paolo, Cam. 266 C1
Stagneri, C. dei 266 B2
Stazione Ferroviaria S. Lucia 262 A3
Stazione Marittima 264 A3, B4
Stella, C.llo 266 B1
Storione, C. del 264 E1
Storto, P. 264 D1
Strada Nova 262 D3, D4
Strazze, C. d. 264 E2
Stretta, C. 264 A3, 264 D1, 266 E3
Stretta, Sal. 268 B1
Strope, C.llo delle 262 B4
Stua, C. della 262 D3, 268 A2
Stua, Fond. 262 D3

T

Tabacchi, d. 264 A1
Tabacco, C. de 264 A1
Tagliacalze, Cor. 266 E4
Tagliapietra, C. d. 262 E3, 264 B3
Tagliapietra, C. del 264 C1
Tana, Cam. della 266 E4
Tana, Fond. della 268 A1
Te Deum, C. del 266 D2
Teatro Goldoni 264 E1
Teatro La Fenice 264 E3
Teatro Malibran 262 E4
Teatro Rossini 264 E2
Teatro, C. 266 A2
Teatro, C. del 262 C4, 264 D3
Tedeschi, Fond. d. 266 B2
Tempio e Museo 262 B2
Terco, C. del 268 B1
Terese, Fond. 264 A3
Terrazzera, C. 266 D3
Testa, C. della 266 C1
Testori, C.llo 266 D3
Tetta, Fond. 266 C2
Tette, P. delle 262 C4
Tintor, C. del 262 C4

Tintoretto, C. 262 D2, 264 C1
Tiracanna, C. d. 262 C2
Todeschini, C. 264 D1
Tolentini, Cam. d. 264 B1
Tolentini, Fond. dei 262 A4
Toletta, C. d. 264 C3
Tomà, Rio Terrà S. 264 C1
Torre dell' Orologio 266 B3
Traghetto d. Madonetta, C. d. 264 D1
Traghetto di S. Lucia, C. del 262 A4
Traghetto Garzoni, C. d. 264 D2
Traghetto Vecchio, C. del 264 D2
Traghetto, C. 264 D2
Traghetto, C. d. 264 C1
Traghetto, C. del 262 D3, E4, 264 C3, 266 B1
Tramontin, C. 266 B2
Trapolin, Fond. del 262 D3
Tre Archi, P. d. 262 A2
Tre Ponti, Campazzo 264 A1
Tre Ponti, Fond. 264 A1
Trevisan, C. 262 D2, 264 B4
Trivisan, C.llo dei 262 D2
Tron, C.llo 264 A3
Tron, R. e C. 262 C3
Turchette, C. d. 264 B3
Turchi Museo Storia Nat., Fond. d. 262 C3
Turlona, C. 262 B1

U

Uva, S. d. 264 B2

V

Vallaresso, C. 264 E3
Varisco, C. 262 E3
Vecchi, Cor. dei 264 A3
Vecchia, C. 268 A2
Vecchia, Cor. 262 D2, 264 D2, D4
Vele, C. d. 266 B2
Vele, C. delle 262 D3
Vendramin, C. 262 C3
Vendramin, Fond. 262 D3
Venier, C. 262 E3, 264 E2
Venier, C. d. 266 C2
Venier, Fond. 262 B2, 264 D4
Vento, C. del 264 B3
Venzato, C. 262 B4

Verde, C. del 262 E4
Vergola, C. 262 B3
Verona, C. della 264 E2
Veste, C. d. 264 E3
Vetturi, C. 264 C3
Vicenza, Cor. 264 E3
Vida, C. delle 264 C2, 264 C1, E2, 266 E3
Vigna, C.llo d. 268 C1
Vin, C. del 266 C3
Vinanti, C. 264 B1
Viotti, C. Larga 264 A2
Visciga, C. 262 B4
Vitalba, C. 264 C1
Vitalba, Cor. 262 B4
Vitelli, S. del 262 B2
Vittorio Veneto, V. 268 B4–C4
Volti, C. d. 262 E3
Volti, C. dei 264 C1
Volto, C. d. 266 B2

W

Widman, C.llo 266 B1
Widman, C. 262 E4

Z

Zaguri, C. 264 D3
Zaguri, F. Cor. 266 A4
Zaguri, Fond. Corner 264 D3
Zambelli, C. 262 C4
Zamboni, C. 264 D4
Zanardi, C. 262 E3
Zancani, C. 262 D3
Zane, C. 262 B4
Zappa, C. 264 B3
Zappa, Cor. 262 C2, 264 B3
Zattere ai Gesuiti, Fond. 264 C4, 264 C4
Zattere allo Spirito Santo, Fond. 264 D4–E4
Zattere al Saloni, Fond. 264 E4
Zattere P. Lungo, Fond. 264 B4
Zavater, C. del 262 C2
Zen, C. 262 B3, 266 D2
Zen, Fond. 262 E3
Zocco, C. d. 266 B2
Zoccolo, C. della 262 D2
Zolfo, C. d. 262 C2
Zorzi Bragadini, Fond. 264 D4
Zorzi, C. 266 D2
Zorzi, Cor. 264 E2
Zotti, C. 262 D3
Zotti, C. dei 264 D2
Zudio, C. 262 B4
Zugna, C. 268 C3–C4
Zusto, Sal. 262 B4

ART AND PHOTO CREDITS

akg-images 80MR
Alamy 120B, 142, 151, 155, 161, 170T, 193B
Andrea Pistolesi 129
Andrea Sarti/Peggy Guggenheim Collection 7T
Andrew Balet 164T
AWL Images 176
Benjamin W.G. Legde 31, 32
Bridgeman Art Library 44
Clayton Parker 114B
Corbis 46B
David Heald/Solomon R. Guggenheim Foundation, New York 130T, 130B
Didier Descouens 7BR, 126, 135
Dreamstime 10T, 248, 256
Fondazione Musei Civici di Venezia 7MR, 68BR, 139T, 168B, 179B, 206
Fotolia 19B, 84R, 139B
Getty Images 1, 6BR, 7M, 7B, 8B, 10B, 11T, 11B, 12/13, 14/15, 16/17, 18, 20, 21, 22, 23B, 23T, 24, 25B, 25T, 28B, 34, 35B, 36, 40, 46T, 48, 49, 50, 51, 52, 59, 60, 61, 62, 64T, 64B, 66, 67, 69TC, 70, 73,

74, 75, 78, 81B, 81BR, 80/81T, 81M, 82, 83, 84L, 86T, 86B, 88/89, 90/91, 92/93, 94, 98, 112, 113T, 117B, 118, 119B, 122/123T, 123B, 123TR, 124, 125, 133, 134B, 136, 140B, 143T, 145B, 150T, 152, 154, 156B, 156T, 157, 158T, 159, 160, 163, 166, 168T, 171, 172, 173, 175, 177T, 178, 179T, 180B, 181, 182, 184, 185, 186, 187, 189, 191, 192, 194, 196, 197B, 199T, 201, 208, 209, 212BR, 212BL, 212/213T, 213TC, 214/215, 216, 228, 231B, 232, 233B, 235B, 241, 242B, 243B, 243T
Hilton Worldwide 218/219
Hotel Excelsior 235T
iStock 4/5, 6ML, 6BL, 7MR, 9B, 19T, 38B, 54, 55T, 55B, 56, 57, 58T, 77, 80BR, 87, 95T, 99, 101, 102, 103, 104, 105, 107, 108, 109, 110, 111, 113B, 114T, 115T, 115B, 116, 119T, 121T, 122MR, 122BL, 123BR, 128B, 132, 137, 138, 145T, 147, 164B, 169, 181R, 198, 200, 207T, 220, 221, 226, 233T, 234, 238, 239T, 239B, 244, 246, 247, 249, 260

Leonardo 242T
Londra Palace 150B
Nino Barbieri 131T
Pictures Colour Library 131B
Public domain 6MR, 26B, 27, 28T, 30, 33, 37, 65, 69BR, 71, 79, 106, 128T, 180T, 212MR
Rex Features 76
Scala Archives 45B, 68MR, 68BL, 68/69T, 69B, 72, 80BL, 213M
Shutterstock 8T, 9TR, 29, 58B, 63, 85, 95B, 117T, 134T, 140T, 144, 149, 153, 158B, 167, 170B, 177B, 183, 188, 193T, 195B, 195T, 197T, 199B, 204B, 204T, 207B, 210, 211, 217, 218, 222T, 222B, 223, 225, 229, 230
Son of Groucho 227
Starwood Hotels & Resorts 120T, 121B
SuperStock 9BR, 141, 143B, 146, 162, 231T
The Art Archive 26T, 35T, 38T, 41, 42, 43, 45T
The MOSE Project 53
TIPS Images 39, 122B
Villa Pisani 240

Cover Credits

Front cover: Gondolas at sunrise *iStock*
Back cover: The Grand Canal *iStock*
Front flap: (from top) I Gesuati *Shutterstock*; Gondolier

Shutterstock; Spaghetti vongole e cozze *Shutterstock*; Murano glass *Shutterstock*
Back flap: Castello *Shutterstock*

INDEX

A

Aalto, Alvar 170
Accademia 8, 211
 collection 68, **212**
Accademia Bridge 60,
 133, **211**
Acqua alta 53, 103, 112
addresses 249
admission charges 249
air travel 247
Ala Napoleonica 45, 60,
 105
Alberoni 235
Altinum 31, 228, 230
Ando, Tadao 202
Angelo Raffaele 206
Aquileia, conquest of
 76
Archaeological Museum
 106
architecture
 building on water 33
 palaces 61
 styles **54**
Armenian community
 43, 242
Arsenale 10, 38, **164**
 architecture 58
 revival of 50
art **63**
 artists' trails 68, 206
 Biennale 169
 courses 192
art museums and
 galleries
 Accademia 8, 68
 best 8
 Ca' Pesaro 141
 Franchetti Gallery 140
 Guggenheim
  Collection 8, **130**,
  211
 International Gallery of
  Modern Art 141
 Museo Diocesano
  d'Arte Sacra 57
 Museo di Pinti Sacri
  Bizantini 152
 Museum of Oriental Art
  142
 Palazzo Grassi 135
 Punta della Dogana
  202
 Querini-Stampalia
  Gallery 152

Spazio Vedova 203
Asolo 141
ATMs 253
Attila's Throne 230
Attila the Hun 31
Austrian rule 45, 60

B

bacari 9, 85, **176**
Bacino Orseolo 109, 111
Bancogiro 11
banking 176
banks 253
Baptistery (San Marco)
 104
Baptistery (Torcello)
 230
barbarian invasions 31
Barbarigo, Doge
 Agostino 40, 225
Barbaro dynasty 115
Barchessa Valmarana
 240
Baroque architecture
 59
bars 85
 Al Remer 141
 bacari 9, 85, **176**
 Caffè Florian 11, 87
 Caffè Quadri 11, 87
 Centrale 11
 Harry's Bar 11, 86,
  114
 Teamo 117
 Zanzibar 152
Basilica di San Marco
 101
 architecture 55
 Campanile 110
 Four Horses 123
Bauer Palladio 59
beaches (Lido) 231, 233,
 234
Bellini, Gentile 63
Bellini, Giovanni **63**
 Accademia 212
 I Frari 183
 tomb 156
 trail 69
Belltower (San Giorgio
 Maggiore) 218
Benchley, Robert 135
Berlusconi, Silvio 49
Biblioteca Nazionale
 Marciana 104

bigoli 210
Black Death 34
Blue Moon complex
 233
boats. See also gondolas;
 vaporetti
 houseboat holidays
  248
 model 183
 vaporetti ferries 247
 water experiences 8
 working 142
boatyards (squeri) 205
bocche di leoni 22, 37
book shops 160
Bossi, Umberto 50
Bottega Tintoretto 192
Bragadin, Marcantonio
 156
Brenta Canal 8, 25, **240**
Brescia 41
Browning, Robert 133
Bucintoro 80, **167**, 168
budgeting 250
building techniques 33
Burano 10, 218, **227**
Byron, Lord 46, 49, 231
 Ca' Mocenigo 118,
  136
 Lido 231
 swimming 241
 Villa Foscarini Rossi
  240
Byzantium 31, 32
 architectural influence
  54
 artistic influence 64

C

Cabot, John 168
Cacciari, Massimo 21
 and flood defences 47,
  49, 53
Ca' Corner della Regina
 140
Ca' da Mosto 56, **139**
Ca' Dario 59, **129**
Ca' d'Oro 8, **139**, 197
cafés 86, **87**
 San Marco 87, 112
Caffè Florian 11, 87
Caffè Quadri 11
Ca' Foscari **136**, 210
Ca' Genovese 129
Ca' Grande 129

Calatrava Bridge 59,
 145
Calle degli Albanesi
 147
Calle della Toletta 211
Calle Larga XXII Marzo
 121
Calle Lunga San
 Barnaba 210
Ca' Loredan 56, 137
Ca' Mocenigo 136
Campanile 110
campi 56
Campo dei Mori 192
Campo de l'Abbazia 192
Campo del Ghetto Nuovo
 198
Campo della Madonna
 dell'Orto 191
Campo dell'Arsenale
 164
Campo della Tana 165
Campo delle Beccarie
 179
Campo Manin 119
Campo San Barnaba 56,
 210
Campo San Bartolomeo
 56, **120**
Campo San Giacomo
 178
Campo San Giacomo
 dell'Orio 9, **180**
Campo San Luca 56,
 119
Campo San Maurizio
 116
Campo San Moisè 113
Campo San Pantalon
 186
Campo San Polo 56,
 187
Campo San Provolo 151
Campo San Rocco 184,
 185
Campo San Samuele
 118
Campo Santa Maria
 Formosa 9, **153**
Campo Sant' Angelo
 118
Campo Santi Apostoli
 195
Campo Santi Giovanni e
 Paolo (Zanipolo) 155

Campo Santo Stefano 9, 56, **116**
Campo San Vio 131, 211
Canale delle Galeazze 167
Canale di Cannaregio 199
Canaletto **67**
Accademia 213
Ca' Rezzonico 135
canal vessels 145
Cannaregio **189**
Canova, Antonio 183
Cantiere delle Gaggiandre 167
Cantina Do Mori 11
Ca' Pesaro 8, 59, **141**, 180
Ca' Rezzonico 8, **133**
architecture 59
Carnival **75**
Carpaccio, Vittorio **64**
Accademia 213
San Giorgio degli Schiavoni 159
car parks 247
Casa Goldoni 186
Casanova, Giacomo **23**
escape from prison 109, 147
Giudecca 221
Palazzo Soranzo 187
San Samuele 118
Casino 25, **143**
Cassiodorus 32
Castello **146**
Eastern **163**
castrati 71
cathedral. See Basilica di San Marco
children **250**
activities for 201
China 36
Chioggia, Battle of 34
churches
Angelo Raffaele 206
Basilica di San Marco 55, **101**
Gesuati 205
Gesuiti 69, **194**
I Frari 10, 58, **181**
Il Redentore 10, 60, **222**
La Pietà 154, **161**
La Salute 10, 59, 129, **201**
Le Zitelle 60, **223**
Madonna dell'Orto 10, 69, **191**

Oratorio dei Crociferi 194
Ospedaletto 158
San Canciano 194
San Cassiano 179
San Francesco del Deserto 238
San Francesco della Vigna 60, 68, **158**
San Geremia 145
San Giacomo dell'Orio 180
San Giacomo di Rialto 55, **177**
San Giorgio degli Schiavoni 10, **159**
San Giorgio dei Greci 152
San Giorgio Maggiore 60, **218**
San Giovanni Crisostomo 195
San Giovanni di Malta 161
San Giovanni Evangelista 181
San Giovanni in Bragora 58, **161**
San Lazzaro degli Armeni 242
San Lorenzo 159
San Marcuola 145, 197
San Martino 228
San Marziale 193
San Michele in Isola 237
San Moisè 114
San Nicolò 234
San Nicolò dei Mendicoli 55, 207
San Pantalon 186
San Pietro di Castello 169
San Pietro Martire 225
San Polo 58, 69, **187**
San Rocco 185
San Salvador 119
San Sebastiano 10, **206**
San Simeone Piccolo 145
San Stae 142
Santa Croce degli Armeni 121
Santa Fosca 229
Santa Maria degli Angeli 225

Santa Maria dei Carmini 8, **208**
Santa Maria dei Miracoli 59, **194**
Santa Maria dell' Assunta 10, **229**, 230
Santa Maria della Visitazione 205
Santa Maria Formosa 59, **153**
Santa Maria Mater Domini 179
Santa Maria Zobenigo 115
Santa Sofia 197
Sant' Elena 170
Sant' Eufemia 223
Santi Apostoli 195
Santi Giovanni e Paolo (Zanipolo) 10, 58, **155**
Santi Maria e Donato 226
Santo Stefano 58, **117**
San Trovaso 206
San Zaccaria 59, **150**
San Zulian 121
Scalzi 145, 199
cichetti 9, 85, 176
cinemas 186
Cini, Count Vittorio 211, 220
Cipriani, Arrigo 50
Cipriani, Giuseppe 114
Cipriani Hotel 223
classical revival 60
climate 250
coach travel 246
cocktails 86
Coducci, Mauro 59
San Giovanni Cristosomo 195
Santa Maria Formosa 153
Scuola Grande di San Marco 157
coffee 87
Colleoni, Bartolomeo 155
colonial power 39, 43
Columbina 77
Columns of San Marco and San Teodoro 111
commedia dell'arte 77, **79**
conference facilities 50

confraternities. See scuole
Constantinople 31, 32
fall of 41
sack of **34**
convicts 167
Corfu 39, 44
Corner, Caterina 140
Corner dynasty 130
Correr, Museo 8, **105**
Corte del Milion 57, **195**
Corte Vecchia 192
Coryate, Thomas 179
Costa, Paolo 21, 49
cost of living 23, 50
costumes, carnival 79
Council of Ten 37
courtesans 22, 179
credit cards 253
Crete 39, 43
crime 251
Croatian community 43
cruises, Brenta Canal 240
cruise ships 51
Crusades 33, **34**
cuisine 83
customs regulations 251
Cyprus 41, 42, 141

D
da Gama, Vasco 39
Dalmatia 39, 42, 160
da Mosto, Alvise 139
da Mosto, Francesco 21, 139
Dandolo, Doge Enrico 34
Danieli Hotel 9, **149**
d'Annunzio, Gabriele 181
Dante 166
da Ponte, Antonio 59
Rialto Bridge 176
Dario family 129
David, Elizabeth 179
de Goncourt brothers 191
Deposito del Megio 145
Diaghilev, Sergei 237
dialect 22
Dickens, Charles 46, 101
di Michelis, Gianni 49
Diocesano d'Arte Sacra, Museo 57
disabled travellers 251

Dogana di Mar 202
doge 35, **40**
    office of 32, 114
    tombs of 156
Doge's Palace.
    See Palazzo Ducale
Dorsoduro 10, **200**

E

Eastern Castello 163
eating 80
Ebraico, Museo 198
ecological problems 51
electricity 251
embassies 251
emergency numbers
    250
empire 37, 39
Erberia 178
Ernst Max 131
etiquette 251
Evelyn, John 43, 76, 113,
    120

F

**Fabbriche Vecchie e
    Nuove 138**, 175
Falier, Doge Marin 133,
    144
F.C. Venezia 170
fegato alla Veneziana
    210
ferries
    city 247
    islands 219, 237
Ferrovia Santa Lucia
    199
festivals and events 11,
    251
    Carnival 11, **75**
    Festa di San Marco
        80
    Galuppi Festival 237
    Il Biennale 11, **169**
    La Fenice opera
        season 11
    La Festa della
        Madonna della
        Salute 81, 126
    La Festa del Redentore
        11, 81
    La Sensa 11, 80
    La Vogalonga 11, 80,
        145
    Regata Storica 11, **80**,
        140
    regattas and water
        festivals **80**
    Venezia Suona 11

    Venice Film Festival
        11, **232**
film 110, **232**
flood barriers 46, 49,
    53
flooding 47, 49, **53**
Follia, Museo della 241
Fondaco dei Tedeschi
    57, 120, **138**
Fondaco dei Turchi 8, 57,
    144, 180
**Fondamenta degli
    Ormesini** 193
Fondamenta dei Vetrai
    225
**Fondamenta della
    Giudecca** 228
**Fondamenta della
    Sensa** 192
**Fondamenta
    dell'Osmarin** 151
Fondamenta del Vin 177
Fondamenta Nani 206
fondamente 194
Fondamente Nuove 193
Fondazione Giorgio Cini
    220
food and drink 83
    bigoli 210
    cichetti 9, 85, 176
    cocktails 86
    coffee 87
    fegato alla Veneziana
        210
    gelaterie 203
    prosecco 86
    risotto 84
    Sgropin 211
    spritz 86, 191
football 170
Forni Pubblici 167
Fortezza di Sant'Andrea
    234
**Fortuny y Madrazo
    Mariano** 118
Foscari Arch 107
Foscari, Doge Francesco
    41, 107, 136, 183,
    240
Foscarini, Antonio 34
Franchetti, Baron 140
Franchetti Gallery 140
Frezzeria 113
Friuli-Venezia Giulia 41

G

Gabrieli, Andrea 71
Galuppi, Baldassare 71
Galuppi Festival 237

Garden of Eden 223
gas extraction 51
Gautier, Théophile 101,
    149, 189, 194
**gay and lesbian
    travellers** 253
gelaterie 203
Genoa 33, 34
Gershwin, George 72
Gesuati 204
Gesuiti 69, **194**
Ghetto 10, **196**, **198**
    walking tour 10
Ghetto Vecchio 198
Giardini Ex Reali 112
Giardini Pubblici 45
Giorgione 65
Giudecca 10, 218, **221**
Giustiniani dynasty 128,
    136
glass 9, **224**
Glass Museum 226
Goethe, J.W. 173, 235
Goldoni, Carlo 187
Goldoni Theatre 25
gondolas 132, 248
    rides 8, 9, 111
gondoliers 132
Gothic architecture 57
government
    city 34, 40
    Republic 45
Grand Canal 8, **125**
    by night 9, **137**
    vaporetti 128
**Grande di Santa Maria
    dei Carmini Carnival**
    8, **75**
**Gran Viale Santa Maria
    Elisabetta** 233
Great Council 35
Greek community 43,
    151
Grimani, Museo 155
Gritti, Doge Andrea 159
Gritti Palace 9, 116,
    129
Grosso, Giacomo 171
Guardi, Francesco 67,
    134, 213
Guggenheim Collection
    8, **130**, 211
Guggenheim, Peggy
    130, 168
guilds 176

H

Habsburg dynasty 42
Hai, Alex 132

Handel, G.F. 70
Harry's Bar 11, 86, **113**
Hartley, L.P. 223
health 253
helicopter rides 233
Hemingway, Ernest 229
    Burano 227
    Harry's Bar 46, 113
    Torcello 229
Henri III of France 136,
    166
history 34
Hitler, Adolf 240
Hoffman, Josef 170
**Holy Byzantine Paintings
    Museum** 152
Holy League 42
Horses of San Marco
    103
Hospital Islands 241
Hôtel des Bains 234
Hotel Excelsior 235
hotels
    legendary 9, 149
Howells, William Dean
    45

I

I Carmini. See Scuola
    Grande di Santa Maria
    dei Carmini
I Frari 10, **181**
    architecture 58
    art in 68
Il Biennale 11, **169**
Il Redentore 10, 60,
    222
independence bid 49
**International Gallery of
    Modern Art** 141
islands
    lagoon **217**
    minor 236
Italian language 257

J

James, Henry
    Londra Palace 149
    Palazzo Barbaro 131
    quoted 46, 144, 136,
        176, 177, 184,
        201, 211, 230
Januszczak, Waldemar
    170
Jesuits 193
Jewish community 43,
    234
    Ghetto 196, **198**
Jewish Museum 198

K

Keates, Jonathan 137
Knights of Malta 160
Kublai Khan 36

L

Labia family 199
lace 227
Lace Museum 228
La Certosa 239
La Fenice 73, **114**
  fire at 73
  opera season 11
lagoon
  boatmen 242
  ecology of 51, 50
  exploring 219
  ferries 248
  islands of 217
  minor islands 236
  nature tours 10
La Malcontenta 240
language 257
  dialect 22
La Pietà 154, **161**
La Salute 10, 59, 129,
  201
La Sensa 11, 80
La Vogalonga 11, 80,
  145
Lawrence, D.H. 233
La Zecca 59, **111**
Lazzaretto Nuovo 237,
  238
Lazzaretto Vecchio 238,
  242
League of Cambrai 41
left luggage 253
Lega Nord 50
Lepanto, Battle of 42
leper colonies 237, 241
Levant 33
Levey, Michael 44, 67
Le Vignole 239
Le Zitelle 60, **223**
Liberty style 57
Libreria Sansoviniana
  59, **106**
Libro d'Oro 43
Lido 25, 218, **231**
  architecture 57
Lion of St Mark 112,
  165
Lista di Spagna 199
listing magazines 253
Liszt, Franz 143
Little, Alastair 83
Littlewood, Ian 184
Locanda Cipriani 229

Loggetta 111
Lombardi brothers 59
Lombardy 41
Londra Palace 149
Longhena, Baldassare
  59, 201, 220
Longhi, Pietro 67, 76,
  134, 213
Lotto, Lorenzo 181, 208
Lungomare 233

M

Machiavelli, Nicolò 34
Madness, Museum of
  241
Madonna della Salute,
  Festa della 81, 126
Madonna dell'Orto 10,
  69, **191**
Magazzini del Sale 203
mainland
  migration to 50
  stato da terrafirma 41,
  44
Malamocco 235
Manin, Doge Lodovico
  45
Mann, Thomas 46, 132,
  149, 234
Mantegna, Andrea 63
maps 253
Marciano, Museo 103
Marco Polo Airport
  247
Margherita 56, **210**
Marini, Marino 131
markets
  Campo Santa Maria
    Formosa 153
  Erberia 178
  Pescheria 140, **178**
  Rialto 9, 138, **177**
Marriage with Sea 80
Martini, Egidio 135
masked balls 78
masks 9, **77**, 79
Massari, Giorgio 60,
  161, 205
Mastelli family 192
Mazzetto, Roberto 192
Mazzorbo 228
McCarthy, Mary 55, 31,
  101, 132
media 253
medical care 253
Mercerie 112, **120**
merchant fleet 38
Merletto, Museo del
  228

Mestre-Marghera 50,
  51
Michiel, Doge Vitale 34
migrations 31
Mocenigo, Doge Alvise
  81, 179
Mocenigo, Doge
  Giovanni 156
Mocenigo, Doge Tomaso
  136
Mocenigo dynasty 136,
  180
Molino Stucky 50, 223
Molmenti, Pompeo 167
monasteries.
  See churches
money 253
  money-saving tips 11
Monteverdi, Claudio 70
Morand, Paul 139
Morea 43, 44, 192
Morosini, Doge Michele
  43, 117, 156
Morris, Jan, quoted 37,
  110, 121, 173, 183,
  217, 224
mosaics
  San Marco 102
  Torcello 55, 230
MOSE 46, **53**, 166
mudflats 33, 242
Murano 10, **224**
  glass 9, 218, 224, 225
Muro Vino e Cucina 11
museums. See also art
  museums and
  galleries
  18th-Century Life 134
  Casa Goldoni 186
  Museo Archeologico
    106
  Museo Correr 8, **105**
  Museo della Follia
    241
  Museo dell'Opera
    (Palazzo Ducale)
    108
  Museo del Merletto
    228
  Museo del Vetro 226
  Museo di Torcello 230
  Museo Ebraico 198
  Museo Grimani 155
  Museo Marciano 103
  Museo Storico Navale
    168
  Natural History 144
  Padiglione delle Nave
    168

music
  opera 73
Musset, Alfred de 149
Mussolini, Benito 240

N

Napoleon 44
  plunder of art 45, 65,
    182
  redevelopment 45, 60,
    163, 169
Nardin, Roberto 132
Nardo, Livia 237
Natural History Museum
  144
nature excursions 10
Naval History Museum
  168
naval power 34
New Prisons 147
Nietzsche, Friedrich 46
nobility 43, 45
Norwich, John Julius 31
Nuovo Cimitero
  Israelitico 234

O

Old Prisons 147
opening hours 254
opera **73**
Oratorio dei Crociferi
  194
Oriental Art Museum
  142
Orseolo, Doge Pietro 33
Ospedale degli
  Incurabili 204
Ospedaletto 158
Ottoman Turks 39, 41,
  44

P

Padiglione delle Nave
  168
Padua 41, 240
palaces **61**
  names of 125
Palazzo Balbi 136
Palazzo Barbarigo 131
Palazzo Barbaro 131
Palazzo Belloni-
  Battaglia 142
Palazzo Cavalli-
  Franchetti 133
Palazzo Cini 211
Palazzo Contarini del
  Bovolo 119
Palazzo Contarini-Fasan
  129

Palazzo Contarini-Polignac 131
Palazzo Corner Mocenigo 187
Palazzo Corner-Spinelli 137
Palazzo da Mula 225
Palazzo dei Camerlenghi 138, 176
Palazzo del Cinema 235
Palazzo Ducale 8, **106**
  architecture 58
Palazzo Falier 133
Palazzo Farsetti 137
Palazzo Flangini 145
Palazzo Fortuny 118
Palazzo Giustinian 128, **136**
Palazzo Grassi 9, 118, **135**
  architecture 60
Palazzo Greci 151
Palazzo Grimani 155
Palazzo Labia 145, 199
Palazzo Loredan 137
Palazzo Mastelli 192
Palazzo Mocenigo 8, **180**
Palazzo Pisani-Gritti 129
Palazzo Pisani-Moretta 137
Palazzo Priuli 151
Palazzo Salviati 129
Palazzo Soranzo 187
Palazzo Trevisan 153, 226
Palazzo Vendramin-Calergi 8, **143**, 198
Palazzo Venier 130
Palazzo Vitturi 153
Palazzo Zen 194
Palazzo Zenobio 208
Palazzo Zorzi 59
Palladio, Andrea 59, **60**, 220
  Fondazione Giorgio Cini 220
  Il Redentore 222
  Palladian villas 25, **240**
  quoted 222
  San Giorgio Maggiore 218
Palma il Giovane 194
papacy 42
parks and gardens
  Garden of Eden 223

Giardini Ex Reali 112
Giardini Pubblici 45
Parco delle Rimembranze 170
Passarowitz, Peace of 44
passports 255
paterae 56, 61
patricians 43
pavilions, Biennale 170
Pellestrina 235, 237, **243**
Penzo, Gilberto 183
people, Venetian 22
Pesaro, Doge 183
Pesaro family 184
Pescheria 140, **178**
Piano, Renzo 204
Piazza Galuppi 229
Piazza San Marco 9, **99**
  cafés 87, 112
  flooding 112
  restoration in 102
Piazzetta 111
Piazzetta dei Leoncini 112
Pinault, François 135, 202
Pinti Sacri Bizantini, Museo di 152
Pisa 33
Pius II Pope 41
Pius VII, Pope 219
plague 34, 238, 243
Plague Doctor 77
Pollock, Jackson 131
pollution 51
Polo, Marco 22, **36**, 195
Ponte dei Pugni 210
Ponte dei Sospiri 147
Ponte della Sacca 192
Ponte delle Guglie 199
population 47, 50
Porta della Carta 107
Porta Magna 164
postal services 254
Pound, Ezra 237
Poveglia 243
Priuli, Girolamo 114
Procuratie Nuove 104
Procuratie Vecchie 104
Prosecco 86
Proust, Marcel 46, 125
public holidays 254
Punta della Dogana 128, **202**

Q
quarantine 238, 243
Querini family 152
Querini-Stampalia Gallery 152

R
rail travel 246
railway station 145, 199
Redentore, Festa del 10, 81
Regata Storica 11, **80**, 140
regattas 80
religious services 254
Renaissance architecture 59
Renoir, Auguste 46
Republic
  end of 45
  government 35, 40, 41
  history 34
  nature of 22
Restaurants and Cafés 85
  Caffè Quadri 11, 87
  Gam Gam 197
  Harry's Bar 11, 86, **113**
  Magna Bevi Tasi 150
Rezzonico dynasty 133, 134
Rialto **173**
  markets 9, 138, **177**
Rialto Bridge 59, 137, **176**
Ridotto 113
rii 195
Rio dei Tedeschi 195
Rio della Misericordia 193
Rio della Sensa 192
Rio di San Trovaso 205
Rio Giovanni Crisostomo 195
risotto 84
Riva Ca' di Dio 167
Riva degli Schiavoni 147
Riva del Ferro 177
Riva San Biagio 168
Rizzo, Damiano 53
road travel 246
Roden, Claudia 83
Romanesque style 57
Rossini, Gioacchino 71
Rubens, Peter Paul 116
Ruga Giuffa 152
Ruskin, John

Basilica di San Marco 101
Ca' d'Oro 140
Gritti Palace 116
post-Gothic architecture 57
quoted 158, 183, 192, 195, 219
Torcello 228, 230
Russell, Francis 44
Ruzzenenti, Claudia 21

S
Sacred Art Museum **149**
safety 251
Sala del Conclave 219
Sala del Maggior Consiglio 107, 108
salt 32, 37, 203
San Canciano 194
San Cassiano 179
San Clemente 241
sandbanks 33, 242
Sand, George 122, 149, 169, 228, 230
San Francesco del Deserto 228, 237, **238**
San Francesco della Vigna 60, 68, **158**
San Geremia 145
San Giacomo dell'Orio 180
San Giacomo di Rialto 55, **177**
San Giorgio degli Schiavoni 10, 159
San Giorgio dei Greci 152
San Giorgio Maggiore 10, **218**
San Giovanni Crisostomo 195
San Giovanni di Malta 161
San Giovanni Evangelista 181
San Giovanni in Bragora 58, **161**
San Lazzaro degli Armeni 10, **242**
San Lorenzo 159
San Marco **99**
  restaurants, bars and cafés 87, **112**
San Marco, Basilica di 55, **101**
San Marco Centrale 11

San Marco, Festa di 80
San Marcuola 145, 197
San Martino 228
San Marziale 193
San Michele 237
San Michele in Isola 237
San Moisè 113
San Nicolò 234
San Nicolò dei Mendicoli 55, 207
San Pantalon 186
San Pietro 169
San Pietro di Castello 169
San Pietro Martire 225
San Polo **179**
San Polo, Chiesa di 58, 69, **187**
San Rocco 185
San Sebastiano 10, **206**
San Servolo **241**
San Silvestro 137
San Simeone Piccolo 145
Sansovino, Jacopo 59, 129
San Stae 142, 180
Santa Croce 173, 180
Santa Croce degli Armeni 121
Santa Fosca 229
Santa Maria degli Angeli 225
Santa Maria dei Carmini 8, **208**
Santa Maria dei Miracoli 59, **194**
Santa Maria della Salute. See La Salute
Santa Maria dell' Assunta 10, **229**, 230
Santa Maria della Visitazione 205
Santa Maria Formosa 59, **153**
Santa Maria Gloriosa dei Frari. See I Frari
Santa Maria Mater Domini 179
Santa Maria Zobenigo 115
Sant' Andrea fort 239
Sant' Angelo 137
Santa Sofia 197
Sant' Elena 170
Sant' Erasmo 10, 219, 237, **239**
Sant' Eufemia 223

Santi Apostoli 195
Santi Giovanni e Paolo 58
Santi Giovanni e Paolo (Zanipolo) 10, 68, **155**
Santi Maria e Donato 226
San Tomà 136
Santo Stefano 58, **117**
San Trovaso 206
San Zaccaria 59, **150**
San Zanipolo. See Santi Giovanni e Paolo
San Zulian 121
Scala dei Giganti 59, 107
Scala d'Oro 108
Scalzi 145, 199
Scalzi Bridge 60
Scarlatti, Domenico 70
Scarpa, Carlo 153, 170
Schola Canton 198
Schola Grande Tedesca 198
Schola Italiana 198
Schola Levantina 199
Schola Spagnola 199
Scuola della Misericordia 193
Scuola di San Giovanni Evangelista 181
Scuola Grande di San Marco **157**, 182
Scuola Grande di San Rocco 8, **182**, 184
art treasures 67
Scuola Grande di Santa Maria dei Carmini 8, **208**
scuole 56, **182**
Secret Itinerary 10, 106, **108**
secret police 37, 160
Senate 37
separatism 49
service charges 254
sestieri 23
Settecento Veneziano, Museo del 134
Sgropin 211
Shakespeare, William
Merchant of Venice 173
Othello 129
Shelley, Percy Bysshe 46, 231
shipbuilding 39, 164

shopping
Lagoon Islands 234
Sior Maschera 77
slave trade 39
smoking 254
sottoporteghi 195
Sottoportego Ghetto Nuovo 198
Spazio Vedova 203
spice trade 37, 39
spritz 86, 191
squares 56
Squero di San Trovaso 205
stato da terrafirma 41
Steer, John 67
Stirling, James 170
St Mark 32, 103
Strada Nuova 193, **197**
Stravinsky, Igor 72, 237
Stucky, Giovanni 223
student travellers 254
subsidence 51, 52
Sumptuary Laws 133
synagogues 199

T

Tana (Corderie) 165
tax 254
Tchaikovsky, Piotr 46, 149
Teatro Malibran 25, 72
Teatro San Cassiano 71
Teatro Verde 221
telephones 255
television 253
Tezon Grande 238
thanksgiving festivals 81
theatre 25
tickets and passes
arts and attractions 11
transport 11
Tiepolo, Giambattista 67
Accademia 213
Ca' Rezzonico 135
Gesuati 205
I Carmini 209
San Polo 187
trail 205
Villa Pisani 240
time zone 255
Tintoretto **66**
Accademia 213
Gesuiti 194
house 69, 192
La Salute 201

Madonna dell'Orto 191
San Polo 187
San Rocco 184
trail 10, **69**
tipping 254
Titian 65, **183**
Accademia 213
Gesuiti 194
I Frari 183
toilets 255
Torcello 10, 32, 228
basilica 55, **229**
Torcello, Museo di 230
Tornatore, Giuseppe 232
Torre dell'Orologio 59, **109**
Torre Massimiliana 239
tourism
attitude to 21
Grand Tour 46, 67
volume of 50
tourist information 255
tourist offices 255
trade 32, 34, 37, 175
traghetti 248
transport 247
travel agents 255
travellers' cheques 253
Treasury (San Marco) 102
Treviso airport 247
Trieste 45
Turner, J.M.W. 46
Twain, Mark 137

U

Umberto I 171
University 136, 206, 210
Urban II, Pope 33

V

Vecelli, Tiziano.
See Titian
Vedova, Emilio 66, 204
Vendramin, Doge Andrea 156
Venetians 22
Veneto 41, 50, 240
Veneto-Byzantine style 55
Veneziano, Paolo 65
Accademia 213
I Frari 184
San Pantalon 186
Santi Maria e Donato 226
Venezia Suona 11

Venice Film Festival 11, **232**
  Palazzo del Cinema 235
Venier dynasty 130
Ventin, Mario 132
Verdi, Giuseppe 72
Verona 41
Veronese, Paolo 66
  Accademia 213
  Palazzo Trevisan 226
  San Giacomo dell'Orio 180

  San Pantalon 186
  San Sebastiano 206
Vetro, Museo del 226
Via Galuppi 227
Via Garibaldi 168
Viale Garibaldi 169
Vicenza 41
Villa Foscari 240
Villa Foscarini Rossi 240
Villa Pisani 240
Villa Widmann 240
Villa Zianigo 135

Viotti, Marcello 73
visas 255
Vivaldi, Antonio 72, **154**, 161

W

Wagner, Richard 46
  La Fenice 72
  Palazzo Giustinian 136
  Palazzo Vendramin-Calergi 143
  San Giorgio dei Greci 152

walks 10, 202
water festivals 80
water taxis 8, 248
websites 255
weights and measures 255
Wilde, Oscar 78
wine 85
World Wars I and II 46, 51

Z

Zattere 10, **203**, 204

ABOUT THIS BOOK

INSIGHT GUIDES

VENICE

Editor: Carine Tracanelli
Author: Lisa Gerard-Sharp
Head of Production: Rebeka Davies
Update Production: AM Services
Pictures: Tom Smyth
Cartography: original cartography
Berndtson, updated by Carte

Distribution

UK, Ireland and Europe
Apa Publications (UK) Ltd
sales@insightguides.com

United States and Canada
Ingram Publisher Services
ips@ingramcontent.com

Australia and New Zealand
Woodslane
info@woodslane.com.au

Southeast Asia
Apa Publications (SN) Pte
singaporeoffice@insightguides.com

Hong Kong, Taiwan and China
Apa Publications (HK) Ltd
hongkongoffice@insightguides.com

Worldwide
Apa Publications (UK) Ltd
sales@insightguides.com

Special Sales, Content Licensing and CoPublishing
Insight Guides can be purchased in bulk quantities at discounted prices. We can create special editions, personalised jackets and corporate imprints tailored to your needs. sales@insightguides.com; www.insightguides.biz

Printing
CTPS-China

All Rights Reserved
© 2016 Apa Digital (CH) AG and
Apa Publications (UK) Ltd

First Edition 1988
Sixth Edition 2016

This City Guide to Venice was written by **Lisa Gerard-Sharp**, a gifted writer and major contributor to Insight's Italian titles. Although a writer and broadcaster with a special interest in Italy, she was initially wary of tackling Venice, a reluctance shared by most Italians. In foreign eyes, Venice may be a dream city we have all visited, if only in our imaginations. However, in Italian eyes, the slithery nature of the lagoon, coupled with the indomitable Venetian spirit, provoke admiration rather than affection. Like many visitors, Lisa Gerard-Sharp was first drawn to the glistening surface of the city and its stage-set qualities; "In time, this deepened into an appreciation of the deliciously sinister nature of Venice in winter, with its undertow of decadence."

This updated edition of *City Guide Venice* was commissioned by **Carine Tracanelli** and updated by **Maciej Zglinicki**.

SEND US YOUR THOUGHTS

We do our best to ensure the information in our books is as accurate and up-to-date as possible. The books are updated on a regular basis using local contacts, who painstakingly add, amend, and correct as required. However, some details (such as telephone numbers and opening times) are liable to change, and we are ultimately reliant on our readers to put us in the picture.

We welcome your feedback, especially your experience of using the book "on the road". Maybe we recommended a hotel that you liked (or another that you didn't), or you came across a great bar or new attraction that we missed.

We will acknowledge all contributions, and we'll offer an Insight Guide to the best letters received.

Please write to us at:
Insight Guides
PO Box 7910, London SE1 1WE
Or email us at:
hello@insightguides.com

VENICE SIXTH EDITION
Venice
510661/00038 - 1 of 1

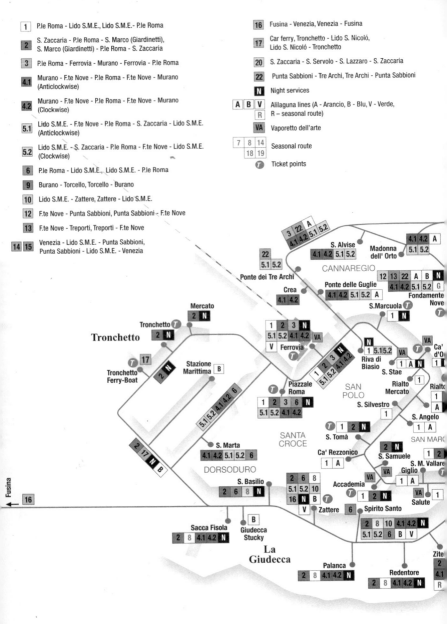

Venice Vaporetti Network